D1116369

The Public Administration
of Economic Development

Irving Swerdlow

The Public Administration of Economic Development

PRAEGER SPECIAL STUDIES IN INTERNATIONAL ECONOMICS AND DEVELOPMENT

Praeger Publishers New York Washington London

Library of Congress Cataloging in Publication Data

Swerdlow, Irving.
    The public administration of economic development.

    (Praeger special studies in international economics
and development)
    Includes index.
    1. Economic development.   2. Economic policy.
3. Public administration.   I.   Title.
HD82.S88   1975   338.9   74-9426
ISBN 0-275-07530-3

PRAEGER PUBLISHERS
111 Fourth Avenue, New York, N.Y. 10003, U.S.A.

Published in the United States of America in 1975
by Praeger Publishers, Inc.

Printed in the United States of America

To my wife, Gertrude K. Swerdlow,
whose encouragement, help, and professional advice
made this book possible.

223821

This book attempts to examine how a government of a less developed country operates in a way to achieve economic development. The thesis of this book is: (1) Economic development is a desirable process, observable, measurable, and capable of being shaped and paced. (2) The activities of government can expedite or slow down the process of economic development. (3) The inadequacies of public administration have become an important bottleneck to achieving a satisfactory rate and quality of economic development. (4) It is possible through training, education and experience to improve the degree to which public administration is useful in the process of economic development.

The viewpoint of this book is focused on the public administrator, not the economist. The economic component of economic development is emphasized, but not given exclusive or even prime importance. Rather, the main stress is on public administration related to economic development, with public administration basically defined as "what governments do!"

I have had a great deal of assistance in the preparation of this book. Primarily, assistance came directly and indirectly from a goodly flow of graduate students from all parts of the world. Their natural bias toward the operating level of presentation is, I think, clearly evident. Several graduate students, notably Agha Ghazanfar of Pakistan, struggled valiantly with my notes. The Brookings Institution of Washington, D.C. helped with funds and secretarial assistance for one year, and I am grateful to Robert Asher and Henry Owen for their understanding and patience. The Maxwell School of Syracuse University, particularly Dean Alan K. Campbell, was very supportive and encouraging. Mrs. Louise Metz contributed markedly to the book by her patience, keen eyesight and capable typing. My wife, Gertrude K. Swerdlow was a constant source of encouragement and direct help. Her questions and suggestions added materially to my effort to present the ideas about the public administration of economic development in a nontechnical yet competent manner.

CONTENTS

The Public Administration
of Economic Development

CHAPTER 1

The inevitability of poverty is no longer accepted by most people, either for themselves or for their fellow citizens. Can this assertion be wishful thinking, or a model of an ideal society, or an explanation of the existing turbulence in the world? Probably all three, combined in different degrees but present in all countries. In those countries commonly classed as "less developed," the conclusion that economic betterment is possible has become a major element in the way a society operates. Together with tradition and with the apathy and hopelessness bred by abject poverty, this realization that a society can be changed to reduce poverty has become widely accepted by many people of many different classes. There may be no simple method of proving this assertion empirically, but it is one of the few obvious generalizations that is supported by casual as well as systematic observation. There may be differences of opinion about the extent and intensity of this conclusion but not about its existence or importance.

The level and composition of economic production and how the products are distributed to the people of a country have thus become an important subject for everybody, particularly those who administer the work of the government. Economic change is inevitable, once people accept the idea that it is possible. Poverty, in spite of all the attempts of some philosophies and religions to justify it, is a painful condition, particularly when it is possible to observe conditions of less poverty and to believe that poverty can be alleviated, or even eliminated, by economic development. But economic development is not costless; it is a painful, complex process in which many people are hurt, with many undesirable results associated with desirable results. Political, social, and cultural changes accompany economic changes, deliberately or unconsciously. Opposition becomes strong to many of the changes, and confrontations can be painful and costly. A willingness to make changes and to accept sacrifices is an essential element in the process of economic development, but it is not sufficient to ensure

1

success. Among the major elements essential are the right kind of governmental operations, and therein lies the essence of the public administration of economic development. What are the right kinds of administration? There is no single, simple answer, and there may not even be any complex set of answers to this kind of simplistic question. But a working knowledge of the economic development process, and of the role of government within that process, is part of the basic capabilities required of public administrators of less developed countries.

CONCEPT OF A MODERNIZING SOCIETY

The familiar Indian fable of blind men examining an elephant aptly illustrates the process by which a changing society is usually described. Each analyst is largely concerned with the part of a society he is examining, and brings to the examination the tools and analytical concepts he derives from his training and experience. Although most modern analysts are aware of the complexity of society, there are implicit and explicit pressures to deal mostly with what is familiar. The part of the elephant he touches tends to become conceptually the central part of the animal.

A society, even the most primitive, is a complex of people, their behavior, institutions, and relationships. This mixture differs greatly from time to time and from place to place. Through lack of alternatives, this complex is arbitrarily divided by most scholars into political, social, economic, cultural, and other overlapping categories. These categories may be useful; but because they are separate only conceptually and not in real life, they often become the basis for misconceptions about the operations of a society.

A changing society is therefore extremely difficult to visualize. So complex are the relationships that a simplifying procedure must be adopted to provide perspective and evaluative capabilities. Consciously or unconsciously, as one examines a society, a model or ideal is established as a frame of reference. The model may be partial or comprehensive, complex or oversimplified; it may provide accurate or distorted measurements. That the model is used, however, is easily verified by reflecting on any experience of observation and evaluation of a society in operation.

A society or nation can be perceived as a dynamic system, a complex of interrelated elements that operate within limits and under constraints. These elements are constantly changing in value, and their interrelationships are also changing. To understand how a system operates means that the important parts or variables must be identified, their interrelationships established in some meaningful way; the constraints to their operations must become known and the limits of operations marked off. The term variable is used here to refer to a

phenomenon or element which changes in value over time, a characteristic of a cause or result that changes under different circumstances.

A developing nation is a social system that has established among
its primary objectives that of becoming modern or developed. Both of
these concepts have acquired a degree of vagueness which makes them
relatively useless in communicating ideas. In a general way, what is
usually meant is that some nations have become "modern" or "developed"
and have acquired some characteristics that the "developing" countries
seek to achieve. These desirable attributes, such as a higher productivity, are generally assorted with other attributes that are apparently
less desirable. Thus, as each developing nation defines its objectives,
it attempts to emphasize what it considers desirable goals and procedures, and minimizes or disregards the less desirable aspects of
development.

While our ignorance of this development process is still monu-
mental, some useful generalizations seem to be supportable. It is
clear, for example, that the modernization process affects all aspects
of a society, all of its important institutions. The most important relationships in a society are affected—economic, political, social,
cultural, and psychological. The church, schools, government, family
relationships, class and group relationships—no important element or
institution can remain unaffected in the process of modernization of
development.

It also seems clear that the economic activities of a society are
particularly affected in this modernization process. Indeed, this is
probably the principal image in the minds of most people, that modernization really means economic modernization, the changing of the
economic activities to achieve greater economic production. It would
be a major error, however, to conclude that economic activities are the
sole or even the major component in the modernization process. Modernization is not just economic development, although that is an important
part of modernization. Further, economic growth is not all of economic
development, just an important part of it. Economic development involves
all the cultural, psychological, political and social changes that make
modern economic processes possible, while economic growth refers to
only one, relatively narrow aspect of economic development. To point
out that economic development is a broader term does not reduce the
importance of economic growth; it merely points out that using the two
terms interchangeably is confusing and misleading. The modernization
process is even broader, encompassing numerous institutions and
activities that may have little to do with economic growth, but are
the very core of the philosophy, ideology, and style of life of a people.
There are few absolute assertions that can be made about the modernization process—and this is one of them—the economic activities of a
society are so interrelated with the other activities, political, social,
cultural, and psychological, that all of them must change as a society
"modernizes" itself. Economic growth is a desirable objective, not

3

merely because the material gains may be desirable, but rather because an economically advanced environment offers a greater freedom of action and choice. Economic growth increases the range of human choice and allows men to choose a greater control over his environment. Development, economic or total, is a means to achieve the creation of a political, social, and economic environment in which the individual can exercise maximum control over his choice of action. Thus the meaning of the three terms should be kept clear, although they are overlapping: (1) Modernization—changing a society and its institutions to achieve political, social, and cultural development as well as economic development; (2) Economic development—changing a society so that production, productivity and income distribution are improved (become higher and "better"); (3) Economic growth—production of more economic goods and services.*

To concentrate only on economic growth is an exercise in economic theory rather than an analysis of how a society modernizes itself. Nevertheless, it is useful to emphasize those parts of a society's behavior that relate most directly to improvement in the production and distribution of goods and services. This economic subsystem in a developing country is undergoing serious modification.† The purpose of these modifications is not just economic growth; it is economic development, to increase production and productivity and to improve distribution of the product. The concept of increasing production and productivity may seem relatively simple; but as will be noted later, it becomes meaningful only as related to cost and time. Even more complicated qualifications must be attached to the concept of improving distribution which goes beyond economic activities and involves moral, ethical, and political criteria as well.

CONCEPT OF A LESS DEVELOPED COUNTRY

Analysis of a country's economic growth and economic development must be in relative terms and at best represents a high level of generalization. A country is "less developed" only by comparison with a "more

---

*These definitions are oversimplified and contain concepts that require much more definition. For example, the concepts of political, social and cultural development imply ideal models or a series of objectives that are far from accepted and are usually modeled on western societies.

†The term economic subsystem emphasizes the important point just made, that other subsystems, loosely divided into political, social and cultural, are equally present and clearly important. The point requires constant emphasis.

developed" country, and not all aspects of a country are at the same levels of relative development. Every one of the so-called "less developed countries" have elements or enterprises that are highly modernized and more developed than the rest of the country. A concept of development presupposes a criteria or objective toward which development is supposed to take place. In this, to apply economic growth mechanically is to confuse the whole process of modernization. It is a misleading simplification to translate the level of production of economic goods into a fixed measure of relative economic development. Essential to an understanding of the process of economic development is the general idea of the economic characteristics of less developed countries at an operating level.

Less developed countries tend to have the following economic characteristics:

Low Productivity of Workers

Most, but certainly not all, of the workers in the less developed countries produce far less than their counterparts in the developed countries. This general characteristic points to a wide number of variables that require consideration by public administrators. If low economic productivity is the essence of the economic problem, then policies must be aimed at improving production per worker. Improved income distribution, an essential part of economic development, is closely related to improving productivity. Governments, in their efforts to improve both productivity and income distribution are often confronted with problems that seem to require contradictory policies. Low productivity per worker means that there must be a large number of poor families in the society and that many of these are so poor that efforts to improve their earning opportunities require new kinds of institutions, a major transformation of the society. Low productivity is shown by the large proportion of workers who are unskilled, by the deficient management and organization of the enterprises that employ them, and by the deficiency in entrepreneurship in the country, the capacity to make appropriate investment decisions. An associated characteristic is population pressure, the startling increase in the numbers of people who must find a place in the economic system in order to live.

High Proportion of Workers in Primary Production, Principally Agriculture

In the less developed countries, agricultural and other primary* work utilizes an overwhelmingly large proportion of the workers. Thus,

---

*Primary production consists of agricultural production, the production of the initial products of forest and stream, and the initial

5

usually between 75-85 percent of the population lives in rural areas, and generally more than half of the production in the country is primary. The principal exports are also often agricultural, being limited to a relatively small number of world-traded commodities. The implication of this basic characteristic on the efforts of a society to modernize itself is arresting. The rural areas are, in most countries, the areas where the traditional way of living is adhered to most completely, where traditional beliefs and traditional values are more fully accepted and transmitted. While many rural areas are undergoing changes, these changes tend to be slower than in the cities. Family influences remain stronger, and outside ideas and influences are fewer and less intense. Rural areas generally have poorer communication and transportation facilities than nonrural areas. The people generally have lower rates of literacy, and the contacts with the outside world are more infrequent. Rural development is not solely, or even primarily, economic growth. It is directly concerned with the basic structure of society, all the institutions that make up the fabric of the society.

A little arithmetic on raising productivity of a society will repeat this emphasis. Where 75 percent of the workers in agriculture produce 60 percent of the product, it takes massive effort to raise average productivity of the country by 2 or 3 percent. Manufacturing, which may occupy about 5 percent of the workers, and provide 10 percent of the product may double in size and productivity and still only effect a relatively small increase in the country's average productivity. The "numbers game" should not be stressed too vigorously, because there are equally misleading impressions that can be given on the other side. The significant point to be stressed is that a large proportion of the labor in the less developed countries is available in the rural areas, unfortunately mostly unskilled and dominated by traditional ideas of production. Average productivity in the rural areas can be improved either by finding more of the same kind of work for the workers, if they are producing something, or by improving the way they work so that more product is produced per worker. So important is the agricultural sector in most of the less developed countries that unless it receives a significant share of the efforts to modernize, the country will advance productivity little or not at all.

Inadequate Economic and Social Overhead Facilities

Overhead facilities, both economic and social, mean the basic, underlying capacities that a society must have. These include roads, schools, hospitals, housing, communication, transportation and power

---

extraction of minerals. Further processing of any other primary products is usually included in the industrial sectors.

facilities. In a sense, these are the infrastructure, the operational foundations of a society that enable it to produce the goods and services it needs.*

Every economic subsystem has some of these overhead capacities. Even the most primitive hunting or fishing society must develop some paths to be used in common by the different production units. As a society develops a higher productivity, its reliance on overhead capacities becomes more explicit and more pronounced. A modern production unit, as measured by its higher productivity, is marked by its increased reliance on the existence of modern power, communications and transportation facilities. Housing, education and health facilities, while not as simply related to production as are transportation, communications and power, are also so closely involved in effects on production as to require little justification for their inclusion among overhead facilities. As a society modernizes its economic activities and raises its productivity, it will require more of the facilities that produce overhead products and services. It will require more and more people trained in using and maintaining these overhead production processes, and a large proportion of its total product will be attributed to overhead production. Indeed, if there were a good way of measuring the adequacy of overhead facilities, it might be placed among the best measures of economic modernization.

Low Savings and Inadequate Capital Formation

The less developed countries have, as a major characteristic of their economic subsystem, a relatively low rate of savings and an inadequate rate of capital formation. This means, in nontechnical terms, that a smaller proportion than is desirable of the goods and services they produce each year are set aside for future use or are used for nonconsumption purposes.

Capital formation is closely related to savings in that it represents the use or expenditure of savings to create capacity for further production. In a sense, capital formation is the reverse side of savings, the use of savings in the development of capacity for further production. But not all savings are automatically used in capital formation. Different institutions may be and usually are involved, and the institutions for capital formation may not be able to function properly because the institutions for savings are inadequate and ineffective. So centrally

---

*The division between social and economic overhead is purely capricious. Both terms are used here to help avoid the charge of overemphasis on economics.

7

important are the processes of savings and capital formation that they are often made the main theme of the whole modernization process. Economists are continually being accused of overemphasizing the importance of savings and capital formation, and sometimes these accusations are warranted. Economics, as a discipline among the social sciences, has developed many concepts and kinds of analysis that are particularly well adapted to the study of savings and capital formation. The opposite error, of underemphasizing the importance of capital formation to the modernizing process, is probably worse than its overemphasis.

TABLE 1.1

Gross National Savings as a Percent of GNP
Compared with GNP Per Capita

Level of GNP Per Capita (In 1964 U.S. dollars)	Gross National Savings as a Percent of GNP
$ 50	9.4
100	12.0
200	14.8
300	16.4
400	17.6
600	19.3
800	20.5
1000	21.5
2000	24.6

Source: Table 1 of Hollis B. Chenery, "Growth and Structural Change," Finance and Development 8, no. 3 (Sept. 1971): 19. Underlying data from IBRD, World Tables, December 1968.

Shortage of Foreign Exchange

A less developed country, determined to raise its production and productivity, requires many goods and services from abroad. First, it requires physical things that it cannot make itself, the machinery, cars, tools, equipment, and instruments that only an industrialized country can make. Second, it requires some raw material and intermediate products for the few industrial or processing plants it has developed, the parts needed to keep its limited capital in operating condition, the steel bars, pipes and copper wire for construction, the specialized oils for lubrication, and the fuels for its power plants. Too often it also requires consumption goods to make up for inadequate production at home, the food, textiles and other consumer goods such as watches, radios, bicycles, and durable consumer goods in general. Some of the consumer goods, like most machinery and equipment, can only be made in industrial economies, as can most chemicals and medicines. Thus, there are many kinds of products that can only be acquired through imports, and these range from essential goods to the most luxurious nonessentials, both consumption and producer goods. Added to the product imports are the importation of technical knowledge and services. The knowledge and skills that are essential to the development and operation of a huge productive economy are imported in many ways: by books and other publications, by sending people abroad to be trained, and by bringing in teachers and trainers. Except for a relatively small amount of technical assistance provided by gifts, all of this imported technical knowledge must be paid for by the importing country.

This brings up a significant point often overlooked, the economic purpose of exports is to pay for imports. If imports were not essential, exporting would be an act of economic irrationality. The less developed countries must emphasize and expand their export capabilities because of their need to pay for imports. Since a country can export only what other countries are willing and able to import, the problems of exports and imports of the less developed countries are inextricably mingled with the problems of cost and price, of trade policies, and of changes in demand in the more developed countries. The whole trading world becomes functionally related to the need for imports by the less developed countries. The rate of construction in the United States, as affected by mortgage and interest policies of the U.S. government, may have more effect on plywood production in Japan and the Philippines than almost anything those countries can do to increase plywood production.

Inadequate Economic Institutions

A less developed country is one that has "inadequate" economic institutions, inadequate measured against a country's ability to raise its productivity and production to adequate levels. A less developed country is one that has thus far been unable to develop the institutions that will provide its people with the level of goods and services achieved by the more developed countries.

Low productivity, the basic characteristic of the less developed countries, can often be attacked only by making major changes in existing institutions or by developing new institutions. The economic forces that work their way in economic institutions result in lower or higher costs, lower or higher production levels, lower or higher imports and exports, as the economic institutions encourage or handicap these forces. However, it would be a mistake to make this approach too mechanically, and individual variation, impulse, even irrationality must be encompassed in the totality of the economic activities of a country. Low productivity, for example, may be approached from the need to adopt improved technologies using more capital and skilled labor. To provide the necessary resources may require new savings institutions and new ways to channel savings to investment. Government action in establishing and operating these new institutions is only one way of looking at public administration, but it is an important and fruitful one.

Market institutions are a particularly important type of economic institution. Unless production is undertaken solely for consumption by the producer and his family, there must be some transaction or exchange associated with the production. These transactions may be limited to exchanging the product for other products or for money that can be used to purchase other products, or may be limited to exchanging some of the product or money for some necessary inputs into the production process. The arrangements that facilitate these transactions of goods and services are a market—a product market for the goods and services produced, a factor market for the factor inputs into the production process, or a money market, an arrangement where money is bought and sold. A market is a subsystem where buyers and sellers decide to transact exchanges on the basis of prices, price movements, price differentials, and the availability of money. A market is thus a place of choices, where buyers and sellers can choose, within limits, to exchange what they own for something else they value somewhat more highly, whether it is another product or money. Market institutions vary in complexity and concreteness, from simple barter markets in low productivity rural areas to highly complicated, nonconcrete arrangements for the worldwide transactions of a wheat market or a gold market. Factor markets, such as labor markets, land markets, and capital markets, may be subdivided into dozens of highly specialized arrangements for specific types of factors, such as urban land markets, long-term and short-term capital markets, insurance markets, and ocean freight markets. A characteristic of the less developed countries is that market institutions are very inadequately developed relative to their needs and to the development of market institutions in the more developed countries. A high productivity society requires a large number of highly specialized market institutions. Without these institutions the adoption of new technologies of production is severely handicapped.

PUBLIC ADMINISTRATION

Public administration is the management of the affairs of government. By definition, each country is free to determine its legitimate areas of governmental operation; there can be no rigid categorization of legitimate and illegitimate governmental functions.* Criteria for the scope of governmental operations must be established in terms of the philosophy, ideology, culture, and social objectives of a people; and to say that these vary from people to people and from time to time is to point out the obvious. A society that is attempting to modernize itself is necessarily changing the scope of its governmental affairs. Whatever these affairs are, they require management in a way that relates the management of complex organizations to their purposes. This management is the concern of public administration, considered as a body of thought and knowledge which can be usefully studied and evaluated.

In a special sense the major job of governments of the less developed countries is to encourage, develop, coordinate, and to make possible the institutional changes that are essential for improved production, productivity, and income distribution. No new institution is begun or old one significantly changed without either the approval or support of government. Economic institutions are the framework by which production and distribution are accomplished. Within this framework move the economic forces that move people to produce goods and services and exchange them for other goods and services. If production in a country is to reach higher levels, these institutions must be so structured and operated that they permit, even press for the general adoption of improved technologies of production. The historical forces that seem to press toward an enlarged role of government in present day economic development can be detailed into many subcategories, obviously present and visible.

Public administration is a scarce input into this process. As a scarce input, it must be allocated carefully; it must be "economized" in that its use must be minimized and its output or return must be maximized. Government, at almost any level of development, is an interdependent mesh of complex organizations. To achieve their purposes as related to economic development, these governmental organizations must be managed by a large number of administrators with a wide variety of background, training, life styles, and objectives. A study of some of the management aspects of public administration is one of the ways of attempting to instill a common approach to problems of operating a government with a commitment for economic development.

The number of ways in which governmental affairs impinge and influence the economic activities of a country are so numerous they almost defy systematic enumeration. By developing some useful categories of these relationships and examining how governmental policies and practices are involved, some idea can be given of how important

---

*This definition is obviously inadequate, but only a long discussion, necessarily full of semantic traps, could try to establish the essential moral and philosophical limits of governmental functions.

is the role of public administration to the process of economic development. The government agencies that employ relatively large numbers of professionally trained economists, such as the central bank, the finance ministry and the central planning agency, clearly encompass only a small part of the relationship of governmental affairs to economic growth. All important institutions, political, social, as well as economic, are involved in the process of modernization and are also involved in the process of economic growth. Public administrators play key roles in the initiation of new institutions and the necessary modification of old ones. While economic institutions play a special role in the process of economic growth, they are not the total and may not even be the critical center of the public administration problems of achieving a more rapid rate of economic growth. Yet, it would be difficult indeed to find an important public administrator who does not in the course of a week's work do many things that affect the economic growth of the community in which he works or the sector of the society's activities in which he performs his governmental responsibilities. A knowledge of how economic growth occurs, how economic institutions relate to governmental operations, must be an important part of the experience and concern of all public administrators, not just economists.

It is an obvious truism, often overlooked, that government sets and enforces the rules under which economic activities are carried out. These rules may have been initiated by ancient custom or may be the result of current legislation or fiat. By enforcing or not enforcing laws or customs, government in its positive or negative action makes the rules under which economic institutions operate. In modernizing countries, no significant economic activity can be carried out without the strong impact of government action, positive or negative. No significant economic institution can be established or important change made without the approval of some government agency. Often government action goes beyond mere approval or disapproval. Direct participation in economic activities is quite common, by governments supplying inputs, making managerial decisions, and selling products and services. By licensing, by control measures, by establishing and enforcing basic rules of property rights, personal rights, and social rights, government accepts, rejects, and modifies the institutional arrangements of a modernizing society.

Government involvement in economic matters is so great that it is possible to study the development and operation of the economic institutions of a modernizing country entirely from the governmental point of view. This has many advantages. It focuses on the aspect of institution building and operation that is most amenable to direct change. Government policies and actions are far easier to change than the actions and the motivations of the numerous individuals involved in the behavior pattern. This viewpoint therefore tends to be more operational than other viewpoints that attempt to cover all points of view. However, it would be a mistake to assume that government policies or actions are the totality of economic institutions. Strong as government influence may be, it often is not enough to move or shape the institution as completely as it wishes. The general purpose of this book is to explore these relationships and to see how government, recognizing the existence and importance of economic forces, can improve its ability to help initiate modern economic institutions.

PRODUCTION AND PRODUCTIVITY

The less developed countries wish to change their economic subsystem to produce more goods and services. This requires far greater changes than merely adding more of the same kind of capital, labor, land and management now in use; it necessarily involves more productivity, a greater return for the work performed. Not only must there be more inputs, more jobs, more machinery, more seeds, and more fertilizer, but the inputs must be improved in quality, and outputs per unit of input must be greatly increased through improved means of production—through improved technology. The elements of production and productivity must be analyzed with a view toward changing their use to achieve higher production and productivity. Some basic economic forces in the supply and demand of improved inputs must be understood because these forces are strongly shaped and influenced by governmental policies and administrative practices. How governments can use these economic forces to help increase the quality and quantity of economic inputs and to raise the technological levels of production becomes the essence of public administration of economic development.

Economic forces, as used here, means tendencies or energies that are channeled through economic institutions. These forces are basic tendencies that are generally present in rational economic behavior. Their exact behavior, the way they work out in a specific institution, will vary with the constraints and limitations of that institution. It is important, however, to identify these forces and to appreciate in a general way how they affect production and distribution of goods and services. The existence of these forces may be derived deductively, from the assumption that man is a rational being and acts rationally in his economic activity. The effect of these forces can be observed empirically. These forces are, therefore, analytical constructs, ways of arbitrarily grouping ideas in order to see how other analytical constructs called economic institutions work in a modernizing society.

The assumption that man acts as a rational economic being has been strongly attacked and can be only partially defended.[1] Man is often not rational in his behavior by any definition of rationality. Beyond that, the criteria and limitations of rationality are obviously culture bound. What our society considers economic rationality may often be determined by environment, by classes of a society, by ethical

13

standards, and by beliefs, superstitions and traditions.* Psychology, with all its insights and experimentation, has offered less than satisfactory explanations of why man acts as he does.

Yet, the analytical method of grouping certain kinds of behavior and ascertaining similarities in behavior is useful, even if crude and subject to exceptions and contradictions. The whole social structure depends on the ability of its members to assume that certain relationships will exist. For example, without assuming that most people are not murderers and are not prone to sudden violent impulses to murder their neighbors, a society cannot exist. In American cities, the painful lesson is being learned that when this assumption is not valid for even a small portion of the general public, cities become desperate places to inhabit. Similarly, in attempting to understand and modify institutions that represent important subsystems of economic activity, it is useful to recognize some basic economic forces that influence and affect these economic activities.

These forces do not operate mechanically or surely. To perceive them in this manner is to miss entirely their importance and their effect. Even a single, simple economic activity will be influenced by many different forces, which may push in many directions at the same time. These forces are manifest in the many different decisions and options or choices available to the individual. An economic institution, as a pattern of economic behavior, in a sense aggregates or adds up these individual behaviors. This important point will become clearer, hopefully, as the economic forces are identified and related to economic institutions.

THE ROLE OF DEMAND

The composition and intensity of demand for the products of the economic subsystem is as important as the supply. Indeed, they cannot be separated in operations although they are usually separated analytically to make their study less complex. In the simplest form of a society, where everybody produces goods only for himself or for his immediate family, the action to create the supply of a product can be

---

*There are concepts of bounded rationality which try to explain how people operate when complete rationality is impossible or unlikely. People only see a few of the possible alternatives and predict only part of the consequences. Even the acceptance of "good enough" shows the force of rationality and a recognition of that force. See H.A. Simon, Models of Man (New York: John Wiley & Son, 1957).

said to have a concurrent known demand; it would be irrational to produce what is not demanded. As soon as exchange becomes a necessary part of economic production, demand must be estimated or assumed by the producer. As a society becomes more complex, with higher and higher levels of productivity, the existence and nature of the demand for products become more complex   subject to more influences that differ from the influences that determine the production decisions. Yet the ability of most people to buy the products they need, the effective demand for products, is to a large extent determined by the process of production.

INSTITUTIONS AND INSTITUTION BUILDING

A society can be viewed as a complex system of interacting subsystems that channel behavior, defined as institutions.* An established institution is an accepted pattern of behavior, a means by which a society accomplishes its purposes of maintaining and ruling itself, of providing the goods and services it uses, of continuing its system of values and beliefs, and, in general, functioning as a social system. The school system, the family, the church, are shorthand ways of referring to important channels or patterns of behavior that a society has developed for nurturing and training its young and for establishing normal value systems and beliefs. By identifying and examining important institutions of a society, it is possible to view how a society operates. This becomes a way of grouping the almost infinitely varied activities of a society into meaningful subsystems and sub-subsystems. Obviously, something is lost in the grouping, some differences hidden, and some important relationships blurred. By selecting institutions that are too broad and general, the relationships explained may be too complex or vague for useful analysis. By selecting very detailed institutions the analysis may become trivial. The level of institutions selected for consideration must be operational in terms of the purposes of the analysis.

The institutions of a given society may be accepted by many or rejected by most. They may be efficient or inefficient in accomplishing their purposes. They may have one purpose or many, even conflicting purposes. Institutions may have their origin in antiquity, in folk beliefs, or may be the result of current legislation. A social system is a complex mixture of these behavior patterns, and specific institutions may

---

*Clearly there are many other definitions of institutions. Institutions may be considered as "systems of rules" or as "normative action patterns." See Chapter 6.

encompass activities that are affected by political, social, and economic beliefs, value systems and objectives.

A society that is modernizing is changing its patterns of behavior. A society that tries to increase its production of goods and services therefore accepts the need for changing its institutions so that more production will result. It is impossible to conceive of a society that can increase its production significantly without drastically changing its existing institutions or adopting new ones. Since it is advanced here that modernization as a process affects all important aspects or elements of a society, including its beliefs and value systems, it follows that its institutions, viewed as behavior patterns, must also be modified.

One further concept is required to make this "institutional" view of a changing society useful in analysis. A particular behavior pattern may be effectively utilized, or may be neglected and ineffective. The concept of becoming institutionalized therefore can be considered the process of adopting a behavior pattern and eventually achieving the objectives of that behavior pattern. Thus, a government agency may design an institution with potentially tremendous impact on a specific area of economic activity; for example, a rural bank designed to loan money to cooperatives. The efforts to establish the bank and operate it can be described as an effort to create an institution, to have the bank become institutionalized. As the bank develops its procedures, creates its flow of authority and funds, its clients, markets, and channels of approval and rejection of loans, its systems of control of expenditures and accountability, its relationships with other government agencies, it is becoming institutionalized. Thus, to be institutionalized is in a sense to become accepted, to become effective as a means of accomplishing the purposes of the pattern of behavior.

Recently, a great deal of attention has been paid to the process of institution building. After many years both the donors and receivers of foreign aid have realized that in a real sense their efforts to utilize resources properly are attempts to create new institutions or to modify existing ones. Resources that were utilized to feed hungry people or to teach rich people were of course important, but it was also important to create the circumstances under which people could be able to produce what they needed. Helping a country to modernize means, in a real sense, to help it create institutions for increasing its production and productivity and improve income distribution. Technical assistance therefore means institution building, if it is not limited to simple relief activities.

By studying many different efforts to create suitable instituions in a modernizing country, it was hoped that some general levels of insights could be established, insights that would be useful to others attempting the same task. Why are some institutions quickly established, while others, similar in general nature, are more slowly accepted or may even be rejected? Are there some general characteristics of the initiation of new ways of doing things or adaptation of old ways that can be helpful in speeding up the achievement of becoming institutionalized? If new institutions were easily established, modernization might be an easy process to undertake. But creating a new institution is not a simple task. Since it is a pattern of behavior, people must act in a new changed way. To become institutionalized, enough people must follow the behavior patterns sufficiently to achieve reasonably well the objectives of the institution. People adjust their behavior patterns very slowly. The power of tradition and custom is difficult to overcome. Problems of motivation and coercion are combined with evaluations of benefits and costs, and it is a difficult process for any new institution to be developed and efficiently operated. Studying institution building is one way of attempting to learn how to change a society so that it becomes modernized. One should be clear, however, that viewing society as a complex of institutions is a limited approach; and an analyst who relies on this view entirely would again be one of the blind men examining the elephant.

The central question to face is whether or not there are ways of speeding up the process of establishing new institutions. Experience and intuition answer this question affirmatively. There are ways that new behavior patterns can be adopted and old behavior patterns modified so that a society achieves a higher level of production. These ways can be grouped into some useful guiding concepts which assist in understanding the process of institution building. Unfortunately, the wisdom on this important aspect of social engineering is neither simple nor complete. The guiding concepts thus far disclosed are partial, contradictory, and far from foolproof. Useful as they may be to some administrators, they must be regarded as tentative indications of directions, rather than a definitive road map.

A major reason why the process of institution building is complicated is simply that an institution cannot be studied in isolation. It must be examined as it operates in a society. It is dependent on other institutions, and in turn it affects older institutions. Institutions are a part of the society in which they exist; they cannot be foreign to that society and be successfully institutionalized. They cannot be unsuitable or "indigestible." It is impossible to take an institution out of one society and fit it, unchanged, into another society. To do so invites failure, even ensures it. Institution building requires innovation and adaptation, the discovery of changes that are necessary for successful operation in a different society, with different psychological, cultural, social, and political value systems.

Economic institutions are the pattern of behavior that a society has adopted in its economic activities, the production and distribution of goods and services. These patterns are importantly affected and closely related to other patterns of behavior in noneconomic activities. Their interrelationships are mutually causative, in that each affects the other. Examining economic activities as they are grouped into economic institutions is thus a process of grouping somewhat similar

behavior so that an infinitely large number of activities can be reduced
to a meaningful number of patterns that can be examined.

Economic institutions can be studied separately because economics,
as a social science discipline, has achieved some insights into their
operations that may be useful in managing these activities or predicting
their operations. This viewpoint is a manipulative approach and, therefore, may be unscientific, in the narrow sense of that term. Yet the
approach is essentially pragmatic and practical. Economic institutions
are studied because in a modernizing society, existing economic institutions are changing and new economic institutions must be developed.
Certain causal relationships and associations have been identified
which may be useful in ascertaining the changes that are required in
the economic subsystem in order to create the opportunity and capacity
for increased production.

The study of economic institutions therefore becomes the analysis
of changes in economic activities, and the forces or tendencies that
induce, persuade, or coerce people into making these changes. A
major contribution of economics to the understanding of the modernization process may be an analysis of the forces or tendencies that are
channeled through economic institutions. In attempting to study how
a society must change in order to achieve higher levels of production,
these forces must be examined as they work in economic institutions.
In a sense, the institutions are behavioral expressions of these economic forces, the resultants of the forces in terms of the actual behavior of people. It is impossible to understand any economic institution
without considering how these economic forces are affecting that institution. To change economic institutions deliberately means that these
economic forces must be channeled differently and therefore changed.
To create new economic institutions means to provide new behavioral
patterns for these forces, as they are revealed in the actual behavior
of workers, managers, sellers, and buyers.

GOVERNMENT ECONOMIC PLANNING

Economic planning has become a major element in a government's
efforts to speed up economic development. The general effectiveness
of governmental economic planning may be in doubt, but its widespread
use and importance can no longer be questioned. Every less developed
country, if it claims economic development as one of its objectives,
develops and advertises its economic planning propensities. Economic
plans have been published and used as guidance for tax policies, monetary policies, resource allocation, international loans and grants, and
almost every type of governmental economic operation. As with many
complex situations, it is often difficult to distinguish between poor economic planning and no economic planning. Yet planning as a major part
of the process of determining how much and what is produced by the

18

economic system is a fact of life that confronts every public administrator in the less developed countries.

To become effective, the economic planning process becomes an exercise of total government, not just a group of trained planners working in a separate agency. Every government agency of any significance becomes involved in both the formulation of the plans and in their implementation and evaluation. To do otherwise is to reduce planning to an exercise in short term public relations with little beneficial effect on economic development. Plans provide operating guidance for public administrators and plan formulation is based not only on future objectives but also on current operating experience and needs. Economic planning not only provides an opportunity to assign priorities to the products of the system, but also determines societal transformation. Political and social development cannot be divorced from their influence on economic planning just as economic development affects the social and political aspects of the life of a country. It is no exaggeration to assert that in economic planning, political and social decisions are often far more relevant than economic decisions.

Thus, it is apparent that all public administrators are involved to a marked degree in the process of economic planning. Decisions of key administrators that do not affect the implementation of economic plans are few indeed. Planning necessarily shapes day by day decisions as well as basic, long time decisions of public administrators. Major resource allocation decisions by political leaders become the basis of far more numerous minor but still important administrative decisions in plan implementation and evaluation. To assume that only planning agency officers develop and implement economic plans is to assure the failure of the planning process. That is why a knowledge of the planning process is so important to public administrators and why, operationally, planning cannot be completely separated from other kinds of governmental activities.

SUMMARY

To recapitulate, this introductory chapter indicates the general direction of the argument in this book:

1. A modernizing society, to achieve economic development, must increase production and productivity of goods and services and improve income distribution.

2. Institutions are patterns of behavior in a society, the established way a society does the things it wants or has to do. Economic institutions are the patterns of behavior which a society uses to produce and distribute the goods and services it values.

3. To achieve higher production and productivity and to improve income distribution, the economic institutions of a country must be

changed. Indeed, all important institutions, arbitrarily classified into political, social, cultural, and economic, will be changed in the modernization process.

4. Government, the means by which a society rules and regulates itself, is clearly important to the continuation and change of economic institutions. Government sets or helps set rules, enforces rules, and is involved in all important changes in existing economic institutions or the initiation of new economic institutions. Through national economic planning, government attempts to establish priorities and develop the means by which the country's rate of economic growth can be sharply increased.

5. Within economic institutions, some basic forces or tendencies are channelled, as expressed in patterns of behavior. These forces, since they affect economic transactions, are important to understand if new economic institutions are to be created or old ones changed.

6. The competition of producers and consumers, of buyers and sellers, becomes involved in the forces that adjust supply and demand in markets, that provide economic signals to the participants of transactions in markets, affecting total production and consumption decisions. Markets, the economic institutions that channel economic behavior involving exchanges of goods and services, are thus a vital part of the whole process of competition. These forces, as they are channelled or developed into acceptable patterns of behavior by the people of a country, become the economic institutions of that country. They are the means by which a country attains a high level of production and productivity and improves the income of its people.

It is the thesis of this book that government administrators are deeply involved in the way these basic economic forces are expressed in the economic institutions of a country. The inadequacies of government administration in the operation of new economic institutions is probably the greatest single cause of the poor economic performance and the slow pace of economic development in the less developed countries. Therefore, administrators must understand more about these forces and how economic institutions channel these forces. Successful economic planning requires that public administrators understand the nature of the planning process and how government proposes to help marshal the country's resources to achieve greater economic growth. The management of the complex organizations of government must be geared to the necessities of improved technology in the production process and of more equitable distribution of the product. To improve public administration in the less developed countries is, to a large extent, to improve the relationship of government to the numerous important changes that are occurring in the institutions of a country, of which the economic institutions are an important part.

NOTE

1. See P.T. Bauer and B.S. Yamey, The Economics of Underdeveloped Countries (London: Cambridge University Press, 1963), pp. 91-101.

2

ELEMENTS
OF PRODUCTION
AND PRODUCTIVITY

THE GROSS NATIONAL PRODUCT

Before examining how production and productivity can be increased, and income distribution improved, it is necessary to examine the basic characteristics of economic production. Production is the process by which inputs are combined or modified to create valued outputs. While there may be some inputs that are free in the sense that they are available at no cost, it is generally true that inputs are scarce; they cost something to use, and therefore their use is related in some fashion to the value of the output. Also, it is clear that the output must be valued by society or some segment of society, or the use of scarce inputs would be senseless. Why produce at a cost something that is known to have no value?

The total production of a country is called its Gross National Product (GNP).* This total consists of all the value of goods and services produced by that country in one year. The time period of one year is of course arbitrary, and is taken for convenience to include all kinds of seasonal production. In aggregating this figure, problems of method and scope arise on all sides. How to add together dissimilar goods, how to account for services, and how to avoid duplication in measuring value as a product goes through several stages of its manufacture, these are the types of problems that economists have answered by developing some reasonably acceptable procedures. Products are valued at their market prices where this is available or at "imputed" market prices if the products are not marketed. Services that are not marketed

---

*The difference between Gross National Product and Gross Domestic Product can be disregarded here. It will be explained later, when the difference has some operational significance.

are usually valued at cost. To avoid duplication in intermediate stages, as in the case of counting wheat as a product, then flour, then bread, only products going to final consumers are included, with adjustments for the products in the production pipeline. The agreements to use these statistical devices have generally been based on the economics of the more developed countries, where markets are more developed and production statistics are more available. The application of these concepts and measurements to the less developed countries becomes increasingly difficult and hazardous. Yet, with all its faults, the GNP is the best measurement available of the total achievement of the production processes of a country.[1]

There are two ways of looking at and measuring the flow of goods and services. One is to measure the value of the products produced, the flow of products to the final consumers. The other is from the viewpoint of the earnings or income of the factors of production, the value of inputs used in the production process. This is similar to measuring the output of a factory in two ways, by saying it produced so much of product A and so much of product B, with a given total value and also by saying that it generated income equal to so much in wages, salaries, interest, profit, and other incomes. By definition, these two methods of measuring product should be exactly the same total if all the arithmetic is correct; but the breakdown is different. Both product and income data are frequently used to present the total production of a country.

Expressing the GNP on a per capita basis is an attempt to meet the problem of the country's population density. Obviously, the production in large countries cannot be compared to that of smaller countries without some adjustment. Similarly, as a country's population grows with time, a comparison of its production between periods of time may need adjustment. For most purposes, the per capita GNP, computed by dividing the GNP by the population, is the best available measure of the average value of goods and services produced per person.

It must be recognized immediately that per capita GNP has only a limited value as a measure of modernization, even of economic growth. Its statistical validity is usually open to serious questions. Its sole emphasis on production, with no account taken of distribution of income, or of the many nonproductive economic functions, as well as the even more numerous noneconomic facets of a society, make this a questionable index of economic growth and an even more questionable index of modernization. Its use as the former can only be justified by the absence of any better indices of economic growth, and its use as an index of modernization is so questionable as to warrant its discontinuance. There are many other measures of economic progress and well-being, but these too have constraints that limit their usefulness. For example, the annual production of electric power is highly correlated with the tendency toward using modern production methods and improved living standards in general. The production of specific products may also be used as indications of economic progress, such as textiles, soap, and petroleum products. The use of newsprint, the availability of radios, bicycles, electric bulbs, miles of telephone and telegraph lines, of railroads and paved highways, all have been advanced as useful indicators of economic well-being. At a different level, measures of how a society takes care of its helpless and unfortunate members would be even better indicators of the degrees of modernization. Thus, the number and percentage of children in school, the number of bankers, doctors, nurses, veterinarians, number of hospital beds, institutions for the mentally ill, all would be directly related to improvement in the well-being of a people. Mortality rates and such measures of human wastage as deaths in childbirth or children's death rates are probably better measures of well-being than per capita economic production. But noneconomic measures are difficult to quantify and interpret. The widespread confusion between economic growth, modernization, well-being of a society and progress in general has left the field to per capita GNP as the most widely used single measure of all the concepts.[*]

In a sense, per capita GNP is a measure of productivity. The concepts of GNP and per capita GNP present quite clearly the difference between production and productivity. Production is the output, the product of a process. Productivity is the measure of the output compared with some measure of input, in order to have a measure of efficiency.[†] True, the basic reason for computing per capita GNP is to have the average production per person in the country. A somewhat more relevant measure of productivity is the product per worker, which is the usual measure of general productivity, and it is often useful to compute other measures of productivity, such as product per acre, and product per unit of capital.

A major caution is necessary to avoid a serious mistake and avert becoming a "prisoner of words and their definitions." GNP may be the best single measure of economic growth; but it has serious limitations

---

[*]Economists protest, somewhat feebly to be sure, at the use of GNP and per capita GNP as the measure of "well-being" and "modernization." The inadequacies are obvious, and economists do not wish to be responsible for the ineffective analysis that inevitably derives from confusing "economic growth" with these other concepts. While related in many ways, there are many substantial and debatable differences. But it is so satisfying to be the "guardians and priests" of the successful measure that the protests of economists are naturally less emphatic than their constant use of per capita GNP as the "one best measure" of nearly everything related to progress and improvement.

[†]Efficiency, in an engineering sense, is output divided by input. Variations of this basic relationship occurs when outputs and inputs are measured in terms of energy, physical product, value, and so forth.

particularly as applied to the less developed countries. The production of a whole country is a tremendously differentiated mixture of thousands of different items. The only useful way they can be combined into a single measure is to place a value on each product and include them in the aggregate index, the GNP, based on each product's total value. This means that the price assigned to an end product is very important in determining its influence on the GNP. If, in a given year, there was an increase in the production of luxury goods, products consumed only by the wealthy few, the GNP would go up, even if the large mass of consumers were relatively unaffected. The product mix of a country is the resultant of many production decisions; but it is largely influenced, particularly as far as the private sector is concerned, on effective demand, on who is willing and able to buy the products of economic subsystems. If the effective demand is drastically changed, the product mix will be changed. GNP can increase with an increase in the same product mix or with a different product mix. If there is an increase in the production of weapons only, the aggregate measure, the GNP, may increase; but this may hardly be an instance of an increase in GNP reflecting an increase in welfare, even if the increase in weapons is judged necessary. An increase in the production of goods needed by the numerous poor may be socially more desirable than an increase of. luxury goods. Clearly, GNP as a measure of production and interpreted as a measure of social improvement must be scrutinized very carefully and used with caution.

Economic growth for a country means producing more goods and services. It also means producing more per capita, a concept that necessarily includes some aspects of distribution and productivity as well as production. The question of how far distribution of income is involved in economic growth will be discussed in Chapter 5; but here it is important to note that in most ways it is impossible to separate production from distribution of income, that implicitly or explicitly, analysis of production involves assumptions and inferences about distribution that are often overlooked. As applied to a country, economic growth clearly requires increasing productivity as well as increasing total production. The relationship between production and productivity is therefore one of the basic concepts that must be explored, if economic growth is to be understood.

FACTOR INPUTS OF PRODUCTION

The factors of production are generally grouped into three categories: land (or natural resources, and therefore nonreproducible); labor (the human input, including training, experience, skill, organization); capital (reproducible physical goods used in further production). The use of these three categories to include all inputs of the production process obviously brings up many kinds of classification problems, most of which are quite irrelevant. The only purpose of this classification is ease of reference. Land is used to represent all nonreproducible resources, all natural resources, not just land itself. Yet a good deal of the quality of land is the result of human labor, which makes it reproducible and therefore, by definition, similar to capital. Labor, too, is a curiously mixed category including quite dissimilar inputs, which require quite different analysis. Yet, there is enough usefulness in the three-category concept to continue to use it in analyzing production and productivity, as long as there is proper recognition of the variety in each category.

One other concept is required to complete our dictionary of terms at this point. The manner in which the factors of production, land, labor, and capital, are combined together in the production process is referred to as technology. A higher level of technology means a better method of combining the factors of production to achieve a higher production. Improved technology is therefore important to productivity, and not merely to greater production. Thus, if a peasant farmer working with a wooden plow and a cow is able to plow one-third of an acre a day, adding another farmer, plow, and cow to that farm will increase the total production of plowed land; but using the same technology will not increase production per worker. However, using a steel plow and better traction power could permit the farmer to plow three acres a day. This, conceptually is an improvement in technology and represents an increase in productivity as well as total production. Production, therefore, is the process of using technology to combine the three factor inputs, land, labor, and capital, into useful goods and services.

Land (Natural Resources)

The natural resources of a country are obviously an important element in its economic activities. To say that a majority of the workers in a country are engaged in agricultural pursuits is another way of saying that land is the most important natural resource involved in the production process. The agricultural land, the minerals, including oil, the forest products, the fisheries, all represent the natural resources of a country, the nonreproducible elements given by the physical nature, the climate, the geography of a country. The location of a country, its nearness to large countries and to ocean transportation, must also be included in the concept of natural resources. It is quite true that often these physical attributes labeled natural and nonreproducible are really produced by human efforts, such as land cleared so long ago, that currently one assumes it was naturally agricultural land. Does the fertility of land, restored by intelligent farming, become classified as a natural resource? Yet the concept of natural resources is a useful one to describe available or potentially available factor inputs that are somehow different for any current production process than the other man-made physical factor inputs. Some form of natural resource is generally required in any significant production process, and the type of natural resource often has a dominant influence on the nature and form of the other complementary factor inputs of labor and capital, as well as the technology used. Natural resources may even be a substitute for capital. Rivers may take the place of man-made roads; and ample, timely rain may make man-made irrigation ditches unnecessary. The natural resources of a country, their availability, ease of use, type, location, and form are clearly of prime importance in determining the nature of the economy of a country, and what can be done to achieve a more rapid rate of economic growth. But availability of natural resources cannot be measured against abstract concepts of adequacy; it must be compared with the actual and potential need of the production function of the economy, with the availability of the complementary labor and capital factor inputs. By this standard many of the less developed countries have to increase the other factor inputs before they can make adequate use of their potential natural resources.

Important as the natural resources are, their role in development must not be exaggerated. Several myth-destroying facts must be kept in mind. First, natural resources do not seem to be a prime determinant of economic development. As one looks at the countries of the world, there seems to be little connection between their natural resources and their relative economic development. Some of the most developed countries have apparently the richest endowment of natural resources. Yet Great Britain and Japan are examples of countries that have achieved a relatively high level of productivity with an apparent scarcity of natural resources. On the other hand, Indonesia is an example of a country rich in natural resources; yet its economic growth has been visibly less than successful. While natural resources are clearly important, they are often a permissive, rather than a driving force in the economy. They need so many complementarities, particularly the improvement in the quality and quantity of associated factor inputs, that their role is often misunderstood. Very rich deposits of oil may provide some apparent exceptions to this generalization. Iraq, Saudi Arabia, Iran, and other countries are of course affected in many ways by their rich oil resources; but they confront many difficulties in economic growth that keeps them at low levels of productivity. It seems clear that mere possession of ample fertile land, rich mineral deposits, extensive forests and fisheries, good climate, and sometimes huge lakes of oil are not, by themselves, sufficient to make inevitable the rapid attainment of a high per capita GNP.

Second, the value of natural resources is determined by market prices and not by any intrinsic value or merit. Every less developed country is familiar with the situation of knowing about mineral deposits that are potentially capable of providing large quantities of a valuable mineral. The reasons for remaining potential rather than having actual production are generally related to costs of production, costs of transportation, costs of opening and operating the mines. These costs are market phenomena, often worldwide in nature. The difference between potential and actual inputs often represents the difference between planning and doing.

It is understandable but still regretable that the leaders of many of the less developed countries have exaggerated notions of the natural resources of their countries. Many of their nationalistic aspirations prior to independence reflected reactions to economic exploitation by imperial powers. The mineral and agricultural products exported under colonial rule were visible evidence of natural resources that were exploited, largely for the master country's benefit. Nearly every colony had stories of rich natural resources that were not developed because it served the interests of the colonial powers to keep them unused. Some of these stories were probably true, although most were exaggerated. Independence not only meant the elimination of the lion's share of profits that went to the masters; but probably more important, it meant the opportunity to develop the country's natural resources in accordance with the country's own needs, and not the best interests of the faraway imperial power.

These beliefs had enough elements of truth to be strongly and widely held. However, they really are only partial pictures of reality and are usually misleading in their inferences. There can be little doubt that many rich natural resources were developed with the interests of the imperial power in mind, and that the share of the product taken by the master clearly warranted the use of the word exploitation. Yet the overwhelming influence of market prices was also present and for the most part dominated production decisions. After independence, the potential riches often remained potential and not actual, because it simply wasn't profitable to develop them. The lion's share of the product which was supposed to have been drained off by the colonial power was often somewhat illusionary, but actually remained quite small relative to a country's riches. It, too, was still a market determined phenomenon, a resultant of costs of production and transportation and of market prices of the product.

Agricultural land has an additional quality which is important to remember. Basic quality may be fixed by nature, but it often may be used up in the production process and is renewable only with effort. While climate and physical location may be natural, fertility, physical condition, topography and access to markets and water are often manmade qualities depending on capital investment rather than natural resources. It is not important to illustrate the arbitrary composition of a category called land. What is important is the point that even natural resources are often largely the result of market forces that determine costs and prices.

Labor

Labor is the human input, in all its wonderful variety. It encompasses the physical efforts of unskilled workers, the creativity of skilled workers, the knowledge and experience of managers and professional workers, the will, decisions and actions at all levels of human endeavor in the production process. Clearly, it is a very mixed bag, and only the need for a shorthand way of expressing a complicated input justifies the use of this single word.

What makes even more complex the use of labor as one of the factor inputs in the production process is the realization that the human element is an end of production as well as a means of production. To treat human effort as only one of the elements of production along with land, oil, trucks and horses, is to create an opportunity for misjudging the purpose of the whole production process—the increased well-being of people. A long time ago, economists discovered that while labor had many commodity-like qualities, it could not be considered only as a commodity. The labor market was not just a commodity market. In many important ways, it was the purpose of the other markets, as well as operating as a market in its own exchanges. While it is useful to use labor as one of the three factors of production, and to analyze its market price, its fluctuations in supply and demand, its relative scarcity and availability, as if it were just another element in the production process, it is always necessary to recognize the unique characteristics of this input factor, its role as a major element in the purpose of the whole process. Market prices of labor can be determined and are critical in all examinations of market relationships, as well as decisions to invest and to produce goods and services. However, one becomes involved in another kind of calculation when one considers health, and even life or death of persons. Yet, if one wishes to examine production, all input elements must be considered, labor along with land and capital.

The concepts of employment and unemployment are particularly difficult to apply to undifferentiated labor and to most of the workers of the less developed countries. The total quantity of work is often divided among a parent and all children capable of working, as on family farms in a peasant agriculture, or in family owned shops and small factories in villages and cities. Everybody is equally employed and unemployed, and all except the smallest children are in the labor market. To count the unemployed as one would count factory workers or skilled mechanics who are looking for jobs is quite a distortion of logic. Yet some way must be found to express the degree of use of this factor input, the availability of unutilized capacities for further use of this input. Since distribution of the product of the production process is to a large extent associated with contribution of inputs in

the production process, unutilized labor inputs represent lower availabilities of goods and services to the people of a country and lower
distribution. This is merely an awkward way of saying what is intuitively accepted—that unemployment means that the people are not
earning wages, hence are less well off than when they are gainfully
employed. Economic development and economic growth are often measured in terms of finding more employment for people, of finding jobs
for people who otherwise are merely doing their share of the family
work. While clearly economic growth is more than finding more jobs,
certainly that is one of the essentials and clearly represents a major
aspect of the purposes and methods of economic growth.

The fact that labor is both a means and an end of the production
process introduces some sensitivities in language that must be taken
into account. For example, when one discusses the quality of labor,
it is necessary to avoid any connotation of disparagement and personal inferiority. It seems permissible to measure overt capabilities, to
say that one man is more skilled than another, even more industrious
and hard working than another. But it is also necessary to insist that
as a human being, with all the rights and privileges that connotes,
each human is basically equal, regardless of skill, training, and status.
Yet the concept of market price of a factor input called labor comes
close, in language, to reducing humans to a commodity and to the
status of slave labor. The fact that widespread institutions of slavery
did exist until recently in many parts of the world, and that in many
production units workers are still in visible dependency circumstances,
makes the question of labor as a commodity quite a sensitive one. It
should be clear that questions of quality of labor refer to technical
input characteristics, and not to human desirability and status.

Skills, experience, and organization are included in the labor input because it is impossible to separate them conceptually from any
other kind of human input. To anyone who has observed a skilled ditch
digger doing a job, as compared to a college professor digging a ditch
in his backyard, the problem of measuring skill and experience is indeed subtle. This point will be discussed more fully later, since one
of the major problems of the less developed countries is providing
adequate skills and organizations for higher productivity.

Capital

The third of the factor inputs of production is labeled capital; and
like the other two, it is a shorthand expression, useful but purchased
at a cost. The word capital in the English language has many correct
meanings, including other technical meanings in economics. Some
times these meanings are related and sometimes they are so different

that communication is lessened by use of the word.* Capital, as used in the sense of a factor input of production, refers to physical things used in further production. This includes the buildings, machinery and equipment of factories, and the buildings, roads, power stations and communication systems of a country, as well as all the work in progress, the partially completed buildings, the goods that are in the production pipeline, and the goods en route to the final consumer. It also includes, technically, all inventories of consumers' goods, even those in the hands of final consumers. At any one time, the capital of a country, considered as a factor of production, includes all the products previously produced and those that have not been consumed.†

The difference between capital as "physical products used in further production" and capital as a "financial capacity to command the procurement of goods and services," needs some explanation, since both are used in a technical sense by economists. Financial capital is largely a bookkeeping concept. When an owner of a factory refers to his capital, he is probably referring to the extent of his financial involvement in the concern, rather than its buildings and equipment. To speak of the capital of a bank generally refers to the funds that the investors have pooled together to establish and operate the bank. "Working capital" is another illustration of the concept used in a financial sense, as the resources available to operate a production unit in its buying and selling activities, to be replenished as sales returns are available. The financial meanings of capital are quite essential, and should not be confused with the use of the term capital as a factor input in production. There are important relationships between the two uses, arising from ownership of a means of production; but the danger of misunderstanding should also be evident.

The process of creating capital is termed capital formation. From the definition of capital it should be clear that capital formation is often determined by hindsight, rather than as an initial conscious effort. The construction of a building or the purchase of a metal stamping machine is clearly capital formation in intent. But the production of consumer goods, such as rice or textiles, turns out to be capital formation if the consumer goods are not consumed and become a stock or inventory. While problems of measurement clearly result in omitting most inventories of consumer goods from the statistics of capital formation, sometimes inventories of export products, for example, are a type of

---

*Yet no substitute seems to be available and to pioneer one requires a combination of irritation and ingenuity that is apparently missing among economists.

†The reason for adding to the complexity by pointing out that inventories of consumer goods are part of capital will become clear later, when it is pointed out that this kind of capital can often increase without much contribution to current production.

capital formation too substantial to be disregarded. Capital formation is the creation of capital, and goods that are not consumed are part of that capital.*

Thus, capital is not a simple concept to use in the analysis of economic growth, and its misunderstanding may lead to erroneous or misapplied policies. Often, capital in the developing countries is identified with durable machinery, practically all of which must be imported. When the gap in foreign exchange is characterized as the most important proximate bottleneck that determines the rate of capital formation in a country, reference is usually made to the numerous kinds of expensive machinery that must be imported because most of the developing countries cannot develop the skill, plant capacity, and size or market to make possible plants that produce machinery. Only countries that are highly developed or very large can be efficient enough to make it economically worthwhile to produce machinery. But capital, the physical, reproducible things used in further production consists of far more than durable machinery. It consists of the buildings, roads, hospitals, schools, power plants, and transportation facilities that economic production requires. Further, and not least in importance, it consists of the stock of consumers' goods that a society requires as working capital, as capital that is constantly used and renewed as it engages in all its various activities, economic and noneconomic. A shortage in working capital, either financial or expressed in real terms, is a serious handicap in the production process. In the technical sense of the term capital, it is the stock of food that a society has at the end of the year and that is required to keep it functioning while it produces the economic goods and services it needs, as well as performing the other functions in which a society necessarily engages: its social, cultural, political, and personal activities. The essential nature of this stock of consumers' goods led early economists to deduce a wage fund theory, in which the remuneration to workers in the economic system, in a sense real wages, depended upon the stock of goods that were available for their employment.[2] Later, economists realized that this was only partially correct, since the goods that were used as real wages were constantly being produced and the concept of a fixed wage fund for any period was not a useful insight into the problems of employment and wages. Yet there is some usefulness in considering the

---

*The terms investment and capital formation are not entirely synonymous, although they are often used in the same sense. Investment, like capital, has other meanings that one must be aware of. Investment in land, for example, does not create capital; it merely transfers land from one owner to another. Investment by one person may mean disinvestment by another, when existing capital is purchased. Investment is the expenditure process by which capital is made or acquired.

stock of consumers' goods in the less developed countries as a sort of wage fund, a working capital of things that must be available to keep the economic system going in both its consumption and capital formation functions. This supply of consumers' goods, the food and clothing, as well as the more durable consumers' goods, such as housing, furniture, refrigerators, stoves, and so forth, can be expanded or contracted widely, depending upon many variables. The adoption of new technologies of production, with its increasing use of indirect methods of production, production for unknown, distant markets, increased specialization, and increased production and use of intermediate products, necessarily means that more stocks of consumers' goods are required to compensate the workers producing these additional goods. Other determinants are equally or even more important, particularly facilities for marketing goods and the style of life—the level of ease and psychology that consumers insist on in their acquisition and use of the goods and services they possess or wish to acquire. In other words, while there are strong economic reasons why the stock of consumers' goods will increase as a society modernizes itself, there are also the noneconomic reasons associated with changes in value systems, motivation, and well-being of a society.

A country that has a low level of production and productivity and wishes to move rapidly toward higher levels of production and productivity must acquire more stocks of consumption goods that can be used as working capital. These stocks of consumers' goods serve three important and different types of operations:

1. Additional stocks must be available to meet increased distribution and demand for consumers' goods. The larger working capital of a more advanced economic system with higher standards of living and a style of life in which more stocks of goods means more security and less hardship.
2. Additional stocks, particularly of food, must be available to take care of the workers who shift from food production to urban areas to engage in manufacturing, mining, trade, transportation, and other service areas. Stocks of consumers' goods utilized in this way are clearly incorporated in the rigorous definition of capital.
3. Additional stocks of consumers' goods are needed to provide incentives for stimulating production of goods both for domestic and export purposes. Thus, the stock of watches, bicycles, radios, and jewelry used to induce peasant producers to produce more rice or corn, after meeting their own consumption needs, may be important elements of the capital needed to induce higher production and productivity.

Because stocks of consumers' goods can be used merely to increase consumption, without much direct effect on future production capabilities, it is difficult to assign to their increase the operational importance they should have. Government policies that deliberately attempt to increase supplies of consumers' goods are usually identified completely with efforts to increase consumption, and not capital formation. But government policies often are designed to affect the distribution of consumers' goods either to induce greater production and productivity with existing capital or to create more capital. This is the basic difficulty in converting the larger excess of unutilized or underutilized labor, mostly unskilled, in capital formation projects. The possibility of transferring large numbers of unskilled workers from agriculture to large construction projects, such as irrigation ditches, drainage works, earth dams, and similar earth moving projects that involve little skill and capital equipment, has intrigued many governments and induced many programs that had less than the expected results.

Capital formation is a social process. Almost all elements and sectors of society are involved in important ways in the decisions and activities that result in the accumulation of the capital of a society. These social impacts can be either in the effects on savings or on the expenditures for capital formation. Family savings, for example, is one of the most important processes in the economy of a country. Even in low productivity countries, with most agricultural families living at or even below the subsistence level, the capital formation activities of these low productivity families are important to the economy. Wealthier classes of people may save and invest a larger part of their income, and a large part of a country's capital formation may come from expenditures by business and by government. A society's preferences and value systems play a significant part in its capital formation function, influencing not only how much capital is created, but by whom it is formed, who owns and operates it and what physical forms and in what sectors of the economy it is used. Social habits and customs clearly affect capital formation. Many attitudes and values, expressed through the societies' institutions, present either encouragement or obstacles to capital formation. Thus, a society that places a high value on economic advancement through acquiring business and property would encourage capital formation in many ways, in contrast with a society that overemphasized the ownership of cattle useful only for their display purposes. Social attitudes toward savings and capital formation are often expressed in the pressure for large expenditures of resources for celebrations and important personal, social, and religious occasions, as in births, deaths, weddings, and confirmations. This is often recognized in less developed countries as in this quotation from Mendero: "Capital formation is indeed a social process. There are social forces present in the underdeveloped economy which tend to block this process. Some habits and customs have to be changed, some attitudes altered and some institutions must be created in order to generate an increased rate of capital formation." [3]

The decisions to save or to expend savings on capital formation are so closely related to the value systems and standards that the institutions of a society are key factors in determining the rate of savings and capital formation. This importance is not limited to those institutions that directly operate in the savings and capital formation fields, such as banks, insurance companies, and government financial agencies. Such standard setting institutions as the church and social and educational institutions are important determinants of the level and type of capital formation. Because capital is formed with a view toward future production, the certainties and uncertainties of the future also affect capital formation. Capital that must be used 20 years for it to become a worthwhile investment will have the future incorporated in the capital formation decisions somewhat differently than capital that will be used up in one year. Where property is insecure because of law and order difficulties, the future will be considered quite differently than where property is secure and government stable.

IMPORTANCE OF TECHNOLOGY

Technology, as used in this analysis, means the way the factor inputs of the production process are combined to achieve the outputs. Improved technology therefore means raising the productivity of the process, with either more outputs from the same inputs or less inputs for the same output.[*] Technology cannot be separated from the factor inputs in production, except as an analytical construct. That is, while it is possible to write about a specific technology, say a method of producing shoes, the actual use of the technology always involves working with and using one or more of the factor inputs of production. In a real sense, the technology is embodied in one or more of the inputs. A carpenter making a table in a small shop, using hand tools and unfinished timber as capital, is using specific technology that involves the kinds of knowledge and skills he has, with the kinds of tools and materials he has. He produces a product with a relatively low-level technology—the relatively inefficient way he combines his labor and skills, his shop facilities, his tools, and timber. In a modern table factory, with mechanical saws and planes, the level of technology is much higher, as embodied in the skills and experience of the labor input, and in the machinery and power tools of the capital input. In both cases, the land inputs are relatively unimportant. Thus capital and labor generally incorporate or embody the level of technology within them.

---

[*]For the sake of simplicity, and with no loss in analytical rigor, it is desirable to avoid subtle distinctions that represent technical difficulties for this admittedly too broad definition. Thus, a cost decrease of a supplier may reduce the cost of inputs and therefore change the measurement of inputs and outputs without changing the physical relationship. Is that a change in technology?

While it is impossible in the real world to separate technology from the factor inputs, it is possible to approximate this separation in an analytical sense. It is mathematically possible, where adequate data are available, to infer the increases in production that have occurred over a long period as a result of increases in the quantity of inputs, assuming the same technology and the same quality of inputs. In the United States, it was estimated that only 10 percent of the economic growth between 1900 and 1960 could be attributed to the increase in the quantity of capital and labor inputs; the remaining 90 percent was a residual that could only be explained by an improvement in knowledge, which operationally is an increase in production technology.[4] In the United Kingdom, a similar study for the period 1948 to 1954 indicated a "residual" in manufacturing output of about 75 percent, with factor inputs assigned only 25 percent.[5]

The prime importance of an improvement in technology is also given by studies of Japan, Taiwan, and India. During the 10 year period of the 1950s, GNP increased annually 9 percent in Japan, 8 percent in Taiwan and 3.5 percent in India. In Japan and Taiwan, nearly 60 percent of the increase seemed attributable to an improvement in technology, as distinct from increases in the factor inputs. In India, improved technology was assigned only 10 percent of the growth of GNP.[6] Thus, factor quantity growth is not enough to sustain a vigorous rate of economic growth. It must be associated with marked improvements in the quality of the factor inputs that represent improved technology.

The most detailed study of this type has been prepared by Edward Denison for the United States production from 1909 to 1957.[7] Instead of merely showing how small was the estimated contribution of an increase in the quantity of inputs, leaving a large residual that could be explained by everything else, Denison attempted to allocate the contribution to the growth rate to changes in the quality of inputs, education, and general improvement of knowledge, and to "economies of scale." The increase in inputs of land, labor and capital by themselves explained only about 30 percent of the increase in output. In other words, if the technology, knowledge, organization and quality of inputs had been kept the same as in 1909 (but the quantity increased as it was), U.S. production would have increased less than one third of the increase that did occur. While there are many statistical difficulties in arriving at these data, economists are agreed that the conclusions are indicative of relative importance.

The fact that in the real world technology and the quality of the inputs are inextricably combined does not reduce the need for emphasis on improved technology. The improved quality of inputs means improving them as they embody a higher level of technology. Education of people, for example, means in this technological sense, improving their capacities to utilize and accept improved technologies of production. Of course, education also has many other equally or even more important objectives, such as betterment as social human beings and greater individual fulfillment. These need not be contradictory objectives for education. Acquiring or creating new capital equipment clearly embodies new and improved technology. Providing the same kind of cows and buffalo as draft power for peasant farmers may add to their capital, in a capital inducing effect, but does not involve new technology. Acquiring tractors, with new plows, new seeds, and new cultivation processes, means a new technology, embodied in the capital and in the knowledge, skill, and attitude of the farmer. Some form of capital accumulation generally precedes the introduction of new technology. Even in those sectors where capital is low relative to other factor inputs, new technology means more or new tools, as well as the knowledge and motivation to use the tools. In primitive-level agriculture, the creation of crude hand tools and the clearing or ditching of land is associated with improved agricultural technology as in more advanced agriculture, where farmers must have money or credit to buy production goods embodying technological development, such as fertilizer and seeds. The fact that improvement in technology is generally associated with capital formation means that the capital goods sector of the economy, the sector that actually produces the machinery and equipment used in further production, must be of particular concern to governments that are pushing economic growth. As a country develops, it begins to produce more and more of the kinds of capital goods it needs. Increased specialization of capital goods is inevitably associated with increased production and productivity.

In the more developed countries, technological improvements are likely to be marginal, relatively small changes compared to existing methods and to existing capital, labor, and land inputs. Once in a while, major technological changes occur; and the resulting social dislocations are significant and visible. The introduction of railroads in the United States is a good example of a technological change that involved great structural changes in the country. Improvements in technology in the less developed countries tend to be more of the structural change type. Most of the improvements in technology do not arise out of existing operations. They are imported from abroad, and usually involve substantial changes in the shape, type, and quality as well as quantity of factor inputs. Also, these improvements in technology tend to be accepted more consciously and publicly in the less developed countries. Because they generally involve some expenditure of foreign exchange, a tightly controlled resource, the government generally becomes involved in the decisions to import a significant technological improvement.

In discussing technological improvements, which are close to being the center of the problem of raising production and productivity, it would be useful to distinguish between invention and innovation. Invention is the discovery of new physical relationships, new techniques; while innovation is the application of new techniques to the production process. Inventions are largely taking place in the more developed countries. A modern society must devote an increasingly large proportion of its resources to the encouragement of this type of creativity. The less developed countries must be satisfied for a long time with emphasis on innovation, leaving the very expensive tasks of invention to their more prosperous world neighbors. While occasionally an important invention may make its appearance in the less developed countries, it would be less than responsible to press for inventions rather than innovations. The adaptation of technology to local conditions is far more important that generating inventions and new discoveries. Not just capital innovations but improving the efficiency of existing production of capital goods is necessary for the long continued economic growth of a country. [8]

Every level of technology involves a particular combination of the factor inputs and economists have labeled this factor proportions. This is a quick way of referring to the different combinations of land, labor, and capital involved in the production process. Some production processes use a great deal of labor and less capital; while others, more common in the less developed countries, use more labor and less capital. There can be "capital intensive" cultivation of land, meaning a great deal more capital, relatively; or there can be a "labor intensive" cultivation of land, meaning more labor relatively. The concept of capital intensive or labor intensive is always relative, but the basis of comparison is often implicit rather than explicitly given. What is important to note here is that the factor proportions in the production process, the relative emphasis on using land, labor, and capital, is involved in the level of technology.

The fact that technology is largely imported has severe repercussions in the less developed countries. Technologies that are developed in the more developed countries tend to reflect the availability and relative costs of their factor inputs, which usually are significantly different from those in the less developed countries. The technologies in the United States, for example, tend to stress labor-saving devices, because labor is relatively expensive and relatively well trained to adopt new technologies, and because capital is relatively available at a low cost. In the less developed countries where labor, particularly unskilled labor, is low cost and relatively hard to train, and where capital is relatively scarce, the imported technologies seem to move against the appropriate factor proportions. These relationships will be explained more fully later; but it is only fair to point out here that at best, only uneasy answers are available to the economist. Factor proportions, the relative emphasis on the factor inputs used in the technology of a country, are a continuing concern to a government committed to a high rate of economic growth.

The process of production and the selection of a technology for that production therefore involves factor substitution, the replacement of one factor input by another. The most common case, as technology improves, seems to be substituting capital for labor, machines for human energy. It is quite conceivable, however, that the reverse can be worthwhile, that human muscle power and skill can be used to replace machines, or more land and labor can make up for inadequate capital. Examples of factor substitution are easily seen. A foundry, using a gang of men to shift its large castings from one machine to another, may install an overhead crane that permits one man to do the work that six men previously did. Contrarywise, a contractor, who previously used power shovels and trucks to excavate a building site, may use gangs of unskilled labor using picks, shovels, and baskets to dig and move the earth. Every production process makes conscious or unconscious decisions about factor proportions, and choices about factor substitutions.

Theoretically, there are no limits to technical substitutability of factors. In actual practice, each kind of technology has limitations that are or seem definite. It may be theoretically possible, for example, to produce an automobile engine without machine tools; but it is a practical impossibility. Factor substitution is an operating problem in the transfer of technology from one market to another, and its limits must be appraised as part of the transfer. A government or a private entrepreneur must decide whether he will build a completely automatic glass factory or one that is semiautomatic, with some automatic machines supported by hand operations, or a completely hand-blown glass factory, using a minimum of capital and no automatic machines. The availability of management and skilled labor, of transportation and marketing facilities, of foreign exchange to import machinery and technicians, the size of the domestic market and opportunities for an export market, the costs of production, all these considerations will influence the basic entrepreneural decision that determines the factor proportions of the technology.

Thus, market considerations of all kinds enter into the question of factor proportions and factor substitutability. Relative costs of labor and capital, of different kinds of labor and different kinds of capital, location of the new process and the mix of land, labor, and capital are to a large extent cost determined. There are not simple cost estimates, because future costs and future prices are always involved. While machinery may be purchased at a fixed cost and may be expected to function over a fixed number of years, the cost of capital operation is only relatively fixed and will vary with the cost of maintenance and service, of availability of the required supplies and skills. Since a technology is selected to last for sometime into the future, it is necessary to involve estimates of future costs, prices, availabilities, markets, and even the rules and regulations under which the production process will operate in the future.

From all of this, it should be clear that there is no simple key to understanding the changes that occur in the level of technology as a country modernizes its economy. It is difficult to measure improvement in technology except by measuring productivity. The most simple approach, useful if it is not exaggerated, is to examine the increase in capital. Clearly, improved technology must mean increased and improved capital. As the stock of capital goes up, the level of technology goes up. To be sure, that is not a simple causal relationship, but causality is involved. Improvement in the quality, if not the quantity of the other factor inputs is also usually involved, and is just as important as the increase and improvement in capital; but these changes are more difficult to measure. For example, improved technology involves improved labor inputs as well as improved capital inputs. Men must be qualified to use the new machines in improved technology; organization and management must generally be modified and improved in terms of efficiency and ability to use the new machinery. These types of changes are hard to measure systematically, although they are crucial to the adoption of improved technology. Capital, since it is physical and its increase generally involves financial transactions, can be measured more readily, and therefore is generally assumed to be the best measure of improvement in technology.

This identification of an increase in capital with an improvement in technology is logical, and can be justified empirically; but it is also annoying and sometimes misleading. It arouses irritation particularly among those people whose job it is to improve the quality of the labor factor, and who see in improving the skills and organization of the production process the key to improving technology. There have been enough instances, widely advertised, of importing capital without the necessary skills and organization to use and support the operations of that capital to arouse serious doubts about the assumption that a rise in capital formation means, by definition, a rise in production and productivity. These failures have been for specific production units and for relatively short periods of time. For an entire country, over a significant time period, it is impossible to envisage a situation where a rise in capital is not positively associated with a rise in production and productivity. To accept the opposite as a reality would be to assume that people deny themselves present consumption in order to have less goods in the future. This may be the unfortunate result of some mistakes in judgment, but no society would continue to exist if that were the overall results of their economic decisions over a significant period of time.

IMPORTANCE OF ORGANIZATION AND MANAGEMENT

Improvements in technology are associated with changes in organization and in manner of management. This means that they are both the cause and the result of changes in one or the other. As the productivity of a country increases, the production process becomes more complex, involving a great deal more specialization of operations. There is more reliance on more complicated, more specialized capital, which embodies the new technology or makes it possible. The labor input is also usually more skilled and more specialized than at lower levels of productivity. Production becomes less direct, more roundabout and indirect. The products are not designated for specific customers, as in the case of handmade shoes, but for a general, unspecified consumer, the demand side of the market, as in the case of a shoe factory. This more complicated kind of production operation requires many new kinds of organization. Entrepreneural and managerial functions become more specialized. The procurement function, for example, may split off from marketing, and the direct supervision of machinery operations may be the responsibility of a third set of management officials. Other administrators may make decisions on new investments, on price policies, and reactions to changes in cost. As a production process incorporates a higher level of technology, achieving a higher production and productivity, its organization and management is substantially different than those required at lower levels of technology. As one economist put it, "Organization can be included as a separate factor in the production function, or it can be left as a special sub-class of labor. But between organization and other factors . . . there is an important distinction: all other factors tend to be substitutable one for another. Capital can be substituted for labor, or labor for land or technology for land, and vice versa, etc., but organization is a complement rather than a substitute. The more capital a firm has, the more rather than less, organization . . . it needs."[9]

Higher productivity may also emphasize new kinds of management skills involved in the improved technology. Many professional type skills are required in the most modern technology that simply do not exist or are deeply submerged in the traditional technology. For example, engineers, financial experts, accountants, transportation and communication specialists, all represent the kinds of specialization that the small traditional kind of manager did not need to possess in more than minor capabilities.

Larger production units with improved technology, specialized functions and more roundabout production means more knowledge of the functioning of markets related to the production process. A small shop, producing for specified customers, with owner-manager doing the buying, hiring, work, supervision, and selling, still must relate to many varied markets; but his relationship would be direct and the market's structure, simple. With a large, higher productivity operation, the markets become more distinguishable, more complicated, and more specialized.

1. The labor market involving cost and availability of unskilled labor, of skilled labor, or training potentials.

2. The capital goods market, involving the availability and cost of imported machinery, and of spare parts.

3. The product market, involving future demand, possible competition, stability of markets.

4. The financial market, involving the opportunity for credit and the cost of credit, interest rates, relationships with banks and other financial institutions.

These are not theoretical considerations of possible complications. They represent the most usual and frequent considerations that any management of a production process must face. With simple, traditional markets, the production managers have relatively simple decisions to make, with tradition largely determining many if not most of the production decisions. As production shifts to higher levels of technology with more dependence on wider market considerations, the role of markets becomes more visible, more related to management decisions.

There is a great deal of evidence to indicate that inadequate organization is a significant contributing factor to low productivity in the less developed countries. Studies by the International Labor Office have shown that organizational inefficiency is widespread, and that "relative to existing levels of technique and capital accumulation, the ratio of resource input to volume output of product is very high in underdeveloped economies."[10] Causes for this high ratio, (which means a low productivity) are both external as well as internal to the organizations. These can often be separately identified and their effects estimated. It is clear from these and other studies that organizational difficulties often limit production and productivity to levels below those possible with the given technology and the available capital.

An element of the growth of market influence is the increasing significance of evaluation of the future. Improved technology generally involves more indirect production, more steps between the basic raw material and the finished product. A small shoe shop may make nearly all its intermediate products. A large factory may buy large quantities of special kinds of parts, relying on specialized factories that concentrate on providing special heels, or soles, or tongues of shoes — factories that can produce the specialized parts in larger volume and more cheaply than a general shoe factory. The time span between initiation of the production process and the delivery to the consumer stretches out as the roundabouts of the production increases.* Certainly, the new kinds of capital, involving much greater expenditures,

---

*This may seem contrary to the facts of life to one who has had to wait weeks and months for handmade shoes or clothes from the individual producers. Yet a little reflection will make clear the intuitive merit of this generalization. The time between the making of the machinery, its sale and physical distribution, the making and processing of the raw materials, the making and processing of the intermediate products, must create a generalized production function that stretches over a long time.

require future production prospects that stretch over a longer time. While these attributes of improved technology may be difficult to measure, they are no less valid, if true, and no less important.

More reliance on more complicated market arrangements, and more dependence on ability to evaluate the future is associated in an improved technology with more interdependence among institutions. A country that consists mostly of peasant agriculturists, small shops and village bazaars still requires a great deal of mutual support and interdependence, but nowhere near as much as when its production enterprises become larger and use much more specialized capital and skilled labor; its markets, more sophisticated and widespread; and its consumers, more impersonal and distant. This is another aspect of the growing need for overhead capacities previously discussed. Modern technology requires a flow of parts and maintenance, a reliance on communication, and power, the availability of adequate transportation facilities that far exceeds in scope and intensity these needs in lower productivity or more traditional production. Indeed, the difference is so great and visible that if it were possible to measure this kind of growing interdependence, it probably would be among the best measures of economic development.

The growing interdependence of the institutional framework provides an increasingly complex framework for the production process. It means that those who make the kinds of entrepreneural and management decisions that keep the production process going must rely more and more on a kind of system thinking, rather than on more personalized, individual relationships. This can be readily pictured by comparing a village carpenter, whose major customers are the relatively few families that use his traditional services and pay him an annual retainer, and the owner and management of a modern furniture factory that relies on customers in all parts of the country. Clearly, the production decisions of the latter require a reliance on the evaluation of a system of organized interrelationships, far more complex and comprehensive than the village carpenter. In a sense, there is more reliance on a type of law and order and on an expected pattern of behavior by his suppliers and his customers. Yet the difference in intensity and scope of this interdependence is very significant, often representing the difference between a traditional society with more or less static technology, and a society that is changing almost all of its institutions and constantly adopting more technologies that raise productivity.

The role of the entrepreneur definitely expands as technology improves. In large enough production units, it may become completely separated from most managerial decisions; but the borderline between management and entrepreneur is a difficult one to draw in actual operations. Like the difference between policy and operations, definitions depend largely on where you are sitting. Entrepreneural decisions, the kind of basic risk taking decisions, often involve minor risks compared with routine management decisions that can make or break an individual plant. Without too much concern about the necessities of precise definitions, the need for decisions to undertake a venture, to build a plant and to make a major investment seems to increase at a very fast rate. Thus, forces and institutions that affect the supply and quality of entrepreneural decision making clearly play an important role in the push toward a higher productivity society.

Finally, it is difficult, both conceptually and empirically, to differentiate increases in productivity between those due to changes in factor proportions or in organization and management. When it was asserted above that statistical methods permitted some judgment about the shares of the increased productivity assignable to each of the factor inputs, improved technology is in a sense the residual claimant. That is, improved technology received the credit after land, labor, and capital were kept constant in quality, and increased only in quantity. Embodied, of course, in the improvement of the quality of the labor input was the improvement in skill, experience, and organization that is the very essence of improved technology. Factor proportions, the recognition that countries vary in the availability and scarcity of factor inputs, and therefore vary basically in their optimum economic response to improvements in technology, is so closely related to changes in organization and management as to be inextricable, both conceptually and operationally.*

COMPLEMENTARITIES AND EXTERNAL ECONOMIES

No discussion of the elements of production and productivity could escape a foray into the concepts of complementarities and external economies. In fact, these two concepts have been implicitly incorporated in the previous discussions, particularly when interdependence of institutions and overhead capacities were discussed. Yet so important are they to an understanding of the obstacles faced by a country trying to improve its productivity that they must be identified openly in this section and exposed in all their vague and nebulous glory.

Complementarities is a rapid way of referring to the fact that in real life two or more goods or services are often joined together in a way that makes them complement each other. The range of complement can vary from absolute essential togetherness to some vague desirable relationship. The vague end of the continuum may be disregarded; but the middle or strong end, where there is an element of

---

*In a sense, this is a warning not to take each element of the analysis too seriously, but always to remember the tremendous overlapping of these concepts and their mutual causation.

necessity and strong dependence, presents many problems to the less developed countries. Illustrations of the need to assess the problem of complementarities in the production process are numerous in common experience. Truck tires are a necessary complement to the continuing availability of truck traffic. Also needed are tire repair facilities, air pressure pumps, gasoline distribution facilities, repair services, all complementary to the continued use of trucks. Sometimes the relationship is not so direct, such as small welding shops to repair minor breaks in metal, just as needed as spare parts. As a production process becomes more complex, with more and more complicated capital and skills needed, the complementarities seem to increase.

Complementarities appear to be related to substitution in the production process. That is, often one product can be substituted for another or for a service that is available as a complementarity. This is true of machinery that performs substantially the same kind of service as do truck and railroad freight cars. In a sense, complementarities may provide competition as well as support—a curious relationship that is difficult to handle analytically yet clearly important in the description of obstacles to economic growth.

An added complication of the concept of complementarities is the strain it places on explanations of market values of the related goods. Joint goods often present problems of market valuation or price, where each element receives all or most of the value of the joint goods. If a pair of shoes is valued at $20, what is the value of each shoe? Under some circumstances, each shoe might be valued at $10; but if one shoe were irretrievably lost, it is likely that the other shoe would be tossed out as valueless, implying that the lost shoe was valued at $20.* When investors are examining the potential return on various options of investment, the question of the existence and pricing of complementarities and substitutes must be part of their considerations.

Illustrations of complementarities abound on the supply side of the production process. The illustration given above, of the various products that represent complementarities of the capacity of a country to transport goods by truck, shows how absence of adequate complementarities can affect the supply of a product. A government agency that was given the assignment of developing a new trucking line between two major cities would have to examine all of these complementarities, and more, before it undertakes the job. It would be the height of folly merely to import 50 trucks, hire 50 truck drivers and a timekeeper, and start to operate the truck line. Many of the difficulties of increasing the production of a good or service lie not in the direct production process itself, but in the complementarities that are needed.

---

*The remaining shoe might have a salvage value at $1, establishing the imputed value of the lost shoe at $19.

Illustrations of complementarities in the demand area of the production process, the demand for goods and services, also are numerous and illustrate the persuasiveness of the concept. The demand for each of the mentioned products that are complementarities of the trucking industry is strongly affected by the establishment of a new trucking industry. These intermediate products, required in the production of other goods, have their own supply problems that must be related to their demand. Thus, the establishment of a large new trucking agency may well decrease the demand for used tires among existing truckers. The demand for complementary goods and services usually fluctuates sympathetically since there is a functional relationship between these goods as well as problems of substitutability.

The existence of complementarities, with its obvious conceptual difficulties, has led economists to advance a more precise, but still hazy, concept of external economies or as it is familiarly referred to by the cognoscenti, externalities.* These are goods or services which are made available in addition to, or external to, the sales of the producing unit. Examples will clarify this. A factory may build a road to its source of raw material as a part of its production facility. As external economies, the villages along the road will have increased capabilities to produce and transport their agricultural products; but they will not have to pay the factory for the use of the road. The factory might ask to internalize the economies (or economic advantages) provided by the road, but cannot do so, as it is a public highway. Therefore, the road has produced external economies, external to the enterprise that produced the road. The factory itself will also yield some other external economies. Workers will be trained, and then may leave to work at other jobs. Local people may observe some of the technology used in the factory and copy it for their own production units. The supervisory staff may bring with it some skills that are useful in the village life. External economies in production are clearly present and important as an operating fact of life. There are several kinds of externalities, arising from different characteristics of the process of production and distribution:

- Some externalities are caused by the fact that many benefits cannot be appropriated and therefore cannot be charged for by the

---

*The concept of external economies is so slippery, in a rigorous sense, that it is "waved out of the park" by very technical economists who dismiss it as reflections of the imperfections of the market. But it creeps back in because it is a useful concept, very real in operations of an economy and very necessary to explain what is happening in the less developed countries. For a more detailed analysis, see T. Scitovsky, "Two Concepts of External Economies," Journal of Political Economy 62 (April 1954): 143-151.

producer. For example, a factory that builds a road often cannot prevent others from using the road free of charge. The road may traverse public land, or may be too long to police even though it is a private road over private property.

• Some externalities arise because their costs cannot be assigned to any product. For example, people beside a river may release their sewage and waste into the river, thus polluting it. While large units may be identified, the cost of pollution may be difficult to apply to all polluters.

• Some externalities arise when the production process is such that there are significant economies of scale, when producing on a large scale is less costly per unit than producing on a small scale. Sometimes, the cost of production is almost constant, regardless of how many goods or services are produced. Consider a bridge which is designed for use by cars and passengers. The cost per service depends very largely on the number of persons and vehicles that cross. The charge or price per unit for the service will probably be geared to some idea of returning the costs of building and maintenance, even though the marginal cost, the cost for each additional crossing, would probably be zero or at least negligible.

• Some externalities arise because consumption cannot be exclusive. That is, some kinds of consumption are indivisible, and are "pure public" in that all individuals must have access to the consumption, or none can. Examples of these are fire and police protection, defense, and flood and epidemic control. The consumption by one person does not, in a sense, reduce the consumption of anyone else. An additional person crossing a bridge costs absolutely nothing. Thus, externalities are basic characteristics of the production process.

Economists have attempted to analyze these external economies while denying their theoretical existence. Sometimes external economies are classified as technological and pecuniary. The pecuniary external economies work their way out through cost and price reductions. For example, a factory may be producing its own power through an inefficient diesel generator which limits its production. The construction of a large hydroelectric generator may produce cheaper power in relatively unlimited quantities. The factory pays a lower price for the power, and also gets other external economies for which the power company does not receive payment, although it is of great value to the factory through its ability to expand use of its equipment, to buy more modern equipment, and to receive its power supply with more stability. These advantages show up as economies for the factory but are external to the economies which the power plant can sell in its market. Any good or service which an enterprise produces but cannot sell or receive payment for its use by others is an external economy.

The importance of external economies to the less developed countries is their relative absence. Modern technology, as has been repeatedly stated, requires a great deal of supporting activities, capabilities, and institutions, all complementary or necessarily associated with increased productivity. Among these, and certainly not the least part of these, are the external economies—the production advantages that accrue simply because they are there, and not just because they can be directly purchased. The more economically advanced countries are filled with external economies that do not have to be paid for directly by the consuming unit. For example, if everyone who needed a broken metal part would have to train the welder, few welding possibilities would exist. In a mechanically advanced society, an infinite flow of small welding jobs are almost inevitable. The external economies provide these for most of the people who need small welding jobs as a by-product from the big industries who may spend money to train welders because they need them continually. It is a basic characteristic of the less developed countries that the extent of their external economies is quite limited, relative to the more developed countries. As economic growth takes place, the availability and flow of external economies increases.

Some production is strongly characterized by external economies, while others are only slightly affected. An example of a production unit providing practically nothing but external economies is a public school where the services produced by the school are provided relatively free. Although there may be some small charges, the education becomes a free advantage to an employer who wishes to hire a bookkeeper or clerk. The plant that provides steel construction rods may have very few external economies, since all it may do is to import large bundles of rods and merely straighten out bent rods and assemble them in smaller bundles. The unskilled work here may have little external economies. External economies can be a very important segment of the product, even though the market price may not include this aspect of production. A particular investment may be justified mainly on the grounds that it provides a large flow of external economies. In countries where modern production methods are very scarce, the educational value of the first few modern units may outweigh any financial profits. Obviously this kind of external economy disappears rapidly as more and more modern production units are built.

The concept of external economies must permit the inclusion of external diseconomies, or negative external economies. This occurs where the side effects or noncompensated result of a production process increases costs of others and provides disadvantages to other production efforts. Examples of this are not hard to find. The papermill that pollutes the nearby stream with its waste products, the hydroelectric plant that destroys a beautiful valley, the factory that pollutes the air around it, these are the results of external diseconomies. Hence, the use of the term externalities, which encompasses both positive and negative by-products of the production process.

This brief summary of the basic elements of production and productivity provides some of the concepts that will permit examination of how economic forces work their way through economic institutions to produce the goods and services that a country needs. Productivity has been distinguished from production as indicating the efficiency with which the production process operates. The almost infinite form and variety of inputs into the production process have been grouped into three broad but identifiable categories: land, labor, and capital. The manner of combining them has been identified as technology, and its improvement has been labeled the most important aspect of increased productivity. Technology, embodied in the improved quality of these factor inputs, is so difficult to measure directly and so closely related to improvements in capital, that capital formation has been advanced as the best measure of improvements in technology. But the importance of organization and management has also been stressed as of outstanding importance for improvement in technology. Finally, there was recognition that complementarities and externalities make the production process even more complex than the direct technological process requires. As productivity accelerates, complexity also increases, probably at a faster rate.

NOTES

1. See Arkadie and Frank, Jr. Economic Accounting and Development Planning (New York: Oxford University Press, 1969) for a good explanation of the system of national accounts.
2. See J.R. McCulloch, Outlines of Political Economy, ed. J. McVickar (New York: A.M. Kelley, 1966) for the most rigid statement of this doctrine. It can also be found in Adam Smith, David Ricardo, Thomas Malthus and other giants of the classical school of economics.
3. Mellon M. Mendero, "The Socio-Cultural Aspects of Economic Development," Far Eastern Economic Review (Hong Kong: February 1955): 171.
4. Robert Solow, "Technological Change and the Aggregate Production Function," The Review of Economics and Statistics 29, no. 3 (August 1957): 312-20.
5. W.B. Reddaway and A.D. Smith, "Progress in British Manufacturing Industries in the Period 1948-1954," Economic Journal 70 (March 1960): 17-31.
6. Charles Wolf, Jr., R. Gangoharan, and Kee Chiram Han, Industrial Productivity and Economic Growth, Asian Productivity Organization, Tokyo, 1964, pp. 28-32.
7. Edward F. Denison, The Sources of Economic Growth in the United States and the Alternatives Before Us. (New York) Committee for Economic Development 1962.
8. For a discussion of capital goods and economic growth, see Nathan Rosenbert, "Capital Goods, Technology and Economic Growth,"

Oxford Economic Papers 15 (1963): 217.

9. Charles P. Kindleberger, Economic Development, 2nd ed.,
(New York: McGraw-Hill, 1965), p. 118.

10. Peter Kilby, "Organization and Productivity in Backward Economies," Quarterly Journal of Economics 76 (1962): 303-10.

3

PRODUCTION AND PRODUCTIVITY— BASIC ECONOMIC FORCES

The actual processes of production are organized in many different ways. For analytical purposes here, these processes of production and exchange will be grouped into the following broad kinds of operations that are useful in understanding economic growth problems: savings and capital formation, allocation of resources, operation of markets, economies of scale and technology, and role of entrepreneurs.

SAVINGS AND CAPITAL FORMATION

Concept of Savings and Capital Formation

Saving is refraining from using resources for consumption purposes. Financial savings occur when someone or some organization receives financial income and spends only part of it on consumption uses. Savings in physical form occurs when some part of a product is not used up in current consumption, but is kept in inventory to be consumed later, or is used up in producing other goods and services. Savings can be hoarded or loaned out, can be used immediately for capital formation purposes, or can be kept for future use. The decision to save can be individual, or by the family, by an entrepreneur or by the government. The latter type of savings, public savings, is particularly important in the less developed countries; but even in the most developed countries, it is of significant proportions, Why do people save? Some understanding of this is essential to an examination of efforts to increase the rate of savings in a country. Individuals and families save for many different reasons:

1. Savings against disasters that reduce or eliminate income, such as floods, poor harvests. These may be termed savings for

protection against risks.

    2. Savings to enable expenditures for some desirable acquisition or activity in the future, for additions to capital, both consumption goods and production goods. These savings are designed to promote increased future consumption.

    3. Savings to permit some socially desirable expenditures as in marriage dowries, feasts at confirmation or initiation ceremonies, death services, and similar socially determined occasions. These savings are status motivated.

    Businesses and organizations have the same three basic reasons for savings; protection against risk, increased future consumption, and status; but the form the savings will take, the mix of motivations, and how the savings will be used will be different.

    Risks may be covered by insurance, which is an efficient method of pooling risks. Consequently special reserves for risks in business may not be as necessary when insurance institutions develop.

    Savings for improvement are the very essence of business savings. Self financed capital formation by business organizations is one of the most important elements of savings and capital formation in a society that is attempting to increase its rate of capital formation.

    Status savings may not be as visible in the case of business enterprises as in families and individuals, but they are still important in understanding the motivation to save. In many countries, families and business enterprises are comingled in a complex way. While business enterprises generally become impersonal as they modernize and grow, considerations of status and socially determined savings and expenditures remain important. The form that the savings take is related to the purpose of the savings and to the kind of income from which the savings are made. Savings may simply be storing up food in a corner of the house, to be used when supplies from current production are no longer available. In countries that are unstable, savings will take forms that attempt to adjust to this instability. Peasants tend to distrust bonds and paper money because of previous experiences with depreciation or defaulting governments, or were exposed to myths related to such situations. Savings often reflect the judgments about transferability and liquidity of assets that people consider desirable. Thus, precious stones, gold, and silver may represent savings both for status and risk purposes. The judgments about the relative importance of these purposes is socially determined, and cannot be dismissed as of little consequence. The savings habits of a society are a firm and complex reflection of their values, their fears, as well as their earning capacity.

    The decision to save can be voluntary or involuntary. Instances of coercive savings decisions abound in history, where governments have forced individuals to set aside some of their current money for some more or less desirable future purpose, commonly war. Through taxation, governments may transfer resources from private hands to public control, and may use these resources for capital formation, thus shifting private consumption and possibly private savings to public consumption and public savings. The term forced savings, however, has been given a technical meaning substantially different than simple compulsory savings, which in a sense is always involved in public savings.

Capital formation is the process of utilizing savings to produce goods that are used in further production. Thus, savings and capital formation are functionally related, but not by an automatic process or with a fixed relationship. True, in the accounting system of a country's economic operations, there is a definitional equality between savings and investment. By definition, as the accounts are cast up for a year, savings is always made to equal investment. But this really means that some balancing entries may be used, some negative savings (dissavings) and negative investment (disinvestment) to balance the books. Low rates of savings, so characteristic of the less developed countries, are nearly always associated with low rates of investment. However, countries can borrow savings from others, or can receive them as gifts, or can use other devices for investing more than their current savings. Thus, while savings and capital formation are functionally related to each other, they are not mirror reflections of each other or reverse sides of the same coin. To assume that savings always equals investment is to look backwards at accounting totals that are definitional identities. The analysis of savings and investment is far too important to leave at this superficial level.

One point should be emphasized that relates to both saving and capital formation. The need for evaluating the future is an essential part of each of them. People and organizations save because they wish to affect the future. In saving, there is a judgment between the advantages of present consumption and future use of the resources. In capital formation, there is a judgment between present costs and future earnings from the capital being formed. The method of evaluation and the time periods will vary, but the need to form some judgment about the future compared with the present remains an essential part of every decision in savings and capital formation. The image of the future, some discount of the future to the present, is made consciously or unconsciously. Anything that affects the image of the future therefore has an important effect on both savings and capital formation. The effects will be different, because these two processes are not the same set of behavior, although they are closely related.

Low Rate of Savings

Why is the rate of savings low in the less developed countries? Three reasons are commonly advanced. First, the low income of the people prevents savings. Poor people cannot save much because they need to use all of their resources for consumption to stay alive. Second, there is the absence of a high enough propensity to save, the result of inadequate motivation and other cultural obstacles to savings. Savings simply are not important enough in the beliefs and value systems of the people. Finally, the low rate of savings are attributed to an absence of the kinds of institutions that induce savings or even make them possible. The banks, savings and loan companies, postal savings, and life insurance are only recent insertions in the institutional structures of the less developed countries; and they are only slowly being accepted

These three reasons have enough validity to be taken seriously; but as complete explanations of the low rate of savings, they are quite inadequate. They represent only the beginning of the search for explanations, and their complete acceptance often can lead to feeble efforts to increase the rate of savings.

The intuitive feeling that poor people cannot save much is of course substantially correct, but can be carried too far. People with low incomes do save, sometimes their capital formation activities are quite significant, as when a peasant agriculturalist labors to bring more land into cultivation by clearing trees and grass, or by improving irrigation ditches and bunds. Poor people also dissave, and the total net addition to the capital of the country in a year from the lowest income group may be quite small. Yet it is significant, and most of it may go unrecorded because it is of the nonmonetary type, with few records available and therefore tremendously difficult to estimate. More important is the reality that a low savings rate is a better explanation of a low average income than the reverse, that low incomes explain low savings. While the average income is low in the less developed countries, there are quite a few high income people and some very profitable enterprises. These are in a position to save more than the low average income of the country would indicate. Furthermore, public savings are generally less than they could be in most countries, at least from an economic point of view.

The thesis that the cultural and motivational obstacles to savings must result in a low propensity to save must also be accepted cautiously. Too many countries have already overcome these obstacles or at least substantially diminished them, for this to be accepted as a continuing excuse for low savings rates. That these difficulties exist is obvious, but equally obvious are the illustrations that they may be significantly reduced through appropriate policies and institutions.

Adequate savings institutions help; but they, too, are more a resultant of increased savings than its cause. There are too many instances of new savings institutions, modeled after successful institutions in the more developed countries, that have been established and then left to function inefficiently, to accept the conclusion that the availability of savings institutions alone can raise the rate of savings. There is an association of these two, and both are increasing in the less developed countries. But the relationship between them is far more complicated than the assumption that new banks will create depositors in these lands.

Obstacles to Increased Savings and Capital Formation

Since savings and capital formation are functionally interrelated, many of the obstacles to increase each are the same. However, they may work somewhat differently, because the motivations and institutions of saving are often quite different from those involved in capital formation. While both savers and investors must evaluate the future as compared with the present, what they look for in the future may be substantially different. The saver may compare future consumption with present consumption, both quantitatively and in terms of psychological satisfactions. Security and social status will also be strong elements in the decision. For the investor, both security and social status will also be involved, but a good deal of emphasis will be on expected returns, compared with alternative uses of the resources and the usual and unusual risks of investment.

Even an abbreviated list of the obstacles to an increased rate of savings shows a range of subjects almost as wide as the whole subject of modernization:

Political stability. Savings involves judgments about the future that are closely related to shifts in power and political forms, especially among the rich and the big industries.

Maintenance of law and order. Here not only the quantity of savings but its type is strongly affected.

Unsettled monetary conditions. Most savings, even in peasant societies, are in the form of money or are planned in monetary terms. Unsettled monetary conditions distort the yardstick and distort the kinds of savings achieved.

Lack of complementary facilities. The savings that are directly related to capital formation are seriously affected by judgments about the future availability of necessary complementary facilities.

Inadequate market facilities. Curiously enough, money savings must be marketed, exchanged for something with people who will use the savings, and this is often hard to visualize in the less developed countries.

Lack of adequate motivation. This could be explained by such features of social life as the extended family, the land tenure system, the stratification of social status or by the psychological effects of child nurture systems, or any of the psychological factors that affect personal motivation. That this is risky even for economists (or analysts) is obvious, but it is equally obvious that these are very important in explaining low savings.

A low rate of capital formation is both the cause and result of low average income. All of the impediments to savings are of course impediments to increased capital formation. The decision to save and invest may be a simultaneous one, as when the peasant cultivator works on clearing land. In the more modern sectors of the economy, the savings and investment decisions are quite likely to be completely separate activities. The industrial or the business concern may decide to save money or buy insurance, and this makes the savings transaction. The bank or the insurance company may loan these savings to the entrepreneur, either a private firm or a government agency, and that chain of activities becomes the start of the capital formation transactions. The timing of these two separate processes is of utmost importance. When the savings and investment decisions are simultaneous, there is no timing problem. A business firm may decide to retain some of its profits rather than distribute them to the owners, and use the profits to expand its machinery capacities. In the modernizing sectors of an economy, this is a frequent type of savings and investment decision.

The timing is also relatively simple when small savings are collected from many individuals and firms, and are then loaned to entrepreneurs to invest. The actual investment decision will then be made by both the lending institutions and the individual or government agency that takes the loan. It is not too important to decide which is really the entrepreneur, the lending institution or the borrower. Both share in the entrepreneurial functions, in a real sense, although in any specific case one may be more important than the other. What is important is to recognize that quite often the lender, although he may get a fixed rate of return on his loan and does not own any equity in the enterprise, may perform the dominant part of the entrepreneurial function.

Investment and Savings

One further point on timing of savings and investment is important. Often, investment decisions will be made in the expectation that the savings will be found. While prudent entrepreneurs check with the lending sources before they become too committed to an investment, this check may only be a judgment that savings funds will be forthcoming, for example, from a savings bank. Where money markets are more fully developed, sale of stocks or bonds is a common way of raising means for capital investments. Large buyers of equipment sell equipment bonds, for example, to be paid off as the equipment earns a rate of return through the production of goods or services. In a causal relationship, it may be correct to point out that investments may create savings more often than savings create investment. The crucial difference between countries that are growing vigorously and economically stagnant countries lies more in the use of savings than in the volume of savings. Savings must be put to productive use, and often the decision to invest is the force that creates the savings.[1]

In agriculture, direct investment by peasants is often difficult to measure. Investment expenditures cannot be readily separated from the usual production expenditures. Thus, when a peasant stores some of his product for future use, he is saving; and his stock of produce represents capital formation. After a particularly successful crop, he may store much more than usual, and therefore decide he can direct some family labor to clearing new fields, digging or restoring drainage ditches, and in general improving the land in ways that are not directly related to raising an immediate crop. The use of his stored crop for this purpose is as much capital formation as expenditures by business to expand their factories or by government to build a new road. Since most agricultural families are quite uncertain of their income, their savings tend to fluctuate with production; and the savings of some temporally prosperous families are offset by the dissavings of other families who are temporally less prosperous, and must use previous savings to make up for shortfalls in income. This is why, while gross capital formation in low productivity agricultural sections may be high, the net addition to the agricultural capital coming from low income families will be quite small.

Where the general environment is not favorable to productive investment, the effect is felt on both savings and capital formation. A large part of the savings is likely to be kept in the form of trinkets, precious stones and metals, and in assets that can be easily moved or concealed. Where taxation depends upon personal relationship and arbitrary decisions, buildings and machinery are less likely to be useful forms of savings than jewels and buried hoards of coins. Economic uncertainties tend to encourage savings to take the form of goods that can be easily traded for food or that provide protection against monetary inflation. Trading as an enterprise tends to provide more liquid assets than large scale manufacturing. These are illustrations of how social conditions affect the form as well as the quantity of both savings and capital formation.

Capital Requirements

The questions of how much additional capital a country requires is closely related to how much additional capital a country can absorb and the criteria applied to evaluate absorption capacity. A little reflection will show that social criteria are always present, either implicitly or explicitly, when these questions are discussed. Obviously, if no returns for capital are expected, then the absorption capacity is limitless, and, by that standard, capital requirements are limitless. While this may be useful in a theoretical study, it is totally unrealistic as an operating situation. Capital is formed in order to produce goods and services, and the expected returns from capital formation must be relative to expected costs, with some expected measures of productivity and rate of return implicit or explicit in every investment decision. To exclude these would be to assume economic irrationality, which one may do at moments of despair at inadequate progress but which cannot be an acceptable basis for continuing analysis. The judgments about risks, uncertainties, security, markets, social implications and similar elements of investment decisions may vary from time to time and from country to country, but what will not vary is the fact that each investment decision will be the result of evaluating expected costs, expected benefits, and any options or choices that may be available.

Here the useful concept of opportunity costs may be mentioned. Costs generally refer to the expenditures made for the inputs, or at least their imputed market value if they are not purchased. The cost of a factory is determined by adding up the cost of land, building and equipment generally measured at market prices. But there is another way of measuring cost that is very real and useful, particularly in decision making. It is the opportunity cost, the idea that the cost of anything is the value of the best thing that was given up as an alternative. Thus, the opportunity cost of buying a car may have been a year's schooling, the opportunity cost of a lumber mill may be a sugar mill. To the extent that these options are real and possible, they represent choices that must be made in choosing one investment over another. Competition in a real sense becomes evident through the choosing between alternatives, and the cost calculations must include some judgments about opportunity costs.

The point has been made that in order to achieve an improvement in technology, a country nearly always must acquire more capital embodying the improved technology. The amount of capital required is measured in monetary value terms because that is the only way that different kinds of capital, buildings, equipment, roads, power plants, can be added together. It is generally meaningless, except for publicity purposes, to represent aggregate investment in terms of 22 projects, unless the characteristics of the capital are so similar that there are major common units.* To say that a country requires a certain amount of additional capital must always mean that it requires this additional capital to achieve a certain additional quantity of production in a given time. Both an expected return on the investment and a time period are inevitably involved. This return can be expressed as a rate, as in 8 percent a year for 20 years, or can be in percentage changes in total product. For example, a country may need a capital investment of $200 million for a five year period in order to increase its GNP by $90,000,000 during that period. Thus, each $100 of investment is

_____

*There may be some meaning to 22 small irrigation projects, or 17 factories, but even here the communication sacrifices clarity for vividness.

58

expected to return $45 of product by the end of the five year period. The increase may be a 30 percent increase in GNP over the period, which would mean in this instance that at the beginning of the period, GNP was $300 million. By improving technology, improving the other inputs and adding $200 million of additional capital, the total product was increased to $390 million.

While this example can be used to illustrate many facets of the problem of capital formation, all that it is intended to show here is that any statement of capital requirements to be meaningful must include a measure of expected production return over time. If very low rates of return are expected, the amount of capital that is required can be very large, just as a zero rate of return implies the ability to utilize an infinite amount of additional capital. The less developed countries clearly require more capital. Their experience in adding capital to their existing production process shows some judgment about the expected rate of return, when the additional capital is fitted into the other input factors by the level of technology thus far attained. The wording here has been carefully selected to show that while the additional capital is clearly an essential cause of the improved production, it is not the total cause. The other input factors and, most important, the improved technology associated with improved input factors are also clearly essential for the increase in production. To repeat, it is easier to measure the increase in capital than in any of the other changes, and that is why capital is so often emphasized in the examination of economic growth. Additional inputs of other factors and improvement in technology are created concurrently or primarily by a high rate of capital formation.

The general limitations on a country's capacity to absorb additional capital are the same kinds of shortages and bottlenecks that have been discussed. Primarily, they are summarized as shortages in the availability of the complementary factors of production, the skilled labor, the organization, the management, and the basic goods and services needed to use the additional capital. Straining capital absorption capacity, as will be discussed later, shows up in inflationary price pressures, in balance of payments difficulties, in work stoppages, and in low efficiency. The complementary factors required for efficient use of capital are quite varied and the reasons for their inadequacy are often noneconomic.

Thus judgments about the capacity to absorb capital represent judgments about the requirements for additional capital. The statement is frequently made that many of the less developed countries do not have the capacity to absorb more capital than they are now forming. What is implicit in such a statement is a concept of creating additional capital "without undue strain and with reasonable efficiency." The standards of strain and efficiency that are acceptable may vary from country to country, and from one analyst to another, and from one type of participant to another. A foreign banker will view the standards quite differently than a harrassed government official. The World Bank may view standards of efficiency quite differently than would a national agricultural bank which may have its own view on the aspects of "undue strain." To one, the major question may be "Will the investment yield sufficient returns?" while the other may view the major question as "What will happen if the investment is not made?" Both institutions will use different opportunity costs in making choices. It should be clear, then, that questions of capital requirements and capacity to absorb additional capital are not precise engineering calculations, whose two separate analyses will arrive at substantially the same result. The capital requirements of a country are the result of many judgments and evaluations, both implicit and explicit. These are affected by many noneconomic influences and forces, as well as economic forces. While estimates of requirements often have to be made, they should not be considered as either exact or incontrovertible.

There is a common assumption that capital intensive investment leads to greater savings than a labor intensive investment. If this is so, lower employment in the present time can lead to faster growth of both output and employment in the future. This conclusion involves the following assumptions:

- Savings are a higher proportion of profits than of wages.
- Increased consumption now makes no contribution to future growth.
- Wage rates do not depend on the techniques of production.
- The government is incapable of securing enough savings through taxation of wage earners or through inflation through deficit financing.

But there are questions about the validity of these assumptions. The wage rate is necessarily linked to the production technique, and labor intensive techniques will usually pay lower wages than capital intensive production. In some countries, a large proportion of profits are remitted overseas, or even if saved, are used for conspicuous consumption rather than added to the investible funds of the country. Government savings may be a more efficient way of mobilizing resources than relying on the decisions of the profit makers. The question may really be one of the government's determination to collect taxes.

ALLOCATION OF RESOURCES

The Process of Resource Allocation

The manner in which a country allocates its resources is of course central to its efforts to improve production and productivity. The extent to which it emphasizes improvement in technology and capital formation,

60

the kinds of capital it creates, the kinds of consumption goods it demands and the kinds of discount it applies to future production are the essence of its efforts to modernize production. Every country allocates its resources by means of a bewildering array of decisions and behavior patterns. Almost every important institution is involved either in buying or producing goods and services, in establishing priorities or values that influence how households, businesses and government receive and expend their incomes. Even in that small part of income allocation that determines the rate and type of capital formation, the allocation process is as broad and varied as the whole of society. For investment is not carried out by an insulated set of institutions, separate from other institutions. In the most centrally directed countries, such as the Communist countries of USSR, China and Yugoslavia, allocation of resources is a total societal process and not just the result of a few specialized institutions. While economists and planners understandably focus their analysis on the allocation of resources for capital formation, it is essential to understand that this is only part of the resource allocation of a country; and this part must fit into, and is strongly affected by, all the other parts of resource allocation.

Resource allocation includes the allocation of all factor inputs, not only investment funds. Yet how a country allocates its labor and its capital is, in the long run, determined to a large extent by how it has allocated its current investible funds. That is why economists often present capital allocation as the total problem of resource allocation. Yet resource allocation ultimately means the total production of a society, how it allocates all of its factor inputs. If a country devotes one-third of its economic effort to produce weapons, its resource allocation is quite different from a country that only devotes one-twentieth of its factor inputs to weapons. The product mix is the complete expression of resource allocation, while the allocation of resources in capital formation shapes and ultimately determines the product mix.

Every expenditure of funds, every action to acquire or utilize a good or service, reflects a decision to allocate resources. When a family buys food, or rents a cart to participate in a festival, or buys land, it is allocating its resources for these specific purposes. When government expends funds to plan a steel mill or import trucks, it is allocating resources. For purposes of this analysis, the concept of resource allocation is focused on the behavior of actually expending resources, rather than on the decision to expend, because decisions are internal, difficult to observe and because it is often difficult to distinguish between operational decisions and wishful thinking except by observing actual behavior. Thus, expenditures represent behavioral responses to allocation decisions. By summarizing and analyzing expenditures, it is possible to observe how a country is actually allocating its economic resources.

A part of the resource allocation may be done by specialized institutions which directly control resources. Examples of these are banks and government budget offices; both are designed to make decisions that specify what expenditures will be allowed. The economic planning organizations are also specialized institutions that have as one of their major functions the assessment of priorities in expenditures. In the area of capital formation, special institutions play an important role. However, most of the resource allocation of a country is really decided in other institutions and by the kinds of decisions that sometimes seem far removed from the problem of resource allocation. Indirect influences are often more important than direct allocation. By assigning a low social status to savings, a society may critically cripple capital formation, and its effect may be to reduce productivity far more than any misallocation of savings. An analysis of the specialized institutions for allocating resources gives an important but incomplete picture of resource allocation and can be misleading if it purports to govern the entire scope of a country's efforts to improve productivity.

Because all expenditures have an impact or reflect resource allocation, it is necessary to recognize that there will be many instances of conflicting tendencies or goals. An institution that is operating to improve nutrition and expand expenditures on protective foods is, in a limited sense, reflecting a resource allocation that conflicts with an institution designed to curtail consumption expenditures. A government cosmetic factory, advertising its products to convince more people to buy their cosmetics, is operating against the government policy to curtail consumption. Any institution that establishes or helps to establish priorities in expenditures is involved in the resource allocation process. Schools, hospitals, religious organizations, families, all have strong influences on resource allocation, not just in their own expenditures, but in the values and beliefs they shape. Resource allocation is a social process involving all the priorities of a society, not just its economic priorities. A country that spends a large portion of its resources on military preparedness is expressing a priority in much the same way as expenditures on capital formation and on education express a priority. The reconciliation of conflicting interests and the settlement of relative priorities is a major function of government at all levels, and usually involves many nongovernmental institutions as well.

The Evaluation of Resource Allocation

The evaluation of how a country allocates its resources by examining its expenditure pattern is both harsh and realistic. It is harsh because it disregards statements about humanistic and welfare goals, the rhetoric of what a country wishes to believe about itself, and focuses on what a country is actually doing. It is realistic in that behavior, hard as it is to measure and modify, is far easier to evaluate than ideas, motivation, and ideals. But harshness and realism are not the only virtues in this kind of analysis, and may be often quite less than virtues. Ideals and motivation are of course basic to behavior and to neglect them entirely is likely to be just as misleading as concentrating all analysis on them. Economic analysis of resource allocations, based on expenditure patterns, can be only one among many kinds of analysis of this important subject.

The expenditures of a country can be presented with many different breakdowns, to cast light on the different kinds and intensities of resource allocation decisions. The first, and most obvious area of decision, is that between consumption and savings. What proportion of a country's resources are expended for immediate consumption purposes, and what proportion is set aside for future use? The analysis of how this determination is made and how the proportions can be altered is central to an understanding of a country's ability to raise its productivity. Second, for each of these major segments, a whole series of important questions can be raised, whose answers would shed light on whether the allocation of resources is consistent with the efforts to raise productivity. The questions may include: How much of the consumption and savings should be in the public sector, by government, and how much in the private sector, by individuals, households and businesses? Within consumption expenditures, what should the allocation be among food, other consumable products, services, and durable consumer goods? Within savings, what kind of savings and in what form should the savings be kept, in kinds of money or stocks of goods or in expenditures on capacities for future production?

The answers to these kinds of questions involve government at all levels, local, provincial, and central. They cannot be limited to officials employed in direct economic institutions, but all institutions that set priorities for expenditures, that direct, limit or control expenditures of all kinds and affect the way the future is discounted in present resource allocation.

Economists have developed many concepts and analytical tools for analyzing resource allocation. Most of these can be applied only to economic analysis of capital formation and all are limited by their focus on economic benefits and costs, although noneconomic costs and benefits are clearly important. Even with these limitations, the analysis of how economic forces operating in resource allocation produce some useful insights into how a country can increase its productivity. The first point to stress in the economic analysis is essentially a comparison of costs and benefits. Benefit-cost analysis includes all techniques for evaluation that involve a systematic comparison of benefits and costs, within the context of an output, implicitly or explicitly given. Conceptually, benefit-cost analysis is relevant to both private and public economic divisions, although the difficulties of application and the weight given to different elements may vary in the private and public sectors. All investments, public or private, involve budgetary constraints and opportunity costs. The major difference between the public and private sector lies in the nature of the desired output, the nature of the constraints on expenditures, and the degree of interdependence among individual projects.[2] To the extent that costs and benefits can be measured, the comparison is simple and logical. Unless anticipated costs are less than anticipated benefits, the expenditure would not be justified on economic grounds. But a whole host of modifying questions make this simple cost-benefit approach just the start of the analysis.

There are many questions that relate to how to measure anticipated costs and benefits. There are also the costs and benefits that cannot be measured in monetary terms. For example, the external economies are distinct, recognizable benefits to someone, but are not included in the selling price of the product. There are the social costs and benefits that are not measurable, or if measurable, are not included in the usual statement of costs and benefits. The pollution of air and water, the added crowds on the streets, the additional markets created by the crowds as well as the crime and deprivation that may be the result of crowded cities are real costs and benefits that are social, if not individual. The difference between individual and social costs and benefits may sometimes be too difficult to evaluate in monetary figures, but this does not make them any less real or any less important in resource allocation decisions. It merely makes the decisions more difficult.

Time is also a difficult element to include in a cost-benefit analysis. How long a product will be useful in the future and what discount rate to apply to future values in order to compare them with present costs remains a complicated matter to think through with each investment decision. Benefits in the short run must be compared with expected benefits in the long run, and both of these must be evaluated in terms of present and future costs.

Of all problems relating to the modernization of a country, resource allocation would seem the one most central to the capacities and interests of economics as a discipline. Yet even here, the noneconomic aspects of any important social process are so important that they usually dwarf the pure economic aspects. It would not be difficult to argue persuasively that the most important variables that determine resource allocation are noneconomic, and that economic decisions, important as they are, must fit into a framework of priorities and time preferences that are largely determined by noneconomic judgments and processes. Even with this basic qualification, however, it is important to understand the contribution that economic analysis can make towards understanding resource allocation, not only because it is possible to maximize returns from investment within a given social framework, but also because the economic considerations often sharpen the noneconomic considerations.[*]

---

[*]Implicit in all of this is the assumption, intuitively understandable, that some investment choices are better than others. If one were

Objectives of Resource Allocation

The following are usually given as the general objectives of any improvement in resource allocation:

- Achieving the greatest increase in production and productivity
- Conserving foreign exchange
- Reducing unemployment
- Improving distribution of income
- Promoting economic growth through emphasizing savings and investment.

These are overlapping, and sometimes contradictory, at least at their limits. The first, achieving the greatest increase in production and productivity, would seem to be the most important and least equivocal. Yet these are fearful traps of definition and time conception that can yield far different answers to simple questions of costs and benefits, depending upon the assumption made about social goals and time preferences. Major consideration must often be given to the importance of complementarities and external economies. The product of a contemplated resource allocation must be measured not only in terms of market value, but of its social value that takes into account hidden costs and benefits and side effects, those noneconomic effects that can be very important but are not usually considered in market evaluation of costs and benefits. In strict economic terms, resources should be allocated so that the total income in production is maximized; and the marginal returns in each sector are equal; that is, so that no change in allocation could produce a greater total production. If social evaluation, rather than market evaluation is used, the concept has been labeled social marginal productivity and is one of the most important concepts used by economists to examine the problem of resource allocation in a country.

Formidable and strange as the concept of marginal productivity sounds, it is a familiar idea to all people who must budget resources, and represents the outcome of basic economic forces. People, even organizations, try to pattern their expenditures so that they will provide the greatest return. If they know, and could act on the knowledge that a different pattern of resource allocation would increase their return, they would make the change. A business that keeps asking

---

to believe that it makes little difference in productivity which resource allocation is made, then of course, the whole problem of resource allocation disappears. But this is the viewpoint of complete despair about a country's ability to speed up the modernization process.

itself "What is the best way for us to allocate our resources between production, transportation, markets, and investment?" is asking the same basic resource allocation question as a government that is allocating its expenditures between current and capital budgets and to different sectors within these budgets. The production for each pattern of expenditures is compared with other feasible patterns, to see which will maximize return. Social marginal productivity is the attempt, conceptually, to assure that nonmarket costs and values are included in the calculations of maximizing returns.[3]

The conserving of foreign exchange as an objective in the allocation of resources is so important that it has been separately mentioned, even though it is really subsumed in the previous discussion of maximizing social marginal productivity. Any consideration of costs and benefits which adjusts market evaluation of costs and benefits to their social or real levels would take into account the fact that foreign exchange is usually so scarce that the foreign exchange rate does not reflect its relative scarcity.* For example, investments that encourage the production by domestic producers of products that have previously been imported are, in general, more desirable than other investments. Here, of course, it is necessary to consider whether future imports will be needed to support the investment, the cost of the domestic product compared with its import price, and the employment and income generated by domestic production. Import substitution, as a guide for the allocation of investment resources, is only one of a number of important considerations.

The objective of reducing unemployment is clearly related to the welfare objectives of modernization. Employment is directly related to the distribution of economic benefits, and a direct way of maximizing the distribution of benefits is to achieve the greatest possible increase of employment as a result of the resource allocation. Here too, there are conceptual and operational pitfalls that must be observed. As previously stated, employment is often a difficult concept to apply in the less developed countries, with its family employment and its scarcity of available jobs. The objective of creating the most possible employment may and often does contradict the objective of maximizing the social marginal productivity. An effort to utilize as much human labor

_____

*The technical concept of accounting price or shadow price has been evolved to take this into account. This uses prices that show the real scarcity of foreign exchange in the calculations of cost and benefits. This is particularly important in the calculation on specific projects, when the underevaluation of foreign exchange may clearly influence investment decisions that appear individually profitable, but are too costly from a country's viewpoint. See Tinbergen, Development Planning, McGraw Hill (New York) 1967.

66

as possible in building roads may often increase costs and reduce production compared with highly mechanized road building technology. Here, too, it is often necessary to inject the concept of social costs and benefits as modifying market costs and benefits. This may lead to many judgment factors of political and social significance that often disregard or transcend economic consideration, but are nonetheless more important and more realistic. Because of the close logical relationship between an increase in employment and an increase in well-being of the mass of people, the objective of maximizing employment will continue to be important in the plans of the less developed countries (see chapter 5).

The effort to maximize employment may therefore be considered one of the major elements of a more general objective, to improve the distribution of income. Clearly, this must always remain one of the major objectives of countries trying to achieve more rapid economic growth. Here, too, this may appear to contradict the objective of maximizing social marginal productivity, particularly when the country as a total is considered. Improving the distribution of income is generally considered as a measure of welfare improvement. This means more income, relatively and in absolute terms, for the poor people and less for the well off. This objective may therefore appear to operate as a limitation on efforts to maximize production and productivity. Poor people may want to use increased income to buy products and services that are not available or must be imported. Poor people usually save less than wealthy people, and giving them more income may reduce the amount of capital formation that a country can finance through domestic savings. However, improvement of income distribution has many effects, economic as well as noneconomic, and the net effect may be to improve production, as will be discussed more fully in chapters 4 and 5. Here it is important to note that an important objective of resource allocation, both theoretically and practically, is the improvement of distribution of income in a modernizing country.

This leads to the last of the major objectives of resource allocation, the goal of promoting economic growth through emphasizing savings and investment. Income distribution is only one of the many variables associated with increased savings. Another is the propensity to reinvest profits, which varies from industry to industry. For example, landlords tend to reinvest profits in land, while manufacturers tend to reinvest profits in manufacturing. Investments that produce large external economies, such as transportation and power projects, may encourage future economic growth far more than projects having more immediate effects on production levels. The time horizon used in evaluating future returns of investment becomes a very important element here, and affects resource allocation attempting to maximize the impact on future capital formation. This concept has been refined to one of focusing on the marginal increase of capital formation, which analyzes the distribution of factor payments and the use to which these payments will be made.[4]

The ideal and complete reconciliation of these major objectives of resource allocation is rarely attempted on an overall basis. Rather, allocation decisions are numerous, dispersed over the whole society; and even decisions in a single important sector may not be considered as an entity. Government tries to consider the totality of its resource allocation through an annual budget or a multi-year development plan. But even in the most comprehensive development plans, where total resources are spread out in the best of fashions, the resource allocation is less of a one-time operation than would appear to be the case. Two basic considerations underlie this:

There are many elements or parts of resource allocation that cannot be directed, or even influenced, except in the most indirect manner. The value systems that determine individual and family allocation of resources and the social status that goes with certain types of expenditures are often beyond direct influence. While these do change in time, the changes are usually slow and imperceptible and can only be indirectly manipulated. Examples of these are the social customs of a people that require the expenditure of relatively large resources on births, deaths or on personal religious occasions, and the social status of land ownership. Consideration of resource allocation based on this type of social value system can only be a projection of what is likely to happen rather than be a deliberate set of activities designed to maximize the achievement of specified social objectives.

In any period of time, a large portion of the resources must be allocated in accordance with past commitments and past evaluations. Factories that are started must usually be finished, regardless of any change in priorities. Previous income distribution patterns will have provided patterns of effective demand that have guided investment decisions in certain directions and away from others. Efforts at allocation of resources that will maximize any or all of the objectives will necessarily have to fit into previous judgments, even though the situation will have changed. Budget makers are rarely offered the opportunity to start all over again. Planners must build on what has happened and what is in process of happening. Thus in any operating situation there is a limitation on flexibility, a reduced ability to adjust resource allocation to maximize achievement of objectives.

RESPONSE TO PRICE SIGNALS

Choice

The discussion of savings and capital formation and the description of the resource allocation process in a country have demonstrated that making choices among alternative actions is part of most economic activities. Every time an economic transaction occurs the participants are choosing to act or not to act, and they choose when to act. The purchase by a consumer, the contract to deliver a quantity of goods by a manufacturer, the agreement to import, all these transactions involve some element of choice, and a selection among alternative actions or nonactions. The presence of choice in economic transactions is not vague or nebulous, although it is often involved with some constraints and limitations. The extent of advertising and marketing in a modern society, both at the consumers' level and the producers' level, indicates the importance given by producers to the existence of choice. The constraints on choice placed by necessity or by lack of resources is of course real, but generally it does not eliminate all choice. The starving man with only one coin may have little choice in his purchase of food, and the unemployed worker who must feed his family has little choice about accepting low paid employment. Thus many choices may be more apparent than real, but for most economic activities some operating choice does exist. Indeed, it may be assumed that as a society modernizes itself, as it reduces the hold of tradition and custom, and shifts over to contract and production for markets, the frequency and importance of choice increases with economic activities.

Every economic transaction is based on thinking, even that which seems to be impulsive and irrational. The choice may not be obvious; but with all its constraints, it generally exists as a part of every transaction. The thinking and choice is based on information, as evaluated by the individual or institution undertaking the activity. It is the basic premise of economic analysis that these transactions are, on the whole, rational and are influenced by rational attempts to minimize costs and to maximize returns. The information used by the participants of the transaction may vary from vague rumors and traditional likes and dislikes to the most detailed analysis of market phenomena. Just as a more modern production system produces for the general market more frequently than did the traditional production system, so does it need more and better information on when to make its decisions and choices. A large part of this information is in the form of prices: price of factor inputs, and price of substitute products. The degree of competition may affect the extent and availability of these competitive inputs and products, but that they exist in almost all significant transactions is easily observable. Prices are a way of presenting information that nearly every participant on economic transactions is familiar with and utilizes.

It is not necessary to insist that prices are always the most important element of information in economic transactions. In a situation where tradition strongly governs, economic transactions may take place regardless of price information. A tribesman who owes a day's work to his chieftan may furnish this work regardless of price considerations, although if the wages of laborers in his area double, he might think twice about his "voluntary" offering. Tradition may build some price restraints, although most prices will ultimately adjust to current pressures of scarcity and demand. At this point in the discussion it is only necessary to insist that in most significant economic transactions, over a reasonable period of time, price information is very important in the making of economic transactions.

Prices are usually an attempt to indicate relative scarcity. In a pure market economy, which never did exist and exists only in theoretical models which economists love to display, market prices will exactly reflect relative scarcity. High priced factor inputs will be more scarce than relatively low priced factor inputs, and higher priced products will cost relatively more than low cost products. That exact measurements and precise price responses to scarcity can exist only in theoretical models does not diminish the practical importance of this characteristic of market prices. Prices in actual markets reflect the lack of a theoretically perfect market; they reflect monopoly, tradition, lack of mobility, ignorance of market conditions, government rules, and fixed prices. Yet they also reflect, in the long run, the way participants in economic transactions regard relative scarcities and discount the future. Prices are information about relative scarcities and about market conditions, imperfect and partial as they may be. They are imperfect but important information on which most economic transactions are heavily based.

Competition is generally reflected in prices. When factor inputs are competing for use, their relative prices, reflecting somewhat their relative scarcities, indicate to potential users of these factor inputs what their expected costs may be and how these can be related to potential outputs. The producer agrees on the prices he will pay for these inputs and quite rationally attempts to acquire their use at a minimum cost. This effort to minimize cost may not be the dominant element in his decision. Tradition, apathy, charity, ignorance, mistakes, social and political considerations may be and usually are also involved in the economic decisions, but these should not completely hide the presence and importance of efforts to minimize costs and maximize returns. Price competition is one of the major ways that these basic economic forces work in economic transactions, competition among suppliers of factor inputs, among producers and among consumers of outputs.

Competition exists where there are choices to be made. It is important to recognize this because competition is often subdued and unobtrusive, and therefore, difficult to observe. Two laborers may offer their services to a producer at the same price. Their competition, however, is present in that the buyer of their services may consider their ability, appearance, experience, personality, and need in deciding which of the two laborers to hire. Manifestations of competition between producer and consumer are so clearly visible that they are often taken for granted and disregarded in the analysis of economic institutions. When a producer reduces prices and improves quality in order to persuade customers to buy his product in preference to that of another producer, the effect of competition is quite clear. Tradition and rules provide constraints and limitations in all sources, and it is quite unusual to have a competitive situation in economic activities without these limitations. Yet the forces or tendencies that competition engenders exist in actual or potential form in every important economic activity.

One does not have to believe that all competition is desirable or will lead to desirable ends to accept the importance of competition in the operation of the economic subsystem. Competition can be encouraged, discouraged, moulded, and manipulated. When, in a village marketplace, custom or law decides that all vegetable sellers must be in one place, competition is being moulded. When, in a larger market, the authorities of the market decide at the start of the day what the prices for the different products will be, competition is being moulded. When government decides that no more air conditioners will be imported, competition in the sale and exchange of domestically produced air conditioners is being manipulated. Pure competition is possible only as an analytical construct, in mathematical models of a society, but actual competition is a powerful force in the economic life of a country and is present or absent in any economic decision in a form determined by the institutions of the society. Competition is often the process, in economic terms, by which the "superior" replaces the "inferior," and as such, can be a powerful force toward efficiency.

Price Changes

Do people and institutions really respond to price signals? Is this only theoretical thinking that results from model building and considerations of pure competition? Two or three practical problems in responses to prices will illustrate these questions. First, consider the usual direction or slope of the supply and demand functions. Normally the supply of a product offered for sale increases as the price goes up, and the demand for a product decreases as the price goes up. This is the expected economic response and conforms to economic rationality. It means that as the price of a good or service goes up, the suppliers will respond by making available or producing more of that good or service. For instance, if the daily wage of a worker is increased, more workers will be available for hire, because some people, who would not work at the lower wage, are now induced to work for the higher wage. A producer who makes 100 tables a month will, if the price of tables goes up, try to increase his production even if he has to pay somewhat more for lumber and for his workers. Obviously the increased price of the goods will be considered in relationship to any increases in the cost of making more of those goods available; but the tendency will be there for greater supplies as a response to price increases. Economists call this an upward slope of the supply curve; as price goes up, supply tends to go up.

In a similar way, but in the opposite direction, demand goes down as price goes up. When people are considering buying something, some people are on the borderline between deciding to buy or not to buy. This point of indifference means that at the price they are considering there are alternative choices, including keeping their money, that are about as attractive an alternative as buying the product. A price increase will definitely push them in the direction of not buying, thus reducing effective demand. With the exception of minor kinds of snob transactions, where the higher the price one pays the higher the satisfaction one receives from the purchase, it is safe to say that buyers respond to higher prices by a tendency to reduce the demand for the product.

Several corollaries to these assertions are also true. Supply goes down as price offered goes down, while demand goes up as price goes down. A graphic model shows these two lines as curves, the supply curve going up from left to right, as prices and quantity go up, while the demand curve goes down from left to right, as prices and quantity go up. Competition, resulting from efforts to minimize costs and maximize returns, tends to promote upward sloping supply curves and downward sloping demand curves. A market, as used in this book, is the institution that provides the framework for these kinds of transactions. A village market is one where producers and suppliers meet and transact business with consumers, react to the prices that confront them and that they offer or accept. An insurance market, a money market, a machinery market, a general retail market, all are structured the same basic way, where suppliers and buyers meet, judge prices and other information, and make decisions to involve themselves in economic transactions.

Concrete questions about reactions to prices in the less developed countries can now be raised. Do suppliers in the less developed countries respond to market signals in the expected way, by increasing supplies? More specifically, do peasant farmers react to price increases in the expected "rational" way, or are prices not nearly as important as they are in the economically developed countries? There is ample evidence, gathered in many countries and covering many different kinds of circumstances, that attest to this "rational" behavior. Peasants do respond to higher prices for their products by trying to produce more, and agricultural production is stimulated by higher agricultural prices.[5] These statements, however, must not be considered as mechanical laws but as tendencies or responses that work their way out in the institutions and value systems that a country has developed and within the constraints and limitations of its cultural and social traditions. Where, for example, subsistence farmers bring to the market only enough of their product to satisfy some fixed debts, then higher prices may cause them to bring less to the market. Where day laborers work only to achieve a certain level of income, raising daily wages may reduce the number of days they wish to work; and consequently, in this instance, they would not be increasing the supply of

72

labor as the price increases. But these backward bending supply curves (supply that goes down as price goes up) are unusual and have been proven to be short time phenomenon. As prices of their goods or services go up, workers and producers in the less developed countries respond in the "rational" economic way by producing more and by making more of their services available. Prices are signals for production, even in the imperfect markets of the less developed countries.

Economists have developed a useful jargon in this connection that permits some shortcut references. The concept of elasticity is applied to this relationship. Supply elasticity refers to changes on the supply side and demand elasticity to changes on the demand side. Elasticity compares changes in two variables, and the other variable used in this comparison is prices, as in the price elasticity of supply and the price elasticity of demand. What has been advanced in this discussion is that producers and consumers in the less developed countries do respond to price signals and do display price elasticity of supply and price elasticity of demand. However, their responses are different in degree from similar responses in the more developed countries. A high elasticity means a relatively larger response. Unitary elasticity means that the proportional response of supply or of demand, as the case may be, is equal to the proportional price change. That is, there is unitary elasticity when a 10 percent increase in price is associated with a 10 percent increase in supply offered. On the demand side, there is unitary elasticity if the demand goes down 10 percent when the price goes up 10 percent. An elastic response exists when the percentage change in supply or demand is more than the percentage change in price.*

The fact that price elasticity of supply exists should not hide the fact that this type of elasticity is usually lower in the less developed countries than in the more developed countries. This is just a shortcut way of summarizing the fact that suppliers in the less developed countries may have more difficulties in responding to price signals than do similar suppliers in the more advanced countries. A shoe manufacturer, who sees prices of shoes rise and, therefore, the opportunity to make larger profits, can increase his production only if the increased factor inputs are available and only if all the complementarities and external economies are relatively available for the increased production. In the

---

*Elasticity of supply and demand are often usefully measured against other variables, particularly income. For example, the fact that the income demand elasticity for imported consumer goods is high is a very important reality for most countries. This is a shortcut way of saying that as income goes up, the demand of imported consumer goods goes up faster. A 10 percent increase in income may be associated with a 15 percent increase in the demand for imported consumer goods, giving an elasticity of 1.5.

less developed countries, it will be harder for the supplier to get increased supplies of skilled labor and management, more repair parts for his equipment, more power and transportation, more working capital to support the greater volume of work in progress. To say that a less developed country has a low elasticity of supply is just another way of saying it is less developed; but it does have the advantage of focusing on the response to price and to market transactions that every producer must consider.

One further point must be advanced. The response to price signals must be considered in relationship to the general efforts to achieve higher productivity. Given the assumptions that have been accepted here, the rationality of economic choice, the existence of basic economic forces that tend toward minimizing costs and maximizing returns, and the role of competition as expressed in prices, then the more quickly a country's producers respond to price signals, the more efficient will be its use of its factor inputs. Efficiency in this sense means a greater output per unit of input or less inputs with the same output. The efforts to minimize costs and maximize returns and the competition this involves necessarily mean efforts to make more efficient use of the production process. Prices, as signals in production, are probably used more in the developed countries than in the less developed countries. This is not to say that all competition is beneficial, or that results of price changes are always beneficial and worthwhile. Pure competition rarely, if ever, exists; and suppliers are always confronted with rules and situations that represent constraints and limitations on their choices. Some of these constraints represent basic policies of the countries concerned, policies that are judged worthwhile within the objectives and value systems of a country. Limitations on competition, both consciously developed and inadvertently present, represent operating reality for all producers. To understand the production process of a country and how it can be improved necessarily involves examining these constraints and evaluating their effects on the efficiency of the production process. What is asserted here is that as a country enables its producers to respond more quickly and effectively to price signals, the economic processes will in general be operating more efficiently.

Two major areas of concern relating to response to prices can now be considered. The first of these relates to factor substitution, an important, difficult concept, briefly referred to in a previous section of this chapter, where the relationship between technology and factor substitution was discussed. While theoretically each factor can be substituted to some degree for any other factor, the most common operating problems occur in the case of labor and capital. Labor and land also have important substitution problems, but these can be discussed later under the economics of land utilization. Here, where the relationship of price movements to economic decisions is being explored, it is important to understand why producers substitute labor for capital or capital for labor. Producers in their attempts to maximize their returns and minimize costs choose the best combination of factor inputs and the technology for their enterprise. Of course, profit maximization, while a principal measure of their success in achieving maximum return with minimum cost, is not the only objective of their efforts. Economists learned a long time ago that to emphasize profits only is as unrealistic as to forget the importance of profits. Production decisions are made under a welter of influences and the determinants of one series of decisions may be quite different than the determinants of another series of decisions by the same organization. Status, security, social reasons, ignorance, impulse, and even stupidity have their place in explaining why certain production decisions are made. Yet there is a basic drive, representing the working out of the rational economic forces, that runs as a common thread through almost all production decisions; and the influence of this drive is quite significant. Factor substitution is an important response to price signals. When, for example, the government fixes a foreign exchange rate relatively low compared to the scarcity of foreign exchange and the demand for imported goods, it is in a real sense placing a lower price on imported goods than would otherwise be in effect. Suppose, for illustrative purposes, that the national currency is valued at 8 units of national currency to the U.S. dollar and demand for imports is so high that many people (legally or illegally) are willing to offer 16 units for a U.S. dollar. When a producer is given an import license to buy foreign machinery, the foreign exchange he is authorized to use costs only half of what it might cost, measured by the free market rate. He is encouraged to substitute capital for labor, because the prices of imported capital goods are reduced for him by government policy setting a low foreign exchange rate. If he had to make a decision about installing an imported crane to move heavy loads in a shop or to use six unskilled laborers to do the same work, the fact that the foreign exchange was available at a low cost is important to his final decision. It may not be the only or even the determining influence, but that it is important is clearly demonstrated in many countries. The low prices established for imported capital in terms of the national currency is a force in the direction of substituting capital for labor.

Another important area of concern to illustrate how an economy responds to price signals is that covered by the grandiose term comparative advantage. It will be useful here to reemphasize that costs are merely prices looked at from the viewpoint of the buyer in a transaction. Prices express costs, and comparative costs are comparative prices. The economic activity examined in this term, comparative advantage, is exports; and the examination is directed at the problems of the kind of products a country should produce and export if it wishes to maximize its returns from foreign trade. A country obviously does not export every type of product it possibly can, regardless of cost. It tends to concentrate on those products that it can produce most effectively, with efficiency measured by judgments of producers and the buyers of the exported goods in foreign countries. The concept of comparative advantage, frequently used in discussions of foreign trade, is basically a simple explanation of the fact that "a country exports those products that are comparatively cheap in price at home and imports those which are comparatively expensive."[6] The elements and forces that determine relative prices in export and import goods are varied and complex, relating basically to the fact that different goods require different factor inputs. While there are many complicating factors, the basic economic push in exports and imports is a response to the relative prices of the factor inputs in the production of these products. Burma produces rice for export because it's comparative advantage basically lies in rice production, not in cotton or tobacco or rubber, although these are also produced. That it is possible, under some more or less theoretical assumptions, to show that Burma could have a comparative advantage in the production of cotton does not negate the importance of comparative costs in explaining why Burma exports rice. Costs can be shifted and molded by all kinds of government policies, and costs are clearly not the only determinant of decisions to produce and export certain products. Yet it is important to stress here that the concept of comparative advantage, so basic to understanding the imports and exports of a country, is basically a response of the production system to price signals.

ECONOMIES OF SCALE AND TECHNOLOGY

As a country modifies its policies and develops new or changed institutions to make possible higher productivity, it confronts another set of associated variables relating to productivity that is important enough to deserve separate identification here. Most of these elements have been previously discussed, but they are recognized here from a somewhat different viewpoint as they reflect the basic economic forces in economic behavior. As a producer tries to minimize costs and maximize returns by becoming more efficient in his production process, he is faced with the fact that improved technology is generally associated with a larger volume of production. This association may be the result of several kinds of situations. Improved technology may be associated with more capital per worker, more skilled labor and more fixed costs. These latter are costs that do not increase directly as production increases but tend to lag and therefore do not go up as fast as production goes up. This means that if variable costs go up exactly as much as production goes up, the lag in fixed costs will result in a lower per unit cost as production rises. This is an incentive to increase production, since it lowers unit costs and, if sales prices remain the same, will increase the profit of the producer.

In addition, advanced technology seems to involve higher quantities of production based on the nature of technology. The more specialized equipment is worthwhile if it contributes to increments of output. Illustrations of these situations abound. A factory that uses an automatic stamping machine will need to produce far more articles than one that uses a hand-operated stamping machine. An automatic bottle factory clearly must produce more than a hand-blown glass factory in order to justify the expensive equipment and management involved. Higher production and productivity is the basic reason for specialized equipment, and that such equipment is generally associated with a large volume of output at a lower unit price is not surprising. It is also true that specific technologies come in lumps; that is, there is a finite number of ways to produce a product, and each will be related to an optimum output. For example, different combinations of equipment may be used to establish bottle factories ranging from one producing completely hand-blown bottles to one utilizing completely automatic production. Each combination will result in a level of production; and the producer, in setting up the factory, must make a choice of technology. If he chooses the more automatic kinds of equipment, he is generally choosing a higher quantity of production. Scale economies definitely link technology to the volume of production.

Consequently, what economists call economies of scale are really a manifestation of technology and are a fact of life for the less developed countries. There are many important consequences arising from economies of scale. Take, for example, the question of comparative advantage, just discussed. The less developed countries, in order to improve their technologies are inevitably choosing technologies that are associated with higher quantities of production. To be competitive in world markets with the more developed countries, to concentrate on and retain the improved efficiency that goes with producing the goods and services for which a country has comparative advantage, means that countries must constantly take advantage of economies of scale. To do otherwise would mean to be noncompetitive in world markets.

Equally important is the effect that economies of scale have on specific decisions of capital formation. To select a technology that has the lowest cost feasible may mean selecting a technology that has a higher output than the domestic market can absorb. For some products the assumption can be made that the goods will be in demand when they are produced, and no further consideration of demand is necessary. But modern technology, with its large and important economies of scale, makes this assumption unrealistic. As technology improves, economies of scale become more important and their neglect more costly. As production processes become more specialized and more indirect with more intermediate products used, the necessity grows for more consideration of the type and intensity of demand for the product. The larger the capital investment is, the larger the output; the larger the time period over which the capital will be used, the more necessary it becomes to know more about the price elasticity of demand. Will the market absorb the increased products? At what price will demand absorb the increased product? The small carpenter shop, making a few pieces of furniture a day, must of course think of product demand. The large furniture factory, which produces a large number of tables and chairs with specialized saws, jigs, and automatic tools, will yield economies of scale, but at a greater volume of production. Hence, considerations of size of demand and price elasticity of demand are basic to operating the factory efficiently.

Some countries suffer from problems of economies of scale because the low density of population or small size of the country creates problems in market size. An automatic bottle plant may produce, when operating near capacity, bottles that are one-tenth the price of a less automatic plant. But the quantity of production involved at near capacity production may be five times the number of bottles needed by the country, even when the price elasticity of demand is taken into account. Problems of scale exist for densely populated countries of large size, whose low incomes may mean such low demand that a modern factory could not find enough of a market for a profitable quantity of production. Highly fabricated products, particularly of metal and chemicals, have now achieved a technology where scale economies are very important, even critical to cost of production. Small oil refineries, steel mills, or chemical plants, are generally doomed by their technology to be high cost operations.

But economies of scale do not force the less developed countries to operate only high cost production capacities. In many of the factories providing a wide variety of products, soap, matches, sandals, rice, flour, sugar, textiles, clothing, a wide range of consumer products, the size of the domestic market and efficient technology with significant economies of scale, are not so far apart.[7] The size of the market represents a constraint on technology when it is too small to permit the use of modern equipment. But size of the market is a function of transportation and communication, of organization and of effective demand. These are often capable of improvement in the direction of removing constraints on the size of the market. By improving transportation facilities, making them more available and lower priced, markets can be enlarged to induce larger scale production and new technologies. By improving income distribution through increased payments to low income families, it is possible to increase the effective demand for widely used basic products and to induce producers to seek economies of scale. By guaranteeing markets, by providing some or all of the new capital, and by taking some or all of the risks, government can make possible investment decisions that will push toward economies of scale in production through improved technology. As market organizations improve, they become a source of external economies, making possible further economies of scale.

THE ROLE OF THE ENTREPRENEUR

The definition of an entrepreneur is one who takes the risks and makes the basic decisions to undertake production and operate a business. As in most definitions of this sort, it is not possible to array a host of decisions that are clearly entrepreneurial, as distinct from usual managerial decisions. Yet the concept, however hard to define, is still a useful one, widely used in discussions of economic development. For the presence of entrepreneurial capacity is essential to economic growth. Someone, or some agency, must make the decisions that are necessary to adopt the new technology, hire or train the different management, contract for or build the new capital, decide the basic issues of cost and price, and in general face and overcome the risks and uncertainties of producing for a market. Even a primitive society has some limited entrepreneurs. As a society modernizes, its production processes necessarily involve more and more entrepreneurial functions, until it is quite obvious that these kinds of decisions are a critical element in the process of initiating and sustaining adequate economic growth.

So important is the entrepreneurial function to economic growth that a generation ago economists used to identify it as a fourth factor input, along with land, labor, and capital. The difficulty of exact definition, and the overlap with the management and organization elements of the labor input, has influenced economists to include entrepreneurial functions into the single human input factor, labor. But this does not eliminate the importance of examining this aspect of the labor factor input, since special significance must be attached to it in the efforts to understand the role of public administration in economic growth.[8]

It may be useful to emphasize the major characteristics of good entrepreneurship, as required in the less developed countries:

A willingness to take risks, within limits, that are reasonable to the situation and which do not prohibit all production.

A capacity to impersonalize economic activities, to work with and cooperate with relative strangers.

A tolerance of adjustment, with the capacity to adapt behavior to new conditions.

A desire to improve economic status, to acquire more economic goods or economic well-being.

An understanding of the ways to achieve the economic benefits desired, through some perception about the economic forces that tend toward minimizing costs, maximizing returns and the competition that goes with producing for a market.

Where do entrepreneurs come from? It has long been an article of faith that most of the less developed countries are lacking in the

necessary entrepreneurial capacity and that their ability to generate
sufficient entrepreneurs is less than adequate.* From this belief arose
the conviction that lack of entrepreneurs was one of the most important
bottlenecks to economic growth. Like most beliefs widely held, there
is enough truth in this position to explain its wide acceptance; but as
described in these general terms, it can be misleading and often results in less than useful economic policies. Entrepreneurs are not a
single type of person, with a uniform personality and skill, from a
single class or origin. While it is possible to define a generalized
entrepreneurial function, it is not possible to have the same kind of
people act as entrepreneurs in every type of production. The entrepreneur in the case of a manufacturing establishment must have quite
different characteristics and capacity from the entrepreneur of a motion
picture house, a radio assembly plant, or a farm. All of these must
have knowledge, capacity to make certain decisions, and the ability
to assemble the factor inputs necessary for the production process. But
the actual knowledge, capacity, and financial resources are quite
different; and it is possible to have an excess of one kind of entrepreneur and a shortage of another kind.

In most of the less developed countries, there is an excess of
entrepreneurial capacity in small trading or merchandising establishments and in small agricultural operations. This can be observed in
the hoards of small shopkeepers and small merchants that press in
ever growing numbers in the cities and villages of the less developed
countries. Importing and dealing with import and export goods also
seem to develop large numbers of small traders, even good sized
traders. Manufacturing, however, is another story. Here, while small
manufacturing establishments are common and seem to develop quite
easily, entrepreneurs of large establishments, for resource and technological reasons, seem to be less available. Many entrepreneurial decisions, because they involve great risks and large amounts of
resources, would necessarily have few entrepreneurial participants.
Transportation, for example, provides a mixed picture. Those capacities
that represent small investments and owner operation, such as taxis,
casual trucks, bicycles, and ox carts, are usually in plentiful supply;
and often rules must be established that limit the creation of additional

---

*The usual summary of the subject is, "In economically backward
societies there are difficulties in the way of developing and using the
entrepreneurial qualities. The force of custom, the rigidity of status,
and the distrust of new ideas and of the exercise of intellectual curi-
osity combine to create an atmosphere inimical to experiment and innovation. The collectivism of the extended family, the village, the clan
or the tribe also inhibits innovation because the reward, if any, has to
be shared widely." Bauer and Yamey, The Economics of Underdeveloped
Countries (Cambridge University Press, 1963), p. 103.

entrepreneurs. Large capacities that serve major bus lines, fleets of trucks, railroads, and airlines have a more limited number of applicants so that the less developed countries often suffer from inadequacies of entrepreneurship in these areas.

There is a firmly held belief among some analysts that entrepreneurs are generated from a group or class of people who are dissatisfied with their existing status or have become dispossessed of their rights and privileges. To compensate for this loss or to achieve more status and power, their efforts become diverted to achieving economic gains, and thus they assume more and more of the entrepreneurial functions of a modernizing society. The psychology of these deviants is supposed to be different than the major conforming elements of society—their child rearing habits and customs can be different, and their scale of values can be different. So important has this kind of circumstance been in the case of some countries, notably Japan, Colombia, France, England, and Greece, that this drive toward economic achievement by a dissatisfied class has been designated by some analysts as the only way or at least the most important way to achieve sustained and rapid economic growth.[9] While many economists accept the importance of this element in a country's efforts to modernize itself, most of them feel that assigning prime responsibility for development to this kind of psychological explanation is somewhat of an oversimplification.

More recent studies of the development of entrepreneurs in the less developed countries shows that entrepreneurial capacity can be developed in many ways. In Pakistan, for example, evidence is available to show that the relatively large number of major entrepreneurs in manufacturing come from families of traditional traders who previously had been engaged in buying and selling agricultural products. Some came from refugees from India, but there was no evidence that the larger entrepreneurs were innovators in noneconomic matters or that they came from suppressed groups or that they differed from other Pakistanis in child rearing practices and extent of nationalism.[10] It seems clear that entrepreneurial capacity is often generated within a country by entirely different sets of circumstances. What is also clear is that the function continues and grows and feeds on success. This is not a once-for-all operation, but there is a requirement for a continuous flow of entrepreneurial decisions; and as a country succeeds in achieving a higher rate of economic growth, its need and capacity for entrepreneurial decisions must continue to expand.

The government's role in providing adequate entrepreneurial capacity is quite clear in description, if not in execution. Governments can make entrepreneurial decisions. Whether in the regular governmental offices or in special commissions, corporations, and authorities, the government can make the basic investment and management decisions, commit the capital, and take the risks of venturing into new businesses involving improved technologies. It can also provide resources for others who will perform the entrepreneurial functions. This it does when development banks are government operated or when the government shares the basic decisions to create a new industry. Or the government can establish and maintain the climate of noneconomic conditions that are necessary for the development of adequate entrepreneurship. These include:

The maintenance of law and order, to confirm contractual obligations, prevent capital flight, and shape future stability.
The provision of more adequate social and economic overhead investment.
The maintenance of a political system which does not collapse under the social and economic changes that modernization necessarily involves.
The development of a value system that is not so hostile to entrepreneurship that only strongly deviant groups can be found willing to become entrepreneurs. This last may not be a function of government and is more a resultant of social changes than of governmental activities.

Finally, it is essential to point out that each country determines in its own way the distribution of entrepreneurial functions between government and private interests. There can be no optimum way assignable to all of the developing countries. Different ideologies may come to different conclusions, and there is no way of evaluating these ideologies in economic terms. A pragmatic approach seems best suited for most countries, with the test being the relative efficiency in performance. This point of view will be discussed more fully in later sections of the chapter, but it seems clear here that economics by itself provides little theoretical guidance to the question of how a country's entrepreneurial functions should be divided between the public and private sectors.

NOTES

1. For a discussion of demand-following and supply-leading finance, see H.T. Patrick, "Financial Development and Economic Growth in Underdeveloped Countries," Economic Development and Cultural Change 14, no. 2 (January 1966): 174-77.

2. Jesse Burkhead and Jerry Miner, Public Expenditures. Aldine (1971). For a technical explanation see A.R. Prest and R. Turrey, "Cost-Benefit Analysis: A Survey," Economics Journal (December 1965): 694.

3. For a technical discussion of social marginal productivity, see Hollis B. Chenery, "The Application of Investment Criteria," Quarterly Journal of Economics 67 (February 1953): 76-96.

4. See Otto Eckstein, "Investment Criteria for Economic Development and the Theory of Intertemporal Welfare Economics," Quarterly Journal of Economics 71 (February 1957): 65.

5. See Max F. Milliken and David Hapgood, No Easy Harvest (Boston: Little, Brown and Co., 1967), pp. 175-90 and Raj Krishna, "Agricultural Policy and Economic Development," in Agricultural Development and Economic Growth, ed. Hermann Southworth and B. J. Johnson (Ithaca, N.Y.: Cornell University Press, 1967), pp. 497-540.

6. Charles P. Kindleberger, "International Economics," 5th ed. (Illinois: Richard D. Irwin, 1973), p. 27.

7. For an analysis of production possibilities and the importance of scale in determining the efficient range of production, see W. P. Strassman, Technological Change and Economic Development (Ithaca, N.Y.: Cornell University Press, 1968).

8. For importance of entrepreneurship in economic development see Harvey Leibenstein, "Entrepreneurship and Development," The American Economic Review (May 1968): 72; G. M. Meier and R. E. Baldwin, Economic Development (New York: John Wiley & Sons, 1957), p. 395-97; and C. P. Kindleberger, Economic Development (New York: McGraw-Hill, 1965), pp. 117-19.

9. See Everett E. Hagen, On The Theory of Social Change (Homewood, Ill.: Dorsey, 1962) and David C. McClelland, The Achieving Society (Princeton, N.J.: Van Nostrand, 1961).

10. Gustave F. Papanek, "The Development of Entrepreneurship," American Economic Review, Papers and Proceedings 52, no. 2 (May 1962): 46-58. This was based on a survey of a random sample covering nearly 10 percent of all firms with about 50 percent of the capital of Pakistan's industry, and included the industrialists who controlled 70 percent of the capital.

4

PRODUCTION AND PRODUCTIVITY— INCREASING THE QUALITY AND QUANTITY OF FACTOR INPUTS

QUALITY AND QUANTITY OF FACTOR INPUTS

Production and productivity can be improved by increasing either the quantity or quality of the factor inputs or, in the usual instance, increasing both. The need to stress the difference between quality and quantity arises from the fact that government policies can affect each differently. While some types of factor inputs may be in surplus, other usually are in critical short supply; and quantity increases of the surplus factors can constrain rather than stimulate the rate of economic growth. In most countries the quantity of unskilled labor is more than ample, suggesting that improvement of labor inputs must be focused on quality. Land and capital also represent mixed pictures, but because these groups of factor inputs are usually scarce relative to labor, increases in both quality and quantity often work in the direction of improving production and productivity. It is also well to remember that improvements in technology, the key element, are strongly associated with improvement in the quality of inputs and not necessarily with the quantity of inputs. Bringing in a few trucks to replace a large number of oxcarts could conceivably lead to a large increase in productivity per worker without increasing the total value of the capital or of the production. Of course, there are other considerations involved, such as what happens to the displaced oxcarts and to the income of the people depending on the oxcarts and who gets the benefits from the increased productivity. That makes increasing productivity an important part of social, political, and administrative, as well as economic, problems.

Policies and programs designed to increase the availability of some factor inputs frequently affect both their quantity and quality. Administrators have to analyze the mixture because the impact of a program may work differently on quality and quantity. A program designed to improve the quality of electricians by requiring certificates of training

and qualifications may reduce the number of electricians available
while improving quality. Importing automatic bottle washing equipment
may increase the quantity and quality of capital in the bottling industry,
and may reduce the requirements for unskilled workers while increasing
the demand for semiskilled machine operators and skilled mechanics.
An increase in one factor may change the requirements for many kinds
of other factor inputs. The criteria for judging the desirability of changes
in the quality and quantity of factor inputs must not only include consideration of the mix of both factor inputs and production, but must also
take into consideration changes of mix in time, the future mix. A shortage of electricians because of efforts to improve their quality may only
be a short-run phenomenon, and the long-run supply may be increased
by additional training facilities and the attraction for new trainees that
results from increased earnings resulting from improved quality and
scarcity of qualified workers. Many times programs to improve quality
appear to increase production difficulties when viewed only from a short-
run perspective. Yet reliance entirely on long-term analyses can also
be too limited; as John Maynard Keynes is reported to have once said,
"In the long run, we are all dead." The mixture of product and factor
input analysis must also be tempered by a consideration of the mixture
of short-run and long-term effects and objectives, which adds up to a
complex mix indeed.

IMPROVING LAND INPUTS (NATURAL RESOURCES)

Land, it will be remembered, is the shortcut way of referring to all
natural resources, the original nonreproducible contribution of nature.
It therefore includes not only agricultural land, with its varying qualities
of fertility, location, and weather, but also minerals, advantages of
general location, and even topography of the country. The fact that it
is often hard to distinguish the natural fertility of land from man-made
reproducible fertility does not completely eliminate the usefulness of
considering natural resources separately.

Availability of Natural Resources

It may be useful to point out that the less developed countries
generally have quite exaggerated pictures of their natural resources,
including agricultural land. Most of them have visible evidence of
underutilized natural resources—land that could be productively used
if roads were built, or water made available, mineral deposits that
could be exploited if the right decisions and resources were devoted to
it, or water rapids that could be converted into hydroelectric power.
All this is coupled with myths and hopes of tremendous oil and gas pools

underlying their country if only someone would be intelligent and forceful enough to do something about it. Almost every colonial experience has developed myths of unused or underutilized resources, because the colonial power felt it was in its interest to keep the colony poor and dependent. Again, like most of the myths and folk beliefs about economic development, there is enough of a basis for the exaggerated beliefs so that they cannot be dismissed offhand; but their acceptance must be accompanied by careful scrutiny and with major modifications.

The unpleasant truth is that most countries are not luxuriously endowed by nature with immediately useful, highly valuable natural resources. The specific determination of what is a usable natural resour is largely a market phenomenon, a matter of costs and benefits as eval uated by persons or institutions making investment decisions. For mar decades, the leaders of Burma knew that their country contained tremendously valuable coal deposits. Coal outcroppings were quite common in many parts of the country, and local mining by hand method was quite common. During the colonial period, it was felt that the British did not develop Burma's coal resources because of their vested interests in the coal mines of India. After independence, serious efforts were made to develop Burma's coal resources. Costly field investigations were undertaken to study the quality and quantity of the various outcroppings of coal and to determine which location could be developed most advantageously. The results were quite disconcerting. Most of the outcroppings were found to represent shallow coal deposits too small for commercial development. The only deposits large enough to warrant large investment with modern equipment, in order to acquire economies of large scale production and produce coal at a low price, were in a distant part of the country, far from existing transportation and consumers. The cost of transportation would be overwhelming. In addition, the coal at the site was friable, of a type that rapidly disintegrated into small pieces and dust; and consequently use of that coal would require a plant for briquetting the coal, binding it into small, more durable pieces. The total cost estimates were excessive and would yield unit costs that far exceeded the cost of imported coal. Afte many expensive studies and with obvious reluctance, the development of Kalawa coal deposits was given low priority, if not outright rejectio:

The transformation of potential natural resources to actual natural resources is primarily a market phenomenon, and it has associated witl it all of the advantages and disadvantages of external economies. It may be judged economically impractical to develop a particular mineral deposit because the estimated costs would be greater than the sales price. But the external economies could conceivably be so great that, even if they are not capable of being captured in the sales price, the investment could be very worthwhile. For example, a mineral deposit in a remote but populated area could be costly to develop because of the cost of building roads and providing power. Yet, if the road is buil and the power plant developed, the effect on other economic activities could be important. It might be possible, if the road were built, to

86

bring agricultural products to urban or export markets, to use the power to develop small industries and to stimulate social and political ties and changes that would be essential in instigating a population to accept new ideas about production and productivity. External economies are usually an important consideration in the development of natural resources, but the optimum balance between cost benefits as they are predicted in market calculations and the added effects of externalities is difficult to judge. Economic calculations can give only a partial answer to these types of questions because there are many externalities that are known to exist that cannot be measured or even roughly evaluated.

These considerations of predicted costs and benefits enter into use of all kinds of natural resources, land as well as mineral deposits. Most countries have large areas of land that are not being used intensively for agricultural production, yet tillable land may be quite scarce. Some natural attribute may be missing, usually water. Provision of water, through irrigation schemes or desalination capacities, could add large quantities of productive land to the country; yet cost considerations often make this development unrealistic. The point being stressed is that cost-benefit considerations, largely the kinds of costs and benefits that are market determined, are important elements of any program to increase the quantity and quality of natural resources.

One additional generalization about natural resources should be considered. Not only have the less developed countries an exaggerated evaluation of their natural resources, but they tend to overemphasize the importance of natural resources in the whole modernization process. As with most of the complex variables under consideration, there is a basic condition of mutual causation. Plentiful natural resources encourage economic growth just as economic growth encourages the development of natural resources. Yet throughout the world, there are many instances of countries with obviously inadequate resources attaining high rates of growth and many richly endowed countries with little growth. Consequently, analysts do not accept that the presence of natural resources is an important determinant of the rate of economic growth. At the extremes, where practically no natural resources are available (Lapland, Arctic areas) or where almost limitless quantities of minerals are available (oil-rich countries), natural resources obviously play an important role in development. But in most of the countries the lack of an adequate rate of economic growth can be attributed more persuasively to other inadequacies than to scarcity of natural resources.

By accepting the importance of market determination of costs and benefits in the realization of a natural resource, transportation as an element of cost receives an overwhelming significance. The technology of mineral exploitation is readily transferable and relatively easily available. While large quantities of capital may be involved, the mineral extraction industry has developed a technology and a mobility that is extraordinary in its effectiveness. In practically any place in the world, if transportation costs were no consideration, it is possible to create miracles of production capacities almost overnight. The recent examples of oil exploitation in Libya, Algeria, and now northern Alaska, are obvious. The iron ore development of Liberia, Venezuela, and Canada are examples of metal extraction expansion. Transportation costs, based on the distance from markets and from complementary facilities, are a major determinant of the transformation from potential to actual resources. Most of the less developed countries have potential resources that would be more fully exploited, if they were located in one of the more developed countries. Burma's unutilized coal deposits would have been developed a long time ago, if they had been on one of the Japanese islands. The importance of transportation costs suggests, for example, the powerful impetus to development that can often be provided through lower and even subsidized transportation capacities.

Agricultural Land Resources

Land, as was observed, is the principal natural resource of the less developed countries. Most of the people are engaged in agricultural production, live close to the land and are greatly and immediately affected by any change in any of the important institutions that are related to agricultural pursuits. Land is generally combined with other factor inputs at a technological level that yields a low quantity of products per acre, per worker, or per unit of any input compared with higher productivity countries. Land is for the most part inefficiently used by comparison with known technology. For that reason, as well as for natural reasons, agricultural land is generally of poor quality in the less developed countries. As in the case of mineral resources, most people of the less developed countries have exaggerated ideas of the quality of their agricultural land. Excellent agricultural land in large quantities is relatively scarce in the world, and the less developed countries have only a small part of it. But this is not really as important as is the fact that most of the agricultural land has deteriorated from centuries of poor land practices, so that as an operating constraint the agricultural land resource of the less developed countries is not only relatively scarce, but it is also relatively poor in quality.[2]

There are some agricultural economists who insist that for the most part agricultural land is efficiently utilized, at present, in the less developed countries.[3] The use of the word "efficient" here relates to the quality of the labor and capital inputs and points to the basic problem of improving the quality of the land input. The quality of the land is closely associated with the ability of the farmers to get more and better capital inputs. Thus, considering the small amount of simple

capital (hand tools, oxcarts, cattle, poor seed) and the limited quality
of the labor input (the unskilled agriculturalist, poor credit, and marketing organizations) the land is used efficiently. Until the quality of
the labor and capital inputs are improved, improving the land input may
be a misuse of resources.

The point can be more readily examined when observing the effects
of creating more high cost land through the building of large dams.
Where these dams have been built in areas of good farming, and where
farmers understand improved agricultural practices and the use of improved capital and have access to more capital, the economic results
have usually been favorable. There may be questions raised whether
this was the best way of utilizing available financial resources; but
the economic effects, on a cost-benefit analysis, are reasonably favorable. But there are numerous instances where high cost land has been
made available to the traditional kind of farmers, with the same technology and the same institutions that existed prior to the construction
of the dam. The results were clearly unfavorable, and only the hope
that the future will see an improvement in labor and capital inputs
appears to justify the situation. Massive attempts to improve agricultural land, without prior or at least concommitant improvement of
the capital and labor inputs, appears to be an unwise investment.

An increase in the quantity and quality of agricultural land is of
course closely related to improvement in transportation facilities.
Economically, there is little difference between acquiring more land
through building a dam and irrigation system or through building roads
to areas where a lack of markets had resulted in a low level subsistence
agriculture. The experience of countries such as Turkey, where new
roads helped bring large quantities of additional land into the market
economy, has been repeated in many countries. In the United States
the opening of the west by railroads marked the greatest single addition
to agricultural land as an input.

Land hunger is a common phenomenon in most countries and is
particularly important in the less developed countries. Population
pressure may make this an explosive issue; but even where there is a
degree of political stability relative to this problem, the relationship
between land tenure systems and improvement of land as a factor input
is of consequence. Since the relationship covers tenant rights and
what can be and is being done to improve the land, it bears heavily on
frustrations of sharing the income from farm land. Land ownership is
one of the key elements, as Myrdal says: "Low productivity of labor
and land is related to the social structure and the attitudes supported
by that structure, the wide-spread existence of absentee land ownership and tenancy being of particular importance. . . . If productivity
in agriculture is to increase, there must be institutional reform. Unless
land reform of one type or another is introduced, improved farming
methods have little chance of being applied."[4]

There are many undesirable effects of ownership concentration,
landlordism, and tenancy. Thus under land ownership conditions

prevailing in many developing countries, five obstacles which impede agricultural development are usually singled out. These are:

● Farmers have little or no incentives to increase production, especially under crop-share renting; the returns from any extra effort the tenant makes he must share with the landlord.

● Farmers have no suitable access to production credit; usually they can get credit only at the will of the landlord and at very high interest rates.

● Managerial responsibility is divided between tenant and landlord and the landlord is rarely development oriented.

● The tenant's occupancy and livelihood is insecure as the landlord can dismiss him more or less at will and find another tenant instantly. This discourages the tenant to improve the land, housing, and other facilities for better production and living conditions. If he does, the landlord increases the rent.

● The tenant's social status in the community is low as a result of this quasi-servile dependence upon his landlord, and impairs his participation in community affairs and his access to schools, marketing and other facilities. Landlords may tend to oppose the development of cooperatives and tenants' access to them, because they reduce the landlords' and merchants' bargaining power in the market.

Land reform has taken many patterns and forms in recorded history, and probably precedes recorded history. Nomadic, pastoral, and feudal land systems are today comingled with factory-in-the-field systems that defy classification. Several different kinds of land tenure systems and land reform movements, with varying patterns of success, are a common phenomenon in most countries.

A report on land reform published by the United Nations compiled the definitions of land reform submitted by various governments into the following categories:

● measures for the redistribution of land ownership.
● improvement of agricultural economic institutions.
● policies for increasing agricultural production and improving land use.[5]

The form and size of landownership is important, but taken by itself it is a confusing variable related to productivity. Concentrated ownership does not necessarily mean large-scale farming. Often, the landlord leases out his land in fragments cultivated by peasants with inadequate access to new inputs as well as inadequate security and motivation. Owners of large land may be indifferent to the opportunity for increased income by improving inputs, because they are satisfied with their present income and status and do not wish to invite the social ferment that can accompany increased income for the peasants. In any

90

planned reform major attention must be given to land use rather than mere size of ownership, although the two are clearly related.

A form of landownership, predominantly found in the Communist countries but also extensively tried in South Asia, Africa, and Latin America, are communes or cooperatives. Ownership of the land is held in common and the production from agricultural enterprises are distributed either according to contribution or need. This distributes a large area of land to a large number of people but still allows for economies of scale through central management and fuller utilization of productive resources. This system has been tried with varying success in many areas, but some serious problems have also developed. There has been a general lack of management experience among the members of these cooperatives and trained agricultural technicians were not available or have not been attracted to these farms. These cooperatives also gave rise to local elites who gradually came to control the distribution of profits. In addition, because of strong kinship ties and cultural preferences there was often a propensity to hire labor while underutilizing the farms' existing labor resources. These enterprises also showed, understandably, a great propensity to consume their product rather than to save or to invest it. For example, the ejidos of Mexico and other cooperative farms have shown increases in crop output because of more intensive use of the land, but they have not increased the productivity of the average worker to any great extent.[6]

Most advocates of changes in the land tenure system relate low productivity in agriculture to absentee or disinterested landlords, to lack of motivation to improve some other person's property, and to insecurity and apathy, all of which would be reduced in their undesirable effects if the land tenure systems could be changed. By a wide variety of means, most countries try to reduce the rate of tenancy and to make the tenant's position more secure on the land and to encourage land improvement by making relatively more income available to those that work the land compared to those who own it. Laws that limit the size of individual holdings, that limit the proportion of the crop that can be demanded as rent, that protect the continued use of land by tenants, that involve payments to tenants for land improvement, all these are types of efforts to improve land tenure and land use systems. The economic reasoning and impact of these changes vary greatly from country to country, and from section to section within a country. The economic aspects of land tenure changes are often not nearly as important as the political and social changes, and an evaluation in economic terms only is certain to be misleading.

Basically, in most of the less developed countries, labor is cheap; and land, as a scarce agricultural input, is relatively expensive. The object of economic policies must be to improve both land and labor productivity. By definition, the best means of attaining this increase in these two measures of productivity is to place each worker on an adequate sized farm and to make available to him the appropriate capital and skills needed to operate the farm at its optimum level. This high level generalization encompasses large, industrial-type farms, cooperative or plantation-type operations, as well as small, family farms. As an ideal, its usefulness lies only in the emphasis it places on the need for sufficient capital and the human training or knowledge that must be associated with changes in land tenure systems to improve agricultural efficiency. Operationally, the key words in this generalization are defined in a situational manner, by actual circumstances in each country and locality at a particular time. What is an adequate sized farm, and what are appropriate capital and skills is the essence of the operating problem, and these must be defined by social and political as well as economic criteria. Systems of land ownership are important and are difficult to modify in a way that automatically pushes in the direction of increased productivity per worker and per acre of land. Land ownership affects stability, motivation, capital formation, and choice of technology. It is a dominant determinant of status and credit worthiness as well as strongly affecting income distribution. There is nothing magical in any particular size and ownership system in agriculture except as it is related operationally to the numerous political, social, and cultural institutions of the country. It appears that land reform, unless supplemented by many other essential changes and improvements, is a necessary but not sufficient condition for agricultural efficiency. Improving land as a factor input is inevitably tied to improving the human input and many associated institutions at the same time.

Indeed, where land reform by itself is tried, its impact on the improvement of land as a factor input may be even less than beneficial. Small farmers and tenants are often less capable than large landlords of improving land as a factor input. They usually lack both capital and knowledge; and because of their immediate economic necessity, they often exploit the land rather than build up its long term capabilities. Small land holdings may make necessary improvement too costly for individual owners, and social arrangements for group sponsorship of these improvements may be lacking. In many cases, land reform results in less rather than more employment.[7] No one who has observed the low agricultural productivity in the less developed countries can deny to land reform, both land tenure and land usage, a major role in the variety of means that are required to improve the well-being of the large mass of rural poor. Yet is is important to emphasize that concentration on land reform, without the necessary complementarities of improved labor inputs and more and improved capital inputs, is not likely to achieve the objectives of higher production and productivity. Although land improvement through land reform is a highly desirable, even necessary objective, its achievement must rely heavily on the working out of economic forces that are ever present and ever important. The desire to have as large an income as possible, to minimize costs and maximize returns of effort or investment, the need to recognize and adjust technology and production to changes in cost and price, must be considered as only part of the problem of improving the land inputs, together with the noneconomic determinants included in such summary terms as status, psychological, cultural and political variables.

The improvement of land as a factor input through land reform must be associated with development or change in the following kinds of institutions:

Legal institutions that make land ownership by small families and poor people possible and enforceable. These legal institutions must also reduce the tremendous waste of resources and energy many countries devote to land ownership disputes.

Credit institutions that make possible the acquisition of additional capital widening or capital deepening. Both raise productivity by improving the capital/labor ratio, by increasing the productivity of labor through existing technologies, and by permitting new technologies to be adopted.

Experimental and demonstration institutions that search for better technologies to apply to specific areas and that demonstrate the gains from these new technologies.

Marketing institutions that enable improved factor inputs to reach producers and products to reach buyers. Various market arrangements, whether the market structure is formal or informal, are required for labor, capital, land, credit, and commodities to encompass a widespread improvement in the use of land.

Social and cultural institutions, such as the family, the tribe, the caste, are involved in land tenure and land use relationships. Complex changes in these, as has been asserted, are usually basic, directly and indirectly, to any significant improvement of land as a factor input.

Finally, it is important to reemphasize how important a role government and its administrators play in land as a factor input. Land reform is usually dramatic and very visible; it is so important that it rapidly becomes determined by the motivations and efforts of the highest political authorities. But it is the slow, evolutionary changes brought about by implementation after the announced land reform that decide the ultimate success or failure of the land reform. These changes are basically institutional, through government support for cooperatives, for community development, for supervised agricultural credit, for enforcement of land ownership laws, and for the provision of institutions providing improved agricultural inputs, marketing, storage, research, and extension work.[8] All of these broad types of institutions are either government sponsored, government administered, or strongly affected by government policies and practices. No single subject could be selected that is more related to improvement in economic production and to government than land as a factor input. Its social and political complexities probably outweigh its economic complexities and together, they represent a major component of the whole complex of modernization. Only by sorting out some

of these complexities and attempting to identify relationships to government policies and practices can one examine the role of public administration in this part of the whole process of modernization.

IMPROVING LABOR INPUTS

Meaning of Improving Labor Inputs

Labor factor inputs, it will be recalled, include all aspects of
human contributions to production, not just human muscular effort. It
includes training, skills, experience, thinking, organization, and judgments. Improvement of the quality of labor therefore involves not merely
improved physical capacity to work, but also the improved organizations
within which work takes place. The outstanding importance to production of training, skills, and of the organizations that provide the
framework for their operations has been so clearly demonstrated that it
can no longer be questioned. The remarkable economic recovery in
Western Europe after World War II was conditioned, of course, by the
new resources made available, both domestic and foreign; but the
destruction of capital was quickly overcome and the basic powerful push
toward recovery and increased productivity was obviously manifest.
Improved technology, the principal element in raising productivity, is
embodied in the knowledge, skills, and organization of the labor factor
input. As an analytical construct, technology can be separately identified; but in reality it is not separable from the human contribution to
production. Analytically, it can be usefully separated because the
forces and activities that operate to increase skilled labor inputs are
in many ways different than those that affect human unskilled labor
inputs.
The discussion of economic rationality in chapter 1 asserted that
people in the less developed countries are as economically rational as
in the more developed countries. This means that they try to economize
on scarce inputs, to minimize their costs, and to maximize their returns
from an economic transaction. The judgments of what is a minimum or
maximum, the influence given to different variables, will be different
from culture to culture, from country to country, just as it differs from
individual to individual. But, essentially, labor in the less developed
countries wishes to earn more wages; business men want to make more
profits; buyers want to buy as cheaply as they can; and sellers want
to receive as high a price as they can for their product. In economic
terms, the supply curve slopes upward, and the demand curve slopes
downward. Workers will be more numerous and will be willing to work
harder as wage rates go up, in spite of short-run occasions when they
seem to do the opposite. In the long run, for any significant number of

people, the labor input's response to higher costs and higher benefits is the same in all countries.

A distinction can be made between increasing the number of labor inputs and improving the quality of labor inputs. When shortages of certain kinds of skilled workers exist, the training of more skilled workers improves the average skill of the total labor input by raising the number of skilled workers and reducing the number of unskilled workers. Workers and management learn on the job, and experience tends to upgrade the labor input. Better work organization in modern, large scale industries that permits workers and management to work more effectively clearly improves the labor input. It may also increase the quantity of workers. Even shifting unskilled workers from unemployment to employment both increases and improves the labor input on the assumption, obviously reasonable, that employed workers are better off and can work better than workers who have given up hope of finding productive employment. In a study of the quality of labor and economic development for the ILO, it was concluded that among the factors contributing to economic growth, labor quality was a far better explanation than the number of labor inputs.[9] Quality improvements in the labor factor inputs may be necessary even when the skills exist in the country. Factors that cause the improper skill utilization are unemployment, inadequate institutions, immobility of labor, and the general inadequacies of health and education as they affect motivation and work capabilities.

Labor productivity is always the object of a large number of influences and should be regarded as a multivariate function, a function that has many variables incorporated within it. Labor productivity reveals the changing effectiveness, not only of the labor itself, but of all the factors with which it is utilized in the production process. Only in a theoretical, mathematical model do these other factors remain constant in the production process. Therefore, labor productivity cannot be the measure of the specific contribution of labor; it shows the cumulative influence of a large number of influences, including technical improvement, rates of operation, degree of efficiency achieved in different processes, availability and reliability of supplies and flows of material, maintenance standards, management efficiency, and employer-employee relationships, to mention only a few of the influences that directly affect labor productivity. Thus, improving labor inputs can be examined from two different but obviously related viewpoints, how to improve the laborer himself and how to improve his work situation.

Employment and Unemployment

In societies that are predominantly agricultural, work is usually spread among all members of the family regardless of how low the average productivity falls. The income from the work is also shared, and therefore concepts of unemployment and employment are difficult to apply. At certain times of the year all members of the family may be employed at whatever type of work is available, usually at planting and harvesting time where timing is an important factor. Also, in the casual work between peaks, where an endless number of minor tasks can be done in a more or less desultory fashion such as gathering wood, hauling straw or fodder, watching livestock feeding, communicating and bargaining, the work is spread as thinly and as inefficiently as the number of potential workers require. Everybody down to the beginning school age can point to some efforts that by themselves add something, however small, to the family product. The contribution by some of these surplus workers is so low that it could be zero or even less than zero, so that production could actually increase if some workers were persuaded to leave.*

The best way to improve the labor inputs in production is to provide for increasing employment on jobs that utilize higher skills, more and improved capital and therefore, improved technology of production. All of a government's efforts to achieve economic development are, in a sense, efforts to improve the labor input. Economic plans that provide for increased investment and increased production therefore should call for more employment. But maximizing output may not necessarily maximize employment, and even maximizing employment may leave an increasing number of workers unemployed in the presence of rapidly increasing populations. The output of production is a mix of products; and employment is also a collection of heterogeneous inputs of skills, type of employment and duration, daily, weekly, or seasonal. Both output and employment that occur over time and current levels always influence future levels of both output and employment. Thus the relationship between increased production, increased productivity, and increased employment is neither simple nor unambiguous.

Unemployment has been growing in the less developed countries. Difficult as it is to measure unemployment in the rural areas, it is clear that there are increasing numbers of disguised or invisible unemployed, persons who share the work of the family and share in the returns as members of the family. With a zero or a very low contribution to the

---

*The existence of disguised unemployment, where the marginal productivity is zero or negative, has been argued vigorously and has been denied equally vigorously. The evidence, quite inconclusive, shows that if the marginal productivity is not zero then it is very low. The important point is that in many countries, large numbers of agricultural workers have so low a productivity that the average productivity is quite low; and until these workers are either removed or given the opportunity to raise their productivity very much, the average productivity in agriculture will remain too low to permit a high rate of economic growth for the country as a total.

product, large numbers of these workers could be withdrawn from the production process without seriously affecting the total production.[*] In the urban areas, unemployed workers are more visible, although they attempt to cover their unemployed status in trivial, unproductive tasks with extremely low productivity, such as street sales and irregular haulage. The increase in industrial employment has been less, proportionately, than the growth in industrial production, in urban population, or in general population. Visible unemployment in urban areas has increased, in spite of the relatively high rate of investment. Data from the United Nations show that for all LDC's, industrial output grew at approximately 7.5 percent per annum over the period 1948-61, while employment in industry expanded at less than one-half that rate—by only 3.5 percent per annum.[10]

In developed countries, problems of employment and unemployment generally focus on how to adapt the labor force to changes in the economic systems; in the less developed countries, the problem is often best viewed in terms of how to use the labor force to change the economic system, to transform it from a low-productivity to a high-productivity subsystem. The nature of the problem and the measures to be adopted by government are quite different. Government employment policies in the less developed countries must go far beyond statements of ultimate aims for full employment. They must include more immediate aims and instruments for emphasizing employment in the choice of production technology, to minimize capital intensive

---

[*]The varying definitions and estimates are illustrated in this quotation: ". . . until there is more agreement as to what is meant by underemployment, estimates or surveys attempting to measure it will be of very limited value for comparative purposes. They may, however, be very revealing in themselves.

"In Japan two sets of calculations based on the results of the 1950 Farm Household Economy Survey and with different underlying assumptions yielded estimates that 35 percent and 57 percent, respectively, of the agricultural labour force constituted surplus labour. The Food and Agriculture Organization (F.A.O.) has estimated that from 28 to 64 percent of the agricultural workers in various areas of the Middle East, North Africa and Southern Europe are surplus. In the Nile Valley in Egypt underemployment has been estimated at 30 percent. Surplus labor in agriculture in Spain was estimated to be more than 35 percent in the early 1950s. In Italy it was estimated that in 1952 underemployment among the peasant labour force may have exceeded 29 percent for the country as a whole. There was great regional variation, however, for the rate went up to 49 percent in the south as against 17 percent in the north." Excerpt from International Labour Office Studies and Reports New Series, "Employment and Economic Growth," Geneva 1964, p. 28.

investment and maximize labor intensive production. This includes examination of those monetary and fiscal policies that encourage capital intensive investment, such as underpricing imported capital to substitute equipment for human labor. These policies must also include government efforts to improve labor mobility and work motivation, to improve the use of existing skills as well as the development of additional human capacities. Education and health policies and programs are essential associates of a government's employment policies. Government efforts to provide employment through public works programs have long been part of their efforts to improve the capital of the country by utilizing otherwise unemployed labor. These works programs, usually rural in nature, were often major elements in the hopes and dreams of national leaders as they struggled for independence. Operating realities soon confronted such programs with high costs and with demands for such quantities of administrative requirements that many programs were substantially reduced or eliminated, or were never initiated. Misallocation of resources, even outright corruption, rapidly moves in to these programs where widespread operations make adequate supervision difficult. However, the growing realization that economic growth, particularly in the industrial sector, tends to be capital intensive and will not provide enough new jobs to keep unemployment down, has reawakened an interest in examining the feasibility and desirability of large works programs, both urban and rural. Usually, employing more people means an increase in the current output. If the productivity of additional workers is very low, the wages paid them may be above their production. But as long as their production is above zero, more employment makes for more output; and so long as total consumption does not increase to the extent of reducing total savings and investment, measures to promote employment will tend to promote economic growth and development.

However, total investment may be reduced in cases where large numbers of workers are given wages that are higher than the output they produce. Their consumption will go up; and since there is likely to be a continuing shortage of capital, their increasd consumption is likely to be at the expense of someone else's consumption or investment. If it is at the expense of investment, clearly the objective of more employment is achieved at the cost of less potentiality for economic growth. But even if the workers' productivity is very low, below their average wage, the conflict between growth and employment can be made up by shifting consumption away from the high consumption groups. The redistribution effects occur when progressive income taxation is used to provide resources for the works program. Obviously, it is difficult to tax high income households without affecting savings, and the final result of such a program most likely is a mixture of impact on both consumption and savings. The necessary technical and financial supervision, as well as most of the administration, can only be provided through a close tie-in with the educational system and compulsory public service of graduates. Just as doctors in most countries have requirements of public service after their training, other categories of students may be required to serve in the works program as supervisors, time keepers, planners and administrators, with appropriate training for these jobs becoming part of their educational curriculum.

The possible conflict between output and employment objectives appears more apparent than real. Not only are both objectives complex mixes, but their future levels must be taken into account. It is commonly asserted that lower employment now may make possible higher employment levels in the future through the larger investment made possible by the lower current consumption. But instability and dissatisfaction will also adversely affect investment and future production, as will the reduced human input through ill health and inadequate human development. The general apathy resulting from a poverty that seems hopeless may be the greatest obstacle to future economic growth. Studies have indicated that in many countries, particularly in Asia, "output growth and employment growth are not in conflict as objectives." The dissatisfaction felt has often been "the unsatisfactory rate of employment creation, in relation to the desire and need for employment." In some countries in Latin America and Africa, there have been rapid growth rates with minimal employment increases. Higher real wages and repatriation of foreign-owned capital left scanty funds for reinvestment and left the employment growth less than satisfactory. But here, the dissatisfaction was as much with the distribution of income as with the conflict between output and employment. In most countries, with improving income distribution, the policies that maximize employment and human development will tend to maximize future output.[11]

Labor Mobility

Economic modernization involves shifting many workers from rural to urban centers. No country has ever succeeded in raising its productivity over a long period of time without undergoing this shift. The causal relationship between the two is complex and mutual, but the association of economic modernization and increased urbanization is a fact. Agriculture is usually the largest sector of the economy in the less developed countries, and also usually has the lowest productivity. A small but increasing number of workers in the urban areas are employed on higher productivity jobs in the modern sector, such as manufacturing, processing, and transportation. Most modern industry in the less developed countries will be located in urban areas, where the necessary power, transportation, and communication facilities are more likely to exist. It is in the urban areas that the external economies and complementarities so necessary for high productivity production are most likely to exist. Consequently, urban areas require and induce the development of labor markets, particularly among skilled and experienced workers.

99

Labor mobility becomes one of the important concepts applied to the development of these markets.

Labor mobility is of two types, geographic and occupational. The geographic mobility implied in the migration of rural to urban areas is not taking place in practically all countries, probably faster than is socially desirable because of the inability of urban areas to provide jobs and adequate living facilities for the migrating workers. The causes for the migration are many, and their analysis has provided as rich a field for theoretical and practical studies as any in the social sciences, but with limited usefulness thus far. The "push" forces, which push people out of rural areas because of poverty, hopelessness, restlessness, boredom, and catastrophy are mingled with the "pull" factors of possibility of increase in income, more interesting living, more amenities, more opportunities, and more anonymity. A high productivity society generally develops a higher capability of geographic mobility for its labor force than do low productivity countries. Aside from the sudden mass movements arising from wars, partitions, and widespread natural calamities, movements because of job markets, particularly among skilled workers, are probably fewer in the low productivity countries than in countries that have achieved a large modern sector of production. While many impediments to geographic mobility remain, such as regionalism and language barriers, these usually have not been serious obstacles to economic growth, although they help create serious social and political problems in some countries.

Occupational immobility of labor is a more serious economic problem. By occupational mobility of labor is meant the ability to move from one occupation to another. This mobility need not be direct; it may mean a more general readjustment, where some workers move to replace other workers who move to areas and occupations where shortages exist. Occupational immobility can be caused by:

Ignorance of potential rewards for mobility.
Traditional attitudes against changing occupations or accepting occupations which are different from those of parents.
Prejudice against occupational shifts, involving concepts of relative social status and acceptability.
Specificity of training and experience and reluctance to shift to more general or other specific jobs.
Artificial restrictions against mobility, designed to protect some interests and ward off some possible troublesome shifts.

The lack of adequate labor mobility is an obstacle to increasing productivity that governmental action can often reduce or eliminate. The traditions and prejudices that prevent mobility can be questioned by government administrators and often they can be disregarded or their effects minimized by governmental decisions. The flow of information regarding work opportunities are often affected by the decisions and actions of administrators. Certainly many of the restrictions against

100

mobility are possible only through threat of enforcement by government, and these restrictions can be exposed for what they are, obstacles to improved labor market operations and economic development.

Health and Education

Improving the quality of the labor input is, in a sense, the essence of the way to achieve a higher productivity country and improved income distribution. It should be clear, however, that improved health and education is both a cause and effect of improved income. To stress its role as a cause without examining this circular relationship is a frequent omission. It is not a mere coincidence that the economically advanced countries have a healthier, better educated working force than do the less developed countries. Greater productivity permits the developed countries to spend a much higher proportion of their gross national income on schools, clinics, and hospitals and on the training of teachers, doctors, and appropriate administrators. Every measure of education and health in countries shows a high, positive correlation with measures of economic productivity. The more developed countries have a higher proportion of children in school, of teachers, of high school and college students, and higher school-leaving age, higher average grade completed and higher adult literacy. Sickness and death rates at every age are lower in the more developed countries. This correlation needs little additional proof today, but many of its implications for increasing the rate of modernization and economic growth seems to escape understanding at operational levels. Nor is it necessary to document the critical role that government and public administration play in the planning and operations of the institutions that are involved in the improvement of health and educational institutions. The fact that so little is really understood at operational levels about what government can do in the health and educational fields in order to stimulate a more rapid rate of economic growth, exposes one of the most significant deficiencies in the public administration of economic growth.

Obviously, it is not necessary to justify efforts to improve health and education by emphasizing the effect on economic growth. Both better health and better education are acceptable as goals by themselves. While there are many differences of opinion on the exact composition of better education, perhaps less on better health, it is true that each country tries to achieve a better educated, healthier level for its people. But the improvement of health and education, however, defined, requires the use of scarce resources, and therefore, difficult as measurement of the process may be, someone or some institution must constantly make judgments about the use of these scarce resources and compare these uses with alternative uses, judging the opportunity costs of using resources for expenditures in health and education. Although all the cost-benefit elements are almost impossible to quantify, judgments on some kind of cost-benefit analysis must be and are constantly made, either by positive action or negative omission of action. Yet these cost-benefit relationships have not enabled governments to establish operating policies and programs that satisfy observers and participants, however difficult the measurement and criteria may be. Most countries are basically unhappy with their health and education programs, not only because they may be starved for resources but also because the composition and substance of the programs do not seem to be well articulated with the changes in their societies.

Health is a simpler affair than education, although it is far from easy to understand. Almost all countries stress health improvement in their government plans for operation. Health has a very high priority in family preferences for expenditures, but in many parts of the world knowledge of what can be done in the field of health is limited to a relatively small sector of the population and to government. Very few governments spend a high proportion of their GNP on health activities. In India, only 0.6 percent of GNP was spent in 1958 on public health activities, compared with 1.2 percent in the United States and 3.2 percent in Sweden.[12] Few studies have been made on the relationship between health deficiencies and efficiency of labor, but there is enough clinical evidence to know that the relationship cannot be doubted.

Because of the certainty of the existence of this relationship, it is correct, but simple, to assert that in order to help achieve a more rapid rate of economic growth, government must push for the improvement of health of workers. Apparently, there is no way of analyzing costs and benefits to measure returns on these expenditures, to see if any particular allocation of funds is more productive than an alternative allocation. Myrdal writes: "Practically no effort has been made to quantify the complicated causal relationship between health deficiencies of various sorts and labor input and efficiency, although a few experimental studies have been made of the relationship between nutritional deficiencies and labor input and efficiency. These studies corroborate in a general observation that sub-optimal food intake has a marked direct effect on peoples' ability to work."[13] It is apparently impossible to impute to any single health measure or groups of health measures a financial return based on the value of the improved health conditions. Where malaria, for example, has been reduced or eliminated, and agricultural production has gone up, other societal and economic changes have proceeded concurrently with the health programs. While the relationship between improved health and improved productivity is intuitively obvious, it does not provide guidelines for specific resource allocation. This must be left to judgments about intensities of pressures and preferences, and intuitive judgments that are a major element of administration. Evaluation about relative efficiencies and alternative resource uses are clearly involved, but economic analytical tools offer little assistance to administrative judgments in these areas.

Progress in formal education is even more difficult to assess than public health. The school system of a country uses considerable resources and its inadequacies are more obvious. The less developed countries have adopted universal literacy as a goal, and most have made valiant, costly efforts to move in that direction. Some have adopted compulsory education laws that demonstrate the high priority that governments wish to give to improved education. In their turn, the people of the less developed countries have turned to education with great enthusiasm, and there can be little doubt that a larger number of people are being exposed to education than ever before. But here the clarity of the situation ends, and these high level generalizations provide little understanding of operating problems.

As an economy raises its productivity, it requires a better quality of labor input. "It simply is not possible to have the fruits of modern agriculture and the abundance of modern industry without making large investments in human beings."[14] New technologies need understanding; and persons who can read and do arithmetic can understand and receive training far better than those who do not. Industrial workers and technicians must be able to read and follow instructions. Farmers who can read newspapers and pamphlets are more progressive than illiterate farmers, and can participate far more effectively in extension programs and group sessions on agricultural improvement. Efforts to induce local planning and community development depend on the availability of literate people in the localities. It is not too grandiose a generalization to assert that to have meaning, modern government depends to a surprising degree upon a literate population. A higher rate of adult literacy may be accepted as a must in a high productivity society, but how and when it is attained are still hotly debated questions. If literacy is pushed more rapidly than is the opportunity to use and profit from reading ability, there is evidently a tremendous waste of resources and even the creation of additional social problems. Is literacy best attained through teaching adults or through the expansion of primary school to all children? The latter may be merely an ideal, but the large proportion of children dropping out of school at an early age shows that this method of attaining adult literacy is less than successful.

The composition of the school system and its quality is a pressing problem in every country. Few countries, if any, have succeeded in establishing adequate principles for judging the relative emphasis on primary schools. The expansion of school enrollment has strained countries' capacities for teacher training and administration, and standards that were low originally are now even lower. It is not true, unfortunately, that all education is necessarily good for both the individual and for the society, and that any kind of education will necessarily lead to progress and therefore is better than no education. No one has succeeded in developing tools that measure in unambiguous terms the relative returns to society and to individuals of teaching 1000 children to read and count when most of them forget what they learned within five years, compared with training 100 college graduates in humanistic studies, most of whom will be unemployed for 10 years after leaving college. While the relationship between higher educationsl attainment and higher productivity is intuitively obvious, the operating relationships that government must work out cannot be so readily perceived or easily established.

It is an unpleasant fact of life that the effectiveness of the educational policies and programs of government cannot be determined by what is done only in the educational field. Success depends very largely on policies and achievements in other fields, particularly in the way that the economic activities of the country require and reward achievement in education. A government's administration of the educational system will be most important to development, and to the economic growth component of development, if the educational system is so arranged that it keeps pace with its environment. Outpacing the need for the type of education provided is not only wasteful of resources but may produce the social unrest that is counterproductive of economic growth. In the early periods of the development process, when only a small proportion, less than required, can read or write, the economic reward for literacy is usually large. Clerks and teachers are paid far higher salaries than other workers; and the incentive to acquire the training is great, although facilities are so limited that only a small number can be trained. Soon this situation changes. More and more people attain the minimum standards to achieve this increase. The economic return to the individual who becomes trained is substantially decreased until, as in some countries, teachers and clerks receive less than urban factory workers. The comparison with unskilled wage earners may still be favorable, but by a much smaller margin while many of the trained workers become unemployed. Where there is acute unemployment of educated persons, a correlation between education and income could lead to the conclusion that the relationship is negative, that a higher education produces, in general, a lower economic return to those that undertake the training. Ultimately, however, an economy can absorb any number of educated persons. The earnings of educated people, the prices in the factor input market, are reduced, and employers raise their job requirements. Where jobs previously called for minimum ability to read and write, employers may require high school diplomas. In economic terms, the supply of educated persons should go down; but since education and people are more than commodities, the response to price signals are not always the same as in product markets. While the basic economic forces are there, other forces, noneconomic in nature, are often far more important in the determination of supply and price.

Although many studies have been made of training and educational requirements in the less developed countries, the guidance for government operations that these provide are difficult to interpret.[*] The

---

[*]We have found, in almost every respect that a correlation exists between "educational deficiencies and a low economic level:deficiencies

general tenor of these studies pushes in the direction of the following:

A revision of the substance of the educational system, with a view toward relating more to the current needs of the country, a heavier scientific, vocational, technical, practical curriculum as compared with humanistic and literacy contents.

An emphasis on improving quality, rather than increasing the number of students.

An examination of the balance between the levels of the educational system, with most countries attempting to place more stress on the high school and on the technical and vocational school, rather than the lowest grades of primary school or the college levels.

Compulsory education accepted as an ideal, but not an operating necessity or feasibility until some time in the future.

The current interest of economists and planners in examining education as an "investment in human resources" is useful, if not pushed too far. It is evident that education increases earnings, and a high school graduate generally earns more than a grammar school graduate. Attempts to measure the returns to expenditures in education are generally crude, but still convincing. For most societies, the return on investment in human resources is probably greater, at the margin, than in most kinds of physical capital. That is, if a country spent more on education and less on capital formation, on the average it would receive a greater increase in production and productivity. But decisions of administrators are difficult to make on the average. Where resources are allocated by sector, for example, specific investment projects may have to be curtailed in order to increase expenditures of specific educational institutions or systems. Here the evaluation of opportunity costs is difficult to keep on an average basis. Cost-benefit analysis and judgments must be made, but these usually will be in indeterminate, intuitive terms. Investment in improved human resources is not a substitute for capital formation; it must be considered a complementarity, a necessary associate if higher levels of productivity are to be achieved.

IMPROVING CAPITAL INPUTS

Increasing capital inputs is also a quality as well as a quantity problem. But here, the nature of the factor input is such that practically every increase in quantity helps raise total production and average

---

are largest and most prevalent in the poorer countries. Educational reform, which is generally costly, is most urgently needed in those countries that can least afford to pay for it," Gunnar Myrdal, Asian Drama (New York: Random House, 1968), p. 1826.

productivity. Usually, the more capital that is used, the greater the production will be. While some cases of mistaken judgment may not follow this path, these tend to be minimal. Why refrain from consumption, the satisfaction of immediate needs, if this did not serve to meet future needs? Thus the act of capital formation is usually a deliberate decision designed to increase production. Even capital of the same quality, that embodies or permits no new technology, will tend to raise both total production and average productivity. This addition of capital of the same technology is called capital widening, while adding capital inputs of a higher productivity is called capital deepening. Both kinds of capital additions will increase total production, unless enough other capital inputs are withdrawn or used up at the same time the new capital is added.

New capital, added to the existing stock of capital, tends to be of above average productivity. The reason is quite obvious. It would be an act of economic irrationality to create less efficient capital than is possible. Why would one build a machine factory without trying to maximize its productivity? It is true then that any product is a compromise between what is theoretically possible if costs were not considered and expected returns. No factory contains all the improvements possible and probably no machine embodies all the latest improvements. All capital formation involves, consciously or unconsciously, a cost-benefit calculation. Thus, for a country as a total, the assumption that new capital tends to be more productive than the average and tends to embody a higher level of technology than the average existing capital, is intuitively obvious and is supported by observation.

Since an increase in savings is functionally associated with an increase in capital formation, efforts to increase the quality of capital can begin with efforts to increase savings. Here it is necessary to distinguish between forces influencing the volume of savings and the forms which these savings take. For, as has been previously stated, savings do not automatically result in capital formation, although there is an accounting equality of the two in national accounts.

Because savings and capital formation are both social processes, changes in the structure of society are important for the increase in capital inputs. Illustrations of how this relationship affects governments' attempts to increase capital inputs are numerous:

Savings in the private sector arise from both households and enterprises. In the early stages of development households are the more important source, but as the production processes become more complex enterprise savings tend to create a larger part of the total savings. Since families tend to save more than they invest in productive capital and governments and enterprises tend to invest more than they themselves save, there is a need to channel private household savings into capital formation.

In converting savings into capital, there is a strong tendency to invest in the same sector that produces the savings. Thus, savings from agricultural pursuits tend to be invested in the agricultural sector, and similar tendencies exist in trade and manufacturing. The reasons for this are understandable; experience and knowledge of the field is an important element in evaluating risk and future returns from capital formation. Thus, governments that wish to convert savings from trade into increasing capital inputs in manufacturing have a somewhat different problem than encouraging manufactures to reinvest their profits in expanding manufacturing.

A large share of income is generated by small business, unincorporated enterprises that have a high savings-income ratio. That is, small family enterprises in manufacturing are a fruitful source of both savings and capital formation in manufacturing. Government policies affecting these enterprises are particularly important in increasing capital inputs. The pattern of savings influences how the savings can be used and must be considered in any plan designed to stimulate and mobilize savings.[15] Use must be stressed, as "the crucial difference between economically growing and stagnant societies lies more in the use than in the volume of savings. Unless savings are put into productive investment, hard work and thrift will produce hoards of treasure, pyramids . . . etc., but not economic growth."[16] There are, in an operational sense, five ways of improving domestic capital: reduce hoarding, create savings institutions, more taxation, more use of idle resources and inflation. The causal relations of these may overlap, but they represent fairly distinct policy and program lines.

Reduction of Hoarding

Hoarding, or holding money and precious metals, is a common phenomenon in the less developed countries. In some countries, private gold hoards are as large as 10 percent of the national income. If these were made available for more productive capital formation purposes, they would add significantly to the savings that could be invested. Gold savings, readily convertible into foreign exchange, is a particularly strategic form of accumulated savings. But it is very difficult to capture hoarded savings. The psychology that makes them widespread has been too deeply incorporated into culture patterns to be easily persuaded to change. Only long periods of political stability and rapid economic growth will change the widespread habits of savings by hoarding.

Governments may also hoard. No lesser term can be used to characterize the almost psychotic views that some governments have of the balances of gold and foreign exchange that they assert are needed to support their currency. This viewpoint supported by banking tradition and some forms of traditional economic analysis, results in savings that are kept in the form of stocks of valuables, rather than by being used for expenditures on capital formation. The need for a working balance of foreign exchange is justified by operations, but the need for a gold base and for theoretical conversion rights that do not exist in actual practice can be questioned.

An increase in hoarding of precious metals or money has other important effects. Hoarding of physical assets may result in a drain on some resources used in their production, but hoarding cash balances idles resources which otherwise might be used in consumption, and therefore it creates some potential for capital formation. This kind of hoarding may thus reduce the inflationary impact of other expenditures, as, for example, investment expenditures financed through government deficits.

Creation of Savings Institutions

Hoarding cash balances is often the outgrowth of inadequate financial institutions. The effect of savings institutions is for the most part permissive, rather than deterministic. That is, savings institutions help change the form of savings rather than determine the creation of savings. Because countries achieving large savings generally have many specialized savings institutions, the conclusion has often been drawn that in order to have large savings, specialized institutions such as banks, savings and loan associations, and postal savings accounts had to be established. While these institutions make savings a greater possibility, they may do little to induce or coerce families or business enterprises into savings. In some areas where, for personal and social reasons, people who are accustomed to save may find it difficult to do so because of the absence of savings institutions, savings will tend to take the form of hoarding money or precious metals or in the possession of valuable jewelry and ornaments. Here, the creation of savings institutions may be a means of directing the savings to a form that can be converted more readily into investment resources. The ease of savings with adequate institutions may even induce more savings, but this is likely to be a marginal response. Countries that have hoped to multiply their savings by creating new institutions designed after those of the more developed countries have learned, to their disappointment, that low savings determine savings institutions more than the reverse. Adequate savings institutions are important, but their role in increasing savings is usually quite limited.

Public lending institutions can increase savings because they become a pressure on the system to provide additional savings. Much of the domestic savings is either created by government policies lowering or restraining consumption or is directed into the public sector through taxation of profits, rents, and incomes from which most of the financial savings arise. The existence of public lending institutions may channel some of the savings back to the private sector, to finance expenditures considered socially desirable by the government. Clearly, the attempt is to have these kinds of loans supplement, not replace, the loans that would be made by private lending establishments. Since, in a modern economic system, investment often precedes savings and may even be said to induce savings, the establishment of public lending capabilities represents an important addition to both the pressure to increase investment expenditures and the pressure to use government resources for investment purposes.

Increased Taxation

Taxation shifts purchasing power from the private sector to the public sector. To the extent that the tax receipts are used for nonconsumption expenditures, they become public savings. They may be used to build up inventories of goods, such as warehouses full of unsold rice or cotton textiles. They may be used to increase hoards of gold or foreign exchange owned by the government. They may be used to meet expenditures on capital formation projects, such as building roads, factories, schools, and so forth. The current operating costs of government, such as salaries to government officials, teachers, consumable supplies, welfare payments and services of all kinds, are usually taken to constitute government consumption. Whether increased taxation as a process results in an increase in savings and therefore makes possible an increase in capital formation, is a question of how government uses the increased tax receipts.

Taxes reduce consumption in the private sector, and they may also reduce private savings. If the latter is true, taxation may merely shift savings from the private sector to the public sector. The desirability of this shift is determined by the usefulness of the two kinds of savings. If the private sector savings constituted jewels and durable consumer goods, or luxury housing construction, or new factories, or the importation of capital equipment, it would be simple to evaluate the desirability of the shift. But these illustrations are two kinds of extremes. It is usually very difficult to judge how much increased taxation has restrained or reduced private savings, altered the composition of private savings, or affected the utilization of increased public revenues. Many other changes in public and private savings and expenditures are occurring at the same time, caused by other forces; and analysts have little or no basis for allocating specific expenditures to specific resources. In a general way, it is possible to make some long-term comparisons, but these must be quite broad and leave a good deal to be desired in the validity of the data used and of the conclusions reached.

Increased taxation is expected to be unpopular. While it may be politically palatable to tax the rich, the rich generally do not find this satisfactory. At the same time they may be influential in shaping tax policy and programs. Consequently, while taxation is widely acclaimed as a means to increase savings, its use has rarely been excessive. Each country determines its own taxing capacity and its own priorities. For few government actions are so powerful in their impact and so sensitive to public reaction as the taxing power. It is true that in the old days of traditional autocratic government, with its God-sanctioned king and its rule by divine right and coercive capabilities, taxation tended to be determined by the needs and whims of the power holders without much regard to the mass of taxpayers. This was so ground into the consciousness of people that the attitude "government is the enemy" is part of the folklore of most people. Yet a careful reading of history will show a great deal of attention paid, even by the worst rulers, to the tax machinery, to the continuing capacity of those assessed to pay taxes, to vested interests, and to tradition. The immediate histories of most people would seem to deny this because colonialism has been associated, quite correctly in many cases, with tax exploitation. But it would not be difficult to find much persuasive evidence to show that even colonial powers paid a great deal of attention to the effect of taxation on the economic and political conditions of their colonies.

The taxing process and impact of government is of course much broader than the use of taxation to increase savings. Taxes mold economic activity the way any cost does. Differential taxes can encourage one kind of activity and discourage or prohibit another kind. The power to tax, as was held by the United States Supreme Court, is the power to destroy. It is also the power to build. By adding or subtracting to cost, by changing the relative profitability of different economic actions, it can presumably push toward one set of actions in preference to another. By taxing private production and not taxing government production, it can affect production directly or indirectly. It is important to note that taxation is a widely, but still underused, method of increasing savings and the rate of capital formation. It is also important to note that rarely if ever does a country overtax its economy. The limit of taxation seems to be more a matter of priorities and commitment than a fixed limit determined by the economy. The level of feasible taxation is probably as much affected by how the taxes are used as by the level of economic activity.

Using Idle Resources

Idle resources represent one of the most challenging problems to the less developed countries and one of its greatest potential advantages. Domestic capital formation can be stimulated by the use of these resources in capital formation. Usually, these unutilized resources consist of manpower, the tremendous numbers of people who are only partially employed or whose productivity is close to zero. In a particular sense, they are similar to the gold and money that is hoarded, only since they are human beings their nonutilization represents tremendous personal tragedies as well as lost opportunity for production and for capital formation. It has always been the dream of planners and leaders to utilize this potential resource in a constructive way, to make it additive to the existing production process and thus increase average productivity. For if one man whose marginal productivity is zero is given more productive work, however small his production is, it adds to the total without adding to the workers, and therefore total production and average productivity go up.

Meritorious as this objective may be, its execution in quantities sufficient to be aggregatively significant usually borders on the impossible. The unpleasant consequences of the need for complementarities stands as an obstacle to using productively the mass of unemployed and unskilled manpower. Some capital, however small, is needed even in the most simple operations. Most of all, what is missing are the organization and the skilled managers needed to initiate and supervise the work. Examples of successful use of mass unemployed manpower in capital formation abound, but careful examination will show their attributes and the kinds of complementarities that must exist. Most of these types of capital formation are large earth-moving projects because they can utilize large numbers of unskilled workers with little equipment above a basket and a hoe or shovel. Building country roads, digging shallow ditches and tunnels for irrigation or drainage, small public buildings using local building materials, these are the kinds of local public works programs that may be useful in attempts to utilize idle manpower.

But it is a mistake, often repeated at high cost, to assume that these projects are easily started and managed. Without appropriate engineering, they become costly failures; and without adequate management, they become unproductive and subject to the worst kinds of illegal diversion and corruption. For example, movement of masses of workers to a large dam project, in an innaccessible area with no housing or sanitary facilities, is possible through the kind of coercion that only an authoritarian government possesses. The human cost in terms of dislocation and deprivation can be immense and difficult to face. Few countries that have developed widespread local works programs have been free from roads that are washed out by the next monsoon, wells that become unusable through contamination, poorly leveled ditches that do not irrigate or drain, and local works whose main purposes are political favors and private benefits. This does not mean that all local works are destined to become this way. It does mean that good local works programs, which provide public capital formation using primarily the resources of unskilled labor, are hard to develop and operate because the complementary requirements of adequate capital and management are relatively scarce and are not made available. It is often asserted that this kind of resource utilization is necessary for nearly all of the less developed countries, but its lack of success results largely from the inadequate priorities and management given to these programs by government.

Inflation

Inflation as a means of increasing capital formation requires a great deal of explanation and careful selection of language, because inflation is an accepted sin, a consequence of bad management and worse morals. To choose inflation deliberately as a means of capital formation is not only considered unwise, but borders on the irresponsible. Yet inflation is a fact of life in many of the countries of the world, at all levels of development. While it has many bad aspects, its achievements are often pleasant and profitable, a time of exuberant consumption and useful capital formation. The savings that generally arise from inflati are forced savings where the country reduces its consumption because of higher prices resulting from public expenditures financed by bank borrowing or by creating money. The mechanics and policies of inflati will be limited here to a brief description of how inflation may result in more public savings.

There is no unequivocal evidence that inflation has in the past been associated with a more rapid rate of economic growth. On the co trary, there is some empirical evidence that as many countries have achieved a rapid rate of economic growth without inflation as have wit rapid general price rises. As in most instances of this type, there are so many other variables operating to influence the price level that to assess all causal responsibility to one variable, even an important on could often be misleading. The basic relationship is complicated but direct and observable. Investment expenditures push up purchasing power without adding to the immediate supply of goods to offset the additional pushing power. An increasing rate of investment is thus in- flationary in its influence on prices, although it may not result in actu inflation because of other influences on the supply of purchasing pow and of goods and services. For example, if the current rate of invest- ment is accompanied by an increase in the import of consumer goods, or a decrease in current government spending, or an increase in taxes or private savings, the price level could remain the same. A general price rise is influenced by many variables, of which the rate of invest ment is only one, although an important one.

Inflation results in forced savings when the government finances its investment expenditures through deficit financing. Inflation can th be a pleasant, euphoric period, with the government getting a great de of favorable attention through expenditures on desirable projects while avoiding the unpleasant task of raising taxes to meet the costs. Sever conceptual problems should be kept in mind, however, to reduce, if no to eliminate, fuzzy thinking. Money is basically fungible, interchang able, losing its identity as it passes from hand to hand. If a country raises taxes in order to pay for increased military expenditures and the borrows money from the banks to finance development, the attribution of each of these sources to its use is psychological in base, not be- havioristic. Some people could argue just the opposite attribution, an the government expenditures and resources would still remain the same In other words, assigning the deficit financing to investment is an exe cise in assessing public response, rather than a logical structural phe nomenon. Borrowing for investment purposes is considered safer, more businesslike than borrowing for military purposes or for other current expenditures. Yet public reaction to government policy is most impor- tant, and the forced savings label usually assigned to those financial deficits of governments that are met by borrowing from banks is probably a useful device.

It is important to note that forced savings occur only when the deficit is covered by creating money through borrowing from banks. If the borrowing is done from private institutions, or from business that would otherwise spend the money, the expenditures resulting from the deficit financing would not be inflationary. It would merely shift expenditures from the private sector to the public sector. If the government deficit is covered by borrowing savings from either individuals or business or banks, this also represents a shift of savings and not a forced savings that is an addition to the intended savings. If, as is usual, all kinds of borrowing, and transfers and increases in both current and investment expenditures of government happen at one time, attribution of the deficit to capital formation is arbitrary bookkeeping.

Inflation can be viewed as an instrument of economic growth or as a byproduct of economic growth. In the former, only a mild inflation can be included, since the difficulties of a severe inflation are readily apparent. The benefits of a mild inflation follow from the fact that they are unexpected; if the inflation is expected, too many people can protext themselves against the effects for there to be any benefits from redistribution. Inflation may give the economic system some mild flexibility. It is, in a sense, a tax on money holdings and on some debts. For short periods of time, inflation has sometimes made possible a forward thrust for public savings; but in the long run, it has often proven a significant impediment to economic growth.

IMPROVEMENTS IN RESOURCE USE AND ALLOCATION

Increasing the quality of the factor inputs in production is of course an integral part of raising the level of technology in the production process. The improved technology is embodied in and can only be seen by the improved quality of the workers, managers, engineers, and the tools and equipment they use. These is a further source of increased productivity that is important enough to mention, that associated with the improved use and allocation of resources. In a sense, this is also included under improved quality of the factor inputs, but additional insights need specification here.

Resource allocation is, as was previously emphasized, the prisoner of the "lumpiness" of capital, the fact that production processes are discrete operations of a particular size, and that there are not an infinite number of sizes and kinds to choose from. Also, the resource allocation of a society at any one time is the prisoner of previous commitments. Changes which appear more productive cannot be made, because the pattern of previous decisions have involved future commitments of resources. Consequently, while improvements of resource allocation must constantly be pressed, it is unrealistic to look forward to large increases in production and productivity through improved resource allocation as a general overall process. The resource allocations of a society are too complex, too involved in the whole structure of economic institutions to be changed drastically or radically. Establishing a new planning office for government capital formation or attempting to shift some resources from one sector to another through government monetary policy and fiscal operation may have important effects in the long run, but it is often hard to distinguish between improvements resulting from the changed allocation and what would have happened if the new allocation had not been made. This is not to argue against the importance of trying to improve resource allocations, but rather to point out that efforts to improve allocation, even if successful, are fairly sure to operate within narrow limits and the increase in productivity will generally not be drastic.

There can be no question about the importance of improving the use of existing capacities to increase productivity and production. Perhaps this could be considered part of improving the quality of the labor input, as part of improved management. Potentially, this is probably the greatest single source of improved production and productivity. Even if the thesis is accepted that, considering the quality of the factor inputs, agriculture is an efficiently operated production process, the point must be stressed. A small amount of additional capital, coupled with some improvement of the quality of the labor input, could conceivably bring about substantial increases in production and productivity. So important is this point that it can be stretched to support the following generalization. In resource allocation, cost-benefit projections are more a function of the predictions regarding the capacity of management than they are on options in equipment and production technology. Very often, it is better to allocate foreign exchange to an efficient company that wishes to expand its mill, rather than a new company of unproven efficiency that proposes to adopt newer technologies with lower capital requirements.

The present use of capital in the less developed countries is often below the level of reasonable expectations, based on technical considerations only. In other words, there is a large measure of waste or inefficiency in the present use of factor inputs, particularly capital. These are generally due to such inadequacies as lack of understanding and skill in using capital, lack of proper maintenance, and lack of externalities.

Whatever the combination of causes, very few productive enterprises utilize their capital as effectively as they can. When productive capacity is built and not used sufficiently, the economy derives little benefit from the investment. Over emphasis on capacities may require use of foreign exchange that could be avoided if existing capacities were more fully utilized.[17] One manifestation of this is the widespread absence of multiple shifts in factories. There is, of course, a reduction in production per worker on night shifts, due to less competent supervision, less externalities, and a slowdown of individual effort; but a large part of this reduction is supposed to be compensated for by greater use of the capital. However, with the drive to increase capital inputs often expressed in an underevaluation of foreign exchange for capital import purposes, it sometimes becomes easier to build more capacity than to utilize existing capacity on more shifts. While improving allocation of capital will undoubtedly yield greater productivity, it is likely that direct efforts to improve use of existing capital capacity may have even more important effects on productivity.[18]

PUBLIC AND PRIVATE SECTORS OF PRODUCTION

A most common classification of the production sectors is that of public and private, a useful if ambiguous distinction. While it is possible to set verbal perimeters to each of these sectors, actual operations are difficult to classify. The public sector is defined as those production units that are owned and operated by government agencies. All other production units not owned and operated by government are in the private sector. This definition is simplistic, in that it oversimplifies numerous instances where production units are owned only partially by government or are owned by government and operated by nongovernment agencies. Where, for example, is a cooperatively-owned factory classified when it is run by government rules and partially financed by government; but it is legally owned by cooperative farmers? Is a public agency established to coordinate the imports of private importers a public or private enterprise? Establishing a mixed category, such as paragovernment or a "joint" may help in some kinds of analysis, but still presents definitional problems on degrees of "jointness." The hazy areas of definition are so common that comparisons of public sectors between countries is almost meaningless unless care is taken to examine definitions.

From a technical viewpoint, the simple concept of public owned and operated is difficult to apply realistically in specific cases. A production unit may be financed by a loan from government, the government may in effect insist that only that particular unit shall operate in the country and the government may be the only customer of the products of that business; but if it were owned by a group of individuals, even though they were selected by government, the business would be classified in the private sector. Consider the question of classifying businesses that are entirely controlled by government, the so-called government corporations that may have sold some stock to private individuals. The sharing of government ownership and government operations becomes, under examination, a sharing of government financing and of government control. But if these are the definitional criteria, there are many privately owned and operated concerns that are entirely under government domination. The government may nationalize a brewe and keep the same management and may not arrange to compensate the former owners. Production policies may be unchanged, but the concern is not in the public sector, yet with no more government influence than in the past. The range of government ownership control or influence is not a simple continuum in one direction, in which an arbitrary point can be selected for classifying the two sectors. The continuum runs in sev eral directions at the same time, a sort of "n" dimensional surface, which is impossible to visualize. Setting verbal limitations becomes arbitrary along several lines of the continuum.

Simplistic as it may seem, the dichotomy between public and private sectors of production is useful, and its use is almost compulsory. For no matter how arbitrary and chaotic the separation seems to be in actual practice, the analytical constructs are used by everybody— technicians, planners, political leaders, and the communications medi The differences in operations are often so real and important that the classification is useful, despite its difficulties. It is not unusual to find an exception to every statement about the public and private secto whether it be a reference to pricing policy, resource allocation, distri- bution of income, or management control. All kinds of public-sector concerns may operate as if they were in the private sector, and many private concerns are almost completely controlled by government. Yet the generalization about private- and public-sector production units ca be empirically supported and may be useful guides to public adminis- trators if these guides are not accepted too literally.

A survey of experiences over the past several decades would revea that there are no valid economic guidelines for determining the optimum mix between public and private sectors for any country. For every case where a criterion would indicate that a particular concern should be in the public sector, a similar case in another country would point to the opposite direction. There are some general tendencies that are discern ible, and these should be examined and their implications evaluated; but they cannot be based solely on economic considerations. Rather, political and social considerations are often far more important in the determination of which corporations are in the public sector in a coun- try.*

---

*It is clear that, "... the main issues which arise in formulating investment criteria for public enterprises are far from settled. There is no agreed code of practice which is available for general adoption, no manual of instruction which can be taken as an authoritative guide by governments and by public enterprises themselves. In part, this results from inevitable differences of opinion about what is practicable in tactical use. When it comes to translating broad objectives into decision rules and operating procedures, what appears to be the most

Ideology

Many of the less developed countries have accepted the general validity of what might be called a socialist society. Without becoming too involved in the semantic morass that inevitably opens when words like "socialism" and "capitalism" are used, it is valid here to use socialism as an expression that the people, or at least the political leaders, of many of the less developed countries wish to emphasize community values, community control, and even community ownership far more than do the so-called capitalistic countries such as the United States, Japan, and those of Western Europe. This can be a matter of degree, since a mixed economy is usually visualized as a mix of private and public sector production units. The point being stressed is that in many of the less developed countries the public sector is often determined by an ideology that emphasizes a kind of socialistic point of view, often quite different from Marxian socialism. Nationalism, as witnessed by national socialistic labels, is usually a strong partner in this ideology. Thus, Burmese socialism and the Indian socialist pattern of India are expressions that show the nationalist tinge of generalized ideology. But while ideology is a factor in the determination of the size and composition of the public sector, it cannot be stated as a dichotomy of socialism and free enterprise. To put it in those terms is to exaggerate the importance of ideology. Since these terms are more polemical tools than analytical constraints, ". . . there seems to be a good reason for deflating the issue of the public versus the private sector as an ideological choice between socialism and free enterprise. The differences in economic policies and in accomplishments in regard to industrial development among the South Asian countries are not closely related to their ideological positions." [19]

History

The history of a country, as interpreted by its people and its political leaders, has a very important impact on the determination of

---

suitable course of action is bound to depend on judgments about how much can be done in given circumstances, and about the extent to which existing practices or institutional arrangements can be altered within a specified period of time. It is not surprising that economists and practical men should disagree about such matters, both with each other and among themselves." P.D. Henderson, "Investment Criteria for Public Enterprises," in Public Enterprises, R. Tunney, ed. (Middlesex, England: Penguin Books, 1968), pp. 153-54.

public and private sector definitions. Often, where a country's history has been colonial rule, with little opportunity to have independently developed its own middle class, the colonial rule was largely considered an exploitation process. Independence meant the end of foreign exploitation, with public ownership the only acceptable alternative in many cases. This history often explains the strong socialistic leaning of many political leaders and the political desirability of emphasizing community ownership of production facilities.

Economics

Most of the economic overhead capital required by a high productivity society is monopolistic in character and needs large amounts of resources over a long period of production to be worthwhile. All these, as has been explained previously, push in the direction of public-sector ownership and operation. The apparent high profits of mineral extraction particularly oil, and the need for specific governmental authority to make possible the use of most natural resources, tend toward general acceptance of the idea that the gains from a country's natural resources should belong to all the people of that country. It is not a far jump from this to the idea of public ownership and public operation.

There are some general guidelines provided by economic concepts that indicate in what situations public ownership may be desirable. It is assumed, quite properly, that regardless of the ownership and the degree of government control, enterprises are seeking efficiency in production, trying to use a minimum of scarce resources and to produce as much as possible. On the need to strive for production efficiency, there can be no distinction between public and private sectors. Enterprises are best considered for inclusion in the public sector when the market mechanism for either factor inputs or products is not working well, or when the market mechanism is operating in a direction that the society does not wish to go, or when the market mechanism is not working at all.

These are often matters of judgment that require examination not only of how the enterprise is expected to operate as a production unit, but how it relates to its environment. These relationships will often be reflected in market prices, either of the factor inputs or the sales price of the product. But the evaluation goes beyond price reactions; it must fit into the noneconomic values and norms that a society has established or wishes to establish. This is why, even in economic terms, the question of public-sector composition must be resolved largely by noneconomic considerations.

It is possible to provide other, more detailed guidelines for the composition and extent of the public sector; but these, too, are to a significant extent determined by judgments based on noneconomic values. The public sector is indicated, or is worthy of serious consideration, where the following situations exist in the market mechanism:

1. Products that require a very large investment will, by their nature, be monopolies and place a severe strain on any market mechanism. Examples are telephone and telegraph services, harbor facilities, railroads, and airlines. Even when these are privately owned, the government must take an active interest in their prices and the distribution of the product.

2. In enterprises where large external economies exist, government ownership may be necessary because the externalities cannot be captured in the market price of the product. Examples are health and educational institutions and economic overhead facilities like roads and bridges.

3. In situations where using existing market mechanisms for determining ownership or prices could lead to socially undesirable results, public ownership or strong public control must be examined. Schools and hospitals are good examples of enterprises where market mechanisms could lead to very narrow bands of consumers.

4. Where market mechanism could push the enterprise into severe exploitation of a limited natural resource, in order to maximize returns, public ownership or control is required. For example, where forest practices based on market considerations would remove just the most valuable trees and leave the forests in an unworkable state, the government may need to attempt to average out costs and benefits. Similarly, situations may occur in mineral extraction enterprises, where only high-priced ore would be removed by enterprises dominated by short-run objectives to maximize profits.

5. Market mechanisms may determine a type of income distribution that is undesirable from social and political points of view. Where direct subsidies or differential taxes are needed to adjust the income distribution that results from market mechanisms, government ownership may be the most efficient approach to the problem of overall distribution of income.

6. Where market pricing simply is not practical, as in the case of public goods, public ownership is clearly indicated. Public goods are products or services that are available to all because of their nature. Examples are police and fire protection and national defense activities. Usually, everybody receives these services, and the quantity available for any one person is not diminished by the availability to others.[20]

There is one other assertion to be advanced. There appears to be no fixed relationship between the rate of economic growth achieved by a country and its emphasis on the public sector. Obviously, the rate of economic growth is strongly affected by the vitality and aggressiveness of the government in pursuing economic growth and in giving economic growth adequate priority. Yet this is quite different from emphasis on public ownership and operation, although sometimes the two are strongly associated. While the rate of economic growth is not completely separable from determination of public sector policy, the relationship is not direct and positive. It would be argued that often unwise emphasis on public ownership and control has acted counterproductively and has reduced the rate of economic growth. It may be that "private enterprise may be more efficient than the government in constructing and operating enterprises, so that the best policy may be to stimulate private enterprise by tax concessions, subsidies, and the provision of cheap credit. Similarly, it may be preferable to stimulate private saving by offering high interest rates, rather than by forcing savings into the hands of the state by taxation or inflation."[21]

In discussing the role of government in increasing production and productivity, the difference between the public and private sector is often meaningless. Many governmental policies affect all production units, with variation of impact by kind of production technology rather than kind of ownership. Agricultural policies of government tend to affect the private sector more than the public sector, because most agricultural production units are in the private sector. Government controls of banking may be quite complete, with private banking affected almost as much as publicly-owned banks. Government regulations of buses may affect both publicly-owned and privately-owned bus companies but may affect them differently, since they may have different access to resources, to foreign exchange import licenses, and to redress of local difficulties. Thus, the relationship of government and of public administration to economic institutions will vary, and the factor of public ownership is only one of the facets to be considered.

There is serious disagreement among economists concerning economic criteria to be established for pricing products of publicly owned enterprises. Even where the questions asked are purely economic, there is no unambiguous answer generally acceptable to economists. Should only cost benefits be used in evaluating investment? And what time limits can be established, what interest rates used to evaluate the future in terms of discounted rates of return?

NOTES

1. See Louis J. Walinsky, Economic Development in Burma 1951-1960, p. 326.
2. For further information on the subject see the following references: Gunnar Myrdal, Asian Drama (New York: The Twentieth Century Fund, 1968), pp. 676-81; also see Appendix 10 to Vol. 3, p. 2109; S.C. Jain, ed., Problems of Agricultural Development in India (Allaharhad: Kitrte Mahal, 1967), pp. 86-87; and George Blyn, Agricultural Trends in India—1891-1947: Output, Availability and Productivity (Philadelphia: University of Pennsylvania Press, 1966), pp. 188-89.

3. See T. W. Schultze, <u>Transforming Traditional Agriculture</u> (New Haven: Yale University Press, 1964).

4. Myrdal, op. cit., p. 1546.

5. United Nations, Department of Economics and Social Affairs, <u>Report on Progress in Land Reform</u> (New York: United Nations, 1954), ST/ECA/21, p. 49.

6. See Schultze, op. cit.; and Herman M. Southworth and Bruce F. Johnston, eds., <u>Agricultural Development and Economic Growth</u> (Ithaca, N.Y.: Cornell University Press, 1968).

7. See Toya Zinken, <u>India</u> (London: Thames and Hudson, 1965).

8. See Philip M. Raup, "Land Reform and Agricultural Output," <u>Development Digest</u> 8, no. 2 (April 1970): 3.

9. Walter Galenson and Graham Pyath, <u>The Quality of Labour and Economic Development in Certain Countries: A Preliminary Study</u> (Geneva: I.L.O., 1964).

10. See <u>The Growth of World Industry: International Analysis and Tables, 1938-61</u> (New York: United Nations, 1963), pp. 4-18.

11. Frances Stewart and Paul Streeten, "Conflicts Between Output and Employment Objectives in Developing Countries," in <u>Oxford Economic Papers</u> (New Series) 23, no. 2 (July 1971).

12. Myrdal, op. cit., p. 1578.

13. Ibid., p. 1617.

14. Presidential Address by T. W. Schultze—Seventy-third Annual Meeting of the American Economic Association, St. Louis, Missouri, Dec. 28, 1960.

15. A. C. Minocha, "Capital Formation and the Pattern of Savings in Developing Economies," <u>Asian Economic Review</u> 7, no. 4 (August 1965).

16. S. S. Tangri and H. P. Gray, <u>Capital Accumulation and Economic Development</u> (Boston: D.C. Heath, 1967), p. 8.

17. See UN-ECAFE, "Economic Development and Planning in Asia and the Far East," <u>Economic Bulletin for Asia and the Far East</u> (December 1961): 12.

18. See Harvey Leibenstein, "Allocate Efficiency Versus 'x' Efficiency," <u>The American Economic Review</u> 56 (June 1966): 392-413.

19. Myrdal, op. cit., p. 845.

20. See G. Campa, "On the Pure Theory of Public Goods," <u>Public Finance</u> 22, no. 4 (1967): 401-22.

21. H. G. Johnson, "Is There a Role for Market Forces in the Developing Countries?" in <u>Economic Development: Challenge and Promise</u>, S. Spiegelglas & C. J. Welsh, eds. (Englewood Cliffs, N.J.: 1970), p. 38.

IMPORTANCE OF DEMAND

Effective Demand

The demand for goods and services seems a simple concept, so obvious that is would appear to merit little attention. Yet many of the problems of achieving a high rate of economic growth arise from a neglect or misinterpretation of demand considerations. Examining the different effects that various changes in demand have on changes in production provides new insights into what can be done to increase production and productivity and also, what the optimum role of government can be in this increase.

It is, of course, a truism that there must be an effective demand for all goods and services that are produced. Only irrational people would continue to produce goods and services that were not valued or used by somebody. Here, consideration of costs and prices are obviously involved, either implicitly or explicitly. People may want goods, but effective demand goes beyond this; it means demand with potential purchasing capacity, so that a beggar's dream of owning an automobile is not effective demand, while the shopkeeper who is deciding between a diamond ring for his wife or a car is involved in determining the effective demand for rings and automobiles. The assumption of economic rationality involves some evaluations of costs and prices, of choices between different options to use resources, whether it is the demand for raw materials, or for basic consumer goods, for luxuries, or for different kinds of necessities. The demand side is as much an intrinsic part of economic activities as the supply side. Just as the assumption of economic rationality means that the supply of a product, the quantity offered for sale, goes up as the price goes up, so, on the demand side, the assumption is made that the quantity that buyers wish to purchase tends to go down as the price goes up. This is generally assumed for all kinds of products and for all kinds of buyers. At times, this tendency may seem to be absent; but, given the underlying assumptions of economic rationality, it is reasonable to assert that demand for a product rises as the price falls.*

Demand for Factor Inputs and for Products

For some purposes, demand must be thought of in two major categories: (1) Demand for factor inputs including raw materials and intermediate products and services; intermediate products incorporated in other products used by the final consumers. (2) Demand for final products and services by consumers, the goods and services used by households, business, and government.

The ultimate purpose of an increase in the rate of economic growth is, of course, to increase final consumption. When a country assigns a high priority to increasing its production and productivity, it does so because, at some time in the future, it hopes to satisfy increasing demands for goods and services by final consumers. Increasing a country's capacity to produce products requires increased investment in facilities and in improvement of factor inputs and technology. At any one time, this requires increased investment expenditures and relatively decreased consumption expenditures. Thus, a less developed country must be interested in the various increases in demand: demand for consumer goods, demand for capital goods, and the demand and utilization of factor inputs. This is simply another way of looking at the different means of increasing production; for production always involves actual or potential demand, and changing production means changing demand.

Increasing production necessarily means increased demand for factor inputs, but not necessarily an increase of the demand for specific final products. Therefore, it is useful to keep in mind this difference in demand. When a producer decides to increase the production of a product, he almost always affects his demand for the quality and quantity of his factor inputs. He may need more skilled labor and less unskilled labor, more capital of a new kind and less capital of the old kind, more raw materials or he may change his technology, thus improving productivity. But he does not necessarily change the demand

---

*The difference between movements along a single demand schedule and shifts of demand schedules over time often explains the apparent discrepancy of a sellers' market, where higher prices seem to call forth greater demand. These really are caused by other forces shifting the demand schedule, so that at a given price, a greater quantity of the product is demanded by buyers willing to pay a higher price.

for his product, which may be controlled and determined by a different set of economic variables. He may and probably does affect total demand for all products, which is affected by the changes in income he pays out to the factor inputs, and upon how they, the factor inputs, expend their changed income. The total of all the changes in demands by producers for factor inputs may result in drastic shortages and price increases in some products and in surpluses and falling prices in others.

Thus, the question of whether an increase in demand is good or bad, in terms of a country trying to modernize itself and modify its economic institutions, is answerable only when one considers the type and the timing of that increase in demand. Ultimately, an increasing demand for a product is a good thing, and is operationally necessary. It means that production can and probably will increase. But the composition and timing of the demand determines its desirability. Since changes in demand may affect the operations of the economic system in several different, sometimes contradictory ways, it is always necessary to assess the different impacts before making an evaluation. For some objectives of a society, an increase in a certain kind of demand may be meritorious; while for other objectives, the increase may be an obstacle and therefore harmful. Finally, to add to the complexity of assessing the impact of changes in demand, there is the unpleasant reality that there, as in most of the variables that have been discussed, the relationship is interdependent and mutually causative. A higher demand can cause a large supply response; but equally true, low production may be a cause of low demand. Empirical data may provide evidence about the association of changes in these variables, but logic and interpretation must sort out the interdependence and causal relationships.

An increase in demand can be a powerful force or impulse for increasing production or productivity. It can also result in inefficient use of resources and be harmful to the modernizing efforts of a country. When the statement is made that demand must be kept down to permit capital formation, it is, of course, understood that the demand in question here is for consumption purposes, since increased capital formation means necessarily an increased demand for factor inputs in the production of the capital goods, or an increase in the demand for imported capital goods. It is useful, in thinking of the kinds of increased demands for factor inputs, to separate them into the following types:

Labor inputs:

1. Increased demand for unskilled labor—usually this factor input is in surplus in the less developed countries.
2. Increased demand for skilled labor—usually this is a relatively scarce input.
3. Increased demand for management and organization—usually this is a scarce input, but imports can add to domestic capabilities.

Capital inputs:

1. Domestic capital—usually scarce and in the domestic production of capital goods the problem of imported components must be considered.

2. Imported capital—usually available if there is a satisfactory means of repayment.

Land (natural resources) inputs:

These are usually scarce in the developing countries and are largely market determined. An increased demand may so raise prices that natural resources formerly considered only a potential input can become an available input.

Technology:

The demand for technology is closely associated with and embodied in the demand for increased human and capital inputs. However, sometimes it has to be considered separately, as preceding the demand for improved capital and labor inputs. Thus, a government may decide to improve the productivity of sugar in a country by importing some scientists and engineers, who, with domestic engineers, scientists, and government officials, may study the local situation and decide to recommend some new technology involving different agricultural practices, extraction plants, transportation facilities, and marketing arrangements. In a sense, the demand for increased technology is the basis of the demand for improved factor inputs. Technology, the mode of production, is an aspect of the mind, of the knowledge, skills, organization, and thinking of people, as well as the kinds of capital used in production. The important, even decisive, role of improved technology is constantly reaffirmed in the increased demand for improved factor inputs.

An increase in demand for a product can be the cause of an increase in production of that product if there is a price elasticity in the supply. It will be recalled that supply elasticity is a concept comparing the proportional increase in the supply of a product with some other variable, in this case price. Thus, the price elasticity of supply of textiles is a shorthand way of saying that when the price received by textile producers is increased, they may be expected to increase production, because it becomes more profitable to do so. Producers who were losing money will make money, at the higher price; and production at the margin, where costs barely equalled returns, would now be profitable and producers who are trying to minimize costs and maximize returns would try to produce more. An elastic supply response to an increase in demand for a product occurs when the proportionate change in supply is greater than the proportionate change in price. An elastic supply means that production responds sluggishly to price increases and to increased demand.

Static Demand

A country that is characterized by a static aggregate demand for final products cannot, almost by definition, achieve a high rate of capital formation and improved productivity. It cannot, by definition, be achieving a high rate of economic growth. While there may be shifts between types of products, a stable aggregate demand is completely inconsistent with a modernizing society. Efficiency in production is often directly related to size of market. A small demand for a product may necessarily involve a kind of technology that makes impossible modern high productivity production. In the numerous illustrations of technology cited, the automatic versus the hand-blown bottle factory, the hand-craft versus the factory production of shoes, the size of the market is an aspect of the demand. If the demand for shoes is so low that a modern shoe machine can satisfy all the demand by working only a small part of the time, it may not pay to build a modern plant. The size of effective demand, which is another way of saying the size of the market, often determines the level of technology as well as the level of production. Economies of scale, so important in raising production and productivity, are only possible when the demand is sufficient to warrant a large enough production unit. Demand is thus an integral part of the production process; production always involves demand for factor inputs and for the products of the enterprise. This is true whether one is analyzing a simple production process of a primitive laborer weaving baskets or the complex process of petrochemical production, with its output of hundreds of different products that are both final products and intermediate products used in further production. Thus, a country that has little or no increase in demand, whether it is aggregate demand, or the demand for a particular important product, lacks one of the major forces pushing towards increased production and productivity.

Static demand is particularly prevalent in rural areas, where low productivity, low incomes, low savings, and low capital formation and meagre expectations form a mass of interrelated obstacles to increased production. Increased demand can be both a cause and a result of overcoming these obstacles. By increasing productivity, subsistence peasants increase demands for both consumers and capital goods. The reverse causal flow also can, and often does, exist. The increased demand of peasants for consumers goods can result in increased capital formation that results in improved productivity and increased production. Where the supply is price elastic, that is, where producers can respond to an increase in the prices they receive by increasing their production, an increase in demand can have a good result. Where supply is inelastic because of lack of complementarities or of necessary factor inputs, an increase in demand will cause an increase in price, but not in production. That is why a country proposing to use increased demand as a spur to increased production must carefully relate this policy to elasticity of supply before proceeding. A price increase that does not elicit an adequate production response may merely transfer purchasing power from consumers to producers without necessarily adding to increased production and productivity.

Decreases in demand may be as important as the increases. If the production of a product is undesirable from the viewpoint of the economic growth of a country, it is possible to curtail or eliminate it through changes in demand for that product. For example, the production of certain kinds of luxury goods could be discouraged by placing a high tax on its purchase, thus reducing demand. Changes in demand, actual or potential, affect the production plans of entrepreneurs and managers. These changes in demand are as much a part of the operations of an economic system as are changes in supply. Since demand operates as a passive variable to most observers and is more the result of other decisions than an originating force in economic production, most planning administrators do not give adequate consideration to the impact of changes in demand on production. The important role that changes in demand may have on capital formation, on improvement of labor inputs and on more efficient applications of technology, can influence strategically the desired total goal: increased production and productivity. Changing demand is one of the dynamic forces in economic development. Whether induced by other forces or appearing to be self-generated, changes in demand must be an area of intense concern to governments of countries that wish to increase production and productivity.

CHANGES IN DEMAND

Value Changes

The less developed countries are confronting a massive change in the value systems of their peoples, a change of unprecedented importance to economic growth. The overwhelming majority of mankind, formerly content or at least apathetic to their economic lot, however low the level of subsistence, has accepted the idea that their consumption levels can, and should, be raised. The combination of ideas, philosophies, religions, and cosmology that gave most people the conviction that nothing really could be done to improve their lot has changed dramatically, almost to the opposite extreme. Now, the people of the less developed countries are convinced that a greater supply of goods and services is not only necessary and desirable, but also quite feasible. Value systems have been adjusted where necessary to accommodate the ideas that improved food and health are consistent with improved virtue, and government is considered as substantially responsible for attaining this improvement in well-being. The term revolution of rising expectations is, of course, applied to a broader horizon than merely goods and services; but the core of these rising expectations is based on the hopes and desires for greater economic returns.

This change in values has, of course, affected many patterns of activities. Changes in the desirability and method of savings, changes in the discount applied to future receipt of goods as compared with present consumption of goods, are only some of the basic changes that form part of this "sea change" in demand. The impatience with adequate social and economic facilities, for example, arises not only from producers' drives to minimize costs and maximize returns. It also arises from a general discontent with the quality and quantity of services supplied to the community in general. Poor communications, uncomfortable and slow transportation facilities, and inadequate health facilities are elements of final consumption as well as factor inputs into the production process. The shift from a barter to a monetized economy and the development of market institutions to channel the increasing number of economic activities involved in higher production levels are partly encouraged by these basic changes in demand.

Demonstration Effect

Social analysts have designated many causes for these basic changes. Underlying most of these causes are the changes in demand for final consumption goods and services, the changing requirements of people who want to consume more. This is initiated largely by ideas and examples from outside the country. Isolation of a country is nearly always relative, not absolute. In history, there are periods and countries that have succeeded in isolating themselves from the rest of the world. New ideas and examples of what other countries are producing, writing, and thinking have been excluded by prohibiting travel abroad and refusing to admit foreigners except under the strictest surveillance. But these periods of isolation were short, historically speaking, and were complete only for the most primitive of peoples. It is inconceivable that in this day of international travel and trade, of radio, television, newspapers and magazines, that one country can remain ignorant of what is happening to production and consumption outside its borders. This learning to consume by observing others has been dubbed the demonstration effect, and is a powerful force in stimulating and accelerating changes in demand for consumer goods.

The demonstration effect operates widely within countries as well as between countries. The various income levels of a society learn from the levels above them the kinds of consumption that richer people desire, and try to emulate this in their expenditure. The keeping up with the Joneses is a universal phenomenon, not limited to western middle classes. The demonstration effect may result in fads, as in the case of clothing styles that change rapidly, or may result in long-run, basic changes that meet peoples' long-felt needs, as in the case of improved drugs and medicinal supplies. The changed examples or ideals that a society accepts as desirable or worthy of imitation reflect the changing culture of a society and deeply affect its economic activities, largely through changes in demand. Value systems not only are reflected in abstract concepts as justice, beauty, and humanism, but also are reflected in the type and intensity of desire for physical assets, the clothing, housing, cars, jewels, and food consumed by a society. The kinds of physical assets to be valued are often determined by specific demonstration effects. Where government is in a position of power and prestige, the style of living followed by the admired and envied government civil servants may have an important demonstration effect, emphasizing the types of products and services enjoyed by civil servants. With improved communication a present and growing phenomenon, the demonstration effect can be expected to expand and intensify its influence on demand.

To illustrate the difficulty of assessing specific causes for changes in demand, consider a village that was previously quite isolated, and produced its economic products at a low level of stability with its environment. Its demand for goods and services was relatively stable; and only a few of its people had contacts outside the village, possibly the storekeeper who purchased supplies and sold the few agricultural products he bought from the villagers, and the few village leaders who occasionally went to town or sent a son to school outside of the village. The building of a road and the introduction of a village school teacher could start a string of communications with the outside world that would include more travelers to the nearby town, more newspapers, more radios to listen to government programs, more children leaving for distant schools and returning occasionally to the village with information of the world around them. Traveling merchants may bring goods to the village and buy some of its products. More frequent visits by government officials may expose the villagers to the thinking and consumption examples of persons who are clearly better off and have different consumption patterns. Improved transportation, communication, education, trade, all could be assigned important roles in the creation of a series of demonstration effects that would change the demand for goods and services in the village.

The demonstration effect has been advanced as the cause for the low rate of savings in the lower income classes of the less developed countries. Every income class in a society seems to be affected by the consumption habits of the class above it, particularly the income class that it wishes to achieve. Thus, the lower income families tend to increase their consumption when their income rises, not only because they need to augment their consumption to stay alive, but because they have seen the pleasures of increased consumption demonstrated by the members of the income class above them which they hope to attain or equal. The savings of the lowest income class of a country tends to remain low and constant, almost regardless of the income increases that occur. This has important implications for the stimulation of increases in the rate of private savings. If a large part of the increased income of a country were to go as payments to low income families, the demonstration effect would help keep a constant, low savings rate. This will be discussed more completely in the next chapter which discusses the effect of income distribution on increasing production and productivity. Here, the point must be made that the demonstration effect clearly has an important role in the changes of demand and of savings.

Formal educational systems obviously stimulate and fortify changes in demand. It is inconceivable that any school system could teach literacy and the elementary concepts of mathematics and science without changing the demand for goods and services. The changes may be direct, as would be involved in teaching about nutrition and health and more desirable living practices. The indirect changes, those that are the essence of education, are ideas that improve communication and open up minds to new ideas and to new observations. Thus educational projects are the most revolutionary of all projects, in the basic, long-run sense of that term. Changes in demand are fostered both in the short run and in the long run by school systems; and this may be one of their most important results.

Changes in transportation must also be identified clearly as one of the basic causes of changes in demand. Most of the time, discussions of economic development focus on transportation as an input in the production process, a necessary service associated with the basic economic overhead facilities necessary for higher productivity. But transportation, in its relationship to communication, may have an even more important role to play in the transmission of new ideas, new viewpoints, and new perceptions, the basis for many changes in demand. When an area opens up new transportation facilities, long-run changes in communication and demand may be more important in shaping the nature of the society than changes in production efficiencies, important as the latter is.

Effects of Changes in Demand

In considering the importance of changes in demand, the interrelated effect of expenditures must be kept in mind. An economy is something like a lake in which a stone is dropped. The waves generated by the impact of the dropped stone are a kind of series, one following the other, although of lesser size; and the succession of waves can be considered as theoretically infinite, although only the first few are visible to the eye. When an expenditure is made, the person who receives the money in return for a product or service, makes his own expenditures. He pays bills, buys materials, buys services, deposits in the bank—all the multiplicity of activities that a person, a business, or a government undertakes with the money it receives. Thus, each expenditure generates other expenditures. Economists call this the expenditure multiplier, because it multiplies the demand for goods and services. If an outsider, to make the illustration simple, comes in and spends $100 on a carved set of chairs, he enables the furniture store to pay the worker $40, the mill that supplied the wood $20, the landlord $10, and the owner of the furniture store and master craftsman the remaining $30, as a form of wage and profit. Each of these in turn will spend his income on food, clothing, payment of bills, workers, and so forth until the original expenditure of $100 may generate $300 of expenditures before the waves become too small to be attributed to the original expenditure of $100. The multiplier of expenditures is not infinitely large because there are frictions and leakages in the system, as there is in the waves started by a rock tossed into the lake. The friction and leakages in the expenditure multiplier are savings, funds that are exported, and the fact that it takes time to receive and spend money. Over a year, the multiplier in the less developed countries may run about three to one, with a higher multiplier for the low income earners because they save little, import little, and spend their money as fast as they can obtain the commodities and services.

Changes in demand for products can be translated rapidly into changes in the demand for the factor inputs that are utilized to produce the product. Increases in the demand for certain types of skilled labor and machines arise when demand increases for the products of a factory. Lumber demand goes up when the demand for furniture goes up. To understand the impact of economic forces on economic institutions, it is necessary to translate market transactions into the impacts they have on the supply and demand of the factor inputs, as well as the supply and demand of the product involved in the market transaction. Thus, an increase in the demand for food must be evaluated by examining the kinds of food, what inputs are required for an increase in the production of that food, and the general appraisal of the opportunity costs of the additional production.

Changes in demand that affect changes in requirements of foreign exchange are of particular importance to the less developed countries. If an increase in domestic demand stimulates domestic production by employing resources that would not otherwise be used, it represents a desirable force towards increasing production and productivity. But if domestic resources are only a small part of the factor inputs, and the increase in production involves a significant use of imported goods, then the question of opportunity costs must arise. What other production requiring foreign imports will be deprived by this increase? What are the alternative uses of the scarce import, foreign exchange? Thus, the generalization that increments of demand are positive because they lead to increments of production must be examined to see how much of the increased factor inputs are domestic and foreign, and to understand what the alternative uses of the resources are likely to be.

Elasticity of Demand

In considering the effects of changes in demand on production and on factor inputs of the production process, the concept of elasticity is again useful. It will be recalled that in chapter 3, the concept of elasticity of supply was discussed. This was the proportional change in the supply of a good or a factor input compared with the proportional change of another variable, usually price or income. Thus, the price elasticity of the supply of shoes was the percentage change in the supply compared with the percentage change in price. When supply appeared changed relatively more than the price change, it was called elastic. An inelastic supply was the term used when the supply did not increase or increased only slightly when the price changed.

This same concept of elasticity can be applied to demand. It is useful to talk about products whose demand are price inelastic, which means that the quantity demanded does not change very much when the price goes up or down. For example, the price elasticity of the demand for coffee in the United States is quite low. This means that the quantity of coffee purchased by consumers is approximately the same, regardless of the price change. When coffee is 80 cents a pound, most people in the United States demand about the same amount of coffee as when the price is 50 cents. Of course, if the cost jumped to $2.00 a pound, demand would drop; and if the cost became 10 cents, it is conceivable that more coffee would be demanded, although this is doubtful. This illustrates several points. The concept of elasticity must be applied to reasonable price changes, changes near the existing price. Also, the time period covered must be of reasonable length, not too short, since it may take some time to work out these changes; but the time period must also not be too long, since in the long run everything changes drastically.

The elasticity of demand for product and services, either final products or factor inputs, must be considered relative to the same two variables, price and income. The difference between these two is significant, although sometimes there is an overlap; and they can be confused. To a worker, the price of his labor and his income are almost the same thing. Yet price may be quoted in different time units and the difference may be important. A worker may get a fixed price of $2.00 an hour for his work, but his income will vary with the hours worked. To a businessman, the difference between the price of his product and his income is quite significant. To a country, this difference is also quite clear. Prices may be going up while national income may be going down. Thus, price elasticity of demand and income elasticity of demand are related but they are essentially different and therefore must be considered separately in many problems. Changes in demand play an important role in stimulating and shaping economic growth, and government policies play an important role in changing the demand for good and services.

MAJOR PROBLEMS OF CHANGING DEMAND

Demand for Capital

An intense and increasing demand for capital is a characteristic of all countries attempting to achieve a higher rate of production. The need for improving productivity, hopefully, focuses this demand on the kinds of capital that embody or permit new technologies to be used in production. Thus, the increased demand for capital is both a cause and a result of the development drive in a country. Considering it solely as one or the other, and not both, will lead to erroneous conclusions about the policies best suited to meet operating situations. The demand for capital can be expected to grow as a country develops; there can be no target date when the rate of economic growth will be such as to reduce or eliminate the growing demand for capital. What can be envisaged, usually a long time in the future, is a growth rate, supported by its complex of institutions in a manner permitting the decisions that result in adequate capital to meet the growing demand, adequate in the sense of a resource still scarce but not necessarily the dominant constraint to further vigorous growth.

The demand for capital is constantly being affected by, as well as affecting, the policies and priorities of government. Because capital formation involves judgments about the future in relationship to the present, any government policy that seriously affects the future has necessarily an impact on the demand for capital. Monetary and fiscal policies that affect evaluation of future costs and prices clearly influence the demand for capital. When governments announce an intention to nationalize selected sectors in the future, the demand for capital from these sectors can be expected to be modified. Where the government decides to invest in a large industrial enterprise, this demand for capital can seriously affect the demand of capital from similar private enterprises. The demand for capital is peculiarly related to the supply of capital. As stated in Chapter 3, often investment decisions are the cause for creating the resources or savings that makes the capital possible. This is true in both simple and complex capital formation. On a simple level, a farmer may need a new shed for his livestock. The demand for this capital presses him to go to the forest, collect the wood and other material he needs; and, taking time from his other production activities or his consumption activities, including leisure, he builds the animal shed and adds capital to his enterprise. In a similar but far more complicated operation, the demand for a new factory may culminate in a decision by government or private enterprise to plan the factory, relying on funds borrowed from banks. The economic system is challenged, even forced, in a sense, to provide the financial resources that are expended to end up as a new factory. All the complications of the money markets, including the methods of assembling the foreign

133

exchange needed to import the machinery, cannot obscure the basic rela tionship and timing that exists between the investment decisions, the demand for capital and the meeting of that demand through the adjustments in the economic system.

A demand for specific kinds of capital can be created or seriously modified by creating a new demand for the products of that capital. Thus, a shift in demand from sandals to shoes creates a demand for the tools and machinery that produces shoes. A demand for soft drinks may be reflected in part in the demand for machinery that makes and bottles these liquids. New ideas and new fashions can work their way through demand for final products back to the capital goods that produce these final products. The demand for capital is often derived from other demands, and this adds to the complexity of relating the timing and quantity of capital formation to the demand for its products. Also, the time lag involved between the investment process and the application of the capital to the production process, can find that demand has changed; and the capital does not quite fit the current demand for its products. Thus, coffee trees that are planted in response to high prices brought by increasing demand for coffee may start producing five years later, when coffee prices have dropped and the new trees are no longer required in the same way.

There is an important difference between capital considered as a physical input into the production process, such as machinery, a building, or raw material, and capital considered as the financial resources used in making the expenditures to create the physical product "thing" capable of further production. In broad national terms, the analysis of the demand for capital is properly phrased as the demand for the financial resources to create capital, the demand for the ability to make the expenditures that will buy or create the physical inputs used in further production. Governmental control of capital formation relates to both of these parts of the process. By affecting the quantity and allocation of financial resources, government affects the capital formation process. By licensing and permits, government affects the specific, physical objects used in further production. In specific situations, however a confusion between financial resources and physical capital can create operational chaos. When financial resources are embodied in physical things to be used in further production, the ability to shift from producing one kind of product to another becomes quite limited. At an oper ational level, shifts in demand that are translated into shifts in capital formation must be analyzed in physical as well as financial terms.

The projected demand schedule, the estimates of the amount of output that will be purchased at different alternative prices, is an important component of any investment decision. The projected volume of output that will yield a satisfactory return to the enterprise is clearly related to the effective demand, the desire on the part of buyers coupled with their ability to buy. Income distribution is thus an essential part of production decisions and therefore necessarily a part of investment decisions. No investment can be rationally made without an important reference to the projected effective demand; and investment decisions are influenced, even determined, by projections of effective demand. In the less developed countries, limitations on the size of the effective demand for products often tends to reduce or postpone investment decisions. The fact that capital is generally in short supply does not necessarily mean that all available capital is utilized or is not underutilized. It has been noted that "despite the overall shortage of capital equipment in the less developed countries, a substantial amount of unutilized or underutilized capacity often exists in developing countries."[1] This may be caused either by a deficiency in demand or by a lack of balance between the sectors or industries of the economy.

All capital formation is a result of a cost-benefit analysis, either explicitly or implicitly performed. By modifying either costs or benefits, the demand for capital can be stimulated, redirected, or can be diminished, even eliminated. Thus, by placing a low cost on the foreign exchange to pay for imported capital equipment, the demand for imported capital may be stimulated. By differential taxes on some kinds of capital, demand can be stimulated or discouraged. Refusal to issue necessary licenses may condemn some projects as undesirable and choke off all effective demand for this type of capital, as in the case of factories producing certain kinds of luxuries. The effect of modifying costs and benefits must be judged in terms of other costs and benefits involved in the calculation. Thus, lowering one kind of cost while increasing another adds to the complications of the calculations; and while each element of cost may be evaluated in terms of its force or direction, its influence must be evaluated in terms of the totality of the analysis. Some elements of the climate within which capital demand must operate may be hard to quantify. This does not necessarily reduce their importance, however; it only enhances the difficulty of the evaluation process.

Because the control of capital is clearly one of the most direct ways to affect economic growth, governments have developed many policies that affect the demand for capital. In its monetary and fiscal policies, a government clearly relates to the demand for capital by determining its cost—the rate of interest—the institutions through which many of the arrangements for capital are channeled, the kinds of capital that will be created directly by government activities, and the priorities given to different kinds of capital. Direct governmental demands for capital are usually an important part of the total demand for capital. Because of the government's ability to affect priorities through the issuance of licenses and permits, a government-owned paper mill is almost certain to be assigned the scarce requirements it needs, including foreign exchange, ahead of similar activities by the private sector. The higher priority generally given government demands for capital may not be undesirable, if the government's capital formation results in capital that will be more productive than the capital formation it displaces or pushes to a lower priority. A government paper mill may be more productive than the building of luxury office buildings for the private sector. But simple comparisons of this kind are difficult to make in actual operations, and

135

comparisons of the best kinds of governmental capital with the least d sirable kinds of private capital are hardly proof that they use the same resources. Usually, all that is possible to analyze are broad categori of capital demand with equally broad evaluations of average productivi Cost and benefit considerations must include external economies, not just monetary returns on capital investment. The role that social and economic overhead facilities play in stimulating other production and the need for breaking up pockets of economic stagnation must also be included.

When all of these are considered, the implicit and explicit high priority given to government demand for capital is on the whole salutory and desirable. Specific illustrations of the contrary situation are not difficult to find. There are usually some good capital formation prc jects in the nongovernmental sector of the economy that have not been initiated because of the lack of capital or because government has, fo some reason, withheld approval or support. There are also always son government projects that have less than adequate marginal social productivity. A comparison of these would seem to provide evidence that the priority generally given to government capital demands is counterproductive and handicaps the push for economic growth. These situations are so numerous they cannot be dismissed lightly. They represent areas where the existing system has failed to do as efficient a job of resource allocation as it can and should do, and public administrators must recognize this and make efforts to have the system scrutinize public demands for capital more carefully. However, the answer cannot be to do away with the priority given to government capital demand, because this is not feasible. It must lie in improving the allocation process that is so important a part of national economic plannin and in improving the government's use of capital.

The effective demand for capital goods is, in a sense, different from the demand for consumers' goods because credit is so important a part of the transaction.* Access to credit for capital formation is largely determined by government policies. Credit worthiness, the jud ment that the applicant for credit is likely to carry out the terms of the credit arrangements, particularly the repayment schedule, always involves criteria that express cultural values and social relationships; but these are almost universally controlled and modified by government policies and practices. Credit is often functionally related to assets, since wealthy families are considered better credit risks than poor families. Thus, in nearly all the credit institutions that a modernizing

---

*It will be remembered that effective demand consists of two parts a willingness to purchase and a capability to purchase. While credit may be part of the capability to purchase consumer goods in the developed countries, consumers' credit is not very important in the less developed countries.

country must develop, the nature of the credit-worthiness criteria are related to ownership of assets, even within a governmental framework that attempts to assign priorities for the available credit. In rural areas, particularly, agricultural credit to increase the effective demand for capital goods is strongly correlated to land ownership. Large farmers are, under the usual criteria of market considerations, clearly the best credit risks, and the demand for credit becomes as concentrated as the ownership of land. The same applies in urban areas, where small businessmen and small traders have difficulty in establishing their credit worthiness, and a large proportion of the credit for capital formation goes to large industries.

The demand for capital in the less developed countries is often complicated by capital flight. This is the effort of some people to export their capital, to move it out of the country and beyond the control of government. Such flight is often undesirable and is usually illegal. A country may permit the export of capital as part of its trading relationship with the world, but this must be fitted into the internal needs of the country. While some specific capital export may be desirable from the viewpoint of assuming a source of supply for raw material or a desirable marketing outlet, capital requirements within the less developed countries are generally so intense as to make undesirable any exports of capital. Capital flight is usually prompted by fear of expropriation, the desire to assure resources if it becomes necessary to leave the country. Thus, wherever the social or political process is involved in shifting power from one class to another, or from one ethnic group to another, the social turbulence is generally accompanied by efforts of the displaced group to export its resources to another, safer country. Numbered bank accounts in Switzerland are only one of the numerous kinds of depositories for these efforts to shift resources from one country to another. All of the major world banking centers generally have similar, if less publicized systems. It is impossible to estimate the size of this capital flight because its essence is secrecy, but that it exists and is an important element in the demand for capital in many of the less developed countries cannot be doubted. Government efforts to check capital flight are usually scanty and ineffective because of the difficulty of controlling such commercial practices as underinvoicing exports or overpricing imports. Smuggling of currency, jewels, and goods are also elements of this capital flight. Thus, capital flight can be a serious drain on a country's resources. While a government is forced to make strenuous efforts to curtail capital flight through direct controls, such as customs inspections and police action, obviously the only way to affect it fundamentally is to create and encourage a climate in which capital can be used productively and safely. Capital flight not only drains out resources that are needed; it also expresses a climate in which the demand for capital is so distorted as to make impossible the development of efficient institutions for allocating and using capital.

Demand for Labor

The term labor, as a factor input into the production process, includes all inputs demanded from human resources including skills, experience, organization, and motivation. It involves many specialized institutions whose activities focus on affecting the demand for labor, such as unions, employment services, and regulatory agencies of government, including the police. While some aspects of demand for labor inputs have been discussed in the previous chapters on the production process and the ways of improving the factor inputs, it is useful to focus here on special problems in the demand for labor.

Unskilled Workers

The demand for unskilled workers in most of the low productivity countries is low relative to the supply. In spite of the immobility of labor in traditional societies, even the slightest hint of the availability of jobs brings in a flood of unskilled applicants. Generally these are inferior labor inputs from the viewpoint of experience, habits, health, and motivation. The wages they will accept are generally very low, although this level may be somewhat higher than the average wages in the rural sector. The demand for unskilled labor never seems to keep pace with economic growth and is usually determined by the availability of other kinds of labor inputs, particularly skilled labor, management, and organization, as well as the associated capital inputs needed for the production process. Government programs rarely are devoted to pushing the demand for unskilled labor as such, although such a demand is obviously an important part of any program that involves increasing employment. In other words, the demand for unskilled labor is almost a derived function of the demand for other kinds of labor inputs.

Skilled Workers

The demand for skilled workers is complicated by the poor market organizations for labor inputs in most of the less developed countries. Shortages of skilled workers continue to exist while unemployed skilled workers are seeking employment. This is partly due to the relative immobility of skilled labor and partly to the fact that employment of skilled workers is often based on considerations other than skill, as family or caste connections, nepotism and other nonefficiency considerations. Where job opportunities are relatively scarce, these considerations tend to be emphasized, although they are nearly always present in any labor market. The relatively small and poorly articulated labor market in the less developed countries means that the demand for skilled workers is generally thin at any one time, that a shortage develops rapidly on a specific project or in an enterprise because of the difficulty of communicating with skilled workers who are unemployed. Training programs are only partial answers to this problem, at best, because employers generally want experienced skilled workers who have learned skill on the job as well as in school rooms. Only a vigorously expanding market for skilled labor enables an area to build up the kinds of institutions that make this spot kind of skilled labor shortage a minor irritation rather than a significant bottleneck in production. The wages of skilled workers in the less developed countries are relatively high because of the demand for their services. It can be seen that "the range of wages and salaries is much greater in poor than in rich countries because of the relatively greater shortage of skills. This handicaps development, since it makes relatively expensive all services and industries which depend on skill, and these tend to be the sectors that should grow fastest in a developing economy."[2]

The demand for skilled labor is also strongly affected by government institutions that set standards for specific kinds of workers. The licensing of certain types of skills, and the issuance of work permits is a widespread condition that affects the demand for certain types of labor. The issuance of building permits often involves adjustments between suppliers of different kinds of labor. It is surprising how often the demand for a specific type of labor is dependent upon an appropriate certificate, license, or permit issued by a government official. The government agency that issues these papers, ranging from employment offices, police offices, headmen's offices, courts, or miscellaneous government agencies, affects labor demand directly. The basic purpose of these institutions is clearly focused on attempts to influence production and productivity through a better allocation of labor inputs. However meritorious the purpose of such efforts, they generally add to the sluggishness with which the labor market attempts to meet changes in demand for skilled labor.

The most critical demand for labor factor inputs, in the sense of importance as a bottleneck to more rapid economic growth, lies in the complex bundle of experience and skills involved in the management of organizations. How to organize productive efforts in a new and improved technology constantly remains a major problem in implementing economic growth plans, and will probably remain a critical demand throughout the foreseeable future. Like the demand for capital, the need for management skills seems to multiply at a faster rate than economic growth; and while imported management may meet some of this demand, particularly the narrow technical types, most of the management skills require a knowledge and personal relationship that can come only with being an integral part of the culture. Since the essence of successful management is the establishment of the necessary human relationships involved in the operations of institutions, the development of an adequate number of managers is largely a domestic problem, not merely one of paying for imported management. Management skills are clearly

139

a relevant and scarce input in governmental operations. The ease with which government can create new enterprises clearly conflicts with the difficulties in finding adequate management for these enterprises.

Labor unions directly affect the demand for labor because they try to control access to the labor market. Unions attempt to restrict employment opportunities to their membership and stress efforts designed to improve wages and working conditions. Unions may also be desirabl avenues for education and improvement of quality of labor inputs, but this aspect of union activities is only a vague hope in most countries. Because they have tremendous political and social as well as economic potentialities, unions are the object of intense interest, control, or influence by government officials and political leaders. The interests of unions to stimulate the demand for their workers is coupled with their efforts to increase labor's wages. Reducing labor costs through productivity improvement is one of the announced but scantly emphasized objectives of unions. In many critical areas, such as dockyards, railroads, trucking, factories, power plants, and communications, labor unions have become important parts of labor markets and significantly affect the demand for labor.

Demand for Land (Natural Resources)

The demand for natural resources other than agricultural land is largely market determined. There are some mineral resources, notably oil, that have a universal, growing demand, with a production and distribution system so advanced that adequate deposits in any part of the earth, however inaccessible, can be rapidly exploited. The need for emphasizing the adequacy of deposits arises from the high costs of exploitation that make a large operation almost mandatory. From oil, which is so intensely demanded, there is a gradual shading through mineral resources that are very valuable and readily marketable, such as manganese, chromium, high grade iron ore, cokable coal, diamonds, down through much less valuable and more widespread deposits such as aluminum, clay, cement, and low grade iron ores. Here, the demand is basically a function of prospective returns to investors. Usually, the extraction and transportation of these natural resources require both experience and large amounts of capital, both relatively lacking in the less developed countries. In the colonial period, the usual method of utilizing these natural resources was by enterprises owned and managed by the colonial power. Today, most countries object to these arrangements and require at least partial participation by their own nationals. Many countries utilize the device of either totally or partially publicly-owned enterprises to avoid having key natural resources entirely controlled by foreigners. The government obviously plays a key role in establishing the "right" kind of relationship between the demand for a natural resource and the arrangements that are made to exploit it. Market demand is an essential element, but it is always fitted into the rules and regulations as presented by the existing institutions of the country. If the market demand operates in a climate of insecurity, such as possible expropriation with arbitrary and inadequate reimbursement, difficult rules of employment, and varying, potentially oppressive taxation, the natural resources may remain as potential rather than actual factor inputs. The line between reasonable controls and requirements legitimately advanced by a government and arbitrary, counterproductive requirements is often a matter of judgment, largely determined by the perspective of the viewer rather than by any basic rules of rationality. Often the only reasonable test is whether as a matter of fact the natural resources of a country are contributing as much as they should to the economic growth of the country.

Agricultural land is obviously an important factor input in most countries. In the less developed countries, the demand for land is a combination of its role as a factor input and the position it occupies in the traditional value system of a country. Land is so basic a part of the life and value system of most countries that land values are formed as part of the cultural pattern. The high value given land ownership in the status system is an outstanding characteristic of countries in which traditional agricultural production is by far the largest economic sector of the economy. Several types of institutions do affect land sales, both on the supply and the demand side.

Many countries are developing legal frameworks for the ownership and transfer of land that strongly affect land as a factor input. Limitations on size of land holdings, prohibition or limitation of absentee ownership, land inheritance laws, tenancy rights of sale and possession, are examples of the types of institutional framework that has developed for the marketing of land. Most of these are attempts to mold the land market in a way that will make land more available to actual farmers on the smaller farms or landless agricultural workers. Included in the legal framework for the marketing of agricultural land are the judicial systems designed to authenticate ownership and settle ownership disputes. The number, complexity, and ferocity that land disputes often assume are almost unbelievable to persons who have not appreciated the status role of land in agricultural societies. The legal institutions about land that are being formulated in the less developed countries go far beyond economic analysis in their scope and objectives. In economic production they have several main purposes.

A major purpose of the legal institutions developing around the demand for agricultural land is to enable production costs and market prices of products to influence land values and land sales. At present, speculation and social status create a demand for agricultural land that raises prices, particularly near cities, beyond any cost-benefit relationship to production. Social and political purposes are of course extremely important in this sector, but the economic impact of violent changes in demand for land is also important. The efforts to create the legal instituitions that will make land a more flexible input, responsive to drives for increasing efficiency in production, strongly affect the legal programs of the less developed countries. There does not seem to be any good way to prevent land speculation or even to capture some of the gains from successful land speculation through the imposition of taxes. Not only is the administration of such taxes difficult in the extreme, but the requirement of a direct confrontation with a powerful group of landlords and wealthy speculators is often more than the political system can achieve. Even the dimensions of the problems relating to the speculative demand for land are usually beyond the reach of empirical studies. As a consequence, government policies in this area are largely politically determined; and their ineffectiveness in economic terms is usually overlooked.

As in the case of capital, the demand for land is often related to the credit institutions being developed, and how these credit institutions assess credit worthiness. Demand for land is an intense and widespread feeling in most peasant areas, particularly among the landless peasants and small landowners who see income improvement only in terms of ownership of land. Credit arrangements to make this demand effective represent one of the greatest challenges to government within the limitations provided by the society as it now exists and as it wishes to become. Land value must be related to land use, actual or potential. Credit arrangements for the acquisitions of improved factor inputs such as seed, fertilizer, insecticide, water, tools, and machines are directly related to improved land use and higher land values; and credit arrangements are largely the resultant of government policies and administration.

There are many institutions, often initiated and fostered by government, that affect the demand for land and are utilized by government to affect production and productivity. Land ownership in many countries is heavily involved in cooperative ownership or in the operation of some system of common land, available to all the inhabitants of the community. The legal framework for the support of these kinds of land usage affects the demand for land and how land is used in the production process. Similarly, credit institutions, both within and without cooperatives, often provide government funds for the purchase of land by tenants and landless workers. Here it is important to note that the twofold economic objectives of increasing production and productivity must be reconciled with the social and political objectives of determining the kind of society that is being developed. The development of ejidos in Mexico and the village settlement schemes in Tanzania are examples of efforts to mold agricultural institutions that require consideration of complicated economic and social problems. The demand for land is so basic and powerful an element of the value system that it necessarily becomes an important part of a government's economic policies.

General Level of Demand for Consumer Goods

One of the most crucial policy areas of the less developed coun-
ries relates to the question of level of consumption. This has been
iscussed from several viewpoints in previous sections, in the exami-
ations of low productivity, savings, capital formation, and in the
llocation of resources. The way the monetary and fiscal policies affect
avings and capital formation are, almost by definition, the way they
ffect consumption, since the variables are so interdependent and inter-
elated. Tax policies, for example, obviously affect the general level
f consumption by affecting the transfer of purchasing power to the gov-
rnment and affecting consumption and savings in the private sector.
ligh interest rates and tighter money may contract consumer credit,
ence reducing consumption. The purpose of this section is not to re-
iew these policies and practices, and the institutions they affect, but
o focus on specific government policies that deliberately affect the
evel of overall consumption demand as a tool or device for increasing
roduction and productivity.

Most governments have an incomes policy implicit or explicit in
heir practices that covers wages and profits. As in the case of most
asic policies, an incomes policy has conflicting objectives as well
s complementary objectives; its instrumental goals are often at vari-
nce with more ultimate goals, and short-run and long-run objectives
re sometimes quite different. This is inherent in the nature of the prob-
em, and does not denigrate the usefulness of such policies. A knowl-
dge of these complexities often may help improve their implementation.
he most usual incomes policy adhered to by the less developed coun-
ries is to keep industrial wages as low as possible. This has several
conomic influences of importance:

1. Demand is kept down, particularly demand for consumer goods
ecause most wages are spent on consumer goods. This is part of the
eneral goal of encouraging savings and discouraging consumption.

2. When wages are kept low, profits are increased. This encour-
ges savings, because profits are the type of income most likely to be
aved, particularly profits from manufacturing and other modern indus-
rial enterprises.

3. By keeping wages low, unit production costs are kept down,
elping the producer compete in foreign markets and earn foreign ex-
hange to pay for imports.

There are, of course, many other relationships affected by this
ind of wage policy. Some of these will be discussed in other con-
ections later in this section. It is necessary to point out again that
conomic effects are only one kind, and that political, social, and
ther kinds of relationships may be essentially involved and may be

more important than the economic results of governmental policies. F
example, a wage policy that holds wages down, regardless of an increase in profits, is quite disturbing politically. The mass of worker
at or near subsistence resent this wage policy, particularly if prices
rising and they are in effect receiving less real wages while profits g
up, both in an absolute and relative sense. Wage policies that are ri
are often impossible to operate, in spite of the way they emphasize
profits, savings, and capital formation. Low consumption is another
way of saying poverty, and poverty is unquestionably the major economic and social problem confronting the less developed countries.
Low consumption exists because effective demand is low, because lo
productivity permits only low effective demand.

Price Demand for Food

Food, because it plays so important a role in production and consumption, requires more consideration than was given in the previous
section. There are several useful demand elasticities for food that ca
be identified:

Price Elasticity of the Demand for Food

This refers to the change in the demand for food when prices go u
or down. The demand for essential food tends to be price inelastic. 1
purchaser tries to buy his necessities even if the price goes up. Othe
purchases may have to be reduced; but the essential food requirement
tends to be the same, even if a substantial rise occurs in food prices
Luxury foods tend to be price elastic, where the demand will go up wl
price goes down and vice versa. However, often to the consternation
of rigorous economists, there is a snob appeal to high prices, so that
the demand may go up because it becomes more a status symbol to ha
a high priced luxury. This applies particularly to imported goods, including imported luxury foods. The relationship to note is that the es
sential foods tend to be price inelastic, to maintain their level of demand even though prices rise substantially. On the down side, a
subsistence economy tends to have a more elastic demand for food tha
a more affluent society. While coffee consumption will not respond to
a price drop of 15 or 20 percent in the United States, in India, the de
mand for rice increases significantly when the price goes down. Poor
people can afford to buy more rice at the lower price even though
wealthier people will not demand more at this lower price since they
already consume all the rice they wish. Thus, the price elasticity of
the demand for food varies significantly from country to country and
from income level to income level within a country.

144

The Income Elasticity of the Demand for Food

The relationship between changes in income and changes in the demand for food is also important. Proportionately, income elasticity of the demand for food is high in the less developed countries. This means that when income goes up, say 10 percent, the demand for food goes up faster, say 15 percent, or an elasticity of 1.5. The importance of this should be apparent immediately. Because the income elasticity of the demand for food is high, as investment and production in the nonagricultural sectors of a country increase, the income of the factor inputs, particularly wages, increases, and the effective demand for food goes up relatively more rapidly. Unless there is an increased supply of food to meet this increased demand, the price of food will go up. Farmers, or at least the people who own the food for sale, will receive more income in this case from the higher prices; but the people who buy the food will receive less for their money, which is the same as saying higher food prices and lowered real income. If the increased demand, and the resultant tendency for increased prices, calls forth more supply, more production through better use of factor inputs, then the price increase will not be high or may not even occur; and the result of the increase in demand is a higher level of production or productivity.

If the supply of food is price elastic, the producers will respond to the price increases by increasing production. This increased production will generally come from using more factor inputs and using them more fully and productively, so that both quantity and productivity will increase, which is a highly desirable outcome. Since there are large supplies of unutilized or poorly utilized labor in most rural areas, the efforts to increase agricultural production will increase productivity per worker. Land may be a relatively static input, but even here there will be a tendency to bring new land into cultivation, to shift land to more productive uses, and to double crops, if possible. Capital inputs in the form of better seeds, added fertilizer, more water, insecticides, and other investments will be increased and improved as farmers have more income to procure them and as production becomes more profitable due to higher prices. But while these basic relationships do develop, there are frictions and gaps that prevent the system from working rapidly or smoothly. These gaps may be shortages in essential inputs, such as fertilizer or water. They may be transportation inadequacies and the lack of communications. Most likely there will be difficulties arising from the structure of the agricultural production process. The technology of agriculture is subject to a time lag in the production process. In the case of added units of acreage, an additional cultivation may take a year or two to result in increments of output. For some land tenure systems and because of marketing inadequacies, the bulk of the increased profits in agriculture may go to dealers and large farmers, leaving small farmers, tenants and agricultural laborers with only scraps of the increased return. The incentives for increased production may soon lose their force, and the production response to price increases may be slow and uncertain.

The demand for food must be considered in relation to two other problems, urbanization and the shortage of foreign exchange that chara terizes nearly every one of the less developed countries. Urban populations, defined as people living in concentrations of population of 2500 and over, are increasing rapidly. The World Bank points out that:

> During the decade of the 1950's the urban population of the developing world expanded about 50 percent. Today, the major cities are doubling in size roughly every decade. By the year 2000, their total population will be some 500 percent higher than today. That means that from 1.2 to 1.6 billion more people will be living—if "living" is the proper word—in these sprawling centers of urban decay.[3]

Most of the workers in the modern production sector of the econom live in these urban areas, since these modern production units general need the complementarities and external economies that only populatio centers can provide. In examining the demand for food, the first concern of a government must be to assure that the supplies of food to the urban centers are adequate to meet demand, or else food prices will ri. As the incomes of the workers in the urban areas increase, the demand for food increases even more rapidly, and pressure on food prices is strong and sustained. If food prices rise too rapidly, several unpleasa effects are likely. The workers are unhappy and struggle for higher wages to offset the higher food prices. If costs of production go up, then general prices go up and an inflation is in progress. The increasi costs of domestic production will slow up exports and encourage imports, which will present prices that seem relatively lower if the domestic inflation is significant. The only people who will benefit direct will be the sellers of the food, and these benefits may or may not drift back to the agricultural laborers and peasant farmers. The economic effects of a sharp increase in the price of food are both widespread and serious.

Countries faced with rapidly rising food prices and a slow production response in agriculture have several alternative lines of action They can import enough food to slow down the price increase and make it tolerable, providing they have the foreign exchange to do so. They can concentrate enough of their capital and administrative capacity on helping agriculture increase its production. Or, what is more likely, they mix these two options, importing what they can and attempting to raise agricultural production as much as they can. Imports are the plea ant way out, if the loss in foreign exchange is not too drastic and visible. If some arrangements can be made for borrowing the foreign ex change for food at subsidized costs, or receiving it free as under the U.S. program for the disposal of surplus food (PL 480) or the Food for

Freedom Plan of the United Nations, then the importation of food to meet the rising demand becomes more pleasant and relatively painless. The real costs of such an import program, however, tend to be hidden. They are empirically unmeasurable but may be reflected in a loss of incentive to accelerate domestic food production. For short-term emergencies, as when monsoons fail and food production drops, imports of gift food may be a good response. But for the long run, when food demands from growing urban centers and from rising incomes create tendencies toward sharp increases in food prices, a country can best concentrate on the bottlenecks that limit the supply response. Since agricultural production takes time, the pressure of increased demand for food must be anticipated.

The Demand for Luxury Goods

The increasing demand for luxury goods is a common phenomenon in the less developed countries. The concept of a luxury good as nonessential is obviously relative, and one person's luxury may be considered another person's basic necessity. Luxury goods generally refer to higher priced foods, to some consumers' durable goods such as cars, air conditioners, radios, refrigerators, jewels, and fancy textiles. The definition is clearly arbitrary, and the many essential uses to which these goods are placed makes the definition less than accurate. Anyone who has lived through the heat of a summer in many of these countries will doubt the desirability of including air conditioners among nonessential goods. Yet, overlooking for the moment the question of accuracy in definition, there is no doubt that the rising income in the less developed countries is associated with an elastic demand for more expensive, less essential goods and services—the luxuries that are so often railed against by government planners yet continue to be demanded and purchased in ever increasing volume.

Two aspects of this problem are involved, the use of scarce factor inputs and the effect on savings and capital formation. If it could be assured that all factor inputs in the production of luxuries were relatively abundant, or that unutilized production capacity existed for the increased production of these luxuries, then the high income elasticity of the demand for luxuries would be useful in stimulating increased production and improved productivity. But generally, the only factor input in abundance is unskilled labor. All the other factor inputs, including skilled labor, materials, factory capacity, fuel and energy, and transportation are relatively scarce in most of the countries. To add to these difficulties, a significant number of these factor inputs have to be imported and often the luxury product, itself, is imported. This is an added consideration in the use of foreign exchange plus the opportunity cost of the alternative uses of foreign exchange in evaluating the desirability of producing or importing luxury goods.

147

The second consideration, the effect on savings and capital formation, arises from the fact that luxuries are generally demanded by the higher income classes of the population—those that provide the largest share of savings by individuals and families. Presumably, if luxuries were less available, there would be a greater possibility of savings. Limitation of the demand for luxuries is a widely held objective in almost all countries. It fits into nearly all moral codes, particularly in countries where so many are poor. It fits well into all schemes for shaping a better society. The less developed countries must particularly place visible emphasis on restricting the expansion of the demand for luxury goods, and of directing the resources that might be available for the production of luxuries to the production of products needed by the majority of the people. Thus the considerations against meeting the increased demand for luxuries seem compelling along both lines of analysis, the scarce factor inputs and the undesirable effects on savings and capital formation.

Yet, inevitably, governments that face sharply rising demands for luxuries are confronted with difficult choices and dilemmas that defy simple solution. First, there is the definitional problem, so easily waved aside in the previous paragraphs. Statisticians can handle this with a footnote, explaining the arbitrariness of these definitions; but governments are faced with concrete operating decisions that affect the lives and property of individuals and institutions. These arbitrary decisions always generate many deserving exceptions, and only an administrative system that is honest, trained, and flexible can handle these exceptions without producing public scandals that shake confidence in the entire administrative structure.

The point is worth illustration. The need for commercial and industrial air conditioners may be accepted because production records can be shown to prove that in a hot, humid climate, factory production and store operation increases significantly when air conditioning is installed. But the essentiality of home and office air conditioning is not so obvious, although the same elements enter into the consideration. If room air conditioners are limited to hotels frequented by tourists and to the houses of imported technicians, some relationship of cost benefits can be attempted. But the office air conditioners of foreigners leads to licensing of import sales of air conditioners, resale after the specific foreigner leaves, and the obvious cases where domestic ofcials and experts also could use air conditioners productively and with equal justice. The arbitrary limitation of use, the system of a government official's approval or disapproval, can and often does become the basis for favoritism and black market activities that drain both competence and self-respect from government administration. The public reaction to this is equally undesirable. Limitations, however, are often necessary, because the same resources involved in the production or import of air conditioners have opportunity costs far greater than the benefits of air conditioning for a relatively small proportion of the population.

The problem of controlling air conditioning is further complicated by adding to the illustration the fact of domestic production of air conditioners, using a substantial amount of imported materials and parts. Here considerations of employment and factory capacity add to the government's dilemma. A sharp curtailment of production, after it has once been permitted, means unemployment and a reduction of profits that may result in a loss of savings and a waste of existing capital that could not easily be converted to other uses. The amount of foreign exchange utilized by production must be compared with these immediate effects on employment, profits, and capital utilization; and the answer is never easy or devoid of well founded criticism.

To summarize, the demand for luxuries in the less developed countries is both price elastic and income elastic on the increase side.* Every one of the less developed countries faces sharp increases in the demand for luxuries and soon develops an administrative system that is supposed to define and control the production, import, and distribution of luxuries. The balance between effects on local employment and savings can only be roughly compared with opportunity costs and the complexities of administrative controls. It is an easy generalization, frequently made, to observe that in most countries the line of least resistance is to continue the domestic production of most of the products defined as luxuries, if this production has assumed significant size and involves considerable employment and capital. Few governments have been able to face the problems of actual closing of domestic facilities. Some efforts may be made to steer production toward more essential uses, as directing more closely that home and office air conditioners require certificates of productive use or medical certificates; but the effects are usually quite trivial and merely add to the administrative ineffectiveness of the control. It is not an exaggeration to assert that a large part of the industrial expansion in the less developed countries has been in the production of goods that are easily classified as luxuries from the viewpoint of a majority of the people. The need to economize in the use of foreign exchange has pushed import-substitution industries, to provide for the domestic production of luxuries previously imported. When incomes rise rapidly, high income families sharply increase their demand for luxuries; and this is reflected in the increased opportunities for higher profits in these industries. Low income families, unable to acquire the necessities they need, are impelled to question

---

*Only the increase side is considered, because prices of luxuries never seem to go down, and, in a developing country, incomes shouldn't go down. For most luxuries, the pent-up demand is so great that were prices and income to go down, it would probably be found that the demand for luxuries is inelastic, and would not change relatively as fast. Luxuries are very important to people who think they can afford them.

the integrity of an economic system that increases production of luxuries while unable to meet what seems to be reasonable minimum levels of production of necessities. Thus, the increasing demand for luxuries is not just an economic question requiring economic policies from government. Its social and political aspects far exceed its economic dimensions.

Demand for Foreign Exchange

In every discussion of the demand for goods and services in the less developed countries, there is either implicitly or explicitly a consideration of the demand for foreign exchange. In the examination of the demand for food, for capital, for luxuries, the impact on the demand for foreign exchange is so ubiquitous and essential that it must appear a part of every significant economic change in demand. Governments, consciously or unconsciously, have recognized this by making control of foreign exchange one of its most critical functions. Government allocation and control of foreign exchange is a part of the development and operation of nearly every economic institution, and presents to governments, rightly or wrongly, a powerful tool that can affect the operation of all important economic institutions. In a discussion of the changes in demand that affect changes in economic growth, it is useful to emphasize some general considerations of governmental policies and priorities that affect the demand for foreign exchange.

Government sets the climate and tone of the demand for foreign exchange. In this case, governmental practices may be more important than governmental policies; and the difference between policies and practices may be quite astonishing. The shortage of foreign exchange and the crippling constraints this applies to economic growth are a continuing subject of governmental announcements, press releases, and directives. No major allocations of resources, control orders, or licenses are issued without some reference to the hope that it will ease the foreign exchange shortage by reducing imports, or encouraging exports, or in some way change the demand for foreign exchange. While this aspect of scarcity is sometimes overemphasized to avoid scrutiny of other aspects more nearly related to the ability of government to change, the emphasis on the scarcity of foreign exchange is both understandable and real. Foreign exchange scarcity is unquestionably a critical scarcity and a major proximate bottleneck to increased production. Yet, while emphasizing the critical scarcity of foreign exchange, the government too often, in its practices, may stimulate the demand for foreign exchange and, by its practices, make more difficult the implementation of its own policies.

For example, some governments anxious to stimulate capital formation, but confronted with the usual shortage of foreign exchange, issue licenses and import permits for the construction of factories as long as the imported equipment is covered by a credit arrangement. Thus, for the construction of the plant, the only foreign exchange costs are those involved in the actual construction, such as the import of cement, steel, pipe, electrical equipment, and similar building materials. Where most of the building materials are fabricated domestically, the foreign exchange impact seems quite light; and many government authorities approve the factory construction without further reference to other long-range considerations that may affect the demand for foreign exchange. These include the repayment of the credit, including interest; the general effect on imports of such raw materials as copper, special machinery to produce building materials, oil, and other energy requirements; and general considerations of the income elasticity of imports. Consideration must also be given to any foreign exchange demands generated by the production that the new factory will make possible. The point is that while on any specific project the desirability of the capital to be formed may justify the increase in demand for foreign exchange, the policy of permitting capital formation based largely on available foreign exchange credits may be wrong. The success of foreign machinery salesmen into extending medium-term credit and thus receiving approval for relatively low priority projects that really increase the demand for foreign exchange in the future is one of the less-than-worthwhile aspects of the growing demand for foreign exchange.

By underpricing foreign exchange in terms of domestic currency, the government directly stimulates the demand for foreign exchange. The existence of this underpricing can be observed in almost all of the less developed countries by the presence of a widespread black or grey market for foreign exchange, where foreign exchange is purchased at exchange rates substantially in excess of the official rate. The demand on the illegal market arises from many diverse situations. Some of it represents capital flight, the efforts to convert money and other assets into a form that can be sent overseas, a process which most governments have declared illegal. Some of the demand comes from a desire to import some goods that otherwise could not be allowed, either goods for final consumption or as inputs into the production process. Thus, individuals may buy foreign exchange in order to pay for luxury imports, like cars, or for special motors needed on durable goods production. Others may buy foreign exchange in order to afford more expenditures on a controlled foreign trip that they are taking, or for sending some family member to school abroad. Usually no one seems to know the extent of the illegal market in terms of the amount of foreign exchange that it could absorb without having the price fall to the official exchange rate. The pent-up demand for foreign exchange is so great that it is likely that a premium for illegal foreign exchange could continue for a long time and cover immense amounts of local currency.

In the legal market, the underpricing of foreign exchange encourages capital formation by changing the factor proportions, favoring imported capital over domestic labor. By making imported capital cheap, relative to the price of that capital in the free or black market, the government encourages an entrepreneur to emphasize imported capital rather than domestic labor, if he has any option in the technology. In other words, because an imported crane may be relatively cheap, the entrepreneur building a foundry may decide to import the crane rather than to use less mechanical and more manual means of moving large castings. When the general rate is half of the free market rate, it seems to the entrepreneur that he is buying the imported capital at half the real price. The immediate effect of this is to increase the demand for foreign exchange. Most analysts would evaluate this as harmful, in net effect, or at least less beneficial than the type of capital formation more reasonable pricing of foreign exchange could be expected to bring out. The question is too indeterminate, given only the usual data, to warrant a definite conclusion. Much depends upon the externalities of imported capital, the opportunity costs, the long-range effects on production, savings and capital formation. In general, the stimulant to the demand for foreign exchange provided by the substantial underevaluation of foreign exchange adds significantly to the importance of foreign exchange control in the functions of government.

The demand for foreign exchange is usually so great, exceeding the supply by such a significant margin, that the authorization to utilize foreign exchange given by government has a market value and is frequently marketable. Import licenses are valuable because they are relatively scarce and are needed. By giving an import license to a specific production enterprise, the government is allocating a scarce resource and acting as an adjusting agency in reconciling the supply of foreign exchange with the demand. If, in the allocation process, the government stimulates demand, it is making its job of adjusting supply to demand more difficult, since the supply of foreign exchange is in a sense not determined by this demand. Where the demand for foreign exchange arises from an enterprise that will produce goods for export or reduce the need for imports through substituting domestic for foreign products, then the supply is directly related to the demand. But these represent only part of the demand for foreign exchange and are more easily identified and given priority.

The bulk of the demand for foreign exchange from producers are not that easily identified and form part of a large generalized mass of interrelated products and services. Thus, in a country that produces only half of the cement it needs, any construction using cement adds to the demand for foreign exchange, even though a specific project may certify that all its cement will be produced locally. The effect of considerations of this type is to make it necessary to examine the total demand for foreign exchange, as well as the specific demand, in order to examine options and alternative uses and costs.

In general, the price elasticity of the demand for imports is low while the income elasticity is high. This means that proportional changes in the price of imports are not associated with as high proportional changes in the demand for imports, but proportional changes in income generally are followed by even higher proportional changes in the demand for imports. As income rises in the less developed countries, they can expect the demand for imports to rise proportionately more, and the need for increasing exports and for the further controls of imports becomes even more pressing. A more rapid rate of economic growth therefore contains within itself the dynamic elements that create economic pressures on both imports and exports. While the intensity and scope of these pressures will vary from country to country, from product to product; and from time to time, it will be useful to examine the general shape of these elasticities as they affect broad classes of imports important in the less developed countries.

Imports of Capital Goods

Imported capital goods tend to have a high income elasticity of demand and a low price elasticity of demand. This means that the pressure for importing larger quantities of capital goods generally arises from increasing incomes, usually profits, and is discouraged by decreasing profits. Because capital formation involves discounting future returns, the cost-benefit analysis made, explicitly or implicitly, by all importers of capital goods involves anticipated as well as current income rates. Thus a possibility of increased profits tends to insure even more than a proportional increase in the imports of capital goods. The price elasticity of demand for imported capital goods is not high. Changes in prices of imported capital are generally associated with smaller changes in the demand for imported capital. Raising the prices of imported capital will, of course, reduce demand, but proportionately less, while lowering prices will not lead to greater than proportionate increases in the demand for imported capital goods. The importance of these differences to government policies is apparent. A government wishing to encourage capital formation using imported capital goods must pay more attention to changes in existing and anticipated profits than to the prices of these goods. Governments often feel that by maintaining a low price for imported capital through undervaluation of foreign exchange, they can encourage investment that would not otherwise be made. While this may be true in some cases, for the most part the effect may be to encourage capital-intensive investment to make it cheaper to import capital than to use domestic labor and to make possible a higher profit rate. Of course, the costs of capital goods and the anticipated profits from using these capital goods are functionally related; but there are other costs and determinants, such as confidence, security, incomes policy, inflation, and competition, that may be even more important than current capital costs in determining investment decisions.

Import of Consumers' Goods

The elasticities of demand for imported consumers' goods can best be examined by considering three classes of goods: (1) essential

153

consumers' goods, primarily basic foods, cheap textiles, medicines, and cheap household equipment; (2) luxury consumers' goods, such as cosmetics, canned fruits and vegetables, high cost textiles, finished clothing, furniture, paintings, and jewelry; and (3) durable household goods, such as refrigerators, stoves, fans, air conditioners, automobiles, and so forth.

It should be noted that the price elasticity of the demand for imported essential consumers' goods is low, while the income elasticity is high. Thus, increased prices do not change proportionately the demand for imported essential goods. Most people, even families with low incomes, will continue to demand imported essential goods and textiles in the face of price increases. The demand response to price increases will not be completely inelastic. Some drop in demand will result from higher prices for imports; but the drop is generally proportionately less than the price increase and may not be apparent at times of extreme shortages until prices are very much higher. Higher income levels, however, will generally be associated with even greater proportionate increases in the demand for imported essential consumers' goods. The reasons for this are quite understandable. Usually imported consumers' goods are not available from local production, or are higher in quality or have status values that domestic products do not have. A rise in income of the low income families, who are the major consumers of imported essential consumers' goods, will be reflected rapidly into an increase in the demand and a willingness to pay a higher price.

The demand for luxury consumers' goods is generally inelastic for both price and income changes. These luxuries are, by definition, generally consumed by higher income families. The demand for these imports do not change proportionately as prices change or as income levels of a country change. An increase in the price of imported perfume will not seriously discourage its demand by wealthy families, nor will an increase in the income of the family significantly increase the demand. This characteristic of the demand for imported luxuries is the basic reason why governments that feel they can afford to use scarce foreign exchange for the import of luxuries can usually place high import duties on these luxuries without destroying their salability. The higher the price, the more they seem to be valued for their status values.

The demand for imported durable consumers' goods is probably price inelastic, but seems income elastic. Durable consumers' goods are purchased largely by upper income families who rapidly become accustomed to the useful and pleasant services provided by refrigerators, cars, air conditioners, and other modern appliances. Usually there is a status value in acquiring these goods; and for these, the higher the price the greater the status symbol becomes. A demonstration effect, both from outside as well as within the country, adds to the desirability of possession. The demand for durable consumers' goods rapidly increases in a society where profits for enterprises are high, and focuses on imports, since most of the durable consumers' goods must be imported. Quality and status considerations may add to the discrimination in favor of imports as contrasted with any domestically produced products.

In general, changes in income levels are far more related to changes in the demand for imports than are price increases. As a country improves its production and productivity, increasing income levels bring increasing pressure for imports of all kinds, both capital and consumers' goods. These reflect not only increasing purchasing power, but also the inability of domestic enterprises to provide the same kinds of products, as well as the demonstration effect—the increasing demand resulting from observing how others enjoy additional or new products. This continuing, ever growing pressure for imports is one of the basic economic forces that confronts governments attempting to speed up their rate of economic growth.

Rural Demand and Production

Demand in rural areas is so important that it involves some additional consideration. The demand for food in rural areas is quite complicated and seems to contradict many of the assumptions about economic rationality and production responses to increased prices. Many, if not most, of the people engaged in agricultural production in the less developed countries consume less food than they wish and are near or even below bare subsistence levels. An increased income, arising from an increase in production or an increase in prices, or a combination of both, will generally elicit an increase in their demand for food. Often, this is manifested by the reduced sale of food to the market since the peasant producer may be able to retain more food and still earn as much money through higher prices. This phenomenon of a smaller supply offered for sale when prices rise has been argued as a contradiction to the assumption of economic rationality among the peasant and subsistence farmers. It should be clear, however, that this is not a basic contradiction and is easily reconciled with rationality. A backward-bending food supply curve usually is a short-term phenomenon, in that over a period of time, with significant price rises, the general tendency even in the subsistence areas is to offer more for sale and to substitute less costly foods at home to achieve both more earnings and more food. In some localities, this backward-bending food supply curve may be a fact for some of the population; but it does not often affect a market enough to be a serious factor. There are usually too many large farmers and farmers who need money for other products to reverse the supply increase completely, although it can be slowed down.

Rural demand for nonfood items is particularly important. It represents the possibility of encouraging or even creating an attitude of effort or achievement in production that is very important among low productivity agricultural sectors of the population. The apathy toward increased effort and the negligible hopes for increased returns make this segment of the working force inefficient factor inputs as well as reducing their effectiveness as citizens of a country that is striving for modernization. Incentives for increased effort and increased productivity are so essential that governments often must overlook the apparent luxury nature of certain products purchased by rural workers. The demand for such desirable consumers' goods as bicycles, watches, radios, clocks, flashlights, and even luxury textiles as nylon and expensive clothing, may become so important as incentives to greater effort that the use of scarce foreign exchange may be justified in order to meet the demand. The problem of controlling supply so that it goes to meet this rural demand, and not urban demand, often presents such extensive administrative and control problems that governments avoid the task and permit imports of these items freely. The availability of some so-called luxury items may be an essential part of achieving higher production and productivity in agriculture.

Coupled with the desirability of incentive goods to meet increased rural demand is the need to develop larger markets for domestic production of industrial goods. Most countries begin developing a manufacturing capacity by increasing the number of small factories producing durable and semidurable consumers goods. Farmers have managed to live without clocks, radios, bicycles, and refrigerators for centuries; yet the new manufacturing industries being developed need large markets for their products, and the largest part of the population live in rural areas. The development of growing markets for the products of a modern manufacturing sector of the economy may be essential to the development of the manufacturing capacity itself. Capital formation to meet pent-up, existing demand in urban areas is soon shown to be too limited to be an appropriate force for modernizing technology. Potential demand increases in the rural areas must be taken into account, or the domestic market often remains too small to require modern production technology. Economies of scale are impossible if only the potential urban demand is considered. Consequently, the increasing demand for manufactured products in rural areas has to be used constructively to stimulate and make profitable the domestic production of consumer goods and capital equipment that forms an increasing part of the modern manufacturing capacity.

The problem of apathy and lack of interest in efforts for improved production and productivity is complex and often misunderstood. That it exists in reality cannot be doubted, but its complex roots defy the kinds of simple solutions that many people think social problems should have. Production apathy can come from many different causes, abject poverty and near starvation, a sense of complete social injustice and hopelessness, a religious attitude towards material possessions and an ignorance of the possibility of achieving any increase in comfort and well-being. These clearly involve the psychological and value systems of a people, its social structure, its systems of political, religious, and cultural relationships, authority and power, that make the economic aspect only one and clearly not always the most important element of this complex.

Yet, if the welfare of a rural people is related positively to the acquisition of more of the economic products of the society, to more goods and services, then the increase in demand of the lower strata of a rural society must be considered as necessary and desirable for the modernization of a society. Certainly, economists and administrators know that it will be almost impossible to achieve higher productivity in the rural areas without modifying this apathy toward more effort and greater efficiency. The need for developing markets of the modern manufacturing sector is associated with the need to increase the feeling in the rural areas that additional effort to produce agricultural products is worthwhile and will be rewarded by acquiring more goods, both agricultural and nonagricultural.

In attempting to interrupt the vicious circles of interrelated inadequacies, any and all break-in possibilities must be utilized. Breaking into the stagnation of productive effort in the rural areas and the constraints on production from small rural markets is essential for countries that wish to achieve more rapid and sustained rates of economic growth. The stagnation in effort, ideas, and expectations that exists in many parts of rural areas is a real obstacle to progress, even if it may not be absolute and may not affect the upper and middle levels of farmers. A large injection of additional purchasing power will, over a reasonable period of time, stir up this stagnation, and provide a possibility for some of the value changes that are necessary if production and productivity are to increase. This increase in purchasing power can be initiated in several ways: by local works programs, by extensive government projects in rural areas, and by specific price subsidies and controls. These have many difficulties. They are all characterized by the need for adequate public administration, which is a scarce input indeed, particularly in the rural areas where it is so important that demand changes be utilized to stimulate production.

By itself, a sharp increase in rural demand for nonagricultural products is unlikely to be very productive. Unless the production enterprises are so adjusted that increased production will be the response to potential or actual sharp increases in rural demand, the net result may be to shift purchasing power from the rural areas to the urban areas. Large injections of purchasing power in the rural areas, to be effective as a tool for modernization, must be associated with policies and priorities by government and by the production system in general that enables a response in terms of higher production and improved productivity.

These necessary assertions can be associated with an observation about the role of transportation and communication in helping break up rural stagnation and apathy. Rural works programs that concentrate on roads and the general improvement of transportation and communication have many externalities. Not only do the labor input requirements generally include large numbers of unskilled labor, but the community response is generally immediate and visible. Roads may mean new market contacts, additional information about costs and benefits, technological changes, the possibility of more choices in both purchases and sales of factor inputs and products, and the possibility of specialization that is so essential to increased productivity. Rural road programs, of course, require much more than unskilled labor. The need for technical skills in design and work supervision are associated with a requirement for adequate public administration. The desirability of both the roads and the jobs on the roads opens a wide variety of opportunities for inefficient, even corrupt priorities. Yet, the possibility and need remains, and a local works program limited largely to roads might readily develop the kind of institutions that would channel an adequate set of management and technical skills for a larger continuing program of more diversified construction.

GOVERNMENT POLICIES AND PRACTICES AFFECTING DEMAND

Government policies and practices obviously are important in determining the size and direction of demand for factor inputs, for intermediate products, and for the goods and services that are available to final consumers. Since changes in demand are an essential and powerful influence in production, they can be used by governments in their efforts to achieve modernization. Indeed, nearly all the economic objectives of modernization can be expressed in terms of the size and distribution of effective demand that is met by the economic system. When the mass of poor people at the bottom of the income distribution pattern are able to receive enough income to provide effective demand and receive enough goods and services for a minimum decency level of living, the modernization process could well be classified as successful, at least in economic terms. The demands for goods and services are affected by many institutions, particularly those economic institutions whose major purpose is to stimulate improvements in production and productivity. Government policies and practices are important elements in these institutions, many times the most essential element. Because changes in demand can cause changes in production, it is useful to examine more specifically the types of government policies and practices that are used to affect demand and the institutions through which many of these changes in demand are channeled to affect production and productivity.

Every economic institution involves some aspects of demand. In examining economic institutions that affect demand, in the context of efforts to achieve a rapid rate of economic growth, it is necessary to have two approaches. First, it is useful to identify some special kinds of institutions that are particularly important in channeling or framing demand—institutions that can help change demand in a way that helps to achieve the objective of modernizing the economy. Second, it is useful to identify those government policies and priorities that, working through these and other institutions, affect demand in ways that are important to achieve the modernization of economic activities. Some of these institutions, policies, and priorities have been discussed as they affect production, since institutions that affect production must necessarily affect the demand for factor inputs. Market institutions are particularly important here.

Market Institutions

Market institutions are institutions that are designed to facilitate the communication between suppliers and buyers, with the objective of encouraging transactions between them. Thus, markets can be for products or for services. They can be for factor inputs, for intermediate products and services, or for products and services in final consumption transactions. They can encompass the whole transaction, as in a food market, or they can facilitate the flow of different elements to the final transaction. In all markets, supply and demand manifest themselves in the selling and purchasing transactions of the participants. Markets are institutions frequently used by governments to shape demand to meet its economic objectives. But markets may be difficult to conceptualize because they are often vague and formless in an objective sense, such as the insurance market or even the money market. Because of this difficult conceptualization, some markets are neglected by government although governmental actions, directly or indirectly, may strongly affect these markets.

Obviously, government rules and regulations for specific markets affect their ability and efficiency in executing transactions. Where, for example, government requires that an entrepreneur receive a license before he can utilize a market institution to purchase large diesel engines, the policies adopted in issuing licenses for diesel engines shape the demand for diesel engines. Where licenses are issued only to large enterprises or persons with influence, the government is shaping the demand in a way that will have important consequences on subsequent production operations that depend on large diesels. Price regulations for specific products or services also affect the market institutions that are organized for transactions in these products. Thus, an arbitrarily low price set for a particular commodity, for example, fish, may remove all fish from the controlled market and send the available supply to other, often illegal, markets. The legal regulations of a market may often shape the quantity and direction of demand that a market institution may channel. Thus, rules for the ownership and sale of land may so affect the nature of the effective demand for land that its price may become very speculative, or very high, restricting new ownership to persons with great risk capabilities rather than those that use the land as factor inputs in a production process.

Often, too, government can make existing markets more effective and efficient in their transactions processes. The effort of government to collect and publish economic data such as prices, imports, exports, retail sales, and so forth, improves the information of market participants. Since market operations tend to decentralize decision making, both on the demand as well as on the supply side, the better the information available to buyers and sellers in the market, the more likely they are to make the correct decisions. One does not have to believe that markets are the only or even the best means of shaping demand to accept the basic concept that market institutions, used within the framework of social purpose, can improve the efficiency with which factor inputs and intermediate and final products are related to the production process.

Institutions Affecting the Demand for Capital

The demand for capital is so strongly shaped by governmental policies and priorities that a large part of the achievements and defeats in capital formation can be placed directly on government. There are several ways of viewing this relationship between government and the demand for capital. Much of the capital fund in a less developed country is directly attributable to government expenditures. Thus, government, in its purchases of machinery and equipment, in its construction of factory buildings, roads, schools, houses, and hospitals, directly creates the demand for capital that strongly affects the demand for factor inputs in the creation of this capital. A government that is vigorously pushing public capital formation is competing in the demand for the resources used in capital formation. Indeed, governments create special institutions to expedite the gathering and availability of financial resources for capital formation such as central banks, development banks, and rural credit institutions. Governments also compete in the effective demand for the resources that these institutions are channelizing. Government projects may draw large shares of resources from these institutions or from government institutions that compete with private institutions for resources used in capital formation.

In any discussion of the ways in which government affects the demand for capital, emphasis must be given to the effect of government policies and priorities on the security and predictability of future production. In the discussions on savings and capital formation, the point was made that evaluation of the future has a critical role to play here. Government shapes the demand for capital by its actions and policies in making the future return for capital formation seem more certain and worthwhile. Here, the term worthwhile is meant to convey more than monetary profitability, although that is certainly a large element of becoming worthwhile. But social status, security, cultural patterns, psychological evaluation—all play important roles when judging the worthiness of future returns and the prospects of monetary profits. Government policies and actions clearly affect the shape and direction of the future and therefore affect the demand for capital. A government that wishes to expand capital formation in the manufacture of textiles and announces that some time in the future (time uncertain) it intends to nationalize all textile manufacturing plants, will not have much success in encouraging the demand for capital to be formed in this sector. Uncertainty about price fixing, about the import policy on specific raw materials, on spare parts, on the continuation of subsidies or of import restrictions on competitive products—these are the types of government policies and priorities that strongly affect the demand for capital and shape its nature to the advantage and disadvantage of the country's efforts to achieve a high rate of economic growth.

Government can also shape the size and composition of the demand for capital through its policies that affect the cost-benefit ratios of capital formation. By underpricing foreign exchange, government can stimulate the demand for imported capital equipment. By issuing licenses for certain industries and not for others, government can help determine in an important way the composition of the capital being formed, whether it concentrates on import substitution products, or luxuries to be produced for the wealthy, or on the production of wage goods used by the big mass of the people. Government tax policies, particularly such measures as tax holidays and tax differentials, clearly affect the nature of the demand for capital and for the future products of capital. Often overlooked, this latter point is important because it gives direction to capital formation. The demand for capital depends, in a basic sense, on the anticipated demand for the products of the capital. The policies of government that shape final demand affect quite clearly the demand for capital. Thus, if a society adopts policies that directly or indirectly shape demand in the direction of those products that are consumed by the wealthier members of the society, then the demand for capital will tend to be of a nature that will produce those kinds of goods. Where the demand for wage goods is different from these goods, the demand for capital will be different. Development banks that are operated to supply resources to enterprises that produce luxury and semiluxury goods demanded by the wealthier fifth of the families may not produce goods required by the lowest income families. For a society as a whole, the nature of the demand for capital may be largely determined by the composition of the demand for final consumers—by the nature of the distribution of income.

The demand for consumption goods and services is the strongest, broadest based type of demand that affects economic production and productivity. The government's role in shaping the consumption demand is both large and critical. Clearly, consumption demand is a function of income distribution, the pattern of payments to the factors involved in the production process. Many institutions affect income distribution and government's income and expenditure arrangements are among the most important. Thus, how a government collects taxes and how it distributes its goods and services, demonstrate the nature of the institutions developed to affect the demand for consumption products. Any institution that affects income distribution affects the shape of the demand for consumption goods and services. Cartels that improve profits, unions that raise wages, credit unions that permit small growers to keep their agricultural surplus until prices go up, transportation that permits more widespread participation in improved market prices—all are instances of institutions that affect income distribution and hence the demand for consumption goods and services.

To the extent that the governments of the less developed countries are able to create institutions that redistribute income by transfer payments to the low income families, they are, through these institutions, affecting the demand for consumption. Thus, payments to the indigent and to the unfortunate make demand for consumers' goods effective where they are badly needed. Where an increase of consumption is considered as a loss to resources available for capital formation, this increase in consumption may be viewed as a drawback to economic growth. But, all consumption cannot be considered as the opposite of savings and capital formation. Some consumption increases may be more important than capital formation, important to future production as well as to the continuity of the society. Consumption that destroys the apathy of the desperately poor and convinces them that it is worthwhile to try to improve their economic status through more effort may be far more important than a new factory or an automatic telephone system. Welfare institutions, systems of reaching the desperately poor through work programs and service programs may be the most important institutions that a government can create to help achieve higher productivity.

Government practices and institutions designed to improve consumer understanding of the use and value of products are another means of influencing consumer demand. Here, such programs as home economics, nutrition, health, and sanitation seem to work against overall policies to hold down consumption; but scarcely anyone would reject these necessary programs because of their general effect on increased consumption. Other effects, for example, the improvement of labor as a factor input and the improvement in general well-being, more than compensate for the tendency to increase consumption.

Institutions Affecting the Demand for Technology

Since technology requires the improvement of factor inputs, the institutions that affect demand for production clearly affect the demand for technology. Yet several additional institutions deserve to be identified because they are important in government efforts to increase productivity through improved technology. First, there are the government institutions deliberately designed to study the application of new methods of production, the laboratories and institutes of research and development. Sometimes these are general, as a Bureau of Standards, or they may be specific, relating to markets such as pulp and paper, wood or agriculture. The latter, the experimental farms and agricultural research centers, are particularly important in this connection.

Government approval and stimulation of the demand for improved technology is demonstrated and participated in by all the agencies that control the efforts to improve the quality of the factor inputs, particularly labor and capital. The ease and freedom with which resources are allocated to new ventures in technology, the importance given to efforts to train labor and to create or import capital including new technology are continuous, visible indications of how government affects the demand for new technology. The resources that the Ministry of Education is devoting to modern vocational and technical high schools, as compared with the allocation to traditional high schools, for example, speaks louder about the government's efforts to increase the demand for technological improvements than do all the public relations press releases of the Information Ministry.

The demand for improved technology is too diffused to be easily identified, yet its importance is basic to an understanding of how government institutions can be effective in raising production and productivity. When a government research agency finds a way to achieve more efficient use of local resources, but cannot influence producers to adopt its recommendations because it is easier and more profitable to secure government permission to import materials, then government influence on the demand for improved technology leaves something to be desired.

NOTES

1. I.I.O. Studies and Reports New Series, Employment and Economic Growth (Geneva: International Labor Office, 1964), p. 54.

2. W. Arthur Lewis, Developing Planning (New York: Harper & Row 1969), p. 90.

3. Address by Robert S. McNamara, President of the World Bank, IFC and IDA, as reported in International Financial News Survey 20, no. 39 (October 3, 1969): 315.

CHAPTER

6

DISTRIBUTION OF
THE PRODUCT OF
ECONOMIC ACTIVITIES

CONCEPTS OF INCOME DISTRIBUTION

The distribution of the product of an economy is of great interest to everybody and of passionate concern to most.[*] Its problems come close to being the center of the ideology of a country, the basic reason for attempting to achieve modernization with its higher level of production and productivity. The well-being of the people of a country is related not only to how much goods and services are available but also to how these are distributed. The changes in distribution are so closely related to how a country is governed and how a country wishes to change or protect its social structure that the economic aspects of distribution are often a minor element, sometimes even irrelevant in decisions on distribution policies and institutions. Yet the changes in income closely and strongly affect both production and demand—sometimes acting as an obstruction to economic growth and sometimes acting as a stimulant. Thus, the economic impact of changes in distribution must be considered in government policies and practices, even though at any point the political and social aspects of distribution of income may be the determining elements. In addition, many economic policies and practices involve distributional changes that may or may not be

---

[*]It is worthwhile again to warn the noneconomists of the pitfalls of economic jargon. Distribution here means the shares of the product of the economic system—who gets the goods and services produced, and not the physical movement of goods. The total production equals the total distribution, by definition. Therefore the total of shares of the product is the same as the total income of the factor inputs.

consistent with other noneconomic objectives of a modernizing society
The increase in the income of the poor is one of the objectives of modernization that may be said to have an "intrinsic value," to use the
phrase of Gunnar Myrdal, as well as an economic impact. Its intrinsic
value lies in the fact that it is one of the basic objectives of modernization, a definition of the generalized objective to improve the general
welfare of the people. It is a good result by itself, considered apart
from its effect on production and productivity.

General Concepts

In examining the distribution of income within a country, several
general concerns must be kept in mind.
It is difficult to select a unit for aggregate analysis that is most
meaningful in all problems. Is income per capita or income per family
the best unit? How should the income of business units, owned by individuals or families, be considered? In the most common analysis of
income distribution, the unit selected is the family or the consumption
unit. Its income is derived from payments to its members as workers
and managers in production enterprises or as owners of property for
which the family units receive property income. Wages and salaries
would be payment for human services performed in the production process, while profits, interest, and rent paid would be income received
by the family because it owns property, either as physical property
(land, buildings, and so forth) or as stock shares, bank balances, part
nerships, or proprietorships of business enterprises. Thus, the concept of income distribution and evaluation of income inequality must
go beyond the business enterprises to consideration of the disposable
income of final consuming units, the families whose members work in
business enterprises or receive rent on property, and interest on saving
and dividends distributed by business enterprises to their owners.*
Both the absolute amount and the relative level of income are important. Income is both physical and psychological, and to neglect
either is to ensure inadequate analysis. It is often difficult to say

_____

*While wishing to avoid technical discussions that are far more
trouble than they are worth, it is necessary to point out that the difficulty of sorting out payments for work from payments from ownership
of unincorporated enterprises makes it necessary to consider all such
income as a return for employment rather than from property. Small
entrepreneurs generally receive a rather low payment for a great deal
of work, rather than property income from owning their property. The
effect of this obvious inadequacy on the limited generalizations that
can be advanced from existing data is only minor.

166

which is more important—the actual physical goods and services that a family receives as its income, or the satisfaction it gains from the recognition and appreciation by others of its ability to receive the goods and services. Psychological income, difficult as it is to measure, is important as an element of motivation, and is therefore an important part of all economic transactions. At the lowest levels of subsistence, the physical level of income may seem to be the most important. The need to supply the minimum necessary amounts of food and clothing seem overriding. But even at these low levels, the relative level of income is important, when all around seem to be receiving the barest minimum. The condition seems more bearable than when some are obviously receiving more. As the level of income rises among classes of people, the relative income becomes an even more visible element in motivation and in economic transactions. The demonstration effect, discussed in chapter 5, is an important aspect of economic behavior that must be considered in examining such problems as the consumption patterns for food, the demand for imports, and the potential demand for industrial products.

Changes in income, both past and prospective, are often as important as actual or relative levels of income. The recognition or hope that levels of real income can change is an important force in the modernization process. In a traditional society, income and status are fixed, more or less static, by the structure of society, by the relationships that are the steel framework of tradition. As a society modernizes and the production process improves its technology and achieves higher levels of productivity, income changes both absolutely and relatively among the different groups within a society. The prospect or hope of income improvement is one of the most explosive elements in social change and in the drive for modernizing a society. Therefore, the changes of income that have occurred in the recent past and the expectations of future income changes are important elements of economic behavior, both as causes and effects of economic actions.

In considering the income of a family or household, it is essential that the definition of income be as broad as possible. Restricting the definition to monetary income would of course be so limiting as to be almost meaningless, particularly in the less developed countries that have large parts of their economic activities carried out in nonmonetary terms. Thus, production for self use, as in the case of agricultural products, is a large part of the total product; even in the developed countries some provision must be made to impute the value of the nonmarketed goods produced. Income technically should include services received from stocks of consumers' durable goods, such as houses, cars, refrigerators, as well as the infrastructure of a society, such as roads, buildings, and so forth. Usually, these present too many statistical problems to be measured, and subsistence income in the less developed countries tends to be substantially understated in the data on income distribution.

167

The serious impact of income changes cannot be evaluated by merely looking at changes in the average income of the total society or even the shares of the different levels of society. Some evaluation, though measurement is practically impossible, must be made of the degree of openness of the movement of families from one level to another. Another way of visualizing this aspect of income distribution is expressed in the term vertical mobility, the capability families in lower levels have of moving to higher segments. The tragedy of inadequate income distribution is epitomized in the extent to which the lowest income group, say the lowest third or lowest half of the income receivers, are locked in to their poverty without the means or hope of moving into a higher level.

Since levels of income are important, both in absolute terms as well as relative to others' income, it is necessary to emphasize the often overlooked point that income is a flow of money, of claims on goods and services, over a period of time. Income is not a stock or inventory of goods. The stock of goods is defined as wealth; and while the two are obviously related, they are not the same. The importance of this distinction is overwhelmingly great because it emphasizes the basic truth that improved income distribution must come largely from greater production, not from inventories of goods. A redistribution of wealth may be part of the income distribution plans of a society, but only because wealth affects the production process and the distribution of income. The ownership of some of the factor inputs, land and capital, will determine who can work and how the shares of the product will be distributed among the inputs. Low productivity usually means low incomes for those who do not own the capital and land that must be associated with their labor. Simply taking the existing stock of goods and factor inputs of a country, its land, capital, and consumers' goods and dividing this inventory among the mass of low income people may be important for political and social reasons; but its importance for economic purposes lies largely in its effect on future production and income distribution. Over any significant period of time the level of consumption of a people must depend on the level of production and productivity of its economic enterprises. Clearly, different kinds of societies will have different methods of distributing income. Even in the most statistician-ridden countries, only partial answers can be given to these questions. It is obvious that there are rich households and poor households, and the poor ones far outnumber the rich ones. But whether the number of each is growing and by how much, is almost beyond our ability to count. No country can completely answer these questions, and only a few of the most advanced countries can provide good hints at some of the answers. The developing countries have provided only fragmentary data that are subject to varying interpretation—most of the answers given by governments are the results of wishful thinking, rather than empirical studies. Research in income distribution is technically difficult. It requires endless questionnaires and careful record keeping, both anathema to most countries. While the data vailable for the developed countries are somewhat more complete and eliable than the data for the less developed countries, they are far om unambiguous. Yet the questions asked are so important to the role f public administration in economic growth that even partial answers ay serve some useful purposes if they are not taken too literally.

The Extent of Inequality of Income

The distribution of household income is about the best overall measre of inequality of income distribution. It includes, or attempts to inlude, not only salaries and wages but also income from property and istributed profits, all before payment of income taxes. Its measureent is so difficult that even conceptually intercountry comparisons are ifficult to make.* Yet enough partial studies have been made to proide ample evidence of wide inequality of income distribution.

There is marked inequality of income distribution in the less deeloped and developed countries, regardless of their level of developent. Table 6.1 shows this clearly.

---

*Questions of public benefits and imputed incomes that vary from ountry to country make consistent definitions almost impossible. Varyng and different price levels add to the confusion.

There are several ways of measuring the inequality of income disribution:

1. The "Gini" concentration ratio or coefficient, which compares n equal distribution (10 percent of the households receiving 10 percent f the income, 50 percent of the households receiving 50 percent of the ncome, and so forth) with a Lorenz Curve showing the cumulative perentages of households and the percentage of the total income they ctually receive. The difficulty of this coefficient is that two quite issimilar distributions can have similar coefficients if their Lorenz urves intersect, which happens quite frequently. [See A. B. Atkinson, On the Measurement of Inequality," _Journal of Economic Theory_ 2, o. 3 (September 1970): 244-63.]

2. The coefficient of variation, which measures the spread of variation of income distribution compared with the average.

3. The standard deviation of the logarithms of the income distriution.

4. The shares of the top income receivers compared with the lowest ncome receivers.

ach of these measures has some advantages and disadvantages, and ll are cast into doubt by the lack of precision of the data. The last neasure, a comparison of the shares of top and bottom groups of houseolds, is used here as the simplest and most expressive of the inequalty that exists in actual income distribution.

169

TABLE 6.1

Cross-classification of Countries by Income Level and Equality

HIGH INEQUALITY
Share of lowest 40% less than 12%

Country(yr.)	Per capita GNP US$	L'st 40%	Mid 40%	Top 20%
Kenya(1969)	136	10.0	22.0	68.0
Sierra Leone (1968)	159	9.6	22.4	68.0
Iraq(1956)	200	6.8	25.2	68.0
Philippines (1971)	239	11.8	34.6	53.8
Senegal(1960)	245	10.0	26.0	64.0
Ivory Coast (1970)	247	10.8	32.1	57.1
Rhodesia(1968)	252	8.2	22.8	69.0
Tunisia(1970)	255	11.4	33.6	55.0
Honduras(1968)	265	6.5	28.5	65.0
Ecuador(1970)	277	6.5	20.0	73.5
El Salvador (1969)	295	11.2	36.4	52.4
Turkey(1968)	282	9.3	29.9	60.8
Malaysia(1970)	330	11.6	32.4	56.0
Colombia(1970)	358	9.0	30.0	61.0
Brazil(1970)	390	10.0	28.4	61.5

MODERATE INEQUALITY
Share of lowest 40% between 12% & 17%

Country(yr.)	Per capita GNP US$	L'st 40%	Mid 40%	Top 20%
Burma(1956)	82	16.5	38.7	44.8
Dahomey(1959)	87	15.5	34.5	50.0
Tanzania(1967)	89	13.0	26.0	61.0
India(1964)	99	18.0	32.0	52.0
Madagascar (1960)	120	13.5	25.5	61.0
Zambia(1959)	230	14.5	28.5	57.0
Dominican Rep. (1969)	323	12.2	30.3	57.5
Iran(1958)	332	12.5	22.0	54.5

LOW INEQUALITY
Share of lowest 40%, 17% and above

Country(yr.)	Per capita GNP US$	L'st 40%	Mid 40%	Top 20%
Chad(1958)	78	18.0	39.0	43.0
Sri Lanka(1969)	95	17.0	37.0	46.0
Niger(1960)	97	18.0	40.0	42.0
Pakistan(1964)	100	17.5	37.5	45.0
Uganda(1970)	125	17.1	35.8	47.1
Thailand(1970)	180	17.0	37.5	45.5
Korea(1970)	235	18.0	37.0	45.0
Taiwan(1964)	241	20.4	39.5	40.1
Surinam(1952)	394	21.7	35.7	42.6
Greece(1957)	500	21.0	29.5	49.5

Income up to US$300

Country (year)	GNP per capita			
Gabon (1968)	497	8.8	23.7	67.5
Jamaica (1958)	510	8.2	30.3	61.5
Costa Rica (1971)	521	11.5	30.0	63.5
Mexico (1969)	645	10.5	25.5	64.0
South Africa (1965)	669	6.2	35.8	58.0
Panama (1969)	692	9.4	31.2	59.4
Venezuela (1970)	1004	7.9	27.1	65.0
Finland (1962)	1599	11.1	39.6	49.3
France (1962)	1913	9.5	36.8	53.7

Income US$300-$750

Country (year)	GNP per capita			
Lebanon (1960)	558	13.0	28.0	61.0
Uruguay (1968)	618	15.5	35.5	46.0
Chile (1968)	744	13.0	30.2	56.8
Argentina (1970)	1079	16.5	36.1	47.4
Puerto Rico (1968)	1100	13.7	35.7	50.6
Netherlands (1967)	1980	13.6	37.9	48.5
Norway (1968)	2010	16.6	42.9	40.5
Germany, Fed. Rep. (1964)	2144	15.4	31.7	52.9
Denmark (1968)	2563	13.6	38.8	47.6
New Zealand (1969)	2859	15.5	42.5	42.0
Sweden (1963)	2949	14.0	42.0	44.0

Income above US$750

Country (year)	GNP per capita			
Bulgaria (1962)	530	25.8	40.6	33.2
Spain (1965)	750	17.6	36.7	45.7
Poland (1964)	850	23.4	40.6	36.0
Japan (1963)	950	20.7	39.3	40.0
United Kingdom (1968)	2015	18.8	42.2	39.0
Hungary (1969)	1140	24.0	42.5	33.5
Czechoslovakia (1964)	1150	27.6	41.4	31.0
Australia (1968)	2509	20.0	41.2	38.8
Canada (1965)	2920	20.0	39.8	40.2
United States (1970)	4850	19.7	41.5	38.8

Source: S. Jain and A. Tiemann, Size Distribution of Income: A Compilation of Data, Development Research Center Discussion Paper No. 4, World Bank, Washington, D.C., 1973.

Note: The income shares of each percentile group were read off a free-hand Lorenz curve fitted to observed points in the cumulative distribution. The distributions are for pretax income. Per capita GNP figures are taken from the World Bank data files and refer to GNP at factor cost for the year indicated in constant 1971 U.S. dollars.

In this table countries are grouped by per capita income and by income inequality.

	Low	Moderate	High
Per Capita Income in US$	Below $300	$300-750	Above $750
Income Inequality Percent of income received by lowest 40 percent of families	Below 12	12-17	Above 17

Source: S. Ahluwalia Montek, "Income Inequality: Some Dimension of the Problem," Finance and Development (International Monetary Fund and World Bank Group, Washington, D.C.) 2, no. 3 (September 1974):

There are developed and less developed countries in all three categories of income inequality. There seems to be some evidence that countries that are just beginning their modernization process have a somewhat more equitable income distribution than the other less developed countries.[*] Of course, this more equitable distribution is for a very low income, as productivity in these countries is among the lowest. As a country develops its modern production sector, the inequality of income distribution seems to increase, although many of the poorer families may be better off because the average income is rising. When the countries achieve a fairly large modern sector, and this sector is beginning to be a large part of the total production process, the middle class of income receivers increases its share by reducing the relative shares of both the upper and lower income families. This conforms to the folk-wisdom that the middle class is relatively small in the less developed countries, seeming to grow as the average income grows.[1]

Income inequality data now available shows that it is not possible to identify the characteristics of a society that are most closely related to income inequality. The level of per capita income, the share of agriculture in the total product, the rate of growth of the economy, growth of education and population explain a large part of the differences in equality of income distribution between countries, but no way has yet

---

[*]It used to be accepted that the distribution of income in the less developed countries was less equal than in the developed countries, but later studies cast doubt on this. Some of the economists and leaders from the less developed countries have resented this conclusion of greater income inequality in their countries, as if it cast aspersions on their ethical and moral standards. It is really an unimportant observation, as the average income is so much higher in the developed countries. See S. Kuznets, Modern Economic Growth (New Haven: Yale University Press, 1967).

been found to include in the analysis such important influences as concentration of wealth, markets and other institutions.

If high income inequality in a country is defined as one of those countries where the lowest 40 percent of the families share less than 12 percent of the income, moderate income inequality as countries where the lowest 40 percent receive between 12 and 17 percent of the income, and low, low inequality as countries where the lowest 40 percent receive about 17 percent of the income, then countries with high income inequality can be found at all levels of development and at all levels of per capita income. Thus, Kenya, Malaysia and France, with per capita incomes of $136, $330, and $1,913 respectively, all had high income inequality with the lowest 40 percent of their families receiving less than 12 percent of the total income received by families.[2]

The absence of large differences in income distribution between countries seems to present an opportunity for generalizing about laws of income distribution, but this temptation must be firmly resisted. There are so many differences in income distribution within a country, urban, rural, regional, ethnic and tribal groups, that the apparent similarity of income distribution between countries may be a statistical phenomen resulting from inadequate data and from the inertia of large statistical aggregates rather than the result of fundamental economic elationships. What seems basic is a firm realization that income distribution arises from the social structure of society, its institutions, and its production processes; and these are in a state of change in the world today.

In the less developed countries the poor are both numerous and very poor. The average income in the less developed countries is so low that the average factory worker is among the top 25 percent of the income receivers.[3] The lowest income receivers are the landless agricultural workers, the marginal farmers, the unemployed, the casual workers and some of the self-employed. Most of the families in any country are low income families; in both the less developed and developed countries the lower 60 percent of the households receive between one-fourth and one-third of the total income. But the average income in these two sets of countries is quite different. In the less developed countries, the level of income in absolute terms is so low that there cannot be much spread around the average. (See Kuznets and Table 6.1.) The average income is close to or even below the subsistence level; and to have many people far below the average would be to have many people far below the subsistence level, a condition that may exist in years of great famine but cannot exist for a long time without a loss of population. The high average income in the developed countries permits the lower income groups to receive only a small portion of the income and still survive. This is not possible in the developing countries. Therefore, the similarity of proportion of income distributed to the lower half or so of the households is not too significant. The identical overall measure of inequality may be of far greater consequence in the less developed than in the developed countries.

On the whole, income equality in the less developed countries ha
not decreased; if anything, the lower income families now receive a
smaller proportion of the total income. In an absolute sense, their incomes may be larger; but relative to the higher income families, their
position has deteriorated. There seems to be some evidence, quite
sketchy, that inequality in income distribution tends to increase in the
early stages of development. Over time, as development proceeds, th
gap in equality may tend to decrease. This may be the meaning of the
data of income distribution in several countries where data for two
fairly comparable years can be secured, as shown in Table 6.2.

TABLE 6.2

Changes in the Distribution of Income:
Percentage of Total Income Received by Households

Country	Years	Top 20%	Lowest 20%	Ratio of top 20% to Lowest 20%
Latin America				
Argentina	1953	50.0	7.5	
	1961	51.6	7.0	Increased
Mexico	1950	59.8	6.1	
	1963	59.6	3.5	Increased
Panama	1952	42.2	7.2	
	1962	45.4	6.2	Increased
Puerto Rico	1953	49.8	5.6	
	1963	50.6	4.5	Increased
Asia				
Ceylon	1953	53.8	5.2	
	1963	52.3	4.5	Increased
India	1952/53	42.8	7.0	
	1960/61	42.0	8.1	Decreased (expenditure data)
Philippines	1956/57	55.1	4.5	
	1965	55.4	3.5	Increased
Taiwan	1953	61.0	4.0	
	1964	41.1	7.7	Decreased

Source: Data summarized in D. J. Turnham, "Income Distribution:
Measurement and Problems," Society for International Development,
12th World Conference, Ottawa, 16-19 May 1971, mimeographed, pp.
3-4.

These data do not take into account price increases at different levels of income, and therefore are additionally unreliable. Yet they do show that with the exception of Taiwan, there has been a slight tendency toward a deterioration of income distribution in these countries as they pushed for modernization. In that time, however, the average income as well as the total income increased significantly, so that the lowest income receivers may have been better off in an absolute sense, although they received a smaller proportion of the total income.

In attempting to measure the changes in the relative levels of living of the poor over time, it has been shown that there is a considerable diversity of country experiences. "In both high-growth and low-growth countries, there are some which have experienced improvements and others that have experienced deteriorations in relative equality. The absence of any marked relationship between income growth and changes in income shares is important for policy purposes. It suggests that there is little firm empirical basis for the view that higher rates of growth inevitably generate greater inequality."[4]

The share of the top 20 percent of the households is such a large proportion of the total income and the lowest 20 percent of the households receive such a small share, that a slight drop in the top shares can add significantly to the bottom. Thus, if the top 20 percent receive 50 percent and the bottom 20 percent receive 6 percent of the total income, a 5 percent decrease of the share of the higher income households would make possible a 40 percent increase in the incomes of the lowest 20 percent of the households. Of course, it is not realistic to assume that reduced consumption of the richest can automatically or even easily be transferred to consumption of the lowest income households. The transfer would involve tremendous changes in production and distribution patterns. It is important to remember that, to reach the lowest income group of a country, not only must the average income be increased, but this group must begin to receive a larger share of the increasing total. To do otherwise would mean that centuries may have to elapse before the lowest third of the population were to attain even a minimum subsistence level. As the poor become aware of their slow growth and deteriorating relative position, these distant horizons must become less and less acceptable.

Income derived from ownership of wealth is usually important in the less developed countries. This importance results not only from the fact that property income is relatively high, but even more so because ownership of assets is a major determinant of ability to participate in improving technology and enjoyment of larger incomes from increases in production and productivity.

Income derived from the ownership of land and capital is, of course, under particular scrutiny in countries that are strenuously trying to increase the income of its poor. Is income inequality primarily a function of the concentration of property ownership in a relatively small number of families? Will reduced property concentration automatically result in more equitable income distribution? Data on which to base answers to these kinds of questions are conspicuously lacking. A large part of the popular ideas about the relationship between property concentration and income inequality arises from philosophical speculation and ideological convictions, rather than from empirical observation. Only a few generalizations can be supported by data, and there are clearly indecisive and less than adequate:

The proportion of property income in total is about the same or may be slightly higher in the less developed countries than in the developed countries.

The fraction of total income that is property income varies greatly between regions of a country; for a particular region, the lower the average level of family income, the lower seems to be the proportion of property income.

Property income seems to be a larger share of total family income in rural areas, as contrasted with urban areas.

Property income, as would be expected, forms a larger share of the higher income families than of lower income families.

There seems to be some evidence that property in general seems to be more concentrated in the less developed countries as compared with the developed countries.[5]

The emphasis on the measurement of overall inequality of income distribution arises from a natural interest in the obvious differences in well-being between the rich and the poor of a country. No government announces that it wishes to make the rich even richer, but the objective of making the poor less poor is given a very high priority. Usually, the implication is that of helping the low income families in both an absolute and relative sense by raising the average income of the poor and by increasing the proportion of the total income received by the poor. But if one wishes to think in operational terms of what can be done by different policies and institutions, the overall measures of inequality of income distribution tend to be misleading not only because the statistical base is questionable, but because there are significant variations within a country that must be considered.

Inequality Among Groups in a Country

Overall income distribution is the aggregate result of distribution by occupation and by sector, by geographic region, by urban and rural households, and by social classes and ethnic groups. To understand how a country's income distribution patterns affect production and productivity requires examination of these subgroups. The average income received in the country and the dispersion about this average is too general to be meaningful in an operational sense. A change in the average is nearly always the result of contrasting changes in important parts of the total. Government policies and institutions can be more easily related in a casual way to the income distribution within the subgroups than with the average. The few studies that give data on subgroup income distribution in the developing countries are fragmentary indeed and must be supplemented by impressions of more or less biased observers. The overall aggregate is nearly always the resultant of so many diverse changes that it tends to mask many deteriorating situations.*

Urban-rural Income Distribution

There appears to be evidence that in the less developed countries there is a greater inequality of income distribution in the urban areas than in the rural areas, as shown in Table 6.3.

TABLE 6.3

Rural and Urban Inequality

Country	Share of Top 20%		Share of Lowest 80%	
	Rural	Urban	Rural	Urban
1. Chile (1968)	48.3	50.2	51.7	49.8
2. Colombia (1970)	50.7	58.2	49.3	41.8
3. Honduras (1968)	55.0	55.8	45.0	44.2
4. India (1964)	43.0	57.0	57.0	43.9
5. Mexico (1963)	54.0	56.2	46.0	43.8
6. Pakistan(E&W) (1964)	42.5	52.0	57.0	49.0
7. Panama (1968)	46.0	45.3	54.0	54.7
8. Thailand (1970)	51.0	45.5	49.0	54.5
9. Tunisia (1961)	50.0	50.0	50.0	50.0
10. Venezuela (1962)	50.0	50.0	50.0	50.0

Source: S. Ahluwalia Montek, "Income Inequality: Some Dimensions of the Problem," Finance and Development (International Monetary Fund and World Bank Group, Washington, D.C.) 2, no. 3 (September 1974): 8.

---

*Myrdal says, "The entire structure of inequality is bolstered by the caste system, the color line, ethnic discrimination, nepotism and the general set of social and religious taboos. The vicious circle of cumulative interrelation and causation is thus perpetuated, and even accentuated, by existing institutions confronted with divergent sectional growth rates, notably between the agricultural and industrial sectors and serious inflation in several of the countries. Present institutional arrangements, therefore, impede the rise of social, regional and

177

This would seem to contradict the fact that the average income an
productivity of regularly employed workers in the urban areas is higher
than in rural areas. But the urban areas in the developing countries ha
attracted many workers who cannot find steady jobs. They live by performing intermittent services such as street selling and casual labor o
the least productive kind. Their income is probably less than they received in their rural home areas, where they shared the income of the
family. These large numbers of very low paid or unemployed workers
swell the low income ranks in the urban areas without adding much to
the total income, and therefore help establish a greater inequality of
income distribution in urban areas.

Together with the addition of many low productivity workers, the
urban areas also are accumulating many of the successful entrepreneur
those who develop and operate the new business ventures. These entr
preneurs are generally the most successful in the country; and while
their production is small in relation to total production, it is usually
expanding the most rapidly and generating the highest rate of profits.
The demand for skilled workers with high relative earnings are also as
sociated with the operations of these entrepreneurs. Government employment, also relatively highly paid, tends to concentrate in the urba
areas. As a consequence, the high profits and salaries that form the
income of a small portion or the urban areas tend to grow faster than tl
average wage earner's income. Thus, the changes at the two extremes
in the high income group and the much larger low income group, tend t
increase the inequality of income distribution in the urban areas. Furthermore, the more rapid population growth of the urban areas has the
effect of increasing the inequality of income distribution within the de
veloping countries.

There is very little evidence on which to evaluate changes in income distribution in the rural areas. The changes in land tenure and tl
laws limiting rents and other charges and regulating wages for agricultural workers, have left a mixed picture of general income distribution. The productivity increases in agriculture that have occurred in
many of the developing countries are the result, to a large extent, of
increased capital in the form of improved seed, fertilizer, and water.
Obviously, the technological changes require an improvement in the
labor input, but this is generally in farm management rather than in
changes in physical inputs of labor. Due to the essentiality of capital
to the new agricultural technology, it is noted that the largest share o
the increased productivity has gone to the large farmers who can afforc
the new capital and know the new technology. Thus there is a likelihood that the sudden increases in agricultural production will create
even larger gaps between the rich and the poor in rural areas.

occupational mobility and encourage the persistence of multi-dimensio
segmentation of social and economic life." Gunnar Myrdal, Asian
Drama (New York: Random House, 1968), p. 579.

In rural areas, property income, rent, and interest not only constitute a higher proportion of total income, but access to employment and
to the credit necessary to acquire the new capital required by new agricultural technology seems highly associated with property. Landless
agricultural laborers are poor credit risks, even for socially-minded
cooperative credit institutions; and farmers with small plots of their
own seem to become more available and more desirable as workers than
the totally landless laborers who tend to have less roots in the community. In low productivity work in rural areas, it is difficult to separate
wages from property income; but studies of poverty demonstrate low
ownership of land nearly always means greater acceptance by the community and greater opportunity for income.

The significance of the urban-rural difference in income distribution
is often hidden by reference to the difference in average income received. The fact that the urban average income is higher in spite of
the large numbers of totally or partially unemployed is often accepted
as hopeful, since the population growth in urban areas usually exceeds
that of rural areas. In-migration and a lower death rate more than offset the lower birth rate in urban areas, and the growing importance of
the modern production sector in the urban areas means that their higher
productivity will have a greater influence over time on the national average income. But the inequality of income and the degree of vertical
mobility of income earners is not exposed by changes in the average
income.

The lifestyle of peasants and of city dwellers is so different that
it is often argued that merely comparing differences in income can be
misleading and exaggerates the poverty of the peasant. Thus, the city
worker often pays for transportation to work, for water and sanitary
facilities, while the peasant has these at no financial cost, waiving
aside differences in convenience, adequacy, and effort. Yet what is
being waived aside in this comparison is often the essence of improvement in the quality of life, particularly if it includes adequacy of public goods and services relating to health, education, and security. The
importance of differences in income between rural and urban families
can be exaggerated, but to neglect it is to gloss over an important aspect of improving income distribution.

The problem of measuring nonmonetary income is particularly difficult in the rural area. Equally difficult are the problems relating to the
valuation of the costs of living, since prices in the urban areas are
generally much higher than those in rural areas, and this difference
varies for each income level. Thus, a study in India indicated that
while, in general, prices in urban areas were 16 percent above those
in rural areas, the prices of products purchased by the lower income
households were about 13 percent higher, compared with about 20 percent higher for the purchases of higher income households.[6] Thus,
proper inclusion of nonmonetary income tends to reduce the greater inequality of income in rural areas. No data or even educated guesses
exist of the relative openness of the system to the lowest portion of the

income recipients. It is usually assumed that the urban areas with the better educational facilities and expanded labor markets provide more opportunities for the children of the poor. Some form of education, either formal through schools or on the job through some form of apprenticeship, is generally necessary to break out of the straitjackets of poverty, the ill health and untrained capabilities that doom the children of the poor to repeat the sorry work history of their parents. While some rural areas may provide limited opportunities for the children of the lowest level income workers to break out of the existing low productivity work pattern tradition, it is likely that children of the urban poor are less prisoners of poverty than the children of the rural poor.

Social Class and Ethnic Groups

Income distribution is strongly related to social stratification, both as a cause and a consequence. Social groups or castes tend to remain static and resist inroads into their economic share. While there is social movement in terms of changing status in all societies, there is far greater social mobility in the developed countries, whose workers can move more freely from one trade to another and from one geographic region to another. In the developing countries, the social and economic position tends to be static, and the obstacles to social mobility are more severe. Income inequality therefore tends to more of a permanent reflection of status. While in both groups of countries the average income may be rising and the overall income distribution may remain almost unchanged, in the developed countries a larger proportion of the households may be changing their relative income positions. In a sense, the turnover at each level of income tends to be larger in the developed countries.

If it were possible to secure data on income distribution by occupation or by social group, the inequality within each group in the less developed countries might not be so great as in the developed countries. This too would result from the lower social mobility that exists. Income more nearly reflects status in the less developed countries. This consequence, if fixed into the expectations of the people of a country, tends to lower social mobility and decrease efforts to raise income. In this sense, social stratification is both a cause and consequence of income distribution.

Ethnic group differences in income are also part of the distribution picture in many developing countries. Where distinct ethnic groups exist, they seem to be associated with concentrations in particular occupations or economic functions. Examples are the Chinese carpenters in Rangoon, the Indian storekeepers in East Africa, the Chinese merchants in Indonesia and Thailand, and the Greek ship operators in Egypt. These ethnic or national concentrations by occupation generally have historical backgrounds that explain both their origin and persistence. Often, they involve differences in degree of urbanization, as, for example, the concentration of Chinese in urban areas of Thailand. One of

the few studies of income distribution by ethnic groups clearly shows
the pattern of ethnic group income differences in Ceylon.[7]

	Mean Income (Rupees per month)
Indian Moors	215
Eurasians	207
Ceylon Moors	117
Ceylon Tamils	107
Sinhalese	89

These differences are usually based on the occupational specialization
of the group. A traditional society, where status is a very important determinant of relationships and opportunities, tends to prolong the existence of accepted, noncompeting groups. These are usually based on
conspicuous racial differences, such as physical features, skin color,
dress, and language. These differences are culturally determined, and
cultural variations in time preference and choice of occupation are
clearly associated with general community acceptance of the traditional
pattern.

Differences in income of ethnic groups are made even more important by differences in opportunities to move out of the lower income
level. Even within an ethnic group, these differences in opportunity
must be considered. For example, differences in formal education may
be marked within an ethnic group, as in a large number of low paid plan-
tation workers and a few wealthy merchants of a single ethnic group. In
some countries, differences in access to government employment and
to higher paid positions in industry may be involved in ethnic group considerations. No studies have been made of the costs and benefits of
these selection patterns. Policies designed to improve income distribution of the poor in these groups always have to face the problems of
political acceptability. Generally, these efforts have short-run costs
that can only be justified by moral evaluations or by long-term benefits
of increased social stability and income, which are difficult to quantify. For many of the less developed countries, ethnic group values
and social stratification present continuing problems to public administrators engaged in formulating and implementing policies that attempt
to improve income distribution.

Regional Differences in Income Distribution

By far the most important subgroup differences in income distribution is that between regions. Nearly every country has regions that
are economically backward compared with the other parts of the country. These differences may be due to problems of accessibility, to
climate and topography, or merely to lateness of exposure to modern
ideas. Some of these areas are large enough to have the differential
of urban-rural income themselves, a problem within a problem. Economic growth is necessarily unbalanced, in a geographic sense. There

are always some places that are more advantageously situated for specific investments than others. Also, an investment in one place may set tensions and imbalances, compulsions toward growth at subsequent points. If all of these are in the same area, they constitute a force that tends to concentrate the growth, which may produce political and social problems and slow up transmission of growth from one region to another. A country's efforts to raise the income of its poorest segment often become translated into regional competition for investment and for the development of roads, power systems, and communication facilities—the economic overhead investment that forms the necessary foundation for economic growth.

Economic data by regions are more scarce and even less reliable than total national data. However, no systematic data may be required to demonstrate that the rural areas of some regions are producing less product and receiving less income per capita than the rural areas of other regions of the same country. Similar comparisons of the income per capita of cities are somewhat more difficult to base on superficial observation, but tend to yield similar conclusions. The poor regions of a country tend to have lower per capita incomes in both the rural and urban areas than do the more productive regions of a country. Since the different regions of a country usually possess different mixes of urban-rural populations, ethnic groups, occupational and industrial groups, as well as differing natural resources, it is almost impossible to identify the different variables responsible for regional differences. The existence of these regional differences, however, is too obvious to be overlooked, as these differences play an important role in government policies relating to income distribution.

There is some slight evidence that there is a systematic relationship between national development levels and regional inequality. The lower the level of average per capita income of a country, the more likely it is that the regional differences in income are the greatest.[8] However, it is suggested that in the early periods of development, the disparity between regional incomes will tend to widen. This is because the most advanced areas offer the best opportunity for investment; the returns tend to be higher where the skilled labor, complementary capacities, and the external economies of more adequate overhead investment already exist. As a country expands these essential to higher productivity, the income differences between regions will tend to diminish. These regional differences, particularly as they relate to agricultural income, tend to reflect differences in factor endowment—the fact that some parts of the country have much better agricultural land than others.

Income Distribution and Economic Growth

The production of goods and services may be considered one side of a coin; the distribution of income is the other side. Every significant change in production necessarily involves an effect on distribution of income. Conversely, every change in distribution of income affects production, either through the production of the product or through the demand for other goods. This close relationship, both definitionally and causally, is important in examining problems of income distribution. The objective of improving income inequality is necessarily associated with objectives of increasing production and productivity. In some instances, the effort to improve the income level of the poor will have a marked affect on production, though that may not have been the intent. The effect may be in the direction of improving production, which becomes an added gain, reinforcing the desirability of raising the lower incomes. But if a specific reduction in income inequality is an obstacle to increased production, it becomes a cost; and the costs and benefits must be evaluated. These costs and benefits, it should be clear, go far beyond monetary costs, or even beyond those envisaged in the concepts of social costs and social benefits. They necessarily include all those cultural, psychological, political, social and moral values that are involved in social change.

Most economists agree that a more equitable income distribution may result in less economic growth, at least in the short run.[9] However, there is also general evidence that "there need not necessarily be a trade-off between output growth and greater equity" and that "if technological change is sufficiently rapid, if tastes of urban dwellers are changing, if imports of food are readily available, . . . redistribution of income would have the effect of increasing consumption of labor-intensive commodities, employment and growth."[10] The concept that a more equitable income distribution and less economic growth is a worthwhile objective may be the present philosophy of mainland China.

> It appears that within a period of less than two decades, China has eradicated the worst forms of poverty; it has full employment, universal literacy and adequate health facilities; it suffers from no obvious malnutrition or squalor. What's more, it was my impression that China has achieved that at fairly modest rates of growth, by paying more attention to the content and distribution of GNP. In fact, China has proved that it is a fallacy that poverty can be removed and full employment achieved only at high rates of growth and only over a period of many decades.[11]

The effects of an improvement of income distribution, increasing the absolute level as well as the proportion of total income received by the low income families, can be focused, for ease of examination, on three key relationships: the labor input, savings and capital formation, and resource allocation.

Other important relationships, such as in technology and human capital, can be adequately described as part of the above three.

Labor Input

Improved income distribution strongly affects the productivity of the labor input factor.

Physical Capability—There is ample evidence that the poverty of much of the unskilled labor force has created labor inputs simply incapable of doing the kind of hard physical work needed by a high productivity economy. The multiplication of machines and the improvement of technology must not hide the fact that unskilled workers still remain the bulk of the labor force and that the sustained physical effort in a production unit concentrating on improving efficiency is likely to be great over longer periods of time than the unskilled work in traditional occupations. In other words, higher productivity operations required more sustained, systematic physical effort than casual labor. High productivity technology is generally associated with new and improved capital, such as machines or equipment. No matter how important this capital is, its use must be associated with human inputs that require superior physical capabilities. In modern production, work tends to be "machine paced" with timing determined by the most effective use of the capital, since that is the relatively scarce and costly input. This usually means more sustained physical effort than in traditional production units, with its spurts of energy interspersed among long delays and rests and the pace of work usually determined by the workers. Numerous studies have demonstrated what is intuitively felt as true, that near starvation and serious malnutrition, inadequate housing and high turnover rates result in such poor labor inputs that productivity is severely curtailed.[12]

Motivation and Work Attitudes—The improvement of motivation is an essential element in the creation of improved labor inputs. Traditional patterns of behavior are not lightly given up, no matter how basically unhappy they may be. Two areas of motivation may be indicated briefly as of outstanding importance in the less developed countries. First, there is the motivation that is related to personal and family benefits, where higher income, because of the benefits made possible, motivate workers to work harder and more productively. This is the most obvious relationship between higher wages and higher productivity. Pay schemes that base wages on piece work or quantity of product produced are increasingly common in industries that wish to emphasize efficiency. Production bonus schemes are, for example, an important element in the incomes policy of most of the communist countries. High wages are as much a cause for high productivity as they are a result. The importance of adequate motivation is also expressed in the concern that there be an adequate flow of consumers' goods to those rural areas where money incomes are increasing. These consumers' goods, such as watches, radios, bicycles, and shoes, are often important enough to provide the motivation for increased agricultural production in areas where market institutions are beginning to penetrate and where subsistence production is the most common type of enterprise.

The second area of motivation, often neglected except at election times or at revolutionary periods, is the relationship between improved income distribution and a sense of social justice. Continuity of a social system depends to a large degree on the acceptance of its usefulness and even desirability by an overwhelming majority of its participants. Unless the mass of workers, both in traditional and modern enterprises, feel that there is a tolerable existence or a tolerable future, their disturbances and apathy continue to make a high productivity production system almost impossible. A sense that the system is working toward improved income distribution is built in, as a prime requirement, in the desire for modernization.

Work Attitudes—Somewhat narrower than the general subject of motivation, and in a sense a result of motivation change, is the necessity of improving the attitude of the laborer towards his work and towards innovations and changes of all kinds that help his productivity. A worker's attitude toward the new institutions that make possible rapid economic growth will be largely conditioned by what he sees he is getting from these changes; how it affects himself, his family, and his world. If his sense of social justice is confirmed and strengthened, he will react quite differently than if he feels the changes are almost entirely for the benefit of the rich and powerful. The adjustment to new technologies, the acceptance of a different and more demanding "work rhythm," is usually resisted, both consciously and unconsciously. Work attitudes are reflected also in relationships to other workers and to supervisors who direct the work and inspect its progress. The rejection of innovation by workers may result in a slowdown and a longer training period, as well as in inadequate maintenance and lower productivity in general. Work attitude includes a recognition of regularity in employment—for beginning and ending the day's work at the same time, for keeping absences due to ill health or family problems to a minimum, and for creating respect for quotas and deadlines. These kinds of changes in work attitude mean a different pattern of priorities and are related directly and indirectly to how adequately the worker feels income is distributed. Obviously, this is not the only consideration; and at any particular time, it may not even be a major determinant. In the long run, however, the need for proper work attitudes is a basic requirement of higher productivity.

Mobility of Labor and Shifts in Labor Supply—Labor mobility consists of many kinds of changes in the human inputs of production. It includes the familiar changes in geographic location and occupation previously referred to. It encompasses the shift of workers from rural occupations to the so-called modern sector, where productivity is higher and income received by workers is generally higher than the traditional sectors.

Both kinds of mobility are directly affected by the prospects of higher income. Indeed, the prospect of higher income is clearly the major cause of labor mobility, both geographic and occupational. There are some relationships, however, that need further description, and not all the aspects of labor mobility are on the positive side of increased productivity.*

Superficial observation might lead to the conclusion that labor is excessively mobile in most of the less developed countries. Every new factory seems to attract hordes of workers clamoring for employment. The absence of social and economic overhead facilities, such as housing, water, roads, and sanitation, does not seem to deter the people who seek employment. "Instant villages" of huts and shops that, if permitted, surround each new factory, attest to the mobility of large numbers of people, both workers and the petty tradesman that accompany them. A more careful examination would show that practically all of the spontaneous mobility is among the unskilled workers, particularly those that are totally unfamiliar with factory work. Skilled workers tend to be far less mobile, and factory management must usuall make special arrangements for their movement and training. This often involves the training of additional skilled workers and the upgrading of skills to meet the specific requirements of the new enterprise. A large part of this training and upgrading must be done on the job, at actual work, which is of course one of the reasons why starting up a new enterprise involves higher labor costs per unit of product than when the men have become properly experienced and trained.

The shift of labor from rural to urban areas, so significant in practically all countries, represents the result of many different pushes and pulls. The higher income that urban employment usually makes possible the low productivity and limited opportunities in the rural areas, and the greater social amenities and occupational opportunities in the urban areas are partial but important elements in this shift of labor supply. In the long run, this shift from rural to urban is a basic characteristic of countries that are modernizing their production processes. The slums and hut villages that so often appear to be associated with this migration are the results of inadequate balances in the production of housing and other urban facilities, and are understandable from many points of view, social, economic, and political. Yet their elimination

---

*"Labor mobility can be too high as well as too low. It is not desirable that everyone in the labor force shuttle about constantly from job to job. Efficient operation of the market requires only a mobile minority, which may be made up largely of new entrants to the labor force plus the unemployed. For the bulk of the labor force, stability had advantages in terms of productive efficiency as well as personal satisfaction." L. G. Reynolds, Labor Economics and Labor Relations, 5th ed. (Englewood Cliffs, N.J.: Prentice-Hall, 1970), p. 581.

may be far too costly to attack directly and as a short-term objective; only in the very long run can a society make adequate resources available to eliminate inadequate housing. The children of these migrants may avail themselves of the educational and training facilities that are more common in the urban areas. Improved income distribution, in the form of additional employment and in higher wages, is clearly an important element in the improvement of the future situation. It cannot be the total answer, as it must be accompanied by massive programs of capital formation, the result of policies that relate to investment and the allocation of resources.

Rate of Savings and Capital Formation

It is in the relationship between improved income distribution and savings that most of the assessments of the economic effects of income redistribution are made. This relationship seems the simplest to analyze. Raising the income of the lowest segment of the population means, for the most part, increasing wage payments. This appears to mean increasing production costs and reducing profits, which is the share of income going to entrepreneurs. Higher incomes for the entrepreneurs and owners is assumed to mean a higher rate of savings, since most household savings that become investible funds come from high income families and most business earnings come from high business profits. More wage payments mean more consumption since low income families will tend to use any additional funds for essential consumption goods.

If these were the only insights available on savings and capital formation, it would be quite easy to assess the desirability of raising the income of the lowest half of the families. It could be proven, with simple mathematical examples, that by maintaining low wages total consumption is curtailed and thus total savings stimulated. Assuming that a large part of the higher income would go to savings, the capital formation arising from the savings would, in a reasonable period of time, result in more jobs and perhaps more income for the lowest income families than if wages had been increased in the first instance. Improved income distribution through increased wages is thus placed in opposition to increased savings and capital formation as something to be minimized if a country wishes to attain a higher rate of economic growth in a short period of time. But this is not the totality of the relationship, and governmental policies derived from its acceptance would be wrong more often than not.

It is true that at any one period of time all income is consumed or saved. Consequently, increasing wages that will be used largely for consumption, may decrease the profits that are the basis for much of the savings. It is also true that there are two general ways of raising the amount of income received by the poor: by raising the wages of the employed worker, and by providing more jobs for the unemployed workers. But the recognition that it is more important to "share a larger pie" than to fight for a larger share of a "smaller pie" applies to profits as well as wages. If production and productivity rise rapidly, profits also can rise rapidly, even if the share of the output going for wages i increased in both absolute and relative terms. In other words, the dynamic view, that it is important to increase the "size of the pie" as well as to bargain over the relative "share of the pie" does not necessarily justify an incomes policy that keeps wages down. At some level of consumption and at some times in the history of a country, additiona income for consumption may be more important for future productivity than additional capital formation.

The basic difficulty is that the useful but still limited distinction between consumption and savings is not always a good operating guide in the developing countries. At very low levels of consumption, additional consumption goods will have a far more beneficial impact on future production than additional capital stocks. Improved technology, which is so basic to increases in production and productivity, is associated with improvements in the labor input, and some, if not most, of these improvements are associated with the increase of consumption among the lowest income recipients.

Most examinations by economists of the problems of future increases in productivity omit any corrections for the improvement of the labor inputs. The assumption is made that for the time period in question, the future, this factor is not a significant element in the question and that production is largely a question of savings and its related capital formation. Yet stability of the social system, evaluation of the uncertainties of the future, and the discount applied to determine the present value of future production are all closely related to providing more income to the lowest income recipients, and therefore may be far more important to the overall capital formation climate than the narrow assessment that savings and capital formation are directly related to increasing high incomes.

For the production of some very important kinds of consumer goods and intermediate products, increased domestic demand may be a key element in determining production and productivity. Increased demand made possible by improved income distribution may provide expanded profitable product markets for which sufficient effective demand did not previously exist. Some kinds of products sold to low income household such as cheap clothing, food, and household necessities, are often produced at relatively high costs because their demand is limited, particularly when more profits are predictable by producing higher priced goods for higher income families. There are no studies that show whether increased demand for these goods and larger scale production will lower the costs of these products and therefore make possible lowering of prices and further increases in demand. Demand, as has been argued in chapter 5, is often overlooked as a powerful tool in shaping the level and mix of production. This is particularly true in the case of small scale enterprises that spring up to meet effective demand and that are so important to an employer of labor in the less developed countries. Formal economic analysis tends to concentrate on the expansion of production that occurs in large scale enterprises because these are more visible and provide better operating data. Also, the larger enterprises obviously use more modern technologies that require mass markets and there is a "return to scale," a lowering of costs and an increase in productivity as the volume of production goes up under the influence of increased sales. But the improvements of production and productivity in small scale enterprises may be even greater, even though they cannot be measured as readily.

The basic assumption that policies to maintain or increase the income of rich families will increase the savings available for capital formation is of questionable validity. It is true that most household savings come from higher income households, but it is not true that this is a fixed relationship that occurs in all higher income households. The increased income is also reflected in the increased demand for luxuries, land, imports, and the speculative holding of commodities, and even in the flight of capital to safer, less taxable countries. There is no unambiguous evidence that increasing taxation on higher incomes reduces the total level of savings or investment. In many of the less developed countries, there is a continuation of conspicuous consumption and of the traditional, nonproductive form of savings. This suggests that the effect of more progressive income taxes would likely be on the pattern of expenditures and investment, rather than on the rate of investment. Increasing the effective demand for domestically produced luxury goods may provide more employment, and appears to be justified on that basis. However, the proper comparison is with the improved income distribution and production that would result from investment in capacities for goods required by the majority of low income families, and in producing a means for creating an effective demand for these products. The proper comparison is not of investment with no investment, but with the different kinds of investment that could come from a changed pattern of taxation and expenditures.

It is clear that improved income distribution may have significant beneficial impact on production and productivity to offset any increase in savings that may come from holding wages low and increasing profits. The increase in savings, as described in chapter 4, is far too complicated to be treated in a simplistic way. Certainly, the relationship of increases of certain kinds of profits must be considered, together with the need for improving low paid wages, of improving workers' incentives and stability, and of increasing rewards for improving efficiency by both the owner managements and the wage earners of enterprises. The interrelated web of government policies that affect profits and levels of wages and have a significant impact on income distribution must be considered as a total system, and not merely individually, by one isolated cause and response at a time. To justify inadequate income distribution because it may increase savings and capital formation is to assume the validity of a broad generalization while overlooking many relationships between inputs and technology that do not support this broad assumption.

Allocation of Resources

Discussions of revenue allocation are often limited to investment decisions, the process of capital formation for future production. But this is too restricted a view of the problems of resource allocation, important as the capital formation process is. Resource allocation also includes how all the factor inputs are allocated, not merely capital. Further, the assumption that the allocation of investible funds for capital determines the allocation of the other factor inputs is only partially true, and may be a misleading assumption on which to base government policy. There are other important influences on labor allocation that may be present, and it is always necessary to go behind the capital allocation process to examine the policies that affect market conditions (see chapter 3). Changes in resource allocation are both a cause and an effect of changes in income distribution. Wealth and income are a base for access to credit and future income. Efforts to improve present income distribution will obviously have an effect on the allocation of resources, since they will affect production and productivity. In the private sector where investment decisions are closely related to projections of costs and benefits to the entrepreneur, government policies that attempt to raise wages appear to have the effect of raising costs, thus acting as a deterrent to investment. Policies that direct investment resources to geographic areas of low income and greater need may also tend to increase costs and reduce estimates of return to investors. Policies that favor low income recipients in rural areas may reduce resources of wealthier people who are trying to establish economic enterprises in the urban areas. Thus, efforts to improve income distribution not only affect the rate of savings and of capital formation, but also the geographic or sectoral location of enterprises.

Just as increased payments to low paid workers does not necessarily mean a lower rate of savings and capital formation, it equally does not necessarily mean a lower efficiency in the use of the capital. Existing market projections of costs and benefits by entrepreneurs and government do not necessarily result in the best allocation of resources Market conditions are imperfectly known and are continually being changed. When the government prohibits the importation of cosmetics, the market conditions and projections of the domestic producers of cosmetics are drastically changed. Similarly, when the government develops a program that results in large increases in the disposable funds of low income households, market conditions will be changed for many types of products purchased by low income families. Differential taxation may be used to encourage investment in luxuries or in products used largely by wealthy families. Markets are at best imperfect evaluations of the relative scarcity of factor inputs, and in the less developed countries, inadequate markets clearly result in inadequate determination of resource allocation.

Where considerations other than market determined costs and profits are important, government policies and their implementation are often designed to modify or replace market decisions. Thus, differential taxes, tax holidays, rapid depreciation, subsidies, import licenses, tax rebates, construction priorities, and the whole gamut of government actions to direct and influence investment are also involved in resource allocation. They help determine how the entrepreneurs, government, or private sector interpret the market signals that enable them to make the necessary cost-benefit analysis. Often, policies that are designed to encourage investment may result in subsidizing capital intensive investment and in adding to the concentration of wealth and income. The allocation of resources to provide additional facilities for producing air conditioners, refrigerators, electric appliances, automobiles, powered grass mowers, and similar durable consumers' goods may result in inadequate facilities for the production of equipment for health centers, schools, low cost housing, and similar products required by low income families. Policies that attempt to improve income distribution must be evaluated within this complex, as a part of the total economic system. A recent study concludes that at most, an improved income distribution of significant magnitude may reduce economic growth by about 1 percent of GNP. It also suggests that with improved income distribution, the import bill could be reduced slightly, that a more efficient allocation of the factors of production could result, with an increase in employment and a shift toward more labor intensive production.[13]

It would appear reasonable to conclude that improved income distribution in the less developed countries assists rather than hinders economic growth, both in the short run and the long run. This would occur in spite of the shift of income from profits with its higher savings, to wages with its higher consumption. Improved income distribution in the less developed countries would lead to improved labor inputs, resulting from improved physical capacity, motivation, and work incentives. It would also lead to a different product mix that would tend to be labor intensive rather than capital intensive in technology of production. Improved income distribution would lead to more production of the types of goods consumed by low income families, and less production of products consumed by higher income families. The shift in product mix might lead to less imports, since luxury goods tend to have a higher import content than mass essentials. Savings could be reduced by improved income distribution, but this is not necessarily so. It depends upon what economic policies the government adopts and how effectively these policies are implemented. Efforts to improve income distribution are not necessarily limitations on economic growth; they may be essential for political and social stability and may result in a more efficient economic system.

ROLE OF GOVERNMENT IN IMPROVING INCOME DISTRIBUTION

General Concepts

One of the major economic functions of government is to influence and improve the final distribution of income in a country. Not only is that part of the sovereign power of a state but it is also a distinct operating function of a large part of its bureaucracy. The laws and regulatory rules concerning property and contracts that are part of the legal and institutional structure of a society obviously shape as well as support its income distribution. Monetary and fiscal policies involve many kinds of impact on income distribution, in addition to shifting income from the private sector to the public sector. Welfare transfer payments policies and specific decisions on resource allocation, protection of markets, pricing practices, labor policies—all have effects that are important in shaping the income distribution of a country. Deliberately or unconsciously, governmental policies influence, even determine, income distribution.

For some purposes, a distinction may be made between government efforts to improve income distribution and government efforts at redistribution of income. The latter refers to efforts to shift income from one set of recipients to another after payments have been made to factor inputs. Thus, transfer payments by government to recipients, such as pension and welfare payments, may be considered redistributional efforts by taking from wealthy families more than from the others. The distinction between improved distribution and redistribution is often difficult to identify operationally, as when government services are supplied at less than costs in order to help the low income families. Here, the payments to the workers in government enterprises may be considered income distribution, while the provision of essential services to low income consumers at less than cost may be an effort at income redistribution. When production enterprises (in spite of higher costs of production) are located in areas where mass unemployment exists, the question of classifying the government's efforts as income redistribution becomes too subtle to be precise.

A further concept may be useful, that of vertical and horizontal redistribution, which refers to redistribution related to levels of income. Vertical redistribution involves taking income from one level of income and redistributing it to other levels, while horizontal redistribution occurs within the same level. Thus, a progressive income tax that secures most of its revenue from wealthy families in order to provide services for the poorer families would be an illustration of vertical redistribution. However, a use charge for a service that is enjoyed by middle and upper income families may result only in horizontal redistribution. Since who would ultimately pay the government taxes and who would use the government services is mostly a matter of conjecture and too complicated to study empirically, income redistribution is difficult to discuss in operational terms.

To cut through this complex of interrelated activities and tendencies, it will be useful to classify government policies and practices regarding improvement of income distribution into two major types, direct and indirect. Admittedly, there will be some policies that could possibly fall into both types, but most policies will be clearly one or the other. It is important to remember in this classification that the criteria for the classification is intent, which is always a hard yardstick to use, because governments do not always make clear their intentions or even always know them. The intent of a policy may be in one direction for economic purposes and directly contrary, at least as announced, for political purposes. In this, of course, governments are not much different than individuals. Therefore, the classification into direct and indirect has limited operating merit; it does not identify functions, tools, or forces. However, it is useful in describing how governmental policies and practices affect both production and income distribution.

Direct

These include governmental policies and priorities that have as their major purpose the improvement of income distribution in the country. They include all efforts by government, whose major justification is to raise the income of the poorest sectors of the population, such as minimum wage laws, the provision of essential government services at no cost or at a price below cost, and "fair price" stores. Also included are policies and efforts by government to restrain or curtail the income of the wealthiest part of the population, such as progressive tax laws and limits to expansion of business enterprises owned by wealthy families.

Indirect

This category includes all governmental policies and priorities that have a major purpose to affect production, with income distribution often an important but nevertheless a secondary objective. Illustrations are the numerous investment and production decisions of government, foreign exchange allocations, import restrictions, most pricing laws and policies, and the host of policies and priorities designed to stimulate savings and capital formation.

Obviously, the time period to be used in implementing these policies is a necessary but puzzling element. Ultimately, the objective of all production decisions may be to improve the income of the lowest segment of the population. As in the case of most classifications that involve time, if a long enough period of time is taken, all problems are reduced to simple propositions; but in an operating sense, such conclusions are simplistic and unreal. Implicit in this classification is a time horizon that is not too short and not too long, the reasonable future.*

A government's efforts to improve income distribution is represented by its policies and practices in the following:

Government services (education, health, transportation, and so forth)
Taxation
Resource allocation
Price controls
Labor and welfare laws

Many of these have been discussed previously in describing the government's role in improving production and productivity. Here the emphasis will be their use in the improvement of income distribution.

Provision of Government Services

Services here refer to the many functions performed by government agencies or by the facilities built by government, whether or not they are operated by government agencies. Thus, public education is a government service, even if some fees are charged to pay for part of the cost. Hospitals and clinics are examples of government services in the health field. Transportation services are provided by government in many ways, through government operated railroads and by building roads for use by private buses, cars, and trucks, as well as by public buses and government trucks. Public systems for the provision of water, sanitation, communication, marketing, and fire and police protection are other examples of how governments provide services, using funds secured by taxation, by borrowing or through charges for the services.

The provision of government services to low income families is often cited as one of the major methods a government can utilize to improve income distribution. By taxing the rich and using these funds to provide essential services for the poor, a government can theoretically redistribute income from high income to low income families. The effectiveness of this prescription is seriously impaired by the difficulty in taxing the rich. Rich families are generally successful in avoiding heavy taxes and the intense need for tax revenue compels governments to tax the poor through a variety of indirect taxes. Because of the

---

*If the reader insists on something more definite than this "reasonable" future, let it be about a generation, from 15 to 20 years.

bility to pass on taxes, indirect taxes become reflected in prices to
inal consumers, most of whom are poor families.

When government revenues are used to provide free or subsidized
ervices for the people, some effects of income redistribution are pres-
nt. To the extent that these services are pure public goods available
o everybody and where the use by one person does not diminish avail-
bility for another person, the services are available to the poor. For
xample, defense and security derived from military expenditures may
e considered as available to all equally. But most types of government services are not that purely "public" in this sense. Schools, hos-
itals, and health facilities are made available to the general public;
ut even casual observation demonstrates that the very poor receive
ittle from such services. Ignorance, superstitution, and small but
ignificant charges usually limit most government services to the upper
nd middle classes. In the less developed countries the mass of low
ncome families lives in rural areas, where public services are often
estricted to sketchy transportation and communication services; and
ven these services are relatively unused by the lowest income fam-
lies. It seems an unfortunate fact that the provision of government
ervices free or at subsidized prices has little overall effect on im-
roving income distribution. It is difficult to allocate by income group
oth tax incidence and benefits of government services, but it would not
e too wrong to assert that in most countries the lower income families
ay far more in taxes than they receive in government services; and
herefore in a general sense they are taxed to provide government serv-
ces for the middle and upper income families.

Taxation

Taxation is obviously the part of a government's operations that
est reveals its determination and effectiveness in improving income
istribution. But it is essential to emphasize that taxation has major
bjectives other than improving income distribution; the overriding ob-
ective of most of the tax schemes in underdeveloped countries is to
aise public revenue. So important is that concept, that often taxes
re levied despite this regressiveness. They bear more heavily on the
oor than on the rich. Similarly, often taxes whose main objectives
re to encourage investment clearly favor the rich, yet they are con-
idered necessary because of the compelling need to increase the capi-
al stock and to induce economic enterprises to adopt improved tech-
ologies. In colonial days, the clear, prime objective of almost all
axes was to raise adequate revenue to support the legal and security
tructure of the society; and the social desirability of increased ex-
enditures and improved income distribution had little or no influence.
oday, no government can avoid the necessity of publicizing improved
ncome distribution as one of the major objectives of its tax laws. As a

consequence, most countries have adopted the principle of progressive taxation, tax rates based on the ability to pay, and have widely advertised this objective. In actual practice, however, the need for tax revenues dominates tax policies; and there is a wide disparity between the publicized tax policies and the actual incidence of taxes.

The measurement of tax incidence, the determination of who really pays or bears the burden of a tax, is one of the most debated, least understood aspects of public finance. It is the height of economic naivete to assume that the person, household, or business that actually pays the tax money to the government collector really bears the burden of the tax. To be economically rational, the actual payer tries to shift the incidence of the tax to others, either the suppliers of his inputs or the purchasers of his outputs. This is true whether the payer is a laborer, who tries to pay less for his food and the other things he purchases and who tries to receive higher wages to compensate for the higher taxes he pays, or a business that passes on a tax through higher prices to its customers or forces its suppliers to take less for the products they supply. A landlord may pass on increased property taxes in higher rents to his tenants, while a doctor may try to compensate for higher income taxes by raising his rates for certain kinds of services he performs. The success in passing on taxes depends on many things such as (1) the price elasticity of the demand for the product, how the consumer will react to a price increase; (2) the degree of competition and monopoly in the sale of the product; and (3) the general economic and political climate. These vary so much from time to time and from place to place that only the broadest kinds of generalizations can be made about tax incidence, particularly in the less developed countries where the price elasticities of demand and the degrees of monopoly are so difficult to assess.

Income Taxes (Personal and Business)

Taxes on income usually try to be progressive; that is, they have increasing rates as the income to be taxed is higher.* Thus, they are politically acceptable to most of the people, since they are easily publicized as progressive and therefore "fair." This is particularly true of progressive business income taxes, where large enterprises always seem best able to pay heavy taxes. It is commonly assumed that income taxes, called direct taxes, are not passed on to others; but this

---

*Income taxes can be "unitary" (based on total income), or "schedular" (different sources of income have different rates), or a combination of unitary and schedular. Schedular rates can be withheld (more easily) at the source, at a constant rate, and thus are less progressive than unitary rates.

assumption is doubtful in many cases, particularly as applied to business taxes where the concerns have high degrees of monopoly on essential products or services. Income taxes do not form a large part of the revenue of the less developed countries, and the reasons are not hard to find.

1. It is almost impossible to tax nonmonetary income and much of the income in the developing countries is of a subsistence or barter character. Nonmonetary income taxes are nonassessable and almost uncollectable.

2. Record keeping and literacy are basic to adequate income taxation. The illiteracy of shopkeepers and small businessmen makes income taxes on their incomes not worth the trouble to collect.

3. Businessmen tend to avoid bookkeeping or keep multiple books for differing purposes. Incomes are difficult to assess under these circumstances.

4. Noncompliance with tax laws is socially acceptable, even praiseworthy, in many countries. Where tax evasion has no social stigma, administration of the tax is bound to be inefficient and corrupt. Groups or families with political power often avoid taxation through special exemptions, arranged neglect or outright corruption. The firm expectation of no penalty or retribution makes this tax avoidance a "rational" economic position.

Income taxation is probably the most difficult tax law to administer. It necessarily leaves many kinds of discretionary decisions to officials, thus providing numerous opportunities for favoritism and corruption. The development of an administrative staff with adequate training and standards is something that few nations have been able to solve successfully. The high progressiveness of income taxes in the less developed countries is therefore more apparent than real, a type of window dressing for the unpleasant fact that relatively few people pay income taxes in these countries. In order to avoid the political difficulties arising from direct taxation of the poor and to demonstrate their desire to improve income distribution, the less developed countries usually have relatively high levels of exempt income. For example, while the United States and the United Kingdom level no income taxes until income reaches about 100 percent of the average income in their countries, in India the exempt level is 1200 percent of the average per capita income. This tendency for high exemptions is understandable; but when added to the difficulties of administration and the ease of tax evasion, it keeps to a small proportion the number of people paying income taxes in the less developed countries. In the developed countries, between 30 percent and 40 percent of the adult population pay income taxes. In the less developed countries these figures are generally below 2 percent.[14] Assessed incomes for personal income tax purposes amounts to about 75 percent of the GNP in the United Kingdom, but was less than 20 percent in the Carribean countries and less than 5 percent in Africa.[15]

In the less developed countries, where agriculture is usually the largest sector for both employment and value of product, agricultural income is taxed very sketchily if at all. In India, for example, agricultural income is exempt from central government taxes, and only abou half of the state governments attempt to tax agricultural income. Not only is agricultural income hard to assess, but large landlords as a group are generally so politically powerful that they can resist taxatior very effectively. A government that pushes high agricultural income taxes will generally find support for its other programs diminishing rap idly. One might expect that among traders, particularly those engaged in imports and exports, income taxation would be effective, especially taxes on sudden windfall profits resulting from drastic price changes. Traders must keep books and records to supply the necessary documentation for foreign exchange contracts and for shipping and financial documentation. But here, too, there is evidence that the difficulties confronting the administration of income taxation usually outweigh a country's capacity to assess and collect income taxes. On the other hand, employees of the government and of foreign firms seem to be the inescapable prisoners of payroll records to which tax assessors have access. For all these reasons, income taxes, both personal and corporate, provide only a small share of government revenue in most of the developing countries.

> There were six countries which derived less than 10 percent of their revenue from direct taxes—Sudan, Guatemala, Haiti, Iran, Jordan, Thailand. On the other hand, there were only six countries which derived more than 50 percent of their revenue in this way—Canada, U.S.A., Netherlands, United Kingdom, Australia, and New Zealand. Alternatively, if we look at those raising less than 20 percent in direct taxes, we find nineteen countries in all, every one being a member of the underdeveloped class.[16]

Governments have generally been unsuccessful in efforts to increase the percentage of revenues collected through direct assessment While the absolute amount of revenue from income taxes may increase as total production goes up, the proportionate share of total taxes usually declines. For example, in India the percentage of total revenue derived from direct taxes fell from 22 percent in 1958 to 17.1 percent in the 1968 budget. In Pakistan, the decrease was from 20 percent in 1958 to 12.1 percent in the 1968 budget.[17] The picture of declining proportion of government revenues from income taxes is substantially the same in other developing countries.

Excise and Sales Taxes

In view of the difficulties of collecting income taxes, it is not surprising that the developing countries have been relying increasingly on such indirect taxes as excise and sales taxes. Here, too, efforts at making the burden progressive and trying to improve income distribution are usually widely publicized. Excise taxes are often assessed, at high rates, on such luxuries as perfume and cosmetics, fancy textiles and luxury household appliances. But excise and sales taxes are too convenient a method of raising revenue to limit their incidence, so most governments extend these taxes to such commonly used items as cigarettes, petroleum products, matches, beer, and other alcoholic drinks. No studies have been made of the incidence of these taxes, but as a total their regressive nature is not in doubt. Most if not all of these excise taxes are passed on to the consumers; a majority of these consumers are lower income families since they form an overwhelming majority of the nation's population and of the total consumption of these products. The high tax rates on specific luxury items usually do not raise much revenue, indicating either some black market operations or a shift in consumption patterns. The lower sale of luxury goods may demonstrate a highly elastic response to price changes, but essential commodities are usually price inelastic in their demand and therefore are favored for taxation when more tax revenue is needed.

Property Taxes

Property taxes, particularly taxes on land, are an ancient story in the less developed countries. Land taxes were formerly the basic source of a major part of a government's income. In colonial days, government taxation efforts were largely devoted to taxing land in accordance with its actual or potential use, since to have even a semblance of fairness, land taxes require frequent valuation of the land with some attention paid to the value of crops produced on the land. Today, land taxes, particularly on agricultural land, have become a smaller and smaller part of total tax revenues. Inflation of land values has turned many assessment systems into a complex task beyond the administrative capabilities of most countries. The use of outdated values for land taxes have increased the regressiveness of the tax, so that small landowners bear an undue portion of the taxes collected, while large landowners increasingly find new ways of reducing their tax assessments. Few field studies have been made of the nature of property taxes in the less developed countries because of the sensitivity of the problem, particularly as related to the political structure of the country and the quality of administration. Property taxes tend to be regressive by their nature; large properties tend to be undervalued because it is difficult to find comparable market transactions to assist in defining current value. This tendency to underevaluate large property is too often assisted by the favorable attention given to wealthy property owners who can repay favoritism more easily than can the less affluent owners.

Customs and Export Taxes

These are widely used taxes that yield an increasing part of government revenue in the less developed countries. Taxes here may take the form of multiple foreign exchange rates, where foreign exchange is either bought or sold at varying prices in the domestic currency. An attempt is usually made to make the burden progressive by taxing imported luxuries; high tax rates may so reduce demand that the tax yield is lowered or even reduced to zero. High customs duties may provide a hidden subsidy for domestic producers, who can charge higher prices because their market is protected. This protection may also induce greater domestic production of luxuries that are meant to replace imports eliminated through high customs duties. Customs and export taxes are relatively easy to collect, since they tend to concentrate in a few locations and require written records that can be examined. The need to control the use of foreign exchange and to expand government revenues results in custom taxes that are clearly regressive in their incidence. Customs taxes are usually passed on to consumers, and most of the ultimate consumers are the poorer families in the less developed countries. Export taxes are less easily passed on to consumers who are foreign buyers, and therefore must usually be borne by the exporter or the producer. Taxing the export of each pound of rubber or bushel of rice at the same rate, regardless of the income of the producer, can only be considered regressive in nature, to the extent that it is not absorbed by the exporter. There is a general belief that on the whole, customs and export taxes are significantly regressive.[18]

Tax Holidays and Special Tax Exemptions for Investment

Government often provides tax holidays and special tax exemptions in order to induce those kinds of economic behavior considered favorable to the economic program of the country. Thus, new factories of specifically approved industries may be given holidays from property taxes for a term of years. Factories that are located in specified depressed areas may be given tax favors, such as an exemption from customs duties, as well as tax holidays. The purpose is, of course, to make investment more profitable for the entrepreneur, to induce him through higher profits to undertake the kinds of operation or the location desired by the government. This action will improve the incomes of some poor families by providing jobs that the investment expenditures create. The operation of the enterprise will also presumably provide additional jobs and therefore help lower income families. It is clear that such taxation policies increase profits; if not, why would they be effective as inducements? While total income therefore will probably be increased by such investments, relative income distribution will probably not be improved

Indeed, it may even be worsened, because of the special emphasis given to increased profits from the investment. Tax holidays and tax exemptions from approved investments are thus essentially regressive in nature; they provide for reductions in the tax burdens of the wealthier families in the country, even though they may be useful in shaping the allocation of resources.

Summary—Taxation as a Means of Affecting Income Distribution

In general, governments claim that their tax policies are "progressive," that is, based as much as possible on ability to pay but consistent with the tremendous need to attain higher and higher tax revenues. Most of these claims are based on published rates of taxation, rather than on studies of real tax incidence. Empirical studies are so difficult to make, that few, if any, have been attempted; and therefore generalizations must be based on estimates and judgments that can only be fragmentary and impressionistic. It seems clear, however, that the general impact of taxation is not to improve income distribution. Instead, the tax burden in the less developed countries is borne largely by the poor families, those who make up most of the population. Improving income distribution through the redistribution effect of taxation is an objective of the taxation policies; but it must be seriously constrained by the compelling need to raise a great deal of revenue and that requires taxation of the poor. "While in developed countries government influences income distribution by means of differential taxation, practically nothing of the kind happens in underdeveloped countries. Statistics show big differences in income distribution in developed countries before and after taxation, distribution being much more even after taxation. In underdeveloped countries distribution is much the same before and after taxation." [19]

Resource Allocation

The government often attempts to improve income distribution by affecting the allocation of resources. Many methods are used. The most important, and most obvious, is through the allocation of government expenditures to improve income distribution. Government resources can be used for direct transfer payments, through given welfare schemes to especially needy beneficiaries such as children, war veterans, cripples, the unemployed, and the aged. Since the need is so great in most countries, and the government's resources so limited, this is not a widely used method of current operations. Government construction projects may be deliberately located in areas where jobs are most needed, or government may direct that its procurement of supplies be focused on certain needy areas. But using government expenditures to improve income distribution must be fitted into a pattern of goals;

201

and thus far at least, it has been a method that is more discussed and proclaimed than it is operationally effective.

The major method the government uses to affect resource allocation to improve income distribution is through affecting investment decisions. Through tax holidays, differential taxation, concessional interest rates investment is influenced both as to location, ownership, and technolog of production. One of the most publicized areas of resource allocation affecting income distribution is that of attempting to reduce the concentration of wealth and income through licensing. The system of granting industrial licenses has as its major objective the more efficient use of scarce capital, the attempt to maximize production and productivity by allocating scarce capital to its most productive use. Most governments add to maximizing production and productivity the objectives of being "fair" to all applicants, of avoiding concentration of wealth and income and of insuring an equitable geographic distribution of economic opportunities. All of these may be encompassed within the general effort to improve income distribution. Concentration of income is a political liability, and governments publicize their efforts to limit the activities of wealthy families and large scale enterprises and to encourage the smaller sized enterprises.

Yet concentration of wealth is a constant threat in most developing countries. The most efficient applicants for scarce permits and license tend to be the existing large enterprises: they can employ adequate technicians to prepare proposals, they have access to adequate financial resources, and they have sufficient influence in the right places to know how to meet government requirements.

In 1959 seven individual families or foreign corporations through 3000 firms controlled 25% of all private industrial assets in Pakistan. Only 24 owning units controlled nearly 50% of all private industrial assets. Also, only 15 families owned 75% of all shares in banks and insurance companies.[20]

Governments may make strenuous efforts to resist concentration of income by establishing rules for the issuance of licenses that constrain large enterprises. A portion of the licenses may be reserved for small scale enterprises or large enterprises may be prohibited from applying for licenses in certain areas. A portion of the permits may be reserved for new entrants to the industry and special contracts issued to new entrants to encourage competition for existing industries. These efforts receive a good deal of publicity as the government wishes to establish an image of helpfulness to small people and independence from influence by big concerns and wealthy families. Rarely, however, do these efforts have a major economic impact. Either the pressure of ongoing operations or the need to utilize all the experiences and managerial capacities available as determined by efficiency considerations make most of these efforts less than affective. Few countries have been able to use their power to influence the allocation of resources in a way that

educes the inequities of income distribution. Probably the most that
an be claimed for them is that they reduce the inequities that would re-
ult from the absence of such controls, which is, of course, a vague
nd far from satisfactory evaluation.

Price Controls

Price policies that attempt to improve income distribution are of
ourse an ancient aspect of government operations. No matter how mar-
et-focused the ideology of a country, at times of crisis it seems quite
cceptable to replace market prices with some forms of government
rice control or even rationing at a fixed price. Governments of the
ess developed countries often establish "fair" prices for essential
ommodities in order to avoid price gauging by the fortunate few who
ave access to supplies. Sometimes the need for control is judged to
e so great that "fair price shops" are established by the government,
r consumer rationing systems may attempt to control sales through
sual commercial channels. A more sophisticated price control system
ay operate through the establishment of standard markups for either
wholesale or retail traders. Because income distribution may be af-
ected indirectly as well as directly, many other kinds of price policies
ave important impacts on income distribution. Thus, curtailing im-
orts in order to protect domestic production of a higher priced product
ay affect the real income of the ultimate consumers adversely and may
ncrease income concentration by making possible a high rate of prof-
ts for the domestic producer. Similarly, any policy of government that
reates a monopolistic position for a domestic producer may permit
rices that reduce real income of consumers—the mass of whom are
enerally low income families—and increase the incomes of the pro-
ucers.

On balance, price policies usually followed by the governments of
he less developed countries apparently distribute income from the low
o the high income side of the distribution, a result that contradicts the
sserted social philosophy of all countries. This assessment, that eco-
omic policies that increase prices for purposes of protecting or stimu-
ating investments tend to increase the inequality of income distribution,
annot be taken as requiring the elimination of such policies. The poli-
ies may be too important for increased production and productivity to
e eliminated. Rather, there is need for recognizing the importance of
his effect as a constraint on price policies, leading to the associated
eed for implementing other policies that will offset these adverse ef-
ects on income distribution.

Labor and Welfare Laws

These are the laws regulating the wages, working conditions or
organizational activities of laborers. Most labor laws affect the incomes of workers, directly or indirectly. Examples of direct attempts
to improve income distribution for workers are minimum wage laws for
specified occupations or areas. Other laws may encourage or retard th
formations of labor unions whose primary purpose may be to raise
workers' real wages. Examples of labor laws that may be classified as
important but indirect in their impact on income distribution would be
laws that limit the inflow of foreign laborers or that stimulate the out-
flow from the country of a foreign minority of workers. Laws specifying
minimum working conditions also must be considered as part of a government's efforts to improve income distribution for low income familie
Labor laws, particularly those affecting unionization, usually have objectives in addition to improved income distribution. The political cap
bilities surrounding strong unions clearly make them a ready channel
for achieving many objectives, particularly those relating to a government's continuation in power.[21] Yet in the long run, laws that permit
workers to form strong unions may have more effect on future income
distribution than any other single policy of government.

Minimum wage laws and similar direct efforts to improve the incom
of low paid workers are not very effective in terms of overall problems
of improving income distribution. They can be applied only to limited
industries, generally large scale, foreign-owned factories or plan-
tations. The large number of small scale enterprises, both agricultural
and industrial, that employ most of the workers of a country provide
an impossible setting for enforcing any minimum wage or working condition laws. Family employment, partial employment and mixtures of
self-employment and apprenticeships make it extremely difficult to apply wage concepts developed in western, industrialized countries to
the less developed countries. In the context of governmental efforts
to improve income distribution, labor laws can be important, but mostl
in a long-range, indirect manner.

Welfare laws may be categorized as laws that are designed to improve the well-being of poor families through the use of transfer payments, income transferred for the good it may do rather than as paymen
for goods or services used in production. Thus, charity to the poor,
aid to the crippled or blind and to minor children, unemployment payments and pensions to the aged are the usual kinds of welfare laws
that directly affect income distribution. In the less developed countrie
welfare laws are not very prominent or extensive. Their potential costs
at almost any standard would represent so large a proportion of public
income that few countries have done more than make token efforts in
this direction. Welfare expenditures are usually family obligations.
Organized forms of public assistance exist, but these are mostly in the
form of governmental services in the health and educational fields,

rather than through transfer payments that involve the expenditures of governmental resources. As in the case of minimum wage laws, the public relations aspect of such welfare programs as exist far outweigh their importance as a means of improving income distribution. While most countries encourage improved welfare laws as important elements for future consideration, the need to use resources in ways directly related to increased production appears to have reduced to a minimum the transfer payments to low income families.

Productivity and Improved Income Distribution

Efforts to improve productivity often appear to be obstructed or diminished by efforts to achieve more equity, particularly as equity is related to improved income distribution. Thus, when policies are adopted that raise the wages of low income families, the opportunity cost appears to include a potential loss in savings or incentives for entrepreneurs to invest. When resources are allocated to depressed areas rather than booming cities, the attempt to improve income distribution may result in higher costs of production. Where investment decisions are guided by considerations of equity rather than by analysis of costs and benefits, it appears that a lower productivity is necessarily associated with deviations from the market-determined choice. While it would be folly to dismiss this aspect of evaluation as mere semantics, it is necessary to insist that most of these direct confrontations between productivity and equity are more symbolic than real, usually the result of questions framed in simplistic and nonoperational terms. Such questions resemble, for example, the frequently raised question, 'Should government development policy emphasize agriculture or industry?" Phrased this way, the answer could only be nonoperational; both sectors must usually be emphasized; and the best mix or optimum degree of relative emphasis will depend upon the current situation in agriculture and industry, the resources available, the institutions available, the objectives and plans of the country. There may be differences in judgment on relative emphasis in many aspects of the interrelationship between agricultural and other sectors of the economy, but no country can afford to neglect the need for a vigorous growth in all relevant sectors.

Similarly, modernization, with its important component, economic growth, requires increasing attention to evaluations of progress in equity as well as in productivity, in terms that are meaningful to each country. Income is a function of production and is closely related to wealth. The problem facing the government is not so much redistributing wealth from the rich to the poor as it is the elimination of poverty. The necessity of considering both equity and productivity may create some constraints, but it may also create some opportunities and it is by no means clear that modernization need be less rapid as a result. The constraints are given prominence because of the consciou or unconscious comparison with the economic history of Western Euro and the United States. It is true that during the period that Western Europe and the United States achieved their relatively high rates of pr ductivity there was much less emphasis than is currently the case on social justice and on the welfare aspects of income distribution. Gov ernments made many public protestations about their responsibility an effort to improve the lot of the poor, but it was firmly believed by mos leaders that economic expansion occurred when the rich were left free to become richer through increasing economic production. By providin more jobs, the poor were helped; and such welfare transfer payments that existed were largely voluntary and went to the specially needy. I these countries, equity considerations that produced progressive tax-ation and social security systems came only after achieving considera momentum toward a higher rate of productivity. This analysis cannot l readily applied to present efforts of the less developed countries to raise their levels of productivity. The moral climate of the world toda produces considerable pressure on all governments to give social just a major, visible role in the objectives of a society. The desire to achieve the benefits of modernization, economic development, and ec nomic growth are not limited to the top income classes or to a heredi-tary elite; it permeates almost the entire body politic, and political leaders must take it into account. The role of government in organi-zation, and supplementation of market-determined economic activities has significantly changed. Consequently, in its efforts to improve in-come distribution, the government must constantly consider policies that represent joint relationships of productivity and equity and must attempt to select the option that optimizes the mix of productivity and equity better than would be possible if one of these were emphasized to the exclusion of the other. The increased role of government may well be a cause, in addition to being a result, of rapid modernization and of rapid economic growth.

In earlier sections of this chapter, several important problems of income distribution were discussed:

High income families supply most of the family savings. Should this income be taxed to pay for increased consumption of low income families?

Urban investment seems more productive, yet the largest number of poor families live in rural areas.

Poor regions of the country need improved income distribution the most, yet market considerations would indicate that investment in the wealthier regions would be more productive.

Some minority ethnic groups appear to be more frugal, more pro-ductive, and earn more income than the average; yet public policy ap-pears to require deliberate efforts to shift income away from these minorities.

Some policies of government that encourage production may be harmful to consumers. Thus, efforts to stimulate agricultural production through raising the prices of basic agricultural commodities may hurt urban consumers, particularly low income families. Yet higher food prices may improve the income of poor families in the rural areas.

Inducements to stimulate investment may press toward capital-intensive expenditures that increase imports and that reduce employment opportunities.

Any formula for the consideration of problems of this type cannot help but be general and resemble moral precepts. Important as these generalizations may be, operating situations usually require additional guidance and criteria; to know that both increased productivity and improved income distribution are important and that governments must select the optimum mix is of limited value to an administrator considering policies that affect a local labor market or the location of a new food processing plant. A government that resolves all policies with sole emphasis on increasing productivity will soon lose its position to others more attuned to changing social and political objectives. Similarly, an administration that emphasizes equity to the exclusion of productivity considerations would soon be overwhelmed by the problems of poverty. The basic operating posture must be that long before there is a direct, unavoidable conflict on an important operating policy between productivity and improved income distribution, steps must be taken to associate these two broad objectives in a situation of a rising productivity and in improving income distribution. Policies must be associated in a way that makes the options both desirable and feasible, from economic as well as political and social viewpoints. This usually can be accomplished by substituting a climate of growth and optimism for the constraints of stagnation and hopelessness. The choice of timing and phasing of the problems for which the policies and options are examined are thus operationally important. It is also necessary to consider the options in operational terms rather than in symbolic terms. Semantics are important because it is necessary to choose language that discourages simplistic comparisons and choices. Where economic growth is vigorous and sustained, the discount applied to future benefits becomes smaller and deferred benefits seem more realistic. Thus, when real wages are rising, though more slowly, than productivity, the prospect of future benefits may spur workers' productivity. However, if real wages are falling as production and productivity rise, it is difficult to gain acceptance for the idea that the rewards for increased productivity will at some future time be available to low income families.

It would be wrong to insist that where considerations of productivity and equity exist, prime emphasis must always be given to increasing productivity. Such a position is dangerous in the extreme, as it's widespread acceptance would soon create either an apathetic, hopeless country or a seething revolutionary mass determined to change the structure of the society. One of the important aspects of the art of political leadership must be guidance and judgment in ordering the right combination of these two patterns of objectives. Furthermore, an important aspect of public administration must be the achievement to a visible degree of both of these objectives through the economic policies adopted in the administration of economic growth. Administrators must accept that the improvement of income distribution is one of the most important economic objectives of a country that wishes to attain a relatively high level of economic production and productivity. Government policies that indirectly affect income distribution are generally far more important for income distribution than direct policies. Unfortunately, governments have largely neglected the importance of direct, visible efforts to improve income distribution. In general, governmental policies that both directly and indirectly affect income distribution have been unsuccessful in improving the relative position of low income families. This in spite of the fact that there need be no sharp confrontation between the objectives of increasing productivity and improving the equity of income distribution. With vigorous, sustained economic growth, both patterns of objectives can be achieved in visible and effective ways.

NOTES

1. See S. Kuznets, Modern Economic Growth (New Haven: Yale University Press, 1967).

2. S. Ahluwalia Montek, "Income Inequality: Some Dimensions of the Problem," Finance and Development (International Monetary Fund and Bank Group, Washington, D.C.) 2, no. 3 (September 1974): 4

3. Report of the National Commission on Labor, Ministry of Labour Employment and Rehabilitation, Government of India, New Delhi, 1964, pp. 183-219.

4. Montek, op. cit., p. 6.

5. Taken from Simon Kuznets, "Quantitative Aspects of Economic Growth of Nations: Distribution of Income by Size," Economic Development and Cultural Change 11, no. 2 (January 1963).

6. Cited by D. J. Turnham, "Income Distribution: Measurement and Problems," p. 8.

7. T. Morgan, "Distribution of Income in Ceylon, Puerto Rico, the United States and the United Kingdom," Economic Journal 63 (December 1953): 821-34.

8. See J. G. Williamson, "Regional Inequality and the Process of National Development: A Description of the Patterns," Economic Development and Cultural Change 13, no. 4, pt. 2 (July 1965): 3-45.

9. See William R. Cline, "The Potential Effect of Income Redistribution on Economic Growth in Six Latin American Countries," The De-

velopment Digest (October 1971): 9-23; Ronald Soligo and James W. Land, "Models of Development Incorporating Distribution Aspects," (mimeo.) Discussion Paper 22, Rice University, Texas (Fall 1972), pp. 1-27; and Felix Paukert, "Income Distribution at Different Levels of Development, A Survey of Evidence," International Labour Review 108, nos. 2-3 (August-September 1973): 97-125.

10. Soligo and Land, op. cit., pp. 16, 27.

11. Mahbub ul Hag, "Employment in the 1970s, a New Perspective," The Development Digest (October 1971): 3-8.

12. W. Calenson and G. Pyatt, The Quality of Labour and Economic Development in Certain Countries (Geneva: International Labour Organization, 1964), pp. 15-19; 87-88; and Harvey Liebenstein, Economic Backwardness and Economic Growth (New York: Wiley and Sons, 1963), p. 65.

13. Cline, op. cit., p. 22.

14. See A. P. Prest, Public Finance in Underdeveloped Countries (New York: Wiley and Sons, 1972); also the East African Commission of Enquiry on Income Taxes, 1956-57 (Nairobi: East Africa High Commission, 1957).

15. Prest, op. cit., p. 28.

16. Ibid., pp. 27-28.

17. Based on unpublished data from the U.S. Government—Agency for International Assistance, Statistics and Reports Division, 1969.

18. See U Tun Wai, "Taxation Problems and Policies of Underdeveloped Countries" in International Monetary Fund Staff Papers 9, 1962.

19. Maria Negreponti-Delivanis, "The Distribution of National Income in Underdeveloped Countries" in The Distribution of National Income, J. Marchal and E. Ducros, eds. (New York: St. Martins Press, 1968), p. 303.

20. Gustav Papanek, Pakistan's Development (Cambridge, Mass.: Harvard University Press, 1967), pp. 67-68.

21. See Sidney Sufrin, Unions in Emerging Societies, Frustration and Politics (Syracuse: Syracuse University Press, 1964).

THE USEFULNESS OF THE INSTITUTION BUILDING APPROACH

General Purpose of the Analysis of Institutions

The institution building approach views society as capable of deliberate change. It assumes that a society can be changed in important ways if the leaders and people of that society wish to change it and are willing to exert the energy and devote the necessary resources to make the desired changes. Obviously there are limits implicit in this assumption. There are some changes that are impossible physically. A country cannot determine to change its mountains into pleasant, well-watered valleys or to turn its forbidding deserts into fertile farmland. Even these "impossible" physical changes must not be stressed too much, because much has been done by determined effort. Yet limitation exist, limitations that are real and operational. The institution building approach to societal changes assumes that desired changes can be achieved in a reasonable time period and at reasonable cost, as determined by the leaders of the society. This, of course, does not rule out either evolutionary or revolutionary changes, changes that occur slowly over time, almost unconsciously as experience dictates and persuades; or changes that occur suddenly, with explosive impact, responding to pent-up, powerful agents of change. The institution building approach adds to evolutionary and revolutionary processes the belief that there are some important changes that can be deliberately instigated, faster than the evolutionary changes that every society undergoes, less painful and less disruptive than the revolutionary changes that many societies go through. The institution building approach is useful to a society that wishes to modernize itself or achieve development more rapidly At a more operational level of thinking in terms of economic growth, it is a view of societal change that insists that it is possible to achieve, through deliberate creation of appropriate institutions, a substantially higher rate of economic growth than would be possible if no deliberate efforts were made to establish or restructure appropriate institutions. The assumptions underlying this belief must be made explicit:

1. Development and one of its important segments, economic growth, require new institutions. These institutions incorporate new values and new ways of doing things that society wishes to be done differently than before. If totally new institutions are not feasible or possible, existing institutions must be restructured or seriously modified.

2. Some new or restricted institutions must necessarily develop slowly. Others can be planned and established deliberately to speed up the process of change.

3. The more modernized a society becomes, the more specialized will many of its institutions become. Specialization is an essential attribute of development, and economic specialization is essential to rapid economic growth.

4. In the institution building or restructuring process, some aspects are generic and can be learned and applied to all institutions, regardless of their specific nature. Institution building as a process has some operational generalizations that are useful as working rules for a society attempting to modernize itself.

Institution building thus includes an acceptance of the feasibility of social engineering, the belief that society can be deliberately changed and improved. This, in turn, assumes that a society has the ability to judge what is improvement and the will to try to achieve it. When a society wishes to modernize itself and to become more developed, there is some image of what this means in terms that are related to how its people live or want to live. By concentrating on economic growth as an important segment of the development process, the assumption is made here that it is possible to achieve a higher rate of economic production and productivity through the establishment of appropriate economic institutions. Of course, other occurrences are also essential; establishing new economic institutions can be considered a necessary but not the sole condition for economic growth.

Concept of an Institution

An institution is defined here as a behavior pattern, a way of doing something that a society values.* The emphasis here is at the level of

---

*There are almost as many definitions of institutions as there are analysts using the concept. Sometimes an institution is defined as a

activity, of doing something useful. But every organization is not an institution. If it were, there would be no advantage in using the word institution. An institution is a special kind of organization or group of organizations. It is an organization that deals with normative values, with values that identify desirable conduct or priorities. An institution establishes normative relationships with its environment to an important degree. Thus, institutions are important organizations, influential, standard-setting, noticed and valued by their environment and essential to a society's operation.

In a sense, stressing the normative values of institutions emphasizes the instrumental nature of those organizations, the fact that there are purposes beyond the immediate product of the organization. Thus, "to institutionalize is to <u>infuse with value</u> beyond the technical requirements of the task at hand."[1] A more detailed definition is that given by the Inter-University Research Program in Institution Building, where the process of institution building is defined as "the planning, a structuring and guidance of new or reconstructed organizations which (a) embody changes in values, functions, physical and/or social technologies, (b) establish, foster and protect normative relationships and action patterns, and (c) attain support and complementarity in the environment."[2]

"system of roles" or a "normative action pattern." Institutions have been defined as "codes of rational, routine activity" (Daniel Lerner), "interactions pursued by relatively stable patterns of practice which are somewhat specialized to particularly value outcomes" (Harold D. Laswell and Allan R. Holmberg), "functionally specific sound organizations which are valued in the environment" (Milton J. Esman and Fred C. Bruhns), quoted in <u>Comparative Theories of Social Change</u>, ed., Hollis W. Peter, Foundation for Research in Human Behavior (Ann Arbor, Michigan, 1966).

Other definitions are: "Generalized patterns of norms that define <u>categories</u> of prescribed, permitted and prohibited behavior in social relationships for people in interaction with each other as members of their society and its various subsystems and groups." Talcott Parsons, <u>Structure and Process in Modern Societies</u> (Glencoe, Ill.: The Free Press, 1960), p. 177.

Also: "Institutions are patterns of recurring acts structured to condition behavior of their members both within the institution and its relationship with other units of the social system and to project a force in the social system in terms of ethos, or action." Ralph Braibanti in <u>Political and Administrative Development</u> (Durham, N.C.: Duke University Press, 1969), p. 55.

Institution Building

The process of institution building is necessarily dynamic; it involves many different forces of changing direction and intensity. Institution building, to be logically useful, must have a means of measuring progress; and it must involve a concept of institutionalization, a situation where the pattern of behavior may be judged successfully established. The criteria for institutionalization may be summarized as follows:

1. Viability. Survival is the age-old test of the success of any organization. The ability to survive and to grow means something about successful operation, since without it continued successful operation is scarcely possible. Yet, mere survival is not enough for an institution, which must spread new norms and foster innovation and change in its relationship to its environment. Survival must include maintenance and growth in effectiveness. The hollow shell of an institution is too often retained after it has lost all effectiveness as an agent of change.

2. Influence. An institution is successfully established when it becomes meaningful to its environment. This means that its output is accepted and valued by its clients, and its ideas and values are becoming accepted by its environment. An organization that has won the respect and approval of other organizations with which it has relationships is institutionalized as far as its environment is concerned. It becomes accepted as a "complementarity" by other institutions.

3. Autonomy. When an institution is successfully established, it attains a workable degree of autonomy. This means that it is not under the detailed supervision of other institutions, but has a large degree of freedom in making decisions about its own operations. Its procedures and practices can differ substantially, if it wishes, from those of the larger group of institutions from which it receives its authority and that allocate the resources it uses. Autonomy is, of course, never absolute. Its measurement, however, is an understandable preoccupation of administrators who can observe the degree of autonomy in resource acquisition, staffing, pricing, issuance of public releases, and in the many channels of communications both internally and with other organizations.

4. Support. Influence and autonomy of an institution is often demonstrated in the kind of support it receives. Support includes the acquisition of many resources: financial, human, physical, informational, technological, and authoritative. The relative ease with which a new institution receives its support and the adequacy of that support indicate how much the institution is valued by its complementary institutions. Where support is given automatically, because of the great esteem or importance attached to the institution, it can be taken as a measure of its importance to complementary institutions and as its complete acceptance.

5. _Output._ Since all institutions have outputs, the valuation of their outputs by clients and other institutions is a measure of institutionalization. The extent of the use of its output and the value attached to it is often a good measure of the degree of acceptance of the institution.

6. _Innovative thrust._ So important is the concept of innovation to an institution that it is important to emphasize its involvement in the process of institutionalization. In a less developed country, institutions are one of the major ways of inducing social change. The successful institution values its innovative thrust, that is its ability to foster changes in ideas and practices both within itself and with its environment.

These six attributes—viability, influence, autonomy, support, output, and innovative thrust—are interdependent in both concept and measurement. Their interaction and mutual causation mean that measurement cannot be made mechanically; there is no fixed point of success in any one of these attributes. Each one may be considered a complex continuum and the measurement of success or failure in one is related in a complex way to the success or failure in another of these attributes. Success in one may require giving up another, as in the case where viability may require giving up the innovative thrust of an organization. To achieve a necessary degree of support it may be necessary to give up some degree of autonomy, by staying attached at detailed levels to another, more powerful organization. All measurement of institutionalization must be relative and judgmental, and therefore subject to differing evaluations.

Since an institution is always heavily involved with its environment, when its environment changes the criteria of institutionalization must change. Thus, it is impossible to transfer an institution successfully from one country to another without many significant changes in the institution. This is particularly true in the case of those institutions that are successful in the developed countries and are therefore assumed to be necessary in the less developed countries. No greater cause for failure in technical foreign aid programs can be found than the efforts to establish institutions that do not fit into their new environment. Environmental changes are also significant during the life of an institution. Sometimes, the changes in environment made possible by the institution itself mean that it is no longer essential and should be eliminated. The continuing shells of formerly useful institutions are evidence that it is often as difficult to eliminate an organization as it is to establish it successfully.

Thus, the process of institution building is dynamic and its evaluation must provide for dynamic concepts of progress and achievement. Its success is not the achievement of a static position of acceptance but rather of successful operation and of acceptance under continually changing conditions and with continuing evaluation. It is here that a systems approach to analysis is most important. An institution by its

214

definition must be part of a complex of systems and subsystems. As it operates, using inputs, producing outputs, communicating, and dealing with its sources of supply and its clients, it creates and is affected by changes both within itself and within its environment. Important relationships in its transactions acquiring inputs and disposing of outputs are constantly changing, and thus continual adjustments are required in internal operations. There are many variables or changing elements in these operations, and their analysis is the major subject of an institution building approach to directed social change.

> And, because the domain of institution building is the domain of human values, beliefs, aspirations and competence, and the tools of institution building include interpersonal influence, human communication and management of the learning process, it is inevitable that the criteria of success will be complex, difficult to quantify and measurable only within broad margins of error. Goals and objectives are likely to change, not in detail, but even in major components, as the institution building process continues.[3]

Economic Institutions

Economic institutions are those institutions whose major purpose is to effect the production of goods and services for sale to others. Since by definition all institutions provide outputs that society values, there must be some meaningful way of identifying those institutions that are designated "economic;" and the difference between them and the others must be in the way the output is utilized. Economic institutions help produce goods and services for the market; their output is valued by both the producer and the consumer in a manner that directly affects exchange transactions. In more technical economic jargon, economic institutions are those organizations whose outputs can be included in the national product at their market value because a significant proportion of output is marketed. Institutions whose outputs are not marketed are generally included in the national product on the basis of some measure of cost, such as the earnings of the factor inputs. Thus, government in general and organizations that supply education, health, and welfare services are usually included in the national product at cost, since there is little attempt to establish market prices for their outputs.*

---

*However, market forces strongly influence the prices of some of these services. Witness the high price of medical services in some places where demand far exceeds supply. Usually, however, cost and social policy are the major considerations for determining the price of noneconomic services.

It is important to emphasize again that the concept of development must include far more than the outputs of economic institutions. Indeed it would not be an exaggeration to insist that the noneconomic institutions have outputs that a society must treasure far more than its economic products. The desirability of modernization may be questioned precisely because it often stresses improvement in economic products in contrast with the health, education, cultural, psychological, and other noneconomic, quality aspects of human life. Economic institutions are important, but certainly are not the only important institutions; and they may even not be the most important institutions in a society that wishes to improve the quality of its style of living.

The concept of institution building includes only certain kinds of important organizations, those that are valued beyond the technical requirements of mere production; an institution embodies changes in value and somehow affects its environment through these value changes. Thus, economic institutions are those organizations engaged in economic activities that have values and influences beyond mere production. They are organizations that have important influences on other institutions and that embody new ways of producing economic outputs, as recognized by suppliers of factor inputs and by those that demand the product. This definition still involves judgment, as most definitions in the social sciences do. It means that a paper mill can be classified as an institution where there is only one paper mill in a community but not where there are many similar mills. In the former instance, the importance of its presence and operations will transcend the paper products it produces, important as that may be. In the less developed countries almost by definition, all important economic undertakings will be classifiable as economic institutions because of their relative visibility and importance. Economic institutions are utilitarian organizations, in the terms of Amitai Etzioni, in which the major means of control is remuneration. [4] Other kinds of institutions, such as churches, universities, and voluntary organizations, use normative power as the major source of control. A normative organization comes into existence when its objectives are so internalized that they become dominant in evoking participation and control within the organization.

In selecting these economic institutions for study of their relationship to public administration, several additional assumptions are made:

1. Much of the economic growth desired by countries attempting to develop themselves will be produced by economic institutions. While additional government expenditures on health, education, and welfare are of prime importance to development, they are not nearly as large in the aggregate as the increase in economic goods and service. This can be readily ascertained in examining the private sector and government components of the GNP of the less developed countries.

2. Though economic growth is a function of noneconomic as well as of economic institutions, most of the important impacts of the noneconomic institutions are reflected in their relationship with the eco-

nomic institutions. Educational institutions are of prime importance in achieving a high rate of economic growth, but largely as they affect the economic institutions that use the labor factor inputs and as these economic institutions use the technology made available by the educational institutions. By studying the administration of economic institutions, the effects of noneconomic institutions on economic growth will necessarily be examined and evaluated.

3. Public administration is a key input of economic institutions. No economic institution can be initiated or restructured without an adequate relationship to governmental agencies. This obviously applies to economic institutions owned and operated by government, but it applies equally to economic institutions that are nongovernment-owned and operated and any variation between these two extremes.

The exact definition of any single economic institution must be left to the specific situation under analysis. The size of the institution and its limits or boundaries will vary with each situation. Sometimes, the unit will be considered one large organization, such as a railroad or a bank. Sometimes it will be necessary to group some organizations for purposes of analysis, such as a cooperatively-owned bus system or a wholesale fruit market. Sometimes there will be no one clearly definable organization but rather a set of economic functions or services that can be more or less aggregated for analytical purposes, such as a money or an insurance market. While size is not a dominant criterion, clearly trivial organizations can be considered as institutions only as they are grouped into meaningful aggregates. Studying economic institutions means studying significant, important patterns of economic behavior, homogeneous enough so that meaningful observations can be made about the patterns of behavior.

The inevitable movement towards increased specialization in a developing country applies particularly to economic institutions. Increased productivity often means increased specialization of output and the adaption of techniques that require increased specialization of inputs. It also means the development of specialized economic institutions to provide intermediate products, for use by other economic institutions as inputs. Thus the economic institutions that must be established include not only the factories, shops, and industrial units that produce with new technologies, but also the banks, insurance companies, markets, and similar organizations that inevitably are parts of a high productivity economic system. Two ideas must be developed to support this assertion. First, these kinds of economic institutions are essential. Second, they have the attributes to be identified as economic institutions.

4. A higher rate of productivity is necessarily associated with improved technology. In turn, improved technology must be incorporated in the capital and human factors, in the machines, organization, and skills that are the inputs involved in the improved technology. As technology improves and productivity increases, the indirectness of the production process increases. More products are made to be inputs of other

products, the time span between the start of production and delivery to final consumer is lengthened, and the number of transactions involved in the whole process increases. This can be visualized quite simply by comparing a small sandal-maker and a shoe factory. The handicraft sandal-maker buys leather, cotton, nails, and then with a few hand tools makes sandals for specific customers or for sale at the local bazaar. The sandal factory must buy machines and a specialized building arrange for light, power, and transportation, must purchase factor inputs in many different markets and must arrange to sell its products through venders, who in turn distribute the product to retail stores, bazaar sellers and even to merchants who export the sandals. The managers of the factory may become involved in bank loans, credit arrangements for their dealers, insurance and government import licenses. Higher productivity necessarily involves larger production units that form parts of new economic institutions, and new kinds of financial and marketing institutions that are needed to produce and distribute the increased production.

These new financial and marketing institutions are not only necessary for increased industrial production; they are also part of the increased productivity of nonindustrial economic units. It is inconceivable that a significant increase in agricultural productivity will occur without the use of new capital equipment, new inputs of fertilizer, seeds, and water. Additional transportation for both inputs and product are required, and there must be increased marketing of both factor inputs and the greater product. New and expanded market facilities will be required, associated with new and expanded facilities for financing, storing, insuring, and marketing. It is a fact that higher productivity of an economic system necessarily involves new or restructured economic organizations that provide the additional products and services, financial, transportation, insurance, and sales that are required for a sustained, high rise of productivity.

5. New or restructured economic capacities can be labeled institutions because they have an innovative thrust, encompassing as they must new ideas and new ways of production and of assisting production Simply repeating the old ways would not be enough; the new technologies require innovation in the process of acquiring and utilizing new, improved inputs. These new production units are important enough to have significant effects in the environment with which they are in contact, both as suppliers of inputs or as consumers of the output. When a large new factory is established in an area that has no factories or only a few factories, its impact goes far beyond the sale of its product. Its rules and procedures, its methods and ideas, the codes of conduct it requires for its work, its relationship with suppliers of intermediate products and services, all these have a marked effect on the community. Its pricing and sales practices may have a strong influence on many communities. An illustration of this would be the effect of the rate structure of a power company or a transportation system, where a single rate may determine whether an entire village is to be serviced or

only a few wealthy people. The general image of a new industrial plant and the feeling of change and efficiency it gives may be as important as the products it sells in the community. The values it fosters in production and distribution and its responsibility and attitude toward its labor force are "external economies," in the jargon of the economist, and may be as important as its marketed product.

Having argued that the successful establishment of special kinds of economic organizations is essential to development, there remains an additional point to emphasize. If they are not in themselves market institutions, economic institutions are necessarily functionally related to market institutions. It will be remembered that market institutions were defined in Chapter 5 as patterns of behavior that encourage transactions by arranging to have the supply and demand for an economic good or service confront each other in exchanges. Some production units have market aspects incorporated internally as part of their operation, but most production units have to associate with formal or informal market arrangements external to their structure. Thus, a factory may select workers from a relatively unorganized labor market, where no formal organization exists. The factory may receive credit from a more organized money market, in the form of a series of banks that could be classified as financial institutions. It may also arrange to sell its product through a wholesale market, where many dealers may make up an economic institution that performs marketing services for many factories. Whether formally organized into a single unit or consisting of a loosely organized unit, the market institution is necessary for production units that produce for the general client and not for specifically designated customers. Since a high level of productivity requires production for the market institutions, it is important to realize that association with marketing institutions is an essential function of every significantly sized production unit.

THE INSTITUTION BUILDING PROCESS

Selection of Variables

Using essentially the same concept of institution as in this book, the process of institution building has been studied by many analysts.5 The typical study selects an institution in one of the less developed countries and analyzes the process by which it was created and operated, evaluating at the same time its effectiveness and the degree to which it has become institutionalized. Most of these studies concern schools initiated through the technical assistance programs of the United States, projects that were clearly institutional in character because of their emphasis on changing some of the standards of a society.

However, there were also studies of planning agencies, banks, valley development authorities, youth programs, and business organizations as well as schools. All of the studies were based on analytical models that stressed the need for identifying variables or clusters of more or less similar attributes and actions that were important in determining the success or failure in the establishment of an institution.

From these studies, it is possible to select those variables that are important in initiating and operating economic institutions. These variables are not different in broad outline from those of other kinds of educational, political, social, and cultural institutions. But the emphasis is quite different and what each can construe as currently useful generalizations is different. Schools and industrial plants have many similarities in their organizational structure, their need for support, and their relationships to the people and organizations that use their products. They also have many important differences. The educational system cannot be operated in the same manner as the banking system, yet in their operations they may have to appraise many problems and examine many influential forces in substantially the same manner. Thus, it is possible to examine the process of economic institution building using many of the same variables that have been identified as useful in the analysis of other kinds of institutions.

The variables selected for analysis must be operational. That is, they should not be so abstracted from reality that they are difficult to identify in the actual operations of an institution. Further, they must be reasonably similar or homogeneous; they must have sufficiently common elements so that they can be grouped logically and permit some generalizations about the group as a whole. Finally, the generalizations must be translated into guidelines for actual operations of an institution. There is no use in selecting variables that are so heterogeneous and so dissimilar that any generalization about them is so vague as to be a moral precept rather than an operating guide for action.*

The variables that have been identified for analysis have usually been divided into internal and external groups. This is because the successful establishment of an institution is so closely related to its ability to adjust to and affect its environment. The internal variables have been designated as "institutional" variables, while the external variables are called "linkages" to emphasize that they join the institution and its environment, other institutions, people, suppliers of its

---

*This is not meant to denigrate moral precepts; but the analysis must be more useful than are exhortations to be good, efficient, honest, cooperative, and conscientious. Obviously, these are necessary and important, but to be operational it is necessary that the level of generalization be lowered to statements about who does what, and what cooperation and efficiency mean in a particular working situation.

inputs, and consumers of its output. However, the separation into two sets of variables, institutional and linkage, that are so intertwined in their internal and external influences and effects is awkward, particularly with regard to economic institutions. Even as analytical constructs, the separation seems forced and unnecessary. Every group of variables has both internal and external aspects that seem so joined operationally that they must be considered at the same time. Consequently, in this survey of institution building, the analysis of variables is combined into a single set having both internal and external aspects.

It is impossible to select variables that are independent in the mathematical sense of that term. All of the variables are interdependent and mutually related. A specific administrative action may affect one or all of these variables at the same time. Changing one variable changes other variables, even if that was not the intention at the time. The relationship between the variables has not been developed to the point where their dimensions can be clearly identified, even in nonquantitative terms. While classification itself generally implies some theoretical basis for selection of what is important, it is safe to assert that the analysis of institution building variables has not advanced to the point where theories of relationships can be presented. Thus, the variables form a sort of pre-theory, a belief that the process of institution building is capable of identifying important related aspects that seem to be present in all institutions. This is not a model in the scientific sense of that term, but rather a map that guides the analyst to examine different aspects for relevance in any particular situation. It may be possible to draw from this map some useful operating generalizations that help in understanding how economic institutions are successfully established.

The variables that have been identified for study are leadership, doctrine, program performance, resources, and internal structure. Each of these has both internal and linkage aspects that help determine the degree of success in establishing an institution.*

Leadership

The leadership of an institution is defined as those persons who are actively engaged in the formulation of its objectives and rules and who direct its operations and relationships with its environment. How far down the hierarchy the leadership goes is not too important, as

---

*The guiding concepts of the Inter-University Research Program in Institution Building identify four "linkage" variables, enabling, functional, normative and diffused, that have been incorporated into these five "institutional" variables. See Esman and Blaise.

there will always be some leadership below any point. Leadership as a variable used in operating analysis must be assigned to the relatively few administrators who exercise a significant proportion of the direction of the institution. Leadership is thus a collective phenomenon. It is a group of people who have a common acceptance of the objectives of the institution and cooperate in directing it towards achieving these objectives. The image of a single leader may occasionally be presented by a dominant or charismatic personality, but this appearance is hardly ever a reflection of reality. From the very nature of its operations, an institution is too complex an organization to be the work of one man, although one person may be exceedingly important.

Leadership has been identified as the single most critical variable in establishing new institutions. This appears so obvious that its expression may seem unnecessary, except that in actual practice the importance of leadership is frequently neglected. Particularly in government-owned and operated institutions, leadership is often treated with more emphasis on the public image than on technical and organizational competence. The unpleasant fact is that leadership is difficult to measure as a variable, and therefore difficult to evaluate and predict. Literally thousands of books have been written on how to select and train good organizational leaders, and all kinds of practical rules have been advanced by experienced and personally successful leaders. Intelligence tests, psychological probes, aptitude tests, experience ratings—all have been advanced with reason as ways of selecting good leadership. All have demonstrated limited value in this respect. Leadership in institution building can be measured largely by the success of the institution itself, and that is a self-serving test. The point is: "no leadership act is inherently effective or ineffective; it might be either depending upon the goals with reference to which it is assessed."

Successful leadership is committed to attaining the objectives of the institution. The adequacy of the leadership varies directly with the intensity of the commitment. No matter how competent the leadership is, if it is not deeply committed to achieving the objectives of the institution, it will find it difficult to do a good job. This means that the objectives must be of a pattern that can be understood and accepted by the leadership. Further, the leadership must internalize these commitments and objectives; that is, the commitments and objectives must be brought into the consciousness of all people in the organization so that they will act as coordinating and unifying forces. The truthful copybook maxims about the essentiality of "interest in your work" can be translated at management levels to commitment to the objectives of the institutions.

No discussion of the importance of the leadership variable can even pretend to be adequate without some reference to authority, power, and responsibility—the "triangle" that is a favorite subject of management analysts and organizational theorists. Sorting out these three aspects of leadership has been fashionable since the discovery of writing. Present analysts have clarified these concepts, and there is some kind of a consensus about their meanings and relationships. Briefly, authority is "accepted right," power is "influence to affect actions," and responsibility is "obligation to act in certain ways." Their interdependence is clear; and the assumption of a necessary parity between them, one of the maxims of received wisdom in traditional public administration, is still accepted by most administrators. There is an appeal to statements such as "authority is power," "authority must equal responsibility," and "every power establishes its equivalent responsibility." Discussions of the relationship between these three aspects of the leadership variable are of course relevant to any study of organizational operations,[7] but here one major relationship needs emphasis. Authority is often a function of the exercise of power. Leadership is often good because it is effective and develops authority because it exercises authority. That this may be circular reasoning and therefore unacceptable as formal logic is regrettable, but it is an operating reality. Leadership in the creation of institutions is often considered ineffective or inadequate because it does not exercise its authority or use the power it has to achieve the objectives of the institution. In a sense, this relationship resembles a muscle that strengthens because it is used, which of course assumes that the inputs of energy are also available. Leadership as a variable in institution building is often a function of the use of its power; it develops authority, the "accepted right" to do certain things through the use of power it has to do these things. No leadership can be expected to be given in advance and as an initial resource all of the authority it may require to build or operate a successful institution. Leaders must expect to look into problems that they themselves are not adequately authorized to deal with and go on to acquire the requisite authorization as solutions are developed.

Doctrine

The term "doctrine" is applied to the values, objectives, and operational style of an institution. This is what the institution is trying to achieve and the choices of methods it uses to achieve its objectives. It is the basis for the image the institution projects, both internally and externally. It establishes what the institution is expected to do and its style of action.

Doctrine is the most difficult of all the institution building variables to describe and analyze, but this difficulty cannot minimize its importance. It is the core of the administration of an institution; it guides the choices and actions that administrators make. Leadership depends upon the internalization of doctrine, the acceptance of its objectives and methods by the staff of the institution, the central agreement on objectives that coordinates and guides all kinds of group and individual decisions. Without the integrating influence of accepted doctrine, it is virtually impossible to direct a complex organization. Doctrine is also an essential variable in developing the appropriate relationship with the environment. The basic idea of defining an institution as a special type of complex organization emphasizes the essentiality of fostering innovative changes in a society. As stated above, an institution establishes normative relationships with its environment to an important degree. Institutions must succeed in transferring some of their doctrine to other institutions, or they are correctly judged to be failures. Thus, a necessary objective among the multiple objectives of every institution must be some normative relationships linking an institution with its environment.

Program Performance

This variable consists of all the activities of an institution that constitute its output; it is the translation of the doctrine of the institution into action. Program performance is the most obvious variable involved in institution building, the variable most commonly observed and often mistakenly assumed to be the only one of importance. In a sense, it reflects the effectiveness of the other institutional variables; but the assumption of a simple, direct relationship among variables leads to many difficulties and fallacies. Performance is as much a function of leadership as of doctrine; and everyone has observed instances where because of the tremendous demands for the output of the institution good performance has occurred in spite of obviously inadequate leadership.

There is need to stress that program performance is necessarily related to program objectives, the purposes of the institution. These objectives are multiple and often contradictory. They form a complicated pattern against which performance is often difficult to measure. Setting low production targets often makes mechanical measurement of program performance appear relatively efficient and successful. But examination of the inevitable interdependencies among institutional variables usually exposes inadequate program objectives to questioning and invites change. If an institution sets too low an output objective against which its program performance can be evaluated, its low efficiencies and consequent higher costs are usually quite visible to the users of its output and stimulates public demands for adequate program performance. Adequate performance is only one of the many objectives and evaluations that good leadership must continually consider—its importance is obvious.

Resources

This variable represents the cluster of inputs needed by the institution. In noneconomic language, it includes the following:

1. Financial resources are the money and credit that the institution utilizes in its operations, including reserves and "lines of credit" that establish financial credibility.

2. Physical resources are the building, machinery, equipment, raw materials, intermediate and final products that the institution uses.

3. Human resources are the manpower inputs, including management experience and organizational skills.

4. Technological resources are the ways in which the inputs are combined to produce the output and are embodied in the financial, physical, and human resources. Because of the importance of technology, it is identified separately to provide a better opportunity to examine its adequacy.

5. Informational resources are so important to successful management and institution building that this intangible input, like technology, is identified separately. As an input, information must be designated as arising externally from the environment. Yet it is inextricably interwoven with internally generated information and is thus difficult to classify only as an input.

6. Authority is mentioned as a resource because it is so important in institution building. It is identified as an input because it is an essential element whose absence is so often fatal to new institutions. Yet authority is also generated from internal action and cannot be totally given to an institution from without as a resource. It is mentioned here because of its importance and because it is associated so firmly with other inputs. Some analysts have identified a variable called "enabling linkage"[8] to group those relationships that permit an institution to become established and operate. At least for economic institutions, it seems best to include this as a resource and therefore as an input.

Time is often suggested as an input. Certainly it is scarce, and its use must be minimized.[9] In many ways, time does appear to be a resource, just as are the financial, physical, and human inputs of an institution. But time is too slippery a concept to be handled this way. The tools for its analysis are too imperfect and blunt, and its rigorous use as a factor finds the analyst straying into a wilderness from which there is no exit into current social analysis. Time is thus an input only to the extent of its inclusion as a characteristic of other inputs, such as the discounting of capital or as the time it takes to train workers. Time as an independent subvariable is better left to moral theologists.

The importance of adequate resources in institution building is so obvious that it needs little amplification. The analysis of adequacy, however, is another matter. Most of the failures in institution building are attributed to inadequate resources, at least by its administrators. Here again, there arises the necessary but frustrating problem of establishing some kind of independent criteria, or else the circular reasoning involved prevents analysis. If an institution fails or is only partially successful in attaining its objectives, obviously by definition its multivarious inputs were insufficient to do the necessary job. When leadership is weak and uncertain or when there is too much interference from the outside, the reasons for institutional failure can be called inadequate human resource inputs or inadequate input of authority.

It is because of this type of circular reasoning that the acquisition of adequate resources is one of the best tests of the other variables in the institution building process. Resources are not a one-time input; they need constant acquisition and constant improvement. The annual budget sessions of government institutions reflect both periodic and intermittent needs to acquire new resources. Private institutions have similar needs. There is a continuing competition for scarce resources of all kinds, and the ability to compete in this scramble is often a rough but good measure of the leadership variable. But, as has been suggested, the relationship is too complex to permit stopping with this simple analysis. Just as authority is often derived from the exercise of power, so the vindication of the use of scarce resources is often merely their successful use. Adequate program performance, the production of outputs, is the best evidence on which leadership can base its claims for more resources. While there may be isolated cases where too good a program performance, too many outputs, have dictated a reduction in resources, these instances are overwhelmingly surpassed by the instances in which resources allocated to an institution have been reduced because of poor program performance.

Internal Structure

This variable consists of the structure and processes necessary for the operation and maintenance of an institution. It involves allocation of roles and authority patterns within the formal structure of the organization and the informal allocation of roles and authority patterns as well. The internal structure of an institution is the variable most easily identified by observers, and therefore its importance tends to be exaggerated far beyond its merit.

While the internal structure of an institution facilitates or limits program performance and leadership, it is not often the prime determinant in the achievement of objectives. In mathematical terms, internal structure is usually a strongly independent variable. If it were able to be dominant in program performance, it would be possible to increase materially the likelihood of the success of a specific institution building process by adopting the best internal structure. But operational reality dismisses that as an impossibility, and there is no reason in theory why this should be so. Internal structure provides opportunities; it is permissive rather than inherently forceful. In this it resembles savings banks, institutions that make a certain kind of savings possible but which do not by themselves generate savings. This quality of the internal structure variable is overlooked by many administrators, who often rely upon changing the internal structure of moribund institutions for a revival of institutional vitality and effectiveness. While modification of internal structure is often important, it usually is ineffective unless it is associated with changes in other variables. Thus, changing the internal structure to a new pattern of authority may be only mildly helpful if the same quality of human inputs is used, the same people told to utilize a different structure of authority.

The internal structure of an institution is of course related to its innovative aspirations, but the structure is evidently so complicated that no currently useful generalization can be advanced. In other words, there does not seem to be any kind of formal internal structure that fosters innovation more than any other kind of internal structure. For example, no study of the experience of public corporations has indicated that because of their internal structure they are more receptive to innovation than are other types of institutions. Innovation evidently arises more from the image and atmosphere of leadership and doctrine than from the formal organizational structure. No useful generalizations can yet be made about the importance of informal structures of institutions. However, since innovations often disturb formal relationships, innovations clearly can be encouraged more readily by the informal rather than formal structure of an institution.[10]

The importance of its environment to the internal structure of an institution is equally obvious and important, although largely unanalyzed. A great deal of the need to adjust patterns of authority arises from "enabling linkages," the relationships with other institutions in the environment that give an institution its authority, power, resources, and doctrine. This is another illustration of the difficulty of isolating internal from external variables; at an operating level, the internal structure of an institution is very dependent upon certain enabling and functional linkages with other complementary institutions. The fairly widespread opinion that government economic institutions are inadequately structured arises largely from a conviction that the internal structure of authority is controlled in detail by government agencies and consequently detracts from both the effectiveness of the leadership and program performance.

THE BUILDING PROCESS OF ECONOMIC INSTITUTIONS

Program Performance Variable

While each variable is significantly different for each type of institution, the greatest difference is found in the performance variable, the output of the institution. Here, economic institutions have features that are of distinct advantage in understanding institution building, and it is this difference that can usefully be made operational. The major outputs of economic institutions are market oriented, and consequently can be market measured. The dominant objective of economic institutions is the production and distribution of goods and services; and while the other attributes of an institution are present, the emphasis on output production is usual and quite natural. It is dangerous to overlook the intangible, nonmarketable externalities generated by economic institutions but these should not hide the fact that most of the outputs of economic institutions are both visible and measurable. This relative ease of measurement should not be oversimplified or permitted to mask the objectives of the institution that are not directly related to its marketable output. Neither should relative ease of measurement be disregarded just because for other types of institutions it may be misleading to stress output (for which measurement is difficult and for which no adequate surrogates of output are available). The difficulties in measuring the real output of an educational institution should not result in neglecting the importance of evaluating the output of an economic institution.

The fact that market values are often unsatisfactory measures of social values means that the measurement of the output of economic institutions must be considered carefully. It does not nullify the usefulness of market measurement; it merely means that caution and judgment are still required. The measurement of the output of economic institutions has always required consideration of the value of externalities to society. As stated in chapter 1, where there are significant differences between individual and social costs and between individual and social benefits; external economies and diseconomies must be considered in the evaluation of production and productivity. This is another way of insisting that market evaluation is useful but must be adjusted to take into account the other aspects of costs and benefits that are not included in market evaluation.

Since both the output and input of economic institutions can be readily measured, the efficiency of economic institutions is more readily assessable than that of other kinds of institutions. The downgrading of efficiency as a dominant objective of public administration came largely from the conviction that efficiency was impossible to measure without evaluating objectives and that concentration on output measurement and efficiency often neglected other, more important objectives. In the case of economic institutions, output is usually acceptable as the dominant objective; and an emphasis on efficiency by the administrators of economic institutions is clearly defensible. It can of course be overemphasized. Economic institutions have outputs other than those incorporated in marketable products or services; but many, if not most, of these nonmarket values are enhanced rather than sacrificed by efficiency in production of the marketable outputs.

Program performance is often the principal variable by which an economic institution establishes functional relationships with its environment. This is clearly seen in the improvement of benefits occurring to the consumers of the outputs of the institution, whether they are ultimate consumers or use the outputs in further production. This is less clearly seen in the intangible positive or negative benefits that are associated with the use of the outputs. For example, a large number of car and truck owners may be required to use the tires produced by a new domestic factory instead of using imported tires, as they had previously done. If the domestic tires are higher priced and of a manifestly lower quality, many of the benefits of the new factory to the social system, such as employment and improved business conditions, will be offset by higher costs and widespread dissatisfaction with domestic products. The point emphasized here is that program performance is the variable that usually establishes the relationship of the economic institution with its complementary institutions. Unlike institutions in other fields, such as in health and education, the complementary economic institutions have direct ways of observing and measuring what they consider to be the major characteristics of the program performance variable and how it affects their costs. While their view may be limited and biased, it is nonetheless clearly visible and of immediate impact.

Doctrine Variable in Economic Institutions

The doctrine of economic institutions, while still difficult to describe as an institution building variable, is substantially simplified by the relative ease with which output and efficiency are measured. A major objective of economic institutions is to produce goods and services as efficiently as possible. Here, there is a working out of economic forces that tends to minimize costs and maximize returns. At the market for which the products are intended, the forces of competition tend to reward relative efficiency and penalize inefficiency. While these forces are often inadequate to achieve fully their objectives, they are present in enough situations to make them important influences on administrative decisions. Efficiency in production, therefore, necessarily becomes a dominant objective of an economic institution. That it can be overdone and can lead to catastrophy if overemphasized necessarily points to the need for judgment and experience, but it does not diminish the importance of efficiency.

Doctrine specifies the objectives of an institution, its preferences for the various results it can achieve. The improvement of production and productivity clearly ranks high if not highest among the objectives of economic institutions. As discussed in chapter 8, the other objectives, the satisfaction of interests, viability, the mobilization of resources, and the observance of codes and rationality depend to a large degree on the achievement of a satisfactory performance in production and efficiency. The relationships with the complementary institutions involve exchanges of influence on value systems and normative relationships, and these are expedited and strengthened by a record of high production and improving efficiency. An economic institution will greatly expand its influence on the standards of the institutions from which it acquires inputs or to which it provides its outputs if it establishes a general image of success in production and efficiency. Common acceptance by the staff, particularly by the key administrators, of the values and priorities of the institution is a necessary facet of securing cooperation, adjusting conflicts, and making the decision making more automatic and consistent. Economic institutions, with a dominant objective on production and efficiency, can achieve this acceptance of doctrines in a simpler, easier manner than can most other kinds of institutions. Even noneconomic values can be favorably improved as the result of increased production and productivity. Consequently, the analysis and understanding of the doctrine variable in institution building confirms the position that by concentrating on production and productivity, administrators help the institution establish a better normative relationship with other institutions.

In economic institutions, government actions are exceptionally important. The doctrine of an economic institution can be seen in the kinds of efficiencies it attempts to achieve, in its labor practices, its marketing practices and priorities, and its way of doing business. For institutions in the public sector, government affects doctrine through direct promulgation and approval of rules and targets. In the private sector, government standards and regulations of factory and business operations are felt through many channels, ranging from licenses to influencing access to resources. The general image of important private and public economic institutions is, for obvious reasons, of vital interest to the government. Thus, the sense of social justice that every government strives to nurture is tested and modified by the image it helps establish of the doctrine of these institutions.

Doctrine, as a variable in the building of economic institutions, tends to be neglected by administrators, except at the highest level of generalization. Top administrators tend to speak of objectives and style of operation in terms that may be useful for political or polemic purposes, but which provide little substance for operating guidance. References to vague criteria of "well-being" and "higher standards of living" furnish few guidelines for setting wage scales and allowances for housing. Doctrine that is too vague and generalized is probably no worse than doctrine that is too detailed and unimaginative. The difficulty of achieving the right mix of vagueness and specification and of abstractions and concrete realities need not hide the importance of attempting to find the right mix. In a sense, the doctrine of an institution becomes a slogan system which establishes easily recognized themes of decision and action. These slogans become part of the diffused linkages with the general public, linkages particularly important in securing the resources for an economic institution from the public sector.

The role of doctrine in the operations of government agencies is thus both important and elusive. Few people are articulate about their doctrine, though some norms and priorities are the subject of much public discussion and debate. To a surprising extent, the style of action of a class or group is governed by the doctrines they have accepted. This is a proposition at an operating level; it is operational because doctrine is something that can be examined and affected, though with difficulty and only with the passage of time.

The doctrine of an institution has operating influence, as Esman says: "This proposition implies that (a) each elite is motivated in some measure by a doctrine, (b) the doctrine can be identified by the communication content and the behavior of the regime, and (c) doctrine effectively influences action."[11] Doctrine, to be an influence, must be communicated. In societies and institutions where structural changes are so sudden and sharp that people are disturbed and unsettled, doctrine may serve as an important channel to maintain stability.

Leadership Variable in Economic Institutions

In this variable, designated as the most critical in the early stages of institution building, economic institutions probably have their greatest advantage in emphasizing production and productivity. In spite of the importance that should be attached to the external economies of economic institutions, to the fostering of innovation, and to the normative relationships with their environments, leadership of economic institutions can be judged largely on the basis of success in improving production and productivity. This need not be the crude process of setting production and cost targets and dismissing the administrators if the targets are not met. Objectives are multiple and can incorporate many different ways of measuring production and productivity. Allowances can be made for the problems of complementarities, for the need in a complex production process to work with the products and services of other institutions. Yet the basic framework of evaluation of the administration of an economic institution remains and should remain the ability of the leadership to achieve the performance objectives of the institution.

Because doctrine can be internalized more easily if it is simple and understandable, the leadership of an economic institution has an easier job than that of other institutions. Decisions are more easily made because inputs and outputs can be more readily quantified. The flow of information necessary for good decisions, and consequently for good administration, is far easier to establish if the information can be more easily quantified and focused on specific types of decisions. Specificity in doctrinal themes provides firmer guides for administrative decisions. It permits more stable reference points by which administrators can measure their program decisions and their relations both internally and with linked institutions. Again it is essential to point out that the danger of a too narrow doctrine, concentrating solely on production and productivity, makes it important to recognize the other

231

objectives of the institution; but this should not turn leadership away from the advantages of emphasizing production and productivity.

Resources Variable in Economic Institutions

The advantage of an emphasis on production and productivity in the acquisition and maintenance of adequate resource inputs needs little amplification. The relationship is both direct and important. Economic institutions that are recognized as successful in achieving a higher rate of production and productivity find it much easier to acquire the resources they need. Cabinets, parliaments and budget departments allocate financial resources more willingly, good administrators are attracted to the organization, authority seems to grow with recognition of successes, and technological and informational resources become more available. When an economic institution is able to project a general image of greatly increased production and productivity, the quality and quantity of its available inputs increases so markedly that it often arouses the resentment of other institutions that do not have so easy a job. Annoying as this is to other institutions and to planners who recognize the interdependence of institutions and the relative ease with which economic institutions can emphasize production and productivity it should not deter administrators of economic institutions from attempting to derive maximum benefits from this characteristic.

The emphasis on production and productivity is generally appealing to the foreign institutions that control much of the foreign exchange available in the less developed countries. It is much easier to borrow money for a factory than for a school. This is particularly due to the generally mistaken belief that direct production loans are more productive than indirect production loans. Having even recognized the importance to the overall production capabilities of the indirect production loans, the foreign lenders often find it easier to measure and understand the operations of economic institutions where production and productivity can be more easily measured and evaluated. This, too, is often disturbing to the leaders of the less developed countries who must apply other important criteria to the allocation of resources. However, it really does not ease their problems in other areas if they de-emphasize the drive for production efficiency in the economic institutions. The contrary is true.

The resources variable clearly involves relationships with the environment, the source of the resources. For economic institutions, this relationship becomes focused on factor input markets, the formal or informal organizations through which institutions receive their resource The operation of the factor market, particularly for economic institution becomes the key to the successful acquisition of resources. For, as in almost all considerations of institution building variables, the ability to quantify resources as expressed in cost and price data represents an overwhelmingly dominant need of the institutions. Thus, relationships with factor markets are more likely to be better organized, and market information is more clearly available for economic institutions than for other kinds of institutions. This situation also exists at the output side of an institution's relations with its environment.

Internal Structure Variable in Economic Institutions

The interdependency between the formal structure of an institution and its leadership, doctrine, resources, program performance, and the other institution building variables means that the structure of an economic institution can be geared to the emphasis on production and productivity. Authority also can be patterned by this dominant objective. There is probably a more direct relationship between internal structure and the achievement of objectives in the case of economic institutions because the emphasis on output makes the measurement of supervision more easily understood and used. But internal structure remains a permissive variable, one that permits the other variables to be more effective. Aside from extreme cases of obvious misadministration, merely reorganizing an economic institution will rarely improve its capacity to establish itself and to attain its objectives. The downgrading of this variable, at least in the case of economic institutions, is disconcerting to many administrators who hope that the science of administration will leargely meet the problems of inefficient economic institutions. Yet it is clear that of the identifiable variables, internal structure is the least likely to be the critical one that distinguishes success from failure.

Institutionalization of Economic Institutions

The successful establishment of an economic institution is as complex as for any other type of institution. In spite of the fact that the performance variable is more dominant here than in other types of institutions, more easily measurable, more visible, and more likely to affect the evaluation of the other variables, it is still necessary to give a great deal of weight to these other variables. An economic institution that concentrates almost entirely on production, neglecting its needs to establish normative relationships with other institutions and to encourage innovative changes in the society, will not be "institutionalized" successfully, in the meaning of the term used here. This has been the condition of foreign enclaves, of modern business units that develop little relationship with the surrounding traditional society, leading to the dual society that was so abhorrent to the developing countries in their colonial periods. If they are to be successful, economic institutions must place a great deal of emphasis on the impact they have on

ideas of production efficiency, of minimizing costs and maximizing returns, and of adoption of new ideas about production and marketing
technologies. But this need to consider other variables in becoming
institutionalized should not result in a decrease of emphasis on production and efficiency, the components of the performance variable.

Thus, the concept of institutionalization has implications for the
efficiency of economic institutions. From an institution building point
of view, an institution that is accepted as efficient (both within the
organization itself and as an institution interacting with its environment) has greatly improved its chances for continuity and for the accep
ance of its values. It encourages innovation through its continuing
success. It gains resources for itself and for other organizations that
apply its values and attempt to emulate its operation.

MARKET INSTITUTIONS

The successful development of economic institutions is, by definition, the essence of economic growth; no significant increase in production and productivity can be achieved without improvement in the
market arrangements through which production enterprises receive their
improved inputs, adopt their improved technology, and dispose of their
increased output. Implicit in this, and not the least important element,
is improved income distribution, which is associated with the improvement of many kinds of market institutions.

Market institutions have been defined as patterns or channels for
facilitating the transactions of buyers and sellers in producing and distributing the products of a society. It may be useful to think of three
main types of markets, even though there may be some overlap between
these types:

1. <u>Factor market institutions</u>. These are the institutions by which
the factor inputs are procured for use in the production process, the
labor, land, and capital goods markets. Many times these markets are
intangible, having no fixed site or physical presence. Thus, no single
physical building may contain the arrangements whereby unskilled
workers are hired to work on local construction projects. Workers may
be hired in selected locations, on actual construction sites, in several
employment offices, and by work-gang leaders. Yet for analytical purposes, the existence of such a labor market is important to consider,
even though the institution is formless and difficult to visualize. Similar difficulties in visualization may relate to the market for agricultural
land or for agricultural capital goods; yet government is constantly establishing rules and providing resources for these market institutions,
as it does when it establishes interest rates for agricultural loans or
makes resources available to agricultural development banks.

2. Product market institutions. These are the more easily seen as institutions. The five-day market in rural areas and the large urban markets for produce and textiles are common, physical manifestations of product market. Not so easily conceived, but just as important are various types of service markets, imported products markets, used machinery markets, and the large number of specialized commodity markets. A brief listing of the types of activities included in the commodity markets will show their importance and their complexity—buying and selling agencies, storage, communication and transportation facilities, capacity for insuring proper weights, measures, and quality controls.

3. Financial market institutions. These are usually intangible, though some aspects of financial market institutions may materialize in special buildings, as stock exchanges or central banks. Market institutions for loanable funds may be divided into short-term and long-term funds; special sectoral financial institutions, such as agricultural banking systems, commercial banking systems, and industrial development banks may also be examined. The importance of foreign exchange to economic growth has led to many kinds of specialized financial market institutions, such as the arrangements for exchanging bonus vouchers and for import licenses as well as foreign exchange itself.

The economic functions that market institutions perform reveal their all-encompassing presence and importance.

Product markets ration the supply of consumers' goods among consumers. These institutions are based primarily on consumers' choice, the willingness of consumers to pay, and may be considered as socially efficient as long as the income distribution is socially acceptable.

Product markets allocate input factors of production among various uses, establish the relative supplies of specific types of labor and capital made available to production enterprises and distributes income between the input factors.

Product markets provide incentives for economic growth by rewarding correct capital formation and stimulating efficiency by increments to income.

The importance of adequate market institutions in achieving economic growth and improved income distribution is most clearly revealed by the consequences of their malfunctioning. Thus, when markets do not perform their functions properly, either through ignorance or through lack of development, all kinds of misallocation occur. Markets notoriously emphasize individual costs and benefits and tend to ignore social costs and benefits. In doing so, they tend to produce results that are often less than the maximum social benefits attainable and may even be totally undesirable. Market institutions may push in the direction of socially undesirable income distribution (see Chapter 5) or may emphasize luxuries in preference to products essential for the mass of poor people. Imperfect market signals through factor prices that do not reflect the relative scarcities of the factors may emphasize capital formation of the wrong kind and may push toward capital intensive rather than labor intensive investment.

Since every economic enterprise uses factor inputs to produce good and services for exchange, every enterprise is directly related to or is actually a part of market institutions. The malfunctioning of market institutions cannot be met by eliminating them, since given forms of marketing operations are essential to any high productivity society. If financial institutions of a country are too concentrated in ownership, operate too slowly for the needs of the country and are too limited in scope, the solution cannot be to eliminate them, which is impossible. As many countries have found, the most rational approach is to develop new roles and procedures, new kinds of specialized institutions, new ways of operating the financial institutions that meet more completely the needs of the country.

In developing these market institutions, it is expedient to utilize the concepts and generalizations developed in the study of institution building:

1. Program performance is the variable that must be stressed in the successful institutionalization of economic institutions. Performance in market institutions means relative efficiency. If market institutions perform their function of allocating factor inputs and products more efficiently than their operating alternatives, they will become accepted patterns of behavior. If they do not do so, people will circumvent them To meet such operating needs, all types of embryo markets spring up, legal and illegal. Performance in terms of efficiency may be more difficult to measure for market institutions than for economic institutions that produce physical products, but the difficulties are minor compared with those faced in measuring the efficiency of such service producing enterprises as schools, hospitals, roads, housing, and so forth. The operating performance of specific market institutions can readily be evaluated by experienced market users, whose efforts to minimize cost and maximize returns give them an incentive to evaluate alternative ways of transacting their exchanges. In the less developed countries, market institutions, inadequate as they are, are so important and widespread that evaluation and data are readily available for analysis. The problem is to analyze them in constructive ways that lead to modification and improvement in efficiency. Here, vested interests and tradition are likely to be the most difficult obstacles to overcome.

2. The institution building variable of doctrine, always difficult to describe and evaluate, is particularly difficult in the case of market institutions. For here a careful eye must be kept on two aspects of the doctrine that can be considered as mutual constraints, and these aspects must not be allowed to confuse, even thwart, each other. One is the emphasis on efficiency that all economic institutions must emphasize. The other is social purpose, the realization that evaluations based on market prices are rarely complete; they nearly always neglect

236

social costs and social benefits that must be included in any computation of desirability and feasibility. In other words, the doctrine of market institutions that are adequately performing their function in an economic system must emphasize the need for higher productivity, for expediting and encouraging transactions that lead to higher production and higher productivity. But it must also include in its calculations, on a macro as well as a micro basis, the need for adjusting market price calculations to social costs and benefits. The fact is that market prices may be based on too much ignorance, may hide great differences between social and individual costs, and may therefore have to be adjusted in evaluating the efficiency and functioning of the market institution. Acceptance of these two as major elements of the doctrine for market institutions provides government with a framework in which to initiate or modify market institutions.

3. Leadership as an institution building variable is clearly important in the case of market institutions. Since markets are often analytical constructs, intangible, rather than physical entities, it is important that the leadership variable be identified and examined. Because of this vagueness and intangibility, the leadership element may not be clearly identified; it may be a small elite group quite dispersed physically, yet operating in a decisive, cohesive way that establishes the efficiency and image of the market institution. Thus, the leadership of the textile market might be a small group of importers and wholesale traders, or the leadership of a financial market institution might be a small group of expatriate bankers. Here, government, by establishing rules and procedures, by outlining rights of participation and methods of operation, becomes an important influence in the designation and acceptance of the leaders of a market institution. In many cases, administrative officers become the effective leaders. Since production and productivity are major objectives of economic institution, the leaders of market institutions can analyze their operations more easily than in other, less tangible and more diversified institutions. The relationships of market institutions to the environment in which they must operate are usually easy to identify.

4. The resource variable in market institutions needs little clarification. Resources tend to flow where operations show they are most valued. Market institutions are a special kind of institution involved heavily in resource allocation. To the extent that market institutions offer the only or the most efficient way of allocating resources, it will attract resources to its operations and its support. Where government rules and practices limit participation, leadership, and scope, it is essential that government also examine the availability of adequate resources. The resources made available to a market institution usually reflect its relationships with its environment. If the market institution is functioning adequately, resources will tend to flow in its direction, almost by definition. If the market institution represents a tightly held, monopolistic control by an elite group that uses it to abstract revenue for its own use, the market function may receive ample resources, but

clearly requires reshaping by expanding its participation and reshaping its operating rules. In the case of market institutions particularly, resources must be evaluated in terms of social purpose as well as narrow profitability. Efficiency cannot be equated to monetary profits on specific market price comparisons of costs and sales.

5. The internal structure variable in economic market institutions is important as related to leadership, doctrine, and performance. Authority can be diffused, but there is a direct relationship between internal structure and leadership. The emphasis on efficiency in the necessary transactions of all economic enterprises means that all internal structures must be related to the functioning of the market institution. Merely restructuring a market by rearranging the lines of authority within may have little effect on the operations of a market institution. Only as changes affect production and distribution will changes in the internal structure of a market institution be effective. Changes in performance, in leadership, and in doctrine (as it affects performance) are far more important than changes in mere internal structure.

The emphasis on this discussion of market institutions has been on their widespread operations and on their importance to a country's efforts to increase productivity and improve income distribution. Market institutions are man-made, they can be shaped, made more efficien and directed to emphasize social as well as individual objectives. The cannot be eliminated, because their operations are an essential part of any economic system that produces goods and services for a market rather than for specific customers designated in advance and with no choice in their consumption. Where market institutions have developed in forms that are inefficient or stress the wrong objectives, they can be changed; but, generally, they cannot be abolished. Some substitute arrangement for facilitating the economic transactions must be made or will develop under pressure of economic need. A strong case can usually be made for controlling, shaping, influencing, and regulating markets, but rarely can a case be made for eliminating them. No significa market institution can be initiated or operated without government's acceptance or participation in some form. It is essential, therefore, that public administrators appreciate their widespread nature and basic importance.

SUMMARY

The institution building approach adds some operational dimension to the examination of the public administration of economic growth.

Economic growth in the less developed countries is to a large extent carried out by economic institutions, that is, by organizations whose primary objective is the production of goods and services for the market. Government policies and practices have an important impact on these institutions, and therefore the study of the public administration of economic growth can be approached through an examination of government controls of economic institutions.

Economic institutions have other important objectives besides the production of goods and services. They influence and help change their environment by influencing normal standards and value systems and by encouraging innovation and change. These additional objectives of economic institutions must be considered by public administrators.

The institution building variables—leadership, doctrine, performance, resources, and internal structure—present a useful schema for examining the process of successful institution building. These variables are mutually dependent and have important relationships with the other institutions in the environment.

The performance variable plays a dominant role in economic institutions because the principal output is so visible and so easily measured compared with the outputs of other kinds of institutions. While this should not serve to hide the importance of the other outputs of economic institutions, such as influence on normative values and innovative thrust, it can be used to make the building process for economic institutions more effective.

The successful establishment of economic institutions helps in the establishment of other kinds of institutions that are needed in the modernization process: by providing more resources, by reducing the pressure on government to alleviate the poverty crisis, by influencing norms of behavior, and in general by helping to create an atmosphere of receptiveness to social and political change.

Market institutions are particularly important economic institutions. They make possible the exchanges of money, factor inputs and products that are essential to high productivity and improved income distribution.

In establishing or improving market institutions, government plays a key role by its rules, procedures, and practices. No market institution of any significance can operate without government acceptance or participation.

NOTES

1. Phillip Selznik, Leadership in Administration (Row Peterson and Co., 1957), p. 17.

2. Milton J. Esman and Hans C. Blaise, "Institution Building Research—The Guiding Concepts," University of Pittsburgh, Inter-University Research Program in Institution Building, GSPIA, 1966.

3. Eugene Jacobson, "The Institution Building Process and Research" (Paper prepared for the Agency for International Development at Workshop on Agricultural College and University Development, Purdue University, July-August 1969).

4. Amitai Etzioni, A Comparative Analysis of Complex Organizations (Glencoe, Ill.: The Free Press, 1964), p. 10.

5. The material on the analysis of the institution building process is largely taken from the following publications: Esman and Blaise, op. cit.; Milton J. Esman, "The Institution Building Concepts—An Interim Appraisal," University of Pittsburgh, Inter-University Research Program in Institution Building, GSPIA, 1968; Gilbert B. Siegel, "Development of the Institution Building Model," University of Pittsburgh, Inter-University Research Program in Institution Building, GSPIA, 1966; and Marion J. Levy, Jr., The Structure of Society (Princeton: Princeton University Press, 1952).

6. Robert Tannenbaum and Fred Massarik, "Leadership: A Frame of Reference," Management Science 4 (October 1957): 8.

7. See Bertram Gross, The Managing of Organizations (New York: The Free Press of Glencoe, 1964), pp. 281-304.

8. Esman and Blaise, op. cit.

9. For a stimulating if discouraging examination of time as a possible input, see Norman T. Uphaff and Warren F. Ilchman, "The Time Dimension in Institution Building," University of Pittsburgh, Inter-University Research Program in Institution Building, GSPIA, 1967.

10. See Victor A. Thompson, Bureaucracy and Innovation (University Alabama: University of Alabama Press, 1969), pp. 29-60.

11. Milton J. Esman, "The Politics of Development Administration," in Approaches to Development: Politics, Administration and Change (New York: McGraw-Hill, 1969), p. 109.

8

THE NATIONAL PLANNING PROCESS

The Concept of National Planning

Planning is the process of consciously developing a sequence of future actions to achieve specified goals.* There are several key words in this concept that require emphasis:

process—Planning is not a single act or document. It is a continuous and complicated series of acts, consisting of gathering, selecting,

---

*This chapter is not an attempt to describe how to plan. Rather, its purpose is to describe enough of the planning process to enable administrators who are not trained planners to examine their country's plan more effectively, to see how the economic policies and projections of the plan affect public administration. For more complete statements of how an economic plan is developed, see the following publications: Everett E. Hagen, Planning Economic Development (Homewood, Ill.: Richard D. Irwin, Inc., 1963), 380 pp; Brian Van Arkodie and Charles R. Frank, Economic Accounting and Development Planning (Revised American Edition) (New York: Oxford University Press, 1969), 366 pp; W. Arthur Lewis, Development Planning (New York: Harper and Row, 1966), 278 pp; Louis J. Walinsky, The Planning and Execution of Economic Development (New York: McGraw-Hill, 1963), 248 pp; Albert Waterston, Development Planning—Lessons of Experience (Baltimore: The Johns Hopkins Press, 1965), 706 pp; and Keith B. Griffin and John L. Enos, Planning Development (London: Addison-Wesley Publishing Co., 1970).

and ordering information, of judging priorities and relationships, and of initiating activities that lead to expected achievements.

consciously—Planning is deliberate and purposeful. While chance events must be considered by planners, the process of planning is one of making rational choices between possible alternative policies and activities. If there are no choices and the future state is inevitable, there can be no planning in a meaningful sense of that term.

sequence of future actions—Planning involves a related series of actions in the future to achieve objectives that are rationally related to the sequence of actions.

specified goals—Planning must have objectives that can be related to the planning process. There can be no rationality in choice if there are no goals towards which purposeful actions are directed.

Modern organization theory has identified planning as one of three principal processes of administrators.[1] Practically everybody but small children plan, but sometimes it is difficult to distinguish between poor planning and no planning. Planning is thus a generic process, almost universally practiced at all times and in all cultural conditions. Even the most primitive societies planned. Because of its colloquial use, the term planning has so broad and loose a meaning that it usually handicaps rather than helps communications. Planning to be meaningful must involve enough knowledge to relate future actions to objectives. Aimless conjectures about the future and wishful thinking are not planning. Mere consideration of a future situation is only the beginning of a rational planning process. In a realistic sense, planning must involve capabilities to undertake action to achieve considered objectives. Government planning requires translating policies into action, not just setting targets. Without policies and instruments, a target may become a projection, a forecast without much operational significance. "To draw up and publish a list of targets is not to plan, the real planning comes when the government takes action to realize these targets."[2] Planned targets must have operational significance; their achievement must shape the policies and priorities of government. Development plans built on illusions will inevitably result in disappointment and frustration, which will bring either violent reaction or apathy. Both of these are unfavorable responses to the need for growing social discipline and for more and better work effort. Ambitious but not impossible targets related to operating reality are essential parts of meaningful planning.

Planning presupposes a basic rationality in purpose and action. Planning cannot exist if the future is considered as fixed by forces that cannot be affected and that inevitably produce their results. Complete fatalism eliminates all rational basis for planning, and of course no country can exist under such circumstances. The identification of those forces which can influence change and those forces that are impervious to government influence represents one of the most critical, difficult areas of political leadership. Planning for a country requires a degree of social discipline and political stability that many countries have not yet achieved. Above all, planning to be effective requires a commitment upon the part of the political leadership of the country to be disciplined by the plan adopted.* This of course does not require acceptance of the plan as a fixed blueprint, but rather as a guiding framework from which deviations must be justified by new information carefully weighed.

Economic Planning

Economic planning refers to the government's efforts to examine in a conscious, orderly way the sequence of future actions that will achieve a more satisfactory rate of economic growth. All governments plan, in the sense that they must give some consideration to the future, even if this consideration is restricted to staying in power and dividing the booty. The fact that governments collect taxes means that governments plan. But economic planning is more than considerations of future economic situations. To be meaningful, it must involve both the intention and capability to so order actions that they tend to achieve the desired objective of economic growth. Mere projections of what will happen is not economic planning, although projections may be part of the process of knowing enough to plan effectively. Economic planning necessarily involves mechanisms or means of achieving specified economic objectives. If a country has no way to influence the economic activities of its people toward achieving its planned objectives, it cannot have economic planning in the operating sense of that term. Since some kinds of very poor economic planning are indistinguishable from no economic planning, it is quite debatable whether many of the countries that talk loudly of planning do in fact engage in economic planning.

Economic planning is a process, a continuing activity; it must be distinguished from a plan which is a summary of the planning process for a specified time period. Thus, a country's five year plan or annual plan represents a summary of what that country plans to do and achieve in its economic activities during that period of time. The publication of a plan for a specified time period does not freeze the planning process or end the planning process until the next time period. Rather, the

---

*"History demonstrates that where a country's government is reasonably stable and its political leaders give a high priority to development, the country generally develops even where there is no formal plan. Conversely, in the absence of political stability, and firm and continuous government support, development plans, no matter how well devised, have little chance of being carried out successfully." Albert Waterston, Development Planning, Lessons of Experience (Baltimore: The Johns Hopkins Press, 1965), p. 341.

published plan document becomes a bench mark, a reference document from which changes can be measured as needed. Countries that issue plan documents may or may not have the capacity for good economic planning. In order to understand what is happening in a country it is necessary to analyze the process itself, rather than just a plan document.

Economic planning is not social planning, although the relationship between them is obvious and important. Because noneconomic problems and forces are critical determinants of economic growth and vital elements in increasing production and productivity, economic plans have usually included many references to noneconomic aspects of a country's objectives and development. Economic plans generally include sections on educational plans, health and welfare plans, and even some references to possible restructuring of social classes. Since these statements generally invoke public expectations and are often related to economic policies, there are many opportunities to describe them in economic plans. Few countries, if any, restrict their modernization objectives to economic growth, as it is obvious that human well-being encompasses much more. Yet these noneconomic references tend to be fragmentary and misleading, usually as an artificial aside for political or social, rather than economic reasons. This may be due to the sensitivity of the subjects treated, but it is also clearly due to the inadequacy of the planning techniques involved. Planning as a technique of operation has been developed with a significant degree of sophistication in some noneconomic areas. Medicine, health, welfare, and education have provided opportunities for considerable advances in planning technique. But the inability to develop systems of social accounting, as distinct from economic accounts, has severely limited the usefulness of these kinds of sectional planning.[3]

Economic planning has been accepted as the core of national planning, but it obviously is not the total planning that a country undertakes. As part of a comprehensive economic plan, the resources required by all parts of the social system must be stated in order to evaluate economic effect and assess priorities. Consequently, a comprehensive economic plan gives the appearance of encompassing all kinds of economic and noneconomic operations of the society. But the extent to which the clearly noneconomic aspects are considered varies greatly, and these considerations are often merely conclusions for specialized plans that are not included in the comprehensive economic plan. For example, while comprehensive economic plans include, in overt or hidden form, resources to be allocated to the military for the defense of the country, military plans are not stated except at the highest level of generalization. Similarly, educational, health and welfare plans may be summarized in the comprehensive economic plan or may even be argued at great length; but the actual planning process is generally carried on by specialized agencies and fitted into the comprehensive economic plan only as resources are allocated and priorities assigned. In an operating sense, it is possible, even desirable at times, to have these types of sectoral and partial plans developed despite the absence of a comprehensive economic plan.

Why have economic plans been so eagerly accepted by the less developed countries?

(1) The long periods of economic stagnation and poverty that most countries have undergone are no longer accepted as inevitable by the leaders and people of these countries. Government can, according to this belief, speed up the process of social restructuring and change the allocation of resources in a manner that will lead to the improvement of production and productivity in a shorter time, shorter than without economic planning.

(2) Many countries have an ideological basis for economic planning which increases the role of government in economic affairs. Some ideas of socialistic philosophy, ranging from full socialism to the acceptance of social ownership of important economic monopolies form part of the basic philosophy of practically all of the less developed countries today.

(3) A countrywide economic plan appeals to many as the national way to compare competing demands for resources and to coordinate economic policies and programs. A good deal of this influence comes from the foreign countries and international agencies that see the obvious need for a means of comparison and establishing priorities. The fact that most of these foreign countries achieved their improvement without formal planning appears somewhat out of place, but the operating appeal to rationality is still there.

(4) The political leaders and administrators of the country need economic planning for communication and coordination both among themselves and with the people of the country. The budgeting of resources and the coordination of policies form a mesh far too difficult to discuss and use without a formal plan. In a sense, in most countries the basic question is not whether to plan or not to plan. Economic planning is inevitable. The operating question is how to plan, what kinds of plans to develop, how much time can be dedicated to planning and what kinds of policies can be coordinated by the plan.

The desire to be free to choose probably represents a universal human need, and manifests itself differently under different historical circumstances. Freedom of choice is basically an inescapable component of other valued states, such as fulfillment of one's capacities, creativity, well-being and control over the environment. By itself, it is operationally meaningless, since freedom of choice where there is no choice is a nonsensical concept, devoid of meaning. Valuing freedom of choice thus becomes a vital protection against tyranny. In economic planning, where deliberate manipulation of motivation and behavior is paramount, freedom of choice must be given special attention to avoid exaggerating the basic infringement of human dignity that deliberate manipulation implies and often involves. Three desirable steps are suggested to mitigate the manipulative aspects of planning.

(1) Increasing awareness of manipulation, by labeling values of all elements as clearly as possible.
(2) Building protection or resistence to manipulation by ensuring wide participation in plan formulation and evaluation.
(3) Making freedom of choice an important and visible part of the objectives of the plan.[4]

Planning does not necessarily eliminate competition in economic activities. It may not even reduce competition, though it may order it differently. The operating rules for competition in production and distribution may be changed, with some areas of competition reduced and others expanded. A priori, there is no reason to assume that economic planning automatically reduces the extent to which market institutions are essential to the production process or even the extent to which market prices are signals to the producers and consumers. Some analysts, whose judgments are largely derived from a revulsion against the excesses of planning in centrally directed economies, have presented economic planning as a substitute for market mechanisms.[5] Planning is not properly understood when it is posed simply as the opposite of freedom in economic matters; such "grand alternatives" are not realistic in operational terms. It may be a striking phrase for political polemics, to pose the basic problem of economic planning in such simplistic terms, but the sobering problems of managing a society require consideration of government economic policies in a coordinated way, which must be the essence of national economic planning.[6]

All governments intervene in economic affairs, in the sense that they perform or omit actions and pursue policies that directly or indirectly affect the economic activities of their people. It can be assumed that coordination of these policies and actions provides a better condition for conducting these activities than uncoordinated policies and activities. But it cannot be assumed that the formal, detailed process that economic planning necessarily involves is the only or even the best way of coordinating these types of governmental functioning. Up to the last few decades, economic planning as the process is presently defined did not exist. To question the need or ability for economic planning does not necessarily involve questioning the need or ability for economic policy coordination or for the development of economic priorities. In fact, it may be that premature efforts to adopt economic planning emphasize directions and introduce biases whose net effect is to hinder rather than stimulate economic growth. However, the desirability of economic planning may no longer be a worthwhile question since, rightly or wrongly, practically all of the less developed countries have decided to have national economic plans. But as yet there is no definitive study that demonstrates beyond a reasonable doubt that national economic planning actively stimulates economic growth.[7] "Such skepticism about the value of planning as a stimulus to growth tends, prima facie, to be reinforced by the experience of the underdeveloped countries. Most of these countries have plans, but there is no

246

positive correlation between their rates of economic growth and the intelligence, rigour and consistency with which their plans are formulated and executed."[8]

TYPES OF ECONOMIC PLANNING

Economic planning can be classified many different ways: by geographic area, by type of activity, by function, and by scope. Thus, there may be city planning, regional planning, financial planning, educational planning, short-term anticyclical economic planning and long-term planning. Economic planning in a country encompasses all of these in varying proportions and combinations.

Physical Planning

The term "physical planning" has been generally adapted by planners to mean the material, "real things" aspect, the design and physical location of a project, the use of physical units of input and output, such as tons of through-put in a mill, tons of coal produced by the mines, distribution of tons of steel by the different physical categories of steel, as in sheet, plate, stainless steel, steel pipe, and so forth. Physical planning stresses the engineering approach to planning, so necessary for use of the mechanical means of production. But even physical planning must often be expressed in value terms because of the problem of comparable units. Tons of steel and tons of iron may be useful as units in some cases because they are meaningful, but tons of machinery and number of buildings have quite limited usefulness. Thus, even physical planning is often expressed in nonphysical, financial terms as a means of aggregating dissimilar and heterogeneous units. Nearly all economic plans contain some aspects of physical planning, unless they completely omit engineering considerations. Even plans that are designed for public information purposes only include references to targets expressed in physical terms because of their simplicity and the ease with which they can be understood.

Physical planning must be, almost by definition, the basis for all capital investment. It is impossible to conceive of building a factory or improving a harbor without the physical planning that lays out the work that must be done, the machinery that must be installed, and the engineering capacities that must be procured and utilized. Nearly all national economic plans contain references to physical planning. Not only are these useful for general public relations purposes but also for understanding at operating levels what the plan proposes to achieve. There is a great deal of utility in such concepts as ton-miles of freight

247

to be moved, tons of foodstuff to be produced and man-years of employment to be provided. In national economic plans it is important to resist the temptation of loading summaries with physical planning data which are appealing because they give the feeling of thorough and competent engineering.

There does not appear to be an acceptable term for nonphysical planning. The use of financial units for aggregating physical units is not financial planning in any accepted meaning of that term. Financial planning is used to describe the examination of financial resources, income, and expenditures, making its broader use quite confusing. Most plans are mixtures of physical and nonphysical planning. Even though the latter term is not usually used, it is useful to have an expression like "physical planning" which emphasizes engineering and substantive operations.

Project Plans

A more meaningful classification of types of plans is to array them in a hierarchy of scope, with physical planning having a differently conceived importance in each category. Thus, a project is defined as a clearly identifiable unit of operation with a relatively similar kind of production function. A project could be a power plant, a factory, an airport, any enterprise that can be identified relatively specifically as to location and function. Physical planning would make up most of the project plan. Even if two similar factories were to be built at two different locations using substantially the same engineering blueprints, they would normally be classified as two projects. Thus, most project plans have as a major part of their analysis the blueprint and engineering estimates that outline their inputs, the technology and the volume and value of their expected outputs. Individual project plans are usually the basic building stones of the larger types of plans.

Program Plans

These are usually made up of several projects or involve related activities that cannot usefully be broken down into individual projects. Thus, a harbor development program may consist of several projects, such as the building of a new wharf, the repair of existing wharves, the building of new warehouses, and the dredging of the harbor. Each of these smaller units may be considered a separate project because the engineering plans of each will be different. Whether each subunit is officially designated as a separate project or is merely called a part of a program will depend upon administrative experience. Very small subunits of programs can easily be lumped into a general category, and the

248

size and variety of the subunits will usually determine whether it is worthwhile to designate the separate projects within a program. Thus, the line between a program plan and a project plan is arbitrarily established; yet it may have useful operating significance. Further, a coal program or an energy program may be stated in more general physical terms than individual mining projects. A broader improvement program may be stated in both physical and nonphysical terms, with aggregate evaluations that are more meaningful than the more specific individual projects.

Sectoral Plans

These consist of the aggregate economic plan for a distinct part or sector of the economy. Clearly, there is no right way to divide the economy into sectors, and many variations have been advanced by analysts. By general usage, the sectors usually given are agriculture, forestry, fishing and hunting, manufacturing, mining and quarrying, transportation, financial service, power, communication, irrigation, construction, wholesale and retail services, and government. Generally, several "miscellaneous" or "all other service" categories are needed to make up the total of the economy. The classification into sectors depends upon the type of analysis to be made; there can be no correct theoretical classification. Thus, some analysts break up manufacturing into "large industries" and "small industries" because of the operational differences between large and small scale industry. Often, health, education and welfare are given separately rather than lumped into a single sector of government services. Sectional plans are an important part of national economic plans, but there is no standardized way of dividing the total economy into sectors.

Functional Plans

It is often useful to prepare plans that cover a function throughout many or all sectors because of the need to coordinate the various sectoral plans. Thus a manpower plan may cover the expected requirements for various kinds of skills and the outputs of various programs designed to provide trained manpower. Functional plans for education could conceivably be broader than the educational sector of government since they may include educational operations that are part of large scale manufacturing enterprises. Housing programs could cut across the construction sector, government sector, and even the manufacturing sector. Financial plans are broad functional plans that cut across all sectors and are an essential part of the total economic plan as well as of many sectoral plans. In a sense, the differences between functional and

249

sectoral plans are established by the analysis necessary in the particular situation. The division must be such that meaningful analysis is possible even though there is considerable overlapping between functional and sectoral analysis. The overlapping may be eliminated in published documents; but plans for specific functions, such as manpower, education and housing, are very useful in examining the need or impact of governmental policies.

Comprehensive Economic Plans

The final type of economic plan to be designated here is the comprehensive economic plan, the published national plan that is supposed to encompass the entire economy. This is the kind of plan that most countries wish to have or act as if they have. Yet its scope is so broad that very few countries have the capacity for comprehensive economic planning. The best way to indicate the scope of a comprehensive economic plan is to outline its major parts.

Current Economic Conditions

This usually includes recent changes in economic output, exports, imports, and the current status of foreign exchange reserves. Foreign exchange earnings are related to recent price changes and the state of the world market prices for the major exports of the country. The plan also usually includes references to the production situation in the major production sectors, particularly food and agricultural export crops. Occasionally there are references to any critical shortages of power, transportation, communication, and other basic services or resources.

Economic Objectives*

In published comprehensive economic plans, the objectives are usually selected for their public relations impact rather than for their operating usefulness. Thus, they may be a mixture of desirable but vague achievements, like "improved welfare," "health improvement," "well-being," and "security." They also generally include many concrete and specific targets given in physical units, as tons of coal,

---

*Some writers distinguish between the following levels: "targets"—short-run and specific; "goals"—broader than targets, but still quite specific; "purpose"—quite broad and long-term. Since keeping to this kind of hierarchy of definition is often more troublesome than beneficial to communications, they will be used almost interchangably here, relying on the text and on adjectives to keep the meaning clear.

miles of road, number of tractors, and thousands of kilowatt hours of power. Most economic objectives are stated in terms of aggregate costs or expenditures, as in total cost of investment or in total expenditures on health and education. When a plan gives many details and "solid" facts, it gives the appearance of thoroughness and of providing solutions to economic problems that is often more illusory than real. Many sophisticated numbers are used, usually in index form or expressed as percentage of annual increase, such as the increase in GNP or in per capita GNP. Employment and unemployment goals are given in verbal expressions that indicate improvement, rather than in precise quantitative terms. The economic objectives in published comprehensive plans are usually difficult to utilize as operating goals because they cannot be given in enough detail to be operational. The underlying documentation and work sheets available to the planning agencies and to the operating departments and divisions generally include far more usable data on objectives than does the total plan document.

Public Revenues and Expenditures

Public revenues and public expenditures are always a major part of economic planning. Too often they are mistakenly considered the whole of the plan, even in countries that have large active private sectors engaged in the production of goods and services. Government is usually the major planning force and becomes the major force initiating structural economic changes. Thus it is clear that its targets for revenues and expenditures express the priorities it wishes to establish, the compromises it will try to set among the different claimants for public resources, and the differential tax treatment that will be accorded to nongovernmental economic enterprises. The general monetary and fiscal policies of the government are frequently a major theme of a comprehensive planning document, and some of the specific financial policies may also be designated. Deficit financing, support of exports and of import substitution, foreign exchange controls, and banking policies are often reflected and even measured in the public revenue and expenditure statements of the published economic plans.

Investment

Investment, considered the "generating engine" of increased production and productivity, forms the major part of the economic plan. In most countries it will cover both public and private investment, but the latter may be only projections of expected investment rather than statements of goals and of implementations necessary to achieve these goals. Investment patterns contained in the plan are often revealing measures of priorities that confirm or deny the reality of the stated objectives of the planning process and of the published plan document. Investment plans must be related to estimates of public revenue and expenditures, as well as to economic objectives. Since this part of the plan is more easily quantified than most of the other parts, it tends to be presented in greater detail, often with a false sense of concreteness and specificity. Its importance to an understanding of the economic planning process is so obvious that the emphasis in published plans on investment is understandable. Yet its overemphasis and lack of implementation has resulted in skepticism and credibility gaps that limit the usefulness of comprehensive plans in many countries.

Macro-economic Projections of the Economy

Comprehensive economic plans are necessarily macro-economic in nature. They represent the total view of aggregate economic forces and economic objectives. To attempt to maintain a workable degree of consistency, every comprehensive plan requires macro-economic projection There must be some way of relating the total available resources to their aggregate uses; the parts of the total must be related to the total itself; one side of an identity must be related to the other side. Total investment must equal the sum of investment estimated for each of the sectors, and the total increase in production can be compared with the increase in investment and employment. Important as aggregate analysis is, however, its use is suspect. How much aggregate analysis arises from detailed plans and how much is the result of assigning mor credibility to aggregates than they initially possess is one of the major running battles among a country's planners.

STRATEGY OF ECONOMIC PLANNING

Concept of Strategy

The size, location, and factor endowment differ from country to country, probably as much as their history, culture, and social and political development differ. All of these differences are influential in determining the emphasis given to different variables in the economic plan of the country. By definition, each country plan may be said to have an economic growth strategy; that is, a particular set of variables which is emphasized because they are conceived as having central importance in achieving the objectives of the plan. Because of their number and complexity, all variables and relationships cannot be included in the plan. And of those included, some will necessarily be emphasized more than others. Plans that attempt to give many variable equal emphasis may only hide the ignorance of their authors and are less effective than those plans that emphasize those variables that wil lead to optimum results. Emphasis can of course be positive or negative; a decision to treat several variables with the same emphasis is as much a strategy as that of emphasizing one and completely neglectin

252

the others. Therefore, the formulation of an economic plan necessarily involves a plan strategy, although this strategy may be unconsciously developed by planners and leaders through piecemeal, apparently unrelated decisions and choices. Adequate economic planning involves the identification of the major obstacles to economic growth at operational levels where something can be done to overcome these obstacles. The plan strategy is based on the identification of these major obstacles and the choice of ways to overcome them. Plan strategy is of course directly related to the basic ideology of a country, particularly to the kind of society the country wishes to become. Since higher production and productivity and improved income distribution, the highly generalized goals of any kind of economic development require basic changes in nearly all important institutions; the kinds of institutions a country wishes to achieve in its ideology is constantly an important element in the changes that are affected by planning. National leaders have found it both necessary and useful to announce and publicize the planning strategy. Two important reasons underlie this situation. First, there is the obvious political advantage in exposing a plan's strategy to the public, particularly if the strategy seems logical and not too painful. Second, the plan strategy provides a necessary framework for making administrative decisions of choices and alternatives. The need for this kind of framework in coordinating policies is stressed in all administrative studies of complex organizations. No matter how detailed objectives are provided, specific administrative decisions at all but the highest levels of operations must constantly be referred to a policy framework in order to keep the general line of emphasis and the accepted strategy of the planning operation. Operational requirements for any complex system requires a general understanding of the strategy, the policies that give the guidelines, where major emphasis is to be placed and where less emphasis is to be given.

While a plan strategy is both necessary and useful as an operating concept, it does lend itself to imprecise language and loose thinking. There is an understandable but dangerous tendency toward simplistic statements, so that the real strategy is often hidden and unnoticed. Because strategy is a matter of relative emphasis, it is sometimes quite difficult to demonstrate strategy in an unambiguous manner. The usual evidence offered for a strategy of economic development is changes in investment expenditures, which are meaningful only in relationship to many other changes. Thus, to announce that the agricultural sector will receive 13 percent of the investment funds, compared with 11 percent in the previous year, may or may not indicate a shift in strategy. The fact that the agricultural sector received 13 percent of the investment funds, compared with 10 percent for transportation, does not necessarily mean that agriculture is emphasized more than transportation and by itself does not identify the strategy in a meaningful way. The degree of improvement resulting from the expenditures, the relative magnitudes of the sectors, the kinds of capital resulting from the expenditures, and the production response expected over time comprise only some of the information needed to judge the relative significance of investment in the two sectors. Simplistic statements about planning strategies are quite common, and they often hide or ward off criticism of the real strategy.

Still, the concept of a plan strategy is important; and it is useful to look at plans in terms of their strategy. For administrators who are not directly involved in plan formulation and coordination, examining a published plan for its strategy is a particularly useful way of attempting to get at the basic logic of the plan. Because of the difficulties of measuring relative emphasis, there are often debates on what the plan strategy really is, even among the members of the central planning staff itself. The unfortunate discrepancies between announced strategies and what is actually proposed in the plan to implement these strategies also creates ample room for discussion and differences of opinion. These dialogues may be quite useful even if perplexing. They help expose issues and identify the kinds of forces that must be considered in evaluating relationships between important variables. Discussion of plan strategy by public administrators is a healthy way of disseminating a planning framework for reference in the numerous kinds of decisions that administrators must constantly make.

Strategies Based on Sector Emphasis

Industrialization

Most of the people in the less developed countries associate modernization, national power, and national independence with an industrial society. Generally, industrial technology is more productive than traditional technology. Some kind of industrial development seems indispensable as part of the planned effort to achieve a high rate of economic growth. Nearly all countries plan a significant increase in their industrial capacity and label the plan's strategy publicly as "industrialization." This serves the public relations purposes of the political leaders rather than those of the central planning agency.

The kinds of modern industry emphasized in the plan can also be part of the plan strategy.

Heavy industry, largely capital producing. Some countries have deliberately decided to emphasize the development of such capital equipment industries as railroad locomotives, large electric generators, industrial machinery, heavy electrical equipment, railroad cars, large motors, and similar products characterized by the large scale industrial capacity required to manufacture these products in an efficient manner. To adopt a strategy of this type requires assessment of future growth paths of the economy and an evaluation of the extent to which present or near future supplies of consumption and light capital goods

254

can be traded off for increased capacity to produce both capital and consumption goods in the future.

Consumption goods. This kind of emphasis in industrialization is in a sense the opposite of the strategy discussed above, and it concentrates on consumable goods industries. This kind of capacity is easier to achieve, since consumers' goods can generally be produced efficiently in smaller industrial units which are technically less difficult to build and operate than those for capital goods. Light consumers' industries, such as canned and packaged food, food processing, clothing and textiles, and furniture manufacture, seem to spring up almost automatically because of the relatively small amounts of capital required, the easily learned technology, and the immediate pressure of demand and thus readily available markets.

Agricultural Sector

The basic importance of the agricultural sector has been emphasized repeatedly. It is a productive sector, a market for the products of other sectors, and a sector that usually must provide a surplus of both labor and capital for the expansion of other sectors. Almost all countries include in their announced plan strategy a promise that the agricultural sector will receive a great deal of emphasis. Unfortunately, even though many countries have demonstrated the high cost of neglecting the agricultural sector, few plan strategies are really based on a special emphasis for increasing agricultural productivity. There are many important reasons why the obstacles of development in this sector are the most difficult to overcome. This is the sector with the strongest traditions, poorest communication, poorest education, and most inadequate leadership; and it is the sector least able to support and encourage the development of modern ideas and technology of production and productivity. A plan strategy of emphasizing agriculture is easy to proclaim; the demonstration is usually a few ratios showing large investment expenditures in the agricultural sector. But only a careful analysis of the changes that are actually being emphasized based on assessments of both need and capabilities can provide the knowledge required to make a judgment about the agricultural aspects of plan strategy. Probably no other strategy decision has raised more questions among planners themselves than the extent to which the emphasis on agriculture really represents a plan strategy.

Leading Sector

A strategy often advanced is that of emphasis on a "leading sector" of the economy, a sector that will be stressed to achieve so vigorous a growth rate that it will lead the rest of the economy toward higher

production and productivity. The leading sector is strategically selecte
because of special advantages it may have; it may fit particularly well
into the factor endowment of the country or be capable of rapid, efficie
expansion with a strong impact on related and neighboring industries.
Thus, textile production was a leading sector in the development of the
United Kingdom early in the eighteenth century, just as it was a leadin
sector in Japan in this century. The production and processing of oil
in those countries that have large oil deposits is often stressed, for
obvious reasons, as a leading sector. Clearly, to the extent that an
especially favorable constellation of factor endowments and potential
demand make one sector worthy of special emphasis, it can usefully be
stressed as a leading sector. Yet the linkages with other sectors of the
economy must not be assumed. Too often, the so-called leading sector
becomes relatively isolated from the rest of the economy, a modern en-
clave surrounded by a mass of slightly affected traditional technology.
This is often the case of the so-called dual economies, where a productive modern sector exists within a larger far less productive economy, with little impact on each other's technology.[9]

Unbalanced Growth

The previous discussion of the possibility of a leading sector involves the utilization of linkages between sectors as an element of
plan strategy. The more general concept of linkages can also be used
in the strategy of a plan so as to induce more rapid economic growth.
Linkage here means the complementarities and interdependencies that
necessarily exist between different elements or units of the production
process. A modern factory will have both backward linkages going back
to its raw material inputs and forward linkages going forward to the use
of its product in final consumption. Thus, a textile spinning and
weaving mill has backward linkages to such activities as producing
the cotton, the machinery, the transportation of the inputs, the repair
and welding facilities, the supply of power and all the support activities required for establishing and maintaining the mill. The forward
linkages would include dyeing plants, clothing manufacturing plants,
and their support and marketing operations. Linkages are important because their absence can be noted and remedied by many people who are
looking for opportunities to engage in economic production that are
needed and for which they can be rewarded. All major capital projects
provide linkages, but some may have more extensive and powerful
linkages than others. Plan strategy could deliberately stimulate the
investment decisions of others to provide necessary complementarities
and support activities and to take advantage of the market for these
linkages. Thus, a large factory may build a staff dining hall, or alter-
natively it may omit all eating facilities in the plant, relying on the

small restaurants and itinerant vendors that seem to spring up in the vicinity of large industrial plants. The heavy investment on such economic overhead as large power plants and good highways often rely for their economic justification on the unbalanced growth they represent, the unbalance creating a situation where forces are set into play that will push toward a balance by numerous, decentralized investment and executive decisions made by people who sense the opportunity to fill a necessary gap in production. That most forms of planned investment leave such gaps is obvious; all detailed support and complementarities cannot be planned. The question really becomes one of intent and intensity. To plan deliberately for unbalanced growth in most sectors seems unnecessary since disequilibrium almost seems inevitable, particularly in those kinds of investment that require long-term considerations. Yet the degree and type of unbalance often represent a useful way of expressing the plan strategy.[10]

Strategies Relating to Foreign Trade

Export Promotion

The importance of emphasizing export promotion is both obvious and compelling. Most of the less developed countries, particularly those that were colonies previous to independence, have large segments of their economy geared to production of goods for export. The expansion of these segments to earn more foreign exchange in order to pay for more imports is an obvious strategy, but it is frought with difficulties in implementation. The feasibility of this strategy depends largely upon the world market and its characteristics of competition and price elasticity. When many countries are simultaneously attempting to expand production of the same product, the competition for markets may push down prices so that foreign exchange earnings are reduced to the levels associated with lower production. Expanded world demand for products when prices are reduced also affects the success of any export promotion strategy. For most countries, emphasis on export promotion must be given an important part of overall planning, but rarely is a country so situated that it can be the totality of plan strategy.

Import Substitution

As a country increases its income and therefore its demand for products, imports tend to rise. The demand for imports and the usual scarcity of foreign exchange combine to induce the creation of facilities for the domestic production of the imported goods. Governments often plan this substitution of domestic products for imports, and plan strategy can be based on this emphasis. Where imports become severely restricted either by wars or by balance of payments difficulties, the push toward domestic production capacities is immediate and powerful. Indeed, im port substitution as the basis for a plan strategy is quite common and is useful for public relations purposes as well. The general public can see the obvious desirability of providing domestic jobs instead of buyi from foreigners. The basic desirability of import substitution as a stra egy lies in the extent and composition of the induced capacities. Do- mestic capacity to take the place of imported luxuries may be less than desirable, even in the short run. Input substitution may lead to empha sis of capital formation for producing goods that can only be purchased by higher income families. The low purchasing power of the lower in- come families may lead to so limited a market demand that the facilitie to produce these goods may be small and inefficient. These goods may be relatively cheap when imported from countries that have large marke demands, where production facilities can take advantage of increasing returns to large scale production. The substitution of high-cost domes tic production for lower cost imported goods may be a decision that creates substantial economic difficulties in the long run, although the short-run effects of the savings of foreign exchange may be favorable. There is apparently an easy phase of import substitution, when importe material and equipment is used to produce light consumers' goods. As the process of import substitution moves back to intermediate products and ultimately to the capital equipment itself, import substitution be- comes more and more difficult to achieve and justify economically. Th early phases of industrialization seem to be easiest when import substi tution of consumers' goods is an obvious, easily implemented strategy However, if it leads to a high cost, highly protected industrial sector the long-term effect can be a severe drag on achieving a high rate of economic growth.*

---

*For example, this quotation summarizes the situation in Latin America: "An industrial structure virtually isolated from the outside world thus grew up in our countries. . . . The criterion by which the choice was determined was based not on considerations of economic expediency, but on immediate feasibility, whatever the cost of pro- duction . . . tariffs have been carried to such a pitch that they are un- doubtedly—on an average—the highest in the world. It is not uncommo. to find tariff duties of over 500 percent.

"As is well known, the proliferation of industries of every kind in a closed market has deprived the Latin American countries of the ad- vantages of specialization and economies of scale, and owing to the protection afforded by excessive tariff duties and restrictions, a healthy form of internal competition has failed to develop, to the detri- ment of efficient production." R. Prebisch, Towards a Dynamic Devel- opment Policy for Latin America (New York: United Nations, 1963)p. 71

Foreign Investment

Where a country has a natural resource that is both extensive and highly desirable, such as oil, copper, or tin, a strategy based on foreign investment may be an important part of the strategy for economic growth. This may be a kind of emphasis that could also be classified as "export promotion" and a "leading sector," but an essential added element is the foreign involvement in order to provide both financial resources and knowledge to the problem of utilizing the natural resources. The form of the foreign investment is of course important from both a political and economic point of view. Foreign exploitation of natural resources is increasingly unpopular, since it has echoes of colonial exploitation and exported benefits. Joint ventures with both foreign and domestic management is a growing technique to combine the two somewhat contradictory elements of the need for foreign investment and the unpopular reaction to much of the foreign investment. Plan strategy that stresses foreign investment is usually toned down publicly and is surrounded by safeguards for keeping control and for keeping as much of the profits as possible for domestic use.

Strategies Relating to the Public and Private Sectors

The importance of the role of the public sector in development has been repeatedly stressed throughout this book. In the situation in which most of the less developed countries find themselves, the government is constantly being pressed to play a larger and larger role in the process of economic development. Many of these pressures arise because of ideological thinking about the nature of the society that is to be achieved through development. Thus, most of the leaders of the less developed countries have definitely shaped, though quite differently, visions of a socialist state, adapted to the peculiar needs and values of the country concerned. But even in the most capitalistic minded countries, the nature of the development process presses toward emphasizing the importance of the government in investment, in financial and monetary policies, in all of its expenditures, and in the policies it develops to manipulate and control the private sector. Nearly all plans point to the role played by the public sector and to the importance of its expansion as the country develops. Some countries make the expansion of the public sector the major strategy of the economic plan, while others minimize its importance. For example, Algeria and Tanzania have clearly identified a plan strategy that emphasizes public sector investment activities.

While emphasizing the growing public sector, most of the developing countries also provide for a growing private sector. Even countries that have announced their adherence to a national form of socialism as the type of state they wish to achieve, accept and even encourage

the need for a vigorous expansion of their important private sector. Son
countries, such as Pakistan and Mexico, clearly identify an emphasis
on the private sector, although they may surround this emphasis with
cautions about the need for more widely distributing the benefits from
such economic growth. While a strategy that is publicly labeled a private sector strategy is unusual because of its political unpopularity, it
is often the core of the economic plan. Turkey, Colombia, Argentina,
and Mexico are countries whose economic plans really involve strategies that place prime emphasis on stimulating and controlling a vigorou
growth in the private sector. It may be true that "the fundamental task
of planning in the private sector is to remove obstacles in the way of
legitimate private initiative, by increasing the knowledge of resources
and their potential utilization, and by improving infrastructure and the
institutional framework of economic activity."11 Reliance on private
sector initiative requires consideration of the signals that the market is
giving to investment and production decisions. If the signals are limite
to guidance for production of those goods and services that are purchased entirely or largely by high income families, the future shape of
the economy may be quite different from that envisaged by the political
leadership and by most of the people. Since all market operations are
to a large extent influenced by rules and constraints established by gov
ernment, there is a constant need to scrutinize the signals that the mar
kets are giving out to influence production and investment decisions.
A growing private sector emphasizing the kinds of goods required and
fostered by better income distribution, is often announced as an essential part of the planning strategy.

Strategies Relating to Education and Training

Nearly all economic plans of the less developed countries stress
improvement of formal education as one of the major elements of plan
strategy. This has a popular appeal, even though the causal relationship between formal education and economic development is somewhat
difficult to assess. While there is no doubt that a high productivity society is a highly literate society with a well-developed formal school
system that reaches the majority of its young people, the causal relationship is difficult to identify or to use in deliberately changing a
society. High productivity may be more of a basic cause for formal education than a result. By stressing formal school education in its plan
strategy, a country may be providing one of the necessary elements for
high productivity in its economic activities; but formal education by
itself will not be a powerful push to adopt improved technologies. Many
instances of mass unemployment of educated people exist, and it is
essential that advances in formal education be balanced with a growing
demand for such training in the labor market. The time span of this balance is of course one of the most difficult problems to work out, and

many countries have been unable to attain a reasonable mix. The drive for universal literacy often is cited as a plan strategy, but it must be accepted as designed for its public relations effect rather than as a basic spur to rapid economic growth. The shift from an emphasis on primary schools to high schools and vocational schools is often a recognition that formal education must be adjusted to economic realities. Even this recognition is usually insufficient to establish a good correlation between the products of the formal school system and the demand for skilled and trained labor inputs. Unless the economy is undergoing a vigorous, continuous expansion, with a constant internal pressure to upgrade the educational qualification for old as well as new jobs, an expanding school system soon produces graduates that cannot find employment at acceptable levels. The existence of large and growing numbers of educated unemployed is a constant source of instability in a society, and the resources wasted on ill-used education are multiplied by the lost productivity of these unemployed human resources. Thus, while emphasis on school education is necessarily a part of the plan strategy, to overemphasize it is to invite rather than confront obstacles to rapid economic growth.

NOTES

1. See Bertram M. Gross, The Managing of Organizations (New York: The Free Press of Glencoe, 1964), p. 774.

2. W. Arthur Lewis, Principles of Economic Planning (London: George Allen and Unwin, Ltd., 1952), pp. 108-9.

3. See Raymond A. Bauer, ed., Social Indicators (Boston: MIT Press, 1966); Bertram M. Gross, The State of the Nation (London: Tavistock Publications, 1966); and Social Goals and Indicators for American Society, Vol. II, American Academy of Political and Social Science, September 1967.

4. Herbert Kilman, "Manipulation of Human Behavior: An Ethical Dilemma for the Social Scientist," in Warren Bennis, Planning for Change (New York: Holt, Rinehart and Winston, 1968), p. 583.

5. See Frederick A. Von Hayek, The Road to Serfdom (Chicago: University of Chicago Press, 1944).

6. For a valuable summary of this point, see Robert A. Dahl and Charles E. Lindbloom, Politics, Economics and Welfare (New York: Harper & Row, 1953).

7. See Albert Waterston, Development Planning (Baltimore: Johns Hopkins Press, 1968), pp. 31-42.

8. A.H. Hanson, The Process of Planning,(London: Oxford University Press, 1966), p. 2.

9. See Benjamin Higgins, Economic Development: Problems, Principles and Policies (New York: W. W. Norton & Co., 1968), pp. 17-21.

10. For a challenging presentation of the concept of unbalance and the need for inducing many decentralized decisions for production, see Albert O. Hirschman, The Strategy of Economic Development (New Haven: Yale University Press, 1958).

11. W. Arthur Lewis, Development Planning (New York: Harper & Row, 1966), p. 274.

9

.

PLAN FORMULATION

Top and Bottom Planning

National economic planning is a continuous process, but for operational purposes it is divided into time periods. The plans are summarized for scrutiny and appraisal by the highest political levels and published in plan documents for public appreciation and guidance. The plan document relies mostly on macro-economic analysis, with important specific projects mentioned to arouse interest and maintain credibility. The published plan document may indicate certain investment, employment, and production targets in the mining sector. This may even be broken down into two or three of the major mineral outputs such as tin, silver and miscellaneous minerals. The central planning agency, the Ministry of Mines planning unit, or some other agency will have the detailed programs on which this summary is based. Thus, a plan document is a summary document only, containing both macro- and micro-economic summaries. However, plan analysis must go beyond analyzing the plan document alone, although that is where the analysis may start.

The plan document summarizes the planning process for a cross-section in time. Obviously, its arithmetic must be correct; a total must be the sum of its parts. But far more than arithmetic accuracy is required in summing up the parts of a plan. There must be reasonable relationships between working parts, and the totals must bear a reasonable relationship to other totals. There are constraints and limitations that are established by technology and by external situations, and these must be given adequate consideration and influence. Many of these relationships are discussed below under the concept of evaluation of economic planning. Here it is necessary to point out that aggregate or overall planning must mesh reasonably into lower level planning, whether it is

263

sectoral, program, or project planning. Comprehensive economic plans cover much more than investment schedules, although that is an important part of the total plan. Similarly, investment schedules must be mo than a list of government investment expenditures, although that is an important part of the investment program. Government revenues and ex penditures must be included in their totality, with some parts of these revenues and expenditures presented in greater detail than others because of their important relationship to economic growth. In short, the overall analysis must be geared to the detailed plans which are the bas of the totals. To do otherwise would be to plan in the clouds, and the document would not be a planning summary but a political publication.

A plan is thus a summary of the planning process from the top dow and from the bottom up. "Top" planning refers to the aggregates, the overall totals that must be compared with its components. Total resources available during the time period of the plan will be compared with statements of the origin and use of these resources. Total exports will be compared with projections of exports by sectors; total imports will be compared with estimates of sectoral requirements for imports. The planning at the top may be performed by the central planning agenc itself or by the central financial agencies that will make macro-econom projections of resources. These aggregate projections of the availability and use of resources must be compared with partial and sectoral projections made by operating ministries and agencies. In most countries the preparation of a plan summary for a given period is initiated by issuing a call for the plans of the separate sectors into which the economy is divided. Each part of the economy is covered and overlapping between agencies delineated so that these can be reconciled and eliminated in the summary. The planning agency assigns responsibility for plan preparation of those parts of the economy not specificall covered by an operating government agency. Thus, the Transportation Ministry will be required to cover planning projections for transportatio in the private sector, as well as for the railroads and airlines owned and operated by the government. The airline agency may be required to submit its proposed plans directly to the planning agency or else all transportation plans may be coordinated and summarized by the Ministry of Transportation. In any case, submissions to the central planning agency will be required and the central planning agency will make plan for those parts of the economy for which no government agency has bee assigned the responsibility.

The last point requires some emphasis. The private sector of the economy usually represents a mixture of relationships to government, and these relationships are reflected in the mechanism for plan preparation. Some parts of the private sector are closely related to the operations of a specific government agency, and that agency may be assigned the responsibility of preparing the plans for its associated part of the private sector. Summary or coordination of the many parts of the private sector may be in the central planning agency or may be in some other government agency before submission to the central planning agency. Thus, the Ministry of Industries may allocate import licenses to industrial firms in the private sector, and therefore it may be assigned the responsibility of planning for the use of foreign exchange for industrial imports by the private sector. The Ministry of Labor may make projections of labor employment in the industrial sector that have to be compared with the Ministry of Industries' plans for issuing licenses to initiate new factories and the rate at which existing factories will be permitted to import raw materials. Other estimates of the private sector's operations may be made by the Trade Ministry and by the Treasury Department, which may be required to estimate projected revenue receipts from private sector imports. Comprehensive plans must be far more than estimates of singular government operations; they must be built up from plans for all the various parts of the economy that contribute to economic growth.

The call that goes out from the central planning agency for the plans of the different elements of the economy will usually contain some guidelines and bench marks for guidance. To neglect these is to add greatly to the difficulties of summarizing and reconciling differences. The exact guidelines and bench marks will depend on the planning experiences of the country and on the need for firm central direction. They will generally include some reference to price level changes, so that one agency does not have its estimates include a 20 percent price increase for the goods and services it buys while another assumes no increase. Guidelines may include references to previous levels of expenditures, to assumed levels, to world market conditions, and to past commitments. Where social unrest or military operations have been important deterrents of economic conditions, the guidelines given to the individual planning agencies may contain references to macro-economic aggregates in long-term projections, such as future times when foreign aid will not be necessary, when exports will pay for imports, or when investment will equal a desired proportion of total production.

It would be unusual, indeed, if the sum of the plans from the bottom meshed perfectly with the aggregate projections developed at the top. Aggregate planning tends to lose operational reality. The constraints and forces given consideration at the top are generally broad and powerful, but are not those likely to reflect realities at the level of actual operations. Total construction capabilities of the country may be considered, but regional distribution of requirements and capabilities may be considered, but regional distribution of requirements and capabilities may be neglected. On the other hand, the projects submitted at the bottom by the operating agencies will usually reflect their hopes as well as their actual requirements. Estimates are often submitted with the expectations that cuts will be made by the coordinating agencies, so that reserves are hidden. In the process of reconciling the total with the parts and of balancing requirements against availabilities, priorities are established and preference patterns made clearer.

Sometimes these priorities and preferences are established openly and deliberately. They arise more often from the day to day decisions in the reconciliation and summation process, and they can be ascertained only by analysis of the fully approved plan. Thus the announced policy to emphasize agriculture during a plan period can best be evaluated by observing what happens to the institutions and operations that are important to agriculture. These include not merely expenditures clearly labeled "agriculture" but also transportation policies, tax policies, education and health expenditures, import and export policies, price policies, and all the other numerous government policies and activities that affect agricultural production and productivity.

Plan Time

Economic plans usually cover a multiple year period, with an apparent preference for five year plans. There is a major consideration in choosing a plan time. Plan time must provide sufficient continuity to initiate, finance, and implement worthwhile projects, but not so long that accumulated mistakes and inevitable deviations significantly impede the plan. The periodic need to renew and establish priorities and allocations is essential to a government's operations, but too frequent reexamination of priorities is disturbing and wasteful and too long a delay in review can be costly. Three kinds of timing for plans seem to have become most prominent:

Annual plans. These cover one fiscal year and are related closely to annual budgets of a country. They seem to be adopted by countries that feel it necessary to fall back from longer time plans because of critical operating reasons, such as civil war, a change in government, or a major failure in expected resources.

Medium-term plans. These have a duration of from three to seven years, with five years being the most popular time period. The five year period seems long enough to cover most kinds of projects from initiation to completion. By the standards of necessary continuity and adequate review, medium-term plans seem to be the best operationally.

Long-term plans. Covering up to 15 and 20 years, long-term plans are generally considered perspective planning, desirable because it can be used to furnish guidelines for shorter period plans. Perspective plans are generally limited to macro-economic projections, giving a framework of relationships within which medium-term planning can be reconciled. Also perspective planning is generally limited to "top" planning, since very few specific projects are needed to support these kinds of aggregate projections. Population, food supplies, general labor force, and foreign exchange availabilities are generally fitted together within broad sectoral totals to show how the economy will look in 15 to 20 years assuming certain forces, priorities, and relationships

Perspective plans rarely can be built up from more detailed operating plans, although operating agencies may be requested to participate in supplying some projections for long-range plans.

Some countries have tried rolling time periods for their plans. Thus, a three year plan would be revised every year, with one year added as the current year becomes history. The rolling period of three years thus attempts to provide a time span that permits continuity, while offering an opportunity for review and adjustment to actual performance that is more current than plans with fixed time periods. There could be rolling five year plans, with one year added as each year passes. In theory, this type of timing could be useful, but in practice it is difficult to capture the advantages without becoming overwhelmed by the disadvantages. The quantity of paper work and decisions increase at an alarming rate, the changes tend to become marginal and superficial, and the rolling plan tends to become a one year program associated with longer projections that are not binding. Few countries try to establish and retain rolling economic plans, although individual agencies and programs may do so.

Sunk Costs

Plans are committed to affect future behavior, but present and past behavior condition the future and must be taken into account. Administrative decisions made today limit the choices that can be made tomorrow, and past decisions are inevitably a strong force in shaping present and future decisions. This is so obvious that it scarcely warrants exposition. Yet in economic planning, the past, particularly as it is reflected in sunk costs, is so major and dominant an influence that it needs emphasis. Sunk costs are costs that have already been incurred for future benefits. In a sense, all expenditures on capital formation are sunk costs, as are expenditures for training of personnel and for the development of institutions. Administrative decisions to incur expenditures for future benefit initiate sunk costs that continue until they have produced all they are expected to produce.

The planning process must take sunk costs into account in presenting economic objectives and their implementation. Obvious illustrations of this are the need in the planning process to make resources available for projects that have already been started. Only under the direst kind of emergency would a building that has already been started not be completed, although instances of this are not unknown. A poor time indeed to decide that the building is not worth finishing is when a building is designed, its foundation put in, and its walls under construction. The costs thus far incurred would be sunk, and such visible evidence of waste is usually more than a government wishes to expose itself to. Sunk costs in training may be less visible, but they are just as real.

When a plan document is issued covering a stated period, it is difficult to determine exactly how much of the proposed plan is determined by sunk costs. Certainly in the investment program a large number of projects will have been started by the time the plan period begins, and unless they are judged to be outstandingly wrong, the plan is constrained to provide for their completion. At the end of the plan period, there will be many incomplete projects on which sunk costs have been incurred, and these will represent a series of constraints on the next plan period. No country can so organize its economy and planning that time is treated as a discrete variable, with a definite beginning and a definite end. The poet's assertion that time is a "seamless web" is more than a poetic expression: it is a realistic operating analysis. While a five year plan period may be long enough to start and finish many projects, many others will be unfinished; and to force plan implementation within separate pieces of time is unrealistic and impossible.

This means that economic plans are often prisoners of previous commitments. The costs that have already been sunk shape the future costs and benefits from current plans. To a surprising extent, investment decisions in any five year period are conditioned by investments that were previously made. The sunk costs must be considered in any cost-benefit analysis, both for the total time of the project and for the plan period (which may be only part of the time needed for the project). Obviously, the best period for considering cost benefits comes before any substantial sunk costs are involved, when choices are less constrained by the existence of sunk costs.

Quantitative Techniques in Planning

Professional economic planners use many different quantitative techniques in planning. To the obvious use of such aggregate data as investment, savings, employment, and the other elements of the GNP have been added some fairly sophisticated analytical tools, such as growth models, simulation models, input-output analysis, mathematical programming, and regression analysis. These it must be stressed are techniques only. Their importance lies in their ability to expose relationships between variables; and, while surprisingly useful results can be attained from using scanty data, the basic requirement of any technique is always reasonably valid data. A brief discussion of each of these techniques can serve the purpose of showing their scope, but can scarcely be a description of method.

Analytical Growth Models

All systematic thinking makes use of models, either implicitly or explicitly.[1] That is, it is necessary to have a model, an abstraction that simplifies how a complex process operates, in order to gather facts and to think critically about that process. Societies have many goals and there are different ways of attaining these goals. Thus, country plans will have goals in employment, consumption, savings, health, and capital formation, to specify only some of the goals. These can be attained, theoretically, through many sets of a large number of variables and conditions. A brief summary would be: "In formulating an aggregate model, one specifies the major quantities; one guesses which are the variables or factors influencing their magnitudes; one stipulates the likely relationships between these variables; one estimates the values of the parameters (constants) in the equations; and one deduces the outcome."[2] Since analytical growth models select a relatively few goals, sectors, variables, and constraints, they are highly abstract and are generally useful only for broad, long-term perspectives. The nature of the model will be determined by purpose of the analysis. If the purpose is to examine the different paths of achieving economic growth, then the variables and constraints will be related to capital formation, savings, and productivity over the long run. If the purpose is to examine income distribution, the model must include data on changes in the shares of the product, prices, taxes, and other income distribution policies. Growth models are useful in checking on the major strategies used in the development plan. They can be made to show the mix of objectives possible with specified, limited resources, and the degree to which the attainment of one objective involves the sacrifice of another objective, the "trade-offs" that so often represent the realities of operations.

Simulation Models

Simulation models go beyond analytical growth models. They add to the model's reality by expanding the complexity of the model, often making it impossible to solve mathematically, but still useful in tracing relationships between the increased number of variables and sectors. Thus, simulation models may be used to examine the possible effects of policy changes, even though the total model cannot be solved due to lack of data. Because of their complexity, simulation models have been developed for only a few countries; but their use is growing. Planning documents rarely mention such models where they exist, since their results are so problematic and their utility so specialized. In effect, their major use is to point out possible relationships between variables and policies, rather than to predict or to evaluate alternative paths of growth.

Input-output Analysis

Input-output analysis[3] is a statistical technique which describes the interrelationships between many parts of the economy. Usually, input-output analysis focuses on manufacturing, although all the sectors of the economy may be included. The basis of the method is a systematic statement of the sources of the inputs received by each sector and the disposition of its output. The rows and columns of the input-output table show first the receipts and distribution of each of the selected groups, followed by total imports and total supply for each column and total intermediate demand, exports and final demand for each row. Thus, the table is balanced with the total supply available during the period equal to the total demand that has been met during that period. Each square shows the value of product sold by one specified sector or industry to another specified sector or industry. This distribution must be based on past data, what has happened in a given time period in the past, generally determined by manufacturing and trade census data. The values in each square are translated into coefficients that are used to predict changes in supply when there will be indicated changes in demand. Thus, if the goal of the plan is to increase manufacturing production by 10 percent, the input-output tables permit estimates of the increases needed in steel, coal, and the other industries specified in the input-output tables. Not only are the amounts of final demand of each industry predicted, but also the availability of product from each industry group to the other industry groups.

There are obvious advantages in using input-output analysis when planning a balance between demand and supply for such major commodities as steel, coal, oil, timber, electric power. Indeed, commodity balancing was the original method used by the USSR to establish the first few five year plans. The projected supplies of each important commodity were compared with the requirements projected for each important industry and to final demand. Thus, the projected supply of coal was compared with the projected expansion in demand for coal by each individual sector, transportation, power, and final home consumption. By using historical records, it was possible to compute from the production plans of a sector its expanded need for coal per unit of production. The commodity-balance technique required that the computations be adjusted and reiterated until a reasonable balance was struck. Input-output analysis with its coefficients determined by basic operating data is a far more flexible technique and yields more useful projections than commodity-balance. Its major contribution may be that it forces the planner to secure and organize data in a useful way so that even partial data become useful in this form. Most countries attempt to develop input-output statements early in their planning process, to be used as checks on sectoral plans submitted by operating agencies. However, there are some disadvantages to the technique that must be kept in mind. First, the current relationship between a unit of output in a sector and its various types of supplies are often difficult to secure with the required degree of accuracy. Second, the relationship between production and input is assumed to be linear; that is, if production increases by 10 percent it is assumed that each element of input will have to increase by 10 percent. This linear relationship is usually not an engineering requirement, but establishing and using nonlinear relationships is too complicated for input-output analysis.

Mathematical Programming

It is often possible to express a complicated process mathematically in the form of a series of equations that give the relationship between the various elements of the process and its results. By mathematical programming,[4] a process can be made subject to specified constraints or conditions and make possible a choice among the alternative means of achieving the best results. Thus, mathematical programming has a wide use in determining the best mix of outputs in a mill or refinery that has many options of a product mix from which to choose, the best location of storage and inventory facilities, the best mix of transportation services to offer and similar problems involving choice among alternatives. Optimizing solutions that maximize the essence of mathematical programming. Thus, maximizing outputs while utilizing a given amount of a limited resource, such as capital, represents the usual kind of problem for mathematical programming. Limitations of the technique, like those of the input-output analysis, are quite serious. Mathematical programming is more comprehensive than input-output analysis, but does not permit substituting one input for another within the model. Within this limit, and the cautions deriving from the need for good basic data, mathematical programming provides a sharp analytical tool for planning by providing specific solutions of complex problems at operating levels.

Regression Analysis

Regression analysis[5] is a statistical method of measuring the association between two or more phenomena, and utilizing this measurement to estimate, even predict, future developments. It is a basic technique used in many kinds of social science analysis where relationships among combinations of variables are used to analyze so-called dependent phenomenon. Thus, the relationship between parents' wealth and occupation may be used to analyze college attendance or capital stock; size of farm and type of ownership status may be used to analyze agricultural yield per acre. Regression analysis consists of determining mathematically the degree of associated fluctuation, but of course this does not necessarily prove causation. Thus, regression measures the way prices of wheat fluctuate with changes in yield of wheat per acre, total production of wheat and the prices of competing feed and food grains, but does not prove that wheat prices are determined by changes in these other variables. Causation must be logically deduced from the realities of the operating situation and can only be inferred from the statistical evidence of regression measurement. With other statistical measures that show the degree of probability of the regression measures such as the standard error of estimate, it is possible to use regressions to check predictions of future production and to relate predicted changes in inputs to a whole series of outputs. Illustrations include possible price changes when production, imports, exports, and competing products are estimated, or when predicting agricultural yield per acre under a proposed land reform scheme that would change ownership, size of farm, availability of credit and capital inputs.

The use of regression analysis is so widespread among economists that it is desirable to attach a special warning for its use in macroeconomic planning. There are usually severe limitations of data that form real operating constraints on the use and validity of much of the macro-economic regression analysis. In practice, economic research often is unable to supply data on many basic determinants, particularly those that are not measured by market operations. Thus, political, social, and psychological inputs are often neglected because they cannot be expressed easily in quantitative terms. Regressions, like models, are often useful because they are simplified abstractions of reality but their use must be carefully examined to see that the omission of important influences is not overlooked or distorted.

The use of quantitative techniques in economic planning is growing as the less developed countries develop a more adequate statistical base for such techniques. There is a danger that these techniques will give a false impression of validity and precision that are not warranted by either the basic data or methodology. Quantitative analysis cannot be a substitute for systematic thinking; it is merely a tool for its assistance, although a powerful tool. The fact that systematic analysis of complex planning problems requires an implicit or explicit model for gathering facts and for developing the right kind of questions and answers about these problems means that mathematical techniques for summarizing and analyzing these quantitative data are both essential and time-saving. But their use does not guarantee accuracy or indeed logical thinking; improper results can be easily secured from inadequate mathematical techniques as from the misuse of any other kind of tool in analyzing complex problems.

PLAN IMPLEMENTATION AND EVALUATION

Implementation and evaluation of progress are now widely accepted as parts of the planning process and as essential parts of any published comprehensive economic plan. This was not true in the early days of economic planning, when execution of the plan was considered the sole prerogative of the traditional operating agencies of government and quite separate from the responsibility of the planners. As the need for operational feedback and flexibility became apparent, the integral relationship between plan formulation and plan implementation and evaluation became an operating necessity. Political leaders and planners have learned that approving plan objectives and publishing plan documents does not mean that these objectives will be accomplished. The need to plan in realistic terms and to adjust plans to operating realities is the clearest, most persuasive evidence that all important government agencies must participate in national economic planning and that plan implementation and evaluation are parts of the planning process.* It has become fashionable to insist that published plans include strong protestations of determination to implement the plan. Most of these are so worded that it is clear that planners and top administrators have learned well the jargon of planning; but unfortunately, the attention to implementation and evaluation is more verbal than real. Published plans usually omit references to policies necessary to achieve the objectives of the plan, such as interest rates, public enterprise pricing, licensing policies, price controls, rationing of imports, and foreign exchange controls. India, for example, refers very vaguely in its plan to implementing policies. The published plan is really a financial plan, with a few scattered physical targets included, but with discussion of policies minimized or omitted entirely. To meet current problems, implementing measures and operational policies are improvised as time goes on with no systematic relationship to the published plan.† Most planning agencies try to avoid the massive effort that would be required to assemble the data on existing and potential policies requiring coordination. Reliance is placed on emergence of problems that force or at least provide opportunity for evaluation and adjustments of policies.

---

*This point has been emphasized as follows: "The final element of a well-conceived development plan is the provision for its implementation. This includes the organization of the planning function and its administrative relationships with the chief executive, the policymaking and operating departments of the government, and the legislative; the assignment of responsibilities of carrying out its component progressions; the relationship of the plan to the national budget; the roles of the fiscal and monetary authorities; the provisions for progress reporting and evaluation; and the selection and training of planning personnel." Gerhard Colm and Theodore Geiger, "Country Programming as a Guide to Development," in Development of the Emerging Countries (Washington, D.C.: Brookings Institution, 1962), p. 51.
†"Both import and export licensing have throughout the plan decade been controlled ad hoc, and have never been . . . formulated in relation to long term planning." D. R. Godzel, "An Approach to Indian Planning," Economic Weekly (July 1961): 1131.

Sometimes the major monetary and fiscal policies are mentioned, such as intentions to examine the level of interest rates, intentions about holding domestic prices level, or adjustments in policies necessitated by changes in world prices. Few plans, if any, make a serious effort to examine all of the new policies that will be needed or the existing policies that will require modification in order to achieve the announced economic objectives. Yet it is these policies that are the start of plan implementation.

Evaluation as part of the information feedback must be operational; that is, it must arise naturally from the information made necessary and available by actual operations. The evaluation of the success or failure of a plan requires that criteria for success be established and validated. It is not difficult to compare actual performance against given targets, but this leaves open the question of the validity of the targets. Plans often overstate targets in order to arouse public enthusiasm and for political advantages. Equally likely, they often understate targets, either from ignorance or from the political advantage of exceeding the targets. In any case, using the targets as criteria presupposes that the targets are reasonable and that their attainment measures success. The major objectives of a plan are, rather than quantitative in form, usually value judgments, which are far more difficult to assess. Since economic objectives usually incorporate external economies, they are quite difficult to assess directly. Most plans produce some worthwhile results, varying from the experience gained in planning and the social discipline gained in the planning process to the effect of planning on allocation of resources and productivity. But it is impossible to compare actual results with what would have happened if there had been no plan; these opportunity costs of the plan are usually impossible to estimate. Partial attainment of some targets and over attainment of others make the evaluation of implementation even more difficult. But this difficulty does not reduce the essentiality of evaluation as a feedback of plan operation, allowing the adjustments necessary in continuous planning. Overall evaluations may be too simplistic because they are necessary for public relations purposes. Evaluation of programs and projects, of sectors and regional plans, of functional operations and policies as they are implemented and as they affect the economic system—these are the continuous kinds of evaluation that must be made part of any plan and its implementation.

Internal consistency in an economic plan is an obvious virtue. A plan that is inconsistent is one that is illogical or irrational by definition. Yet all economic plans contain inconsistencies since they must necessarily be a series of compromises between the many contradictory objectives of a society. As planning is one of the first steps in translating economic policies into actions, the economic plan must also expose the many policy contradictions inherently present in the complex of institutions involved in economic growth. To examine a plan for its internal consistency is often to examine it in a way that exposes its contradictions and its opposing assumptions. Policies often are the result of adjustments between contradictory objectives at almost all levels of generalization. Thus there are specific operational compromises, as when a decision is made to encourage railroads and to reduce the emphasis on highways. There are the more general policy decisions, as where investment in the public sector is to be emphasized and private sector investment de-emphasized. Sometimes these policy decisions are explicitly stated, but most of the time they are implicit in the planning action decided upon or neglected. Internal inconsistencies may reveal that planners have deliberately neglected to consider some policies, or that they have avoided considering some unpleasant aspects of the plan that will become apparent as the plan is implemented. The economic plan can be examined for internal consistency at two levels. A person skilled in the concepts and statistical conceptions of national accounts can examine the plan for technical competence, for deviation from accepted practices that reveals technical errors or omissions or that assumes technical relationships that do not exist. Another level of consistency, the one examined in this section, is to provide a framework for examining the plan in order to permit evaluation of the policies implicit in the plan. Hopefully this will reveal the compromises between conflicting objectives that are necessarily a part of planning.

Identities and Equalities

There are many identities and equalities in the plan, some arising from the essentials of simple arithmetic and some from the definitions used in national accounting and macro-economic analysis. Identities and equalities "define the possible." That is, they mark off limits where an inconsistency is illogical, and where some adjustment, usually involving policies, must be made or at least identified. Examining these equalities often reveals some implicit or explicit economic policies, or the need for new policies. For example, national accounts are so defined that savings equal investment on an ex post facto basis. That is, in order to have the national accounts balance in any one year, by definition the amount of savings in a country must equal the amount of investment. There are many technicalities involved, including how to cover hoarding, the flow of foreign capital, and the distribution of government expenditures; but the essential equality remains between savings and investment. By comparing the expected changes in each of the savings components, it is possible to examine the relationships between many policies and projections. An expected sharp increase in savings of individuals and householders must be accompanied or related to policy changes that will make this a reasonable expectation. What is being planned that will produce this change in private savings? An expected increase in foreign capital will be somehow related to changes in government policies regarding private foreign investment, or foreign government grants and loans, or international agency loans and grants. The changes that necessarily occur in components of equalities and identities will often indicate where policy changes are assumed and whether or not they are explicitly described in the plan. The criterion for the reasonableness of these assumptions is often a matter of political and social judgment, and should not be only an economic projection The most frequent equalities used for examining the consistency of economic plans are related to resources, either in total or in some part of the economic system. For example, total resources used in a country must, by definition, equal the sum of production, changes in inventory, and the net result of imports and exports. The technical difficulties of securing reliable statistics that do not include duplicate accounting cannot mask the basic relationships that exist and that define the limits of the resources available.

The most useful identities to examine are those that are related to foreign exchange, which is likely to be the immediate bottleneck for many investment plans. Foreign exchange, to be utilized in a plan, must equal receipts and changes in foreign exchange reserves, while receipts must equal earnings from exports and receipts from foreign loans and grants. Each of these elements can be subdivided into more detailed categories; and the more detailed the data, the easier it is to reveal underlying assumptions about new or existing policies and about the expected effect of these policies. The point to be emphasized here is that administrators whose activities are related to resource availabilities or use can examine the assumptions that are made in the estimates presented in the plan. Thus, a plan that projects an increase of 10 percent in the production of timber products, most of which it is assumed will be exported, may raise questions about policy decisions and practices necessary to ensure that most of the increased production will be exported and not used for domestic purposes. These policies may or may not have been included in the plan submissions of the Forestry Department. That they require an examination by appropriate administrators cannot be questioned.

Complementarities

There are many complementary elements in any economic system. Economic plans raise many questions about complementarities varying from relatively specific instances easy to identify to important broad associations that are very difficult to assess. An example of a specific complementarity is the association of hospital and health programs with programs for training of doctors, nurses, and medical technicians, or considering the building of school rooms together with teacher training programs. An example of the type of a complementary often overlooked in the production sectors is the production of coal and the availability of coal cars and barges to move the coal. The whole field of manpower requirements as they relate to specific development plans is an area of complementarities that receives scant attention in economic plans. Quite often questioning the absence of references to necessary complementarities identifies the need to consider new policies or modifications of existing policies in related activities and agencies. The more questions that are raised, the more likely is there to be adequate policy consideration and coordination in operating and informal levels, as well as at top planning levels.

Reasonable Functional Relationships

One of the most useful though difficult means of checking the internal consistency of economic plans is to examine changes in the relationship between only two variables and to question whether the change is reasonable in view of experience or new policies involved. For example, if tax revenue is expected to increase, what are the changes in law or in tax base that are expected to yield the higher tax revenue? If savings are to increase as a proportion of income, why? Is the increase in savings consistent with the increase in income? The comparison with experience can also be considered as trying to judge functional relationships. If savings were only 8 percent of GNP last year, why are they expected to be 10 percent this year, a 25 percent increase? If railroads carried 70 percent of the total freight last year, why does the plan assume they will carry 80 percent during the next plan period? This translates into what increases in railroad capacity are planned, what assumptions are made about changes in competitive freight carriers? Nearly all aspects of the plan are capable of comparisons with the actual performance of the economy in the previous year or planned period. Comparison with experience is of course only a partial guide to reasonableness; it does not provide limits. The purpose of the whole planning exercise is to induce and shape changes in most of the elements of the economy. Many of these kinds of questions will require technical answers and data that do not appear in the published plan documents. But at all levels of generalization, questions of this kind and efforts to identify partial answers and to outline areas of ignorance improve the understanding of what is involved in implementing economic plans.

Materials Commodity Balances

This technical check for consistency has often been the basis for the physical planning technique for some countries, particularly in the early days of planning in communist countries. The method consists of selecting important, widely used materials and examining their projecte availabilities and use by sector. Planners may take coal, steel, coppel oil, and power and examine how much of these resources each sector of the economy will use at the projected levels of production. Where imbalances exist, adjustment either in supply or use will be required; and since a production system is involved, a change in one variable will produce changes in the others. The commodity balance for coal may shc that if steel is to be produced at the projected level, it may need much more coal than projected. Increasing the production of coal will of course require more steel and more power, as well as other inputs. The projected supplies and demand for each of the critical materials must be adjusted until a reasonable balance exists. Carried to its mathematical conclusion, the process ends in complicated input-output tables, a method of studying interindustry relationships that is very important where adequate data exists. In the less developed countries, less sophisticated methods of examining the balances of important materials often reveal assumptions about changes in use patterns that involve numerous administrative decisions and even the development of system of rationing and control.

Policy Consistency

Economic policies are usually neglected in published economic plans, and too often neglected in the plan formulation. Even if full consideration were given to policies, there would still be contradiction and inconsistencies, policies that seem to be going in opposite directions. The reason for these inconsistencies lies in the varied and complex objectives of the plan, in the complex mixture of instrumental and ultimate goals. Often, these goals are not only contradictory at operational levels, but often they are compromises with other goals, compromises that must change as operating conditions change. Thus, examining a plan for its monetary or fiscal policies will often lead to recognition that some policies conflict with others; efforts to increase savings will work against policies that penalize savings and encourage consumption. Some policies will be present because they were followec historically; and although they operate against an increase in investment, they are too difficult to change in the plan period, even though long range plans may call for their elimination. Many policies will be included because they are the best compromise that can be expected under existing circumstances. A policy that is designed to encourage private foreign investment, implied in a projected increase of foreign resources, may conflict with announced policies to reduce foreign employment in the country and to require large increases of supervisory personnel from among the nationals of the country. Tightening controls to reduce the use of foreign exchange for imported luxuries may conflict with estimates of increased revenues from imported luxuries.

THE ADMINISTRATION OF PLANNING

Role of Public Administration

Since national economic planning is a continuous process in which practically all important government agencies participate, the importance of adequate administration of the planning process is decisive to its success. It is difficult to discuss all of the problems of the administration of national planning—including plan formulation, implementation, and evaluation—since this would cover nearly all of public administration of government. It is important to remember that planning is not limited merely to the central planning agency or to a few of the more specialized economic agencies, such as banks, the finance ministry, and resource allocation agencies. Where an agency's operations are importantly related to economic activities, it is generally useful to establish special planning units, although agency planning must necessarily be carried out by all important administrators. A special planning unit is merely a way of organizing agency specialists, to give the function of economic planning the extra attention it often requires. But economic planning as an important aspect of public administration goes beyond the activities of the central planning agency and of special planning units in operating agencies.

The guidance of economic planning is of course diffused throughout government since it forms an important part of the responsibility of many, if not most, administrators. The major guidance, however, comes from a cluster of agencies whose functions bring them closer to the ultimate appraisal of plans. The highest political levels generally dispense final approval, but the central fiscal agencies and the major operating agencies clearly play important roles in the administration of the planning process. A complex cluster of guidance exists that makes plan formulation and evaluation difficult to analyze. So closely are planning policies and activities interwoven into other operating policies and practices that to describe planning guidance and operation is almost as general an undertaking as to describe the totality of governmental operations. Here it is important to recognize that the formal planning apparatus of government is only part of the planning process.

Planning Capabilities of Governments

Not all countries can formulate economic plans that are comprehensive and cover the total economy. But the need and prestige of national comprehensive plans have become so accepted that nearly every one of the less developed countries tries to publish a plan document that purports to be a summary of a comprehensive plan. Three kinds of constraints operate to limit planning capabilities of a country.

Limitations of Trained Planners

Few of the less developed countries possess the trained planners needed to formulate a comprehensive plan. These include the economists, engineers, and administrators in the operating government agencies as well as in the planning units of operating agencies and in the central planning agency. This limitation may not seem too constraining, as it is always possible to employ foreign planning personnel to do special planning work. But the mere statement of the situation exposes its critical shortcomings. While a few foreigners may fill some of the key planning posts, comprehensive economic planning presupposes competence and trained personnel at many points of the economic system. Foreign planners who develop comprehensive plans by themselves are usually engaging in pseudoplanning, a costly and wasteful misuse of resources.

Inadequate Data

Economic planning requires large quantities of economic data, most of which requires systematic collection and analysis. Some of this information is readily available if someone takes the trouble to collect it, as, for example, data in imports and exports classified in a meaningful way. Some data require special effort and considerable skill in statistical inference and sampling techniques and extensive statistical capacity, as data on wholesale and retail prices and on wages and price levels. The less developed countries are characterized by a conspicuous absence of adequate economic data. One of the external economies of their attempts to develop economic plans is the experience gained in developing data necessary for the usual economic operations as well as for planning purposes. A great deal of the economic data used in comprehensive plans is fabricated from unreliable and fragmentary information, and therefore confers a false sense of exactness to economic comparisons and projections. While an inadequate data base can be overcome, it is usually a slow and expensive process—one that must be given continued high-level support and expert guidance. The edge between skillful use of partial data and improper use of inadequate data is thin indeed, and most countries have frequently mistaken one for the other.

Absence of the Means of Affecting Economic Activities

By far the most difficult constraint on economic planning is the absence of institutions and arrangements by which government policies can affect economic actions. These interactions may involve direct government operations or, more frequently, governmental relations with the private sector. A government may be able to control its own investment expenditures, but not those in the private sector. Plans may call for licensing of imports, but the government may be incapable of establishing adequate licensing systems. Projections for increased tax revenues may assume a capacity for tax collection that does not exist, either in commitment or in execution. Economic planning must often assume certain broad capabilities in the initiation and implementation of monetary and fiscal policies that many governments do not have. These means of affecting economic activities may develop in time, but their absence may reduce comprehensive economic planning to an exercise in wishful thinking and to projections of what is likely to happen regardless of attempts at economic planning. "It is my contention that in spite of all claims to the contrary, planning as such does not operate in India today: there are only schemes of public expenditure or of aid to private or cooperative enterprise. There is no coordinated conscious effort to lead development along predefined lines. As a consequence, development proceeds largely as if in a 'laissez faire' regime."[6]

Because of these kinds of constraints, many countries find it impossible to utilize comprehensive economic plans. This doesn't prevent them from publishing plan documents, however, because of their political advantage. Obviously, it would be much better from the operating viewpoint if planning activities of countries that are not capable of comprehensive planning were limited to those partial and sectoral plans where adequate data are available and where meaningful plans can be presented. For key projects in the economy—a selected power project, a harbor improvement program, an agricultural extension service, demonstration farms, or a development bank for agricultural credit—specific projects and programs can be presented as useful partial plans, together with the outlines of government participation. Even a list of proposed government investment expenditures, financially labeled as such, may be better than a pretentious investment program that attempts to hide the fact that little is known and even less can be done about nongovernment investment. When it is not shored up by adequate sectoral, program, and project planning and by adequate statistical data, aggregative planning often presents simplistic and unreal pictures of the economy. A bad economic plan can be much worse than no economic plan. While the idea of economic planning was received enthusiastically in the period after World War II as a prime requirement for modernization, recent years have been marked by a more restrained enthusiasm. The inadequate, and even ludicrous quality of macroeconomic planning in some countries has been too conspicuous to be overlooked and has cast substantial doubt on the feasibility of comprehensive economic planning. "While development plans have proliferated, and the techniques by which they are formulated have improved, the average annual rate at which domestic product has grown in the less developed countries has shown no appreciable improvement since the 1950's, and in Latin America and even more in Southern and Southeast Asia, the annual rate of growth has actually declined."[7]

Public Participation in Economic Planning

It is clear that practically every important agency of government must participate in comprehensive economic planning. To have plans prepared entirely by a central group of technicians, with little or no involvement by the operating agencies of government, is to insure the failure of the plan in operation. The necessary cooperation by the planning agency and by the numerous government agencies establishing and implementing policies is so widely accepted and so obviously important and reasonable that it scarcely needs emphasis. The necessity of such widespread participation has been carried over into the area of participation of the general public, particularly as it relates to the private sector of the economy. Most countries have accepted the general thesis that planning in all its phases—formulation, implementation, and evaluation—must be associated with a vigorous effort to encourage as widespread public participation as possible. Public participation is measured by the extent to which groups and individuals outside of government have an effect on decision making in the process of plan formulation, implementation and evaluation.* There is usually a basic assumption that "expanded participation will enhance growth." [8]

The benefits to be derived from widespread public participation range over many facets of the planning process:

1. Better information on which to base decisions. Interested public participation provides information on preferences and priorities, on the effect of existing policies and practices, on the obstacles to be anticipated and the means that can be used to achieve objectives.

2. Better acceptance of the plan's objectives. Effective implementation is possible only when there is both widespread agreement with the priorities of the plan and an acceptance of the kinds of social discipline that the plan necessarily involves. The extent to which consumers' choices and entrepreneurial decisions lie in the direction that the economic plan wishes to achieve is strongly conditioned by the degree to which the plan reflects accepted priorities, with its implied sacrifices of present consumption for increased future production capabilities.

3. Better plan implementation and evaluation. The planning proces is necessarily continuous and must adjust operations to realities of implementation. Public participation is an important information feedback

---

*One other possible meaning of public participation, participation in the benefits of the economic plan, is excluded from this meaning as used here, not because it is unimportant, but because of its overriding importance as a basic feature of the entire economic subsystem, discussed in chapter 5.

and planners sensitive to public response to the plan's progress will be in a position to evaluate necessary adjustments to the plan.

That there are constraints and possible disadvantages to many kinds of public participation is also evident. General public influence may resist the necessary postponement of consumption in order to accumulate capital goods. The government may be pushed by popular pressure into ventures of public welfare and policies that may be unwise in their timing, if not in their ultimate desirability. Thus minimum wage laws, immediate universal literacy, widespread health clinics, subsidized imports, and unemployment benefits may represent popular priorities, but often at a cost to production and capital formation that is excessive and make their timing unfortunate. The pressure of special interest groups may often be exercised to protect their special status and to avoid government action that is disadvantageous to them. It is quite difficult to distinguish between legitimate expression of interests and needs and the use of influence to protect an undesirable advantage. The difference is often a matter of ultimate value judgment rather than operational necessity.[9]

Public participation is exercised through formal and informal channels and by formal and informal organizations. There may be instruments of expression for important elements of the public, such as chambers of commerce, unions, importers' councils, associations of bankers, merchants, and other business associations. The government may establish special advisory councils and commissions to study particular problems or to represent particular kinds of participants, as in advisory councils on regional balance or commissions to examine the needs of minority groups. Communication media are used to establish public interest in the planning process and to arrive at some kind of consensus on problems of public policy. Thus such media not only transmit information but also are a means of feedback, securing information about public consensus and response to changing policies. At nearly every level of government, voting is in part a method of public participation in the process of establishing public policies, as well as a method for the establishment of a social consensus and the selection of political leaders. Many different kinds of social and political institutions, as well as economic institutions, are involved in the flow of information to and from the public as part of the planning process. The school system, churches, and local and regional organizations represent channels that are used to disseminate and receive information useful for national economic planning. The extent to which these institutions are capable of doing this efficiently is obviously a prime determinant in the extent to which public participation is a useful element in planning.

Several useful generalizations can be made about public participation in the planning process:

The advantages of developing a good mix of various kinds of public participation in the planning process is obviously so important that practically every government examines the role of public participation in the planning process. Basic political and social pressures constantly force the question of public participation to the attention of the top political leaders.

Public participation must be conscious and clearly visible, and it must be operational. It must be recognized as a major concern of government, by government officials not only willing but anxious to listen and learn from representatives of all kinds of interests.

Public participation must occur early enough in the planning process to affect evaluation of objectives as well as their implementation. Limiting public participation to protests against specific operations reduces its usefulness and magnifies some of its worst possibilities.

The structures of public participation must be informal as well as formal and must have permanent as well as temporary form. "It should also be obvious that where permanent machinery has been established through which businessmen, farmers, and workers can regularly and freely express their views, there is a better chance that a plan will reflect the realities in the private sector and induce the cooperation and support required for the plan's successful implementation."10

Many private institutions are essential for successful public participation in the planning process. Some of these institutions require government initiation and encouragement. Government officials must constantly examine these institutions and encourage their increased usefulness in the planning process.

To be most useful, public participation must represent in some form all of the important elements or groups affected by the economic plan, and not merely those that are powerful or articulate.11

Government planning agencies must exercise patience and adopt a realistic time scale in the use and evaluation of public participation, which is often slow and cumbersome. It is easy to lose patience with the sluggishness of adequate public response and to pervert a careful data exchange into polemics and propaganda. While these characteristics have important roles in the functioning of a society, their usefulness in the planning process is not only limited, but may even be negative.

Planning and Market Institutions

Planning does not mean the substitution of directives or coercion for market institutions. Economic development is always a changing mixture of market operations and planning, since a government always either accepts, changes, or establishes the rules by which a country operates its economic system. Thus planning does not necessarily mean a decrease in the importance of market institutions. A higher productivity society requires a greater division of labor, greater specialization of capital and production for wider markets. This increases the exchanges of products and money, and bigger and better market institution must develop to facilitate these exchanges. Planning must provide for adequate market institutions; where existing markets are too limited or are constrained by inadequate transportation, inadequate communication, or improper procedures, planning must attempt to remedy these inadequacies. Any projection of the feasibility of increased production and improved distribution necessarily involves an examination of the associated market institutions.

No country, however centralized its control of economic activities, can completely substitute directed allocation for detailed market operations. Decentralized decision making and choice through some market mechanisms is the major allocating process, whether it is the laborer choosing his job, an entrepreneur deciding on his product mix, or a consumer choosing the particular item of food or clothing he purchases. Central direction, with specific rationing of jobs and products and directed production schedules for each enterprise, would require an administrative apparatus so massive as to be impossible. Even the most centrally directed economies in the world today do not attempt it. Even in times of great stress, such as war or famine, large portions of the necessary allocation of factor inputs and products are assigned to market institutions, and the government attempts to control here through changes in the rules and limits of participation in these markets. This often involves no more than price control. Market allocation by means of prices assumes that the current income distribution is satisfactory or at least reasonable. Since this is clearly not true in most cases, market allocations must be examined and influenced to assist in attaining the objectives generally encompassed in increased production, increasing productivity, and improved income distribution. Thus, the rules of market participation, limits on price changes, minimum prices, regulations regarding product composition, and even specific restrictive measures may be adopted to push market operations toward attaining social as well as efficiency objectives. For example, labor markets may be opened up to previously excluded groups, a skilled trade may be opened to new entrants, new facilities and tax differentials may encourage wider participation and more competition in marketing arrangements; all this to shape the marketing institutions that will encourage improved productivity and income distribution. Planning must examine marketing institutions as they relate to new programs being initiated. The effort to create new agriculture cooperatives must be related to improved marketing institutions for products as well as for such new inputs as better seeds, fertilizer, and insecticides. The impact on income distribution of all new programs must be examined in terms of their reliance on existing market institutions, and planning must become interested in any extensions of market institutions that will be required. To wait for individual needs to express themselves in market extensions or development of new markets will often be to lose many of the advantages that efficient market institutions bring. Yet to establish market institutions without the need will be a wasteful and futile exercise. Therefore, planning the development of market institutions must be carefully related to operational needs by production enterprises. There is little general theory that can guide the planners in specific situation; only operating judgment after careful study of each situation. General theory points to the basic need of market institutions, to the role that market institutions play, and this theory can provide the criteria by which need for markets can be measured. But only the specific operating situation can provide the data that permit positive planning.

The need for positive planning in the extension or improvement of market institutions must be emphasize because psychologically, decreased reliance on market operations is favored by most governments of the less developed countries. Not only are most of them inclined toward socialism in their basic philosophy, but they have images of market institutions that are directly related to colonial exploitation and foreign domination. Markets are the tools of exploitive capitalism, a means by which the poor are coerced to perform their tasks for the powerful and rich. Recognizing the basic importance of markets to any complex economic situation, the reduction and even elimination of markets is assumed to be necessary to avoid the harsh results of low productivity production. An impatience with slowly moving, diffused functioning of intangible markets, mixed with idealism and the desire to take direct action to achieve good results often impels planners to establish direct allocation schemes that attempt to substitute for market operations. The result is often an added administrative burden of serious proportions, a strong impulse toward favoritism and corruption, the growth of hidden, supplementary market operations, and a less efficient allocation system in general. The belief in the personal disinterestedness of government officials, their ability to be fair, and the general desirability of government intervention in the economic system is soon overwhelmed by the tremendous workload and obvious inefficiency.

Planning as a process must constantly review market institutions and the rules and limits within which they operate. The essential function of markets, to allocate inputs, products and financial resources and to decentralize decision making, must constantly be related to new investment plans and to planned production. In most countries, with the exception of major financial market institutions, market institutions are left to develop as needed. The numerous market institutions are probably just as likely to hinder this development as they are to encourage it. Sometimes market institutional considerations form part of specific sectoral projects, as when marketing operations are part of a program to establish farm cooperatives or plans to produce and distribute fertilizer. Usually these changes in parts of the market institutions are grossly inadequate, without any consideration of the larger institutions of which they are a part. Only when a crisis develops, a severe shortage or a shocking inadequacy, are deliberate efforts made to study the market operations and to identify what has to be done to encourage changes. This lack of understanding and appreciation of the importance of market institutions becomes one of the major inadequacies of economic planning.

OPERATIONS OF THE PLANNING AGENCY

Organization

The formal organization for the administration of planning is of course important, but within limits it does not seem to be a major determinant for the success of economic planning. That is, there doesn't seem to be a high degree of correlation between any specific type of formal planning organization and effective planning. Too many countries have adopted "good" organizations and produced poor and ineffective plans for planning organizations to be considered the major determinant of success. The planning organization must be fitted into the administrative structure of the country. That country's level of effective administration, history and culture, value systems, and degree of commitment to economic growth will be more important probably in determining the effective type of planning organization than any theoretical analysis of organization. There can be no optimum planning organization for all countries. But some generalizations about useful characteristics of the central planning organizations can be made:

1. The central planning organization must operate continuously, and not only during a short period when a plan document is being prepared. It must be established by law and have a permanent staff of its own, with career potentials for its professional members, as in any other important government agency. During peak periods of its work, professional staff from other agencies may be deputied to the planning agency; but these people should never dominate the central planning operation.

2. The central planning agency must have enough authority and power to maintain meaningful dialogues with ministries and other agencies involved in financing, sectoral plans, government policies, and government administrative operations involving control of economic activities.

Beyond these two prime considerations, the question of whether the central planning agency should be a commission, a ministry or a separate agency reporting directly to the highest political levels must be settled on the basis of the characteristics of each individual country. It is important that the authority of the central planning agency should be as clear and unambiguous as words can make it, although it should be obvious that what establishes this authority unambiguously is the manner in which the agency is supported by the highest political authorities. A country that is capable of developing a good central planning agency is generally capable of good administration and, unfortunately, the exact reverse can also be true.

3. The central planning agency must be closely integrated at operational levels with all important government agencies. It cannot become

a state within a state and still be an effective planning agency. In order to keep the planning process flexible and adjusted to realities, the central planning agency has a responsibility for keeping in close touch with plan implementation and evaluation; and this means that its staff must have friendly, continuous, and detailed contact with the staffs of operating agencies. For the central planning staff cannot be an important implementing agency; to do so would almost surely result in the neglect of its planning functions in favor of the all-absorbing, crisis-settling situations that seem to be a continuing part of implementing activities. The central planning agency often becomes the training center for planners, whereby its professional planners often transfer to operating agencies either in planning or operating positions. The reverse flow of staff is also usually present, and both flows should be encouraged to the degree that they represent opportunities for gaining experience and for rewarding excellence. Yet, the separation of the central planning agency from plan implementation is not without cost, since

> There can be little doubt that the separation of plan formulation from implementation has been exacerbated by the concentration of planners' attention on economic factors to the virtual exclusion of organizational and management factors which predominate when a plan is being implemented. Professional planners and planning experts appear to be divided into two main groups: one tends to believe that better planning depends upon further improvements in their imperfect planning instruments (as witness the preoccupation with model building, simulation and input-output technique), while the second tends to feel that the shortcomings of the planning process reflect the inadequacies of the administrative and political environment within which plans must be carried out more than any deficiency of planning technique. But whatever their position, planners are little likely to concern themselves with the problems of public administration and politics.[12]

Relationship to Financial Agencies and to the Annual Budget

The relationship between economic planning and the financial agencies of government is necessarily close and not necessarily cooperative. Both agencies may have the same ultimate objectives and may seek their attainment through the same channels of control and influence. Yet the perspective and the day by day operating problems and policies are quite different, and there is likely to be a great deal of difference in institutional judgment of feasibility and desirability, on both the revenue and expenditure side of government finance. Before economic planning was accepted, the financial agencies really performed this function, although it was for the most part an unconscious, unidentified aspect of their work. In their attempt to acquire as much revenue as possible, and to allocate the collected revenue in accordance with the decisions of the political leaders, the financial agencies were exercising the functions that have now been consciously expanded to become national economic planning.

Most countries now have formal or informal annual budgets. An annual budget is accepted as a necessary management device to help assign responsibility and authority to collect and spend government funds. It seems so simple and obviously necessary that it is astonishing to reflect that annual budgets are a relatively modern management tool. Most countries did not use annual budgets until the last century. Today practically all countries have annual budgets as the major means of financial control, and finance ministries and their budget officers usually develop strong administrative influence within the government. The judgments of budget officials are always critical elements in the monetary and fiscal plans of the country. The relationship between these functions and those of the planning agency is so direct that there must be a close relationship between the planning agency and the financial agencies, both in their objectives and in their methods of operation.

The economic plan may call for differential taxes, tax increases, and tax holidays to encourage or discourage different kinds of investment. If the annual budget does not reflect these considerations in its estimates of revenues and expenditures, the commitment of government to implement the plan may be doubted. The expenditure pattern must reflect the pattern of priorities and commitments formulated. To the extent that these two patterns differ, they reflect either nonimplementation or the need to revise the plan. The latter situation should not be overlooked, because the annual budget must be considered as feedback information for the planning process. Annual budgets, which reflect quite clearly the current decisions of government about actual availabilities and existing pressures, must be influential in plan adjustment. This becomes more evident as the plan proceeds, so that the fifth year of a plan period needs more numerous adjustments than the first year.

Annual budgets are documents that reflect financial planning, but by themselves they are poor economic planning instruments:

1. They often omit many kinds of government receipts and expenditures, such as trust funds, segregated funds, defense funds, and independent and semiindependent agencies. They usually omit much of the local governments' revenues and expenditures.

2. Their classification system is usually based on historical precedents and formal governmental organization, rather than on categories meaningful for the management of economic growth. Annual budgets often merely summarize ministry estimates that are cleared at cabinet meetings.

3. Annual budgets are too narrow in scope for their use in choosing and coordinating financial policies necessary for economic growth plans.

Many important policies are not focused on annual income and expenditure of government funds. For example, the need for establishing and maintaining a specialized development bank is scarcely placed in the proper framework for consideration when it is viewed as part of the annual budget. While this bank will use some part of the annual budget, this may be quite minor and the decision to have a bank may be made by an entirely different set of administrators from those concerned with budget considerations.

As a planning device, foreign exchange budgets are likely to be better than the usual annual budgets of governments. Foreign exchange budgets attempt to project revenues and expenditures of foreign exchange in a manner similar to the annual government budget. Few countries (Japan is the most conspicuous example) have really developed this method of organizing the government's financial activity to achieve objectives of stability and economic growth. Most countries have relegated the whole subsystem of foreign exchange planning and control of foreign exchange expenditures to operations entirely removed from the annual budget process, as if to imply that all kinds of financial resources are interchangeable. The need to develop complicated (and usually inefficient) channels of translating annual budgetary decisions into foreign exchange requirements usually becomes a negotiation between the foreign exchange control agency and the individual ministries or operating agencies.

Government has the job of managing its own affiars, as well as managing the whole economy. While the two cannot be separated, because government affairs are so important to the whole economy, there are differences that require separate frameworks for their best consideration. The annual budget concentrates on government affairs; and the budget must be fitted into the planning process, which is the economic management of the whole economy. The need for agreement on projections of government revenues and expenditures and the need for priorities and policies are just as present in the financial sector as it is in any other sector of the economy.

The difference between planning and financing operations lies in the functions of the financial agencies and of the annual budget as it relates to operating control. The financial agencies that issue the budget are often placed in a position of controlling operations by sanctioning specific expenditures within the authorized budget. Thus, they perform functions close to actual execution of plans at points far closer to actual operations than do planning officials. The desirability of having a system of "sanctioning" below the level of a proved annual budget is open to serious question. The need obviously exists for tight financial control, where general authorizations of levels of expenditure are translated into specific actions that expend resources. As an internal check on governmental operations, treasury control of detailed expenditures has historical explanations and even justification. Yet it easily can be carried too far, in terms of detailed controls of individual actions that choke rather than supervise the expenditure of government funds. As it relates to planning and plan implementation, it gives the financial agencies with detailed sanctioning authority over governmental expenditures the opportunity to second-guess planning and budget decisions, an opportunity that often leads to delays and to substitution priorities of the financial agency for priorities in the plan. Where financial checks and double checks become too detailed, too frequent, and too delaying, they must be examined and evaluated, usually at high political levels. In governmental operations, the annual budget and the controls of the financial agencies, such as Treasury Departments or Ministries of Finance, are so essential to day by day operations of government that they must be constantly scrutinized in their role in the plan formulation and implementation process. Since they cannot be entirely eliminated, either conceptually or operationally, their functioning must be improved.

Relationship to Statistical Agencies and Data Improvement

Economic data are the basic building stones of economic planners. Without adequate data, a plan becomes a combination of exhortation and wishful thinking. The central planning agency needs so many different kinds of economic data that its requirements appear to be both insatiable and unreal. No country, no matter how long it has planned and how much it has improved its data base, ever assembles enough data to satisfy its planners, particularly economists. The administrators in charge of the central planning agency must choose a nice balance between strong encouragement of improved data collection and spending too much time and capacity on using and improving economic data, beyond the merits of the problem and the returns for the use of scarce resources. The best economic data are those developed by operating agencies and used in the management of those agencies. Some specialized statistical agencies, such as census bureaus, may be needed for mass statistical work. But in general the gathering of useful economic data is a function of the adequate operations of many government agencies, as well as of institutions and organizations in the private sector, such as banks, clearing houses, and business associations.

As one of the important consumers of economic data, the central planning agency must be a strong force in the direction of improving a country's data base. This may be done in many ways, by supporting any agency's efforts to train personnel and improve its data collection, by strong support of government work, or by using its relationship to top administrators and political leaders to stress the importance of long-range programs of statistical improvement. While avoiding overspending on statistical frills, the central planning agency must be a major supporter of continuous scrutiny of government data to eliminate the less useful reports that always seem to surround operating agencies and to encourage the development of management data that include the economic data required for plan formulation, implementation, and evaluation.

Because data gathering for management purposes is the best basis for any kind of government data gathering, it is not desirable to have the central planning agency act as central statistical office or as a place where data are originally gathered and published. Obviously, where a central statistical office has been established to help government agencies think through their data needs and to publish in a central way the most important economic data collected and compiled by government agencies, the central planning agency must have close working relations with the central statistical office. This relationship, however, should not involve operating supervision. To do so would be to burden the planning agency with a difficult statistical job that could not but detract from its planning functions. It would also reduce the usefulness of the central statistical office, which must be oriented to other government management needs beside central planning. The central planning agency should have constant meetings with a central statistical office, leading to agreements on technical concepts and definitions and even to staff interchange. Without cordial personnel and professional relationships, there can be a wasting, cut-throat competition between the professionals on both staffs that can only be harmful to the planning and data gathering functions of government.

Yet the central planning agency must also be the most severe critic of the data gathering function of government and the numerous agencies that perform this function. The gathering of useless data is one of the most wasteful aspects of government. Every agency seems to fall into the trap of requiring from its staff, its public constitutuencies, and its subordinate agencies, data of doubtful validity and limited usefulness. As agencies' operating responsibilities change, data requirements and capacities should change, but the data gathering mechanism of an agency is one of its slowest parts to reflect these changes. With rapidly changing administrators, so typical in agencies deeply involved in economic growth, the judgments of what data are required for management purposes constantly changes. This is often reflected in the initiation of new reports, and the failure to follow up or use data channels established by previous administrators. The central planning agency must, as a prime consumer of economic data, recognize this kind of vicious circle and use its influence and professional judgment to reduce the large mass of relatively useless data gathering that characterizes many government agencies.

Because of the importance of adequate data to the central planning agency, it is often tempted into supporting grandiose schemes for government-wide data improvement. These schemes are usually modeled after the arrangement in the economically advanced countries, from which statistical advisors are made available. The undesirability of this procedure has become clear after many unfortunate and expensive lessons have been absorbed. What is essential is that the central planning agency must urge and help prepare a program for improvement of the data base, carefully considering the possibility of improvement and assigning priorities in line with the need for data and the resources likely to be available. Advocating and establishing a multi-year field study of consumption by rural families may utilize most of the additional statistical resources in a sector that may be ultimately very important; but this may take a lower priority compared to the gathering of more useful data. The central planning agency is in a strong position to help define statistical priorities and resources, and it must accept this as one of its major objectives in the improvement of the whole planning process.

Relationship to Political Leadership

Planners cannot ignore administrative feasibility; to do so would be to plan deliberately for what they know cannot be achieved. Equally, planners cannot ignore political feasibility since most of the important decisions relating to economic objectives and choice of alternative ways of achieving these objectives must be based on political judgments. All important economic policies have important political implications. Even in countries that do not rely heavily on popular elections to select political leadership, the political effect of economic planning is relevant and important. Consequently there must be the closest kind of collaboration and support between the political leadership and the central planning agency, Political leaders generally do not need much convincing that economic growth is important and that economic planning is a useful method of trying to speed up economic growth. Where political leaders have decided that economic growth is unimportant, as in Indonesia under Sukarno, economic planning becomes a facade with little impact.[13] Political leadership really sets the tasks for administrators, whose commitment to economic planning is usually a reflection of the commitment of the political leaders. Where this is not recognized and administrators are confident enough to think of national economic planning as separate, or even partially divorced from political leaders and priorities, planning soon becomes an exercise in futility.[14]

Planning has as one of its operating necessities the identification of policies that must be adopted if economic goals are to be achieved. Planning thus may raise many fundamental policy questions that require definition and answer, if not solution. These usually have political implications, as important for policy implementation as the administrative aspects. For example, the question of initiating and enforcing rural income taxes in the less developed countries raises problems that are usually as much political as administrative. Can rural income taxes be assessed and collected in a way that still leaves an adequate political base? Planners are forced to consider these kinds of problems, as must the administrators of the Finance Ministry and the political leaders of the country.

Political leaders must consider many different kinds of priorities. Even in problems that seem peculiarly associated with economic growth—such as resource allocation, investment patterns, and foreign exchange controls—the needs for nation building, internal political base, defense, territorial expansion and power blocs become important considerations that must have politically inspired answers. The central planning agency cannot ignore such considerations or assume that decisions will be made only on economic grounds. Whenever sufficient information is available, planners must present alternative options to be chosen, alternative costs and benefits, and alternative ways of attaining objectives with their market costs and their opportunity costs. When planners make these decisions, they are making political decisions; and at relatively low operational levels, this is often the case. The higher the level of operation, the more necessary it is that the planning decisions have the full overt support and concurrence of the political leadership.

How this close working relationship between planners and political leaders is established at an operating level is one of the most difficult problems facing the administrators in charge of the central planning agency. The answer lies to a large extent in convincing political leaders of the integrity of the planning operation and the need for professional approaches to the whole process of economic planning. Recognizing the need for close collaboration with political leadership and giving full weight to the importance of political decisions on most of the important priority questions does not eliminate the need for stressing the importance of systematic examination of plan objectives, policies, and practices. Judgments of feasibility, projections of possible results, and implementation of economic plans require trained personnel that must be used by political leaders to help manage the economy. To minimize the professional inputs necessary for economic planning can be just as costly as to minimize the political inputs; both are essential in a way that integrates and expands their individual contributions.

NOTES

1. See J. Tinbergen and H. C. Bos, Mathematical Models of Economic Growth (New York: McGraw-Hill, 1962).

2. Keith B. Griffin and John L. Enos, Planning Development (London: Addison-Wesley, 1970).

3. See H. B. Chenery and P. G. Clark, Interindustry Economics (New York: John Wiley & Sons, 1959).

4. See R. Dorfman, "Mathematical or 'Linear' Programming: A Nonmathematical Exposition," American Economic Review 43, no. 5 (December 1953): 797-825.

5. See any good elementary statistics book for a discussion of regression analysis. For example, see Werner Z. Hirsch, Introduction to Modern Statistics (New York: The Macmillan Co., 1957), pp. 247-81.

6. D. R. Gadgel, Planning and Economic Policy in India (Poona: Asia Publishing House, 1962), p. 140.

7. Albert Waterston, "An Operational Approach to Development Planning," Finance and Development Quarterly 6, no. 4 (December 1969): 38-42.

8. David Hapgood, The Role of Popular Participation in Development (Boston: MIT Press, 1969), p. 26.

9. See Bertram M. Gross, ed., Action Under Planning: The Guidance of Economic Development (New York: Mcgraw-Hill, 1967), pp. 186-232.

10. Albert Waterston, Development Planning (Baltimore: Johns Hopkins Press, 1968), p. 463.

11. See Wolfgang Stopler, Development Digest 6, no. 1 (January 1968): 6.

12. Waterston, Development Planning, p. 339.

13. See Benjamin Higgins, Economic Development—Problems, Principles and Policies (New York: W.W. Norton & Co., 1968), Chap. 31, "Indonesia, the Chronic Dropout."

14. See Frederick W. Riggs, "Relearning an Old Lesson: The Political Context of Development Administration," Public Administration Review 25, no. 1 (March 1965): 7.

10

THE ADMINISTRATION
OF ECONOMIC POLICIES

THE CONCEPT OF ECONOMIC POLICIES

An "economic policy" is a line of action adopted by government to achieve a certain objective or group of objectives related to the production and distribution of goods and services. Policies specify purposes, and assign priorities and preferences to alternative objectives and to ways of achieving these objectives. Policies therefore necessarily involve value judgments. Normally, an economic policy is deliberate; but a government can have a policy through inaction, delibera or nondeliberate. An economic policy is supposed to be a guide for administrators because it furnishes information strongly affecting, evei determining, the actions they take. But at an operational level, policy administration is not separate from policy formulation; it is part of a single process and cannot be separated except in theory. This is why is so important for public administrators to understand some of the com plexities of economic policy formulation and implementation.

The term, "policy," should be applied to important guide lines onl Language soon becomes too loose for accurate communication if the tit of "policy" is awarded to every governmental decision, however unimportant. Individual instances of action taken as a result of a general line of action cannot usefully be designated as policy. For example, it may be the economic policy of a government to lower the prices of consumers' goods; the order to reduce the price of a specific product is too minor a governmental action to be labeled as a policy.

Policy explicitly or implicitly involves implementation. Without means of implementation, a policy becomes a pious wish or a dream. These may be useful over a short time, particularly for polemic or inspirational reasons; but operationally they may soon become discounte While means and ends can often be separated as analytical constructs, they are inseparable and are mutually deterministic operationally. The means often predetermine the ends, while defining the ends usually involves indicating the means. Thus, economic policies necessarily involve both objectives and the means of attaining these objectives.

Policy formulation must be associated with policy implementation; in operations there can be no separation.

The objectives of economic policies can be both broad and narrow. Widely conceived economic policies can mean a complicated mixture of ends and means, as in a stabilization policy, where the broad goal is economic stability which may involve subsidiary goals relating to money, prices, wages, profits, and imports. The economic policy of stimulating economic growth is so broad as to encompass literally dozens of other broad economic objectives. Too broad a concept of economic policy may make analysis and communication too general for usefulness. Too narrow a concept of economic policy may result in confusion and triviality, as when economic policies are conceived as applying to specific factories or to specific market transaction. Obviously, the type of analysis being made determines to a large extent what is a useful application of the term "economic policy." Broad economic policies can be almost infinitely subdivided and are very closely related to other policies. Foreign economic policy, for example, includes policy considerations for exports, imports, pricing, taxes and commercial treaties.

Economic policies have multiple objectives, often contradictory and mutually constraining. Thus, a foreign economic policy that encourages foreign investment may have a marked impact on policies relating to domestic control of natural resources. Policies that tax imports heavily may constrain policies that encourage foreign investment. The analysis and understanding of economic policies must come not only from an understanding of specific policy objectives, but also how well those fit into the objectives of other, related, economic policies. The conflicting and supporting objectives must usually be judged in terms of the optimum mix or best balance possible, rather than in simple terms of good or bad. It is quite common to find advocacy of contradictory economic policies, largely based on differing views of the importance of the multiple objectives and multiple consequences that are part of each important economic decision. This is another illustration why policy formulation cannot be separated operationally from policy implementation and policy coordination.

A distinction must be made between "proposed" and "actual" economic policies. Proposed policies are generally more rational and neater than actual policies, which must suffer the impact of reality. Implementing an announced policy must establish the boundaries of that policy and much of its substance. Announced policies have to be adjusted through their administration to pressure groups and vested interests and to the environment in which administrative decisions always take place.

Economic policy decisions are always made and implemented in the context of politics and value systems. Economic policies are only part of public policies, which include social policies, defense policies, foreign policies, and political policies. Economic policies are framed within a context of institutions that have a very important influence on their interpretation and implementation. Thus, economic policies, in their implementation, must often encounter constitutional objections and must use the courts for enforcement and for resolution of conflicts and assessment of responsibilities. Economic policies, in their formulation as well as their implementation, must take into account the existing structure of the country, its institutions, values, and capacities Public administration at an operational level is extremely contextual.

IMPACT ON PRODUCTION AND PRODUCTIVITY

Government economic policies affect the production and distribution of goods and services at many different points of the process. An appreciation of this concept helps understand why important economic policies have many different points of impact.

Entrance to Production

Many government policies involve permission or capability to initiate an economic activity. Without such approval, the operation of an enterprise is impossible or is adversely limited. The techniques used by government to control entrance to production form a complex of overlapping activities, sometimes contradictory and always difficult to administer. They vary from general regulations involving all would-be participants to specific operations involving each participant. Government authorization may be open, or it may be quite hidden, a result of some other government action often only secondarily related to the enterprise in question. Licenses or permits are the simplest, most open way of controlling entrance to the market. By requiring a license to establish an enterprise or to engage in operations at a particular location, government controls entrance, shapes competition, and strongly affects the economic activities involved. Sometimes the awarding selection can be fairly open, and licenses are issued to all applicants, in which case licensing may be a revenue producing device rather than a control of entrance to the operation. Building permits are another example of the licensing authority, where permission to engage in the activity is joined with some effort to assure adequate technical competence in construction. Import licenses often determine how many enterprises shall operate or what new enterprises will be allowed to enter a business field. Certificates of essentiality, issued as part of the process of securing foreign exchange, are often the determing element in securing adequate financing. Investment controls, such as those that involve permission to sell lands or make loans, often determine which specific business will be permitted to expand or even to continue, and will strongly affect the kind of competition that exists.

Factor Markets

Factor markets are the general organization of the arrangements by which entrepreneurs secure the factors of production. Many government policies affect factor markets. Indeed, this is the main area in which government policies have an impact on the private sector. The existence of complex, interrelated labor markets can scarcely be doubted, although there may be no visible labor exchanges to observe. Similarly, the capital market exists and operates, although only a few of the less developed countries have visible, physical buildings where money is bought and sold. Land markets are even less visible, although even illiterate peasants are aware of the existence of this complex factor market. The wide variety of ways in which government can increase the quality and quantity of factor inputs were indicated in chapter 4 above. There the problems of improving the factor inputs were discussed in terms of general problems and the kinds of impact these problems have on the availability of adequate factor inputs. Here, it is useful to emphasize how the numerous kinds of governmental policies affect the factor markets, illustrating how diverse such policies are and how important are indirect, sometimes difficult-to-observe impacts on production and productivity.

Government policies that affect factor costs obviously affect the investment and management decisions of production enterprises. Thus, labor legislation and its implementation relating to minimum wage laws, working conditions, hiring priorities, and laws regulating the discharge of workers, illustrate how governmental policies can affect the cost of labor inputs. Similarly, laws regulating loans, interest rates, bank reserves, credit criteria, differential taxes, and subsidies are illustrations of governmental policies and their implementation that affect the availability and cost of capital inputs. Land tenure laws, laws regulating the ownership and exploitation of natural resources, and even laws prescribing rules of inheritance and sales illustrate the wide variety of governmental policies affecting the natural resource input in production. Practically all of the important social legislation adopted by a government involves an impact on factor costs, either limiting or prescribing how a factor input can be utilized in the production process in a way that affects costs.

Not all governmental policies affecting factor markets operate to increase factor costs. Such policies as the improvement of labor information, rationalization of capital credit facilities, and provision of such government services as improved communication, improved law and order, more efficient tax administration, and better training and educational facilities, work in the direction of reducing factor costs. Here it is important to reemphasize that government control does not necessarily mean a position adverse to increasing production and productivity. Costs and benefits, it will be remembered, are not always adequately inclusive of social costs and benefits. Increasing the monetary cost of a factor input may introduce sufficient social benefits to more than compensate for an adverse impact on the individual enterprise. Clearly, government economic policies must be examined in terms of the overall impact they have on factor costs. Policies that increase factor costs must have sufficient merit in other aspects and in their timing to justify them, since cost-increasing forces are, by their definition, suspect of operating against improved production and productivity.

Technology

Government economic policies often have important, direct impact on the kinds and levels of technology utilized in the production process. Thus, governmental sponsored or operated technical schools are important elements in making available required trained personnel. Governmental policies that affect the import of technical books, magazines and papers, and the availability of visiting foreign technicians and of foreign study tours for nationals clearly relate to the level and receptivity of new technologies. These illustrations of direct impact of governmental policies on technology must be supplemented by reference to even more important but less obvious, indirect policies that affect the improvement of the production technologies of a country. Import policies, particularly those relating to the import of capital equipment, may have more impact on the level of technology of a specific industry than the general training and educational programs of a country. Broad governmental policies advocating the adoption of improved technology may be vitally affected by specific implementation of other policies that make such improvements less likely. Thus policies reflecting the government's willingness to permit the employment of foreign specialists may affect a specific technology more than the availability of import licenses or the announced policy of welcoming improved technology. The indirect impact of governmental policies may often be more important to improving the level of technology than the direct policies. For example, government policies regarding the salary and status of trained engineers on certain kinds of government enterprises may have more impact on the level of technology of those enterprises than any announced policies that exhort the benefits of professionalization and advanced education. The attitude of the government toward improved technology, as observed in operations, may be more important than its most widely circulated policy statements.

Product Market

At the point of the economic process where enterprises must sell their products, thus acquiring the rewards for incurring the costs and risks of production, government economic policies have their widest and most visible impact. Such policies as price controls, and licensing of monopolies have long been standard elements in a government's efforts to affect the economic system. Less visible, but equally important variations of these are policies limiting competition, policies that prescribe markup at wholesale or retail levels, and licensing that limits the number of competitors. On the more positive side are government policies that encourage the initiation or improvement of existing product markets, such as cooperative marketing and arrangements in agricultural price supports. Government subsidies often implement policies to encourage certain kinds of production, as do policies on differential taxation. Obviously, government policies that affect entrance into the industry or affect factor costs and technology also have an important impact on the product market, and the multiple impacts may be mutually supportive or may be mutually antagonistic. Thus, a policy that improves the factor market may stimulate or adversely affect a product market. Factory laws that insist a product must be manufactured under highly sanitary conditions may so limit a process that its costs become too high for its usual product market. Laws protecting the rights of nationals in natural resources exploitation may eliminate the only possible method of securing adequate capital for the investment.

ECONOMIC POLICIES—FIELDS OF OPERATION

Economic policies are usually classified by their major objectives. Thus, reference to "agricultural policies" would include all those policies that affect agricultural production and distribution, such as agricultural tax policies, land policies, and agricultural pricing policies. It usually would not include monetary and fiscal policies, yet these strongly affect agriculture. Indeed, they may be the major determinants of changes in agricultural production. There is seldom an economic policy formulated in one area which will not affect, in one way or another, the activities in one or more other policy areas. While a policy may be formulated for the express purpose of achieving a technological objective, for example, it would be very difficult not to have this policy affect such broad areas as education and employment. In many cases the only available method to classify economic policies is to designate the original area of intent. Thus, any classification of economic policies is bound to be overlapping and hazy at the edges. The purpose of classification here is to indicate the wide scope of economic policies, their interdependence and mutual determination, and their inevitable influence on the activities of public administrators at almost all levels of administration.

Monetary and Fiscal Policies

Monetary and fiscal policies of government are among the most obvious functions of a government, the establishment and control of the money of a country and the management of the financial affairs of the government. These functions of government have probably existed since governments were initiated by primitive societies, certainly since the creation of money as a necessary tool in the economic activities of a society. They are among the most highly prized functions of a sovereign nation and have become among the most difficult areas of coordination in regional and international cooperative efforts. The consequences of monetary and fiscal policies are so directly related to the possession or continuation of political power that the decisions on general monetar and fiscal policies must usually rest with the highest political authorities in the country. Yet these policies are permeated with technical relationships that often only trained economists can observe and evaluate. General monetary and fiscal policies are necessarily associated with more specific policies formulated and implemented by administrators, that act as the framework for innumerable economic decisions by producers and consumers. Very few administrators are completely divorced from implementing or establishing the substantive effects of the broad monetary and fiscal policies of their governments.

Monetary policy refers to the government's efforts to control the quantity and quality of money. Only government can establish legal tender and prescribe the rules for creating money. Since the unit of money is associated with independence and is a symbol of sovereignty most of the colonial areas have, upon achieving independence, rushed to establish their own unit of account and their own monetary controls. Often, for technical reasons, their money continues to be linked with the former currency because international monetary transactions are an important continuing element in the economic activities of an independent country. Monetary policy has as its prime objective the creation of a supply of money appropriate to the production level of a coun try. As production and productivity increase, the quantity and sophisti cation of the money supply must also change and increase. Where the supply of money is not responsive to the needs of production, the level of production will be seriously constrained. Money of course refers no only to the coins and paper money used in cash transactions, but the checks, bank drafts and other credit instruments that become increasingly important as production becomes more complicated and technology becomes more advanced. Markets that are mainly limited to bartering can incorporate a relatively primitive, low productivity technology. As markets expand and the production process involves more capital, more intermediate products, more supportive services, and more widespread factor markets, money must become more sophisticated and more responsive, in both quantity and quality, to the needs of the larger, more differentiated markets. Not all of these changes are the direct result of specific government policies and actions. Many arise almost spontaneously, created by need or by demonstration from other areas. Yet government's positive or negative policies form an important, even deterministic, element in this change process. General monetary policy includes such subcategory policies as determining the availability of credit, the existence of investment and savings institutions, interest rates, bank reserve requirements, criteria for credit worthiness, loan regulations, regulations on repayment schedules, enforcement of repayment and prescription of penalties for nonpayment.

The cost of borrowing money, the interest rate, is clearly an important element in the provision of an adequate supply of money to productive enterprises. Usually governments cannot affect all interest rates through regulations and the creation of credit institutions. The commercial money markets in the less developed countries are quite limited, with most household credit extended through personal relationships and highly traditional channels. This is particularly true in the agricultural sector and the area of small loans, where traditional money lenders or local small shop keepers loan money on personal security at astonishingly high rates of interest. Government's efforts to establish more general rates of interest at lower levels usually affect the larger business credit deals and the government rules for the selection of credit clients often determine the cost of capital in the modern sector of the economy.

The government's broad monetary policy is largely affected through the control of banks and credit. As the country modernizes its production processes, demand deposits against which checks or drafts can be written become the largest component of the monetary system. Credit creation based on reserves is a major area of government initiative and control. Legal reserve requirements are established by the central bank and represent the government's judgment of the need for money related to the level of confidence of the people and of the institutions that make credit available. By changing the reserve levels, by buying or selling government securities that are often the basis for creating the reserves, the central bank affects the general quantity and quality of money directly, a manner that is quite visible to the participants in the production process.

The indirect ways that government policies can affect the quantity and quality of money are also important, sometimes more important than the announced direct policies. Broad monetary policies are implemented at operational levels by specific decisions and interpretations. A broad monetary policy whose objective is to provide sufficient, low cost funds for agricultural producers may be seriously constrained by inadequate or poorly designed specific policies establishing credit worthiness or repayment schedules. For example, credit agencies can call a loan for consumption purposes a production loan, thus seriously diverting the government's policy. Implementation of government monetary policies to encourage increases in production and productivity often depends upon the cooperation of private interests, such as private banks, as well as the operation of governmental or para-governmental institutions, such as government banks and cooperative societies. Implementation thus depends not on following governmental rules alone, but also on the sympathetic interest and concern of a large number of private enterprises. Monetary policies are implemented best when they are relevant to the self interest of the private banks and other concerned enterprises. Availability and expansion of credit facilities is often a permissive rather than a deterministic element in the improvement of productivity. That is, such availability makes improvement possible, but by itself is often not enough to force its use. Control of credit may hold down expansion but is not nearly as effective in pushing expansion when the underlying interests of producers and consumers do not lie in expansion. Thus, the climate of cooperation is, explicitly or implicitly, an important element in the expanded use of credit facilities. Public administrators affect this climate, directly and indirectly, by the decisions they make in implementing the specific activities that are guided by the broad policies of government.

Fiscal policies of government refer to the management of government finances, both receipts and expenditures. Fiscal policies affect nearly all important elements in the economic subsystem. Government collects resources from all factors of production and all enterprises, directly or indirectly. How and how much it collects affect the costs and prices of almost everything produced. Similarly, government buys goods and services of almost infinite variety; its expenditures form parts of the sales of all sectors, and its competition in the factor and product markets affects the costs and prices of almost everything. Fiscal policies are closely interrelated to monetary policies; together they form a major part of a government's efforts to initiate, stimulate and shape economic changes.

On the receipt side, tax policies have four major objectives:[*]

(1) To raise sufficient revenue, or as much as possible.
(2) To help stabilize the economy.
(3) To encourage or discourage appropriate investment and consumption.
(4) To improve income distribution.

Government tax policies not only affect the size of disposable income in the hands of households, but have a major role in determining the composition of production. Differential taxation encourages the production of some goods or facilities and discourages others. Progressive income taxation attempts to redistribute income by levying heavier taxes on the high income families. Taxation also shapes the demand for certain products by lowering or raising their prices to the consumer, as in the case of high excise duties on luxuries to prevent or reduce their production. Differential taxation may shape the nature of competition in both factor and product markets in ways that differ significantly from the original objectives when the tax policy was formulated. Thus, a high customs duty on an imported luxury may not only raise government revenue and reduce imports, but may also result in an unwanted increase in domestic production of that luxury good.

---

[*]See chapter 4 for a discussion of the government's efforts to improve factor inputs and chapter 6 on the use of taxation to improve income distribution.

A primary objective of the monetary and fiscal policies of a government must be appropriate stabilization of the economy. This objective includes not only the basic stability arising from adequate security of person and property and of enforcement of contracts, but also the avoidance of the extremes of wildly inflating or deflating prices. The prime importance that the expectations of both consumers and producers play in production and distribution has been constantly emphasized. As the production process moves to higher levels of productivity, the importance of economic stability increases, along with the difficulty of maintaining that stability. When producers know their customers personally, when production is largely for known markets, sales levels can be quite simply judged. As production becomes larger in scale, with production of intermediate products and for unknown consumers, estimates of the direction of price movements are not only more difficult to make, but are also more important to the producers. Consequently, the monetary and fiscal policies of government, in their broad application in the form of interest rates and changes in the money supply, in taxes levied and expenditure incurred, are prime determinants in maintaining the economic stability of the country.

Government fiscal policies affect the money supply and the general level of demand. A government policy to spend significantly more money than it receives from taxes and the sale of governmental services, deficit financing, will have the result of injecting purchasing power into the economy. This increased purchasing power will be utilized primarily by its recipients to purchase goods and services. Under some conditions, the increase in demand will stimulate production and under other conditions, the injection of purchasing power will be inflationary, a tendency for a general price increase. Government fiscal policies thus have an important effect on the supply of money and the domestic price level, particularly as they operate in conjunction with monetary policies. Government expenditures are also important because of their composition. What government spends its money for is intimately related to its social and political ideology as well as its economic policies. Procurement of military equipment, largely imported, has a different social and economic impact on the economy than expenditures on low cost housing programs. Expenditure on rural roads has different consequences than expenditures on public buildings in the capital city. Government expenditures on providing goods and services that are available to the lower income families have a different economic impact than expenditures that largely benefit upper income families. Government expenditures form the incomes of the recipients of these expenditures, and the way these recipients spend their income has an important impact on the production pattern as well as on the rates of savings and capital formation.

Debt management and borrowing policies of the government have both direct and indirect effects on the money market and on general conditions for production. Price stability is seriously affected by the method and size of government borrowing and spending. Government debt instruments may become the basis for a well-managed credit structure or may be a disturbing element that absorbs much of the available credit, to the detriment of investment in nongovernment enterprise. The rates of interest paid by government and the source of the credit advanced to government affect all domestic credit markets, not only through their impact on the climate of the market, but also on the criteria established for credit worthiness. Foreign borrowing, which appears so easy and costless when it is initiated, becomes a serious component of a country's fiscal operations when repayment becomes inevitable. Increasingly, as the less developed countries enter the second and third decades of their drive for economic modernization, the management of public debt, both domestic and foreign, becomes a more important part of their fiscal problems.

Monetary and fiscal policies are major tools in the government's efforts to achieve a higher productivity society with improved income distribution. Through taxation and expenditure patterns, it can forge or encourage institutions of social change. Government cannot wait until institutions that are obstacles to change are modified by other nongovernmental forces. Differential taxes can help establish appropriate new economic institutions and discourage restrictive institutions. Tax reforms can help change the relationships between tenants and landlords as part of more general changes in land tenure institutions. Progressive taxation, effectively administered, can have significant effects on the social structure. Monetary and fiscal policies are so complex and pervasive that elements of each often work in contradictory or mutually constraining directions. Thus, fiscal policies may work in the direction of increasing money supply through borrowing, while monetary policies may attempt to contract the money supply in order to constrain inflationary forces. The existence of such contradictions are unavoidable and do not necessarily represent inadequate coordination. Rather, they attest to the multiplicity of objectives and effects of major economic policies and to the constant need for scrutinizing the mix in order to encompass these mutual constraints into an optimal totality that presses in the direction of increased production and improved income distribution.

The implementation of monetary and fiscal policies are clearly related to the adequacy of the government's administrative apparatus. This is reflected not only in technical matters, as in establishing the correct variety and level of interest rates, the changing supply of money and technical central bank operations, but also in the day by day decisions at many levels and points of administration. Correct tax policies, for example, are closely related to the way they fit into a country's web of interrelated economic, political, and social institutions. It is surely harmful to transfer tax policies unchanged from developed to less developed countries. Differences in institutions, relationships, and value systems make a total transfer dangerous and bordering on irresponsibility. Generalizations about monetary and fiscal policies may be useful; but at an operational level, they must be adjusted to the needs and capabilities of each country.

Resource Allocation and Investment Policies

In chapter 3, a discussion of the basic economic forces operating in production emphasized that capital formation is a social process, affecting and involving every important institution of a country. While a large number of specialized institutions have been developed to allocate resources, most of the decisions that affect resource allocations are really decided in other institutions and by kinds of decisions that sometimes seem far removed from the problem of resource allocation. Basically, resource allocation reflects all the priorities of a country, not just the economic priorities. The allocation of resources between consumption and savings and the allocation of savings to the numerous sectors of the economy reflect all of the major economic policies of a government and all of the major activities of public administrators, not merely those that directly relate to capital formation. Obviously, the monetary and fiscal policies discussed in the previous section form a framework for investment decisions both in the public and private sectors of the economy. Government affects costs and sales prices of all products through its tax and expenditure policies, through its policies that determine the cost and availability of credit, the competition it develops for the limited financial resources, the availability of economic overhead facilities, the stability of the economy, the climate for "discounting the future"; all part of the complex results of formulating and implementing a government's monetary and fiscal policies. The direct and indirect effects of government policies on resource allocation and investment decisions mean that many of these policies will often have constraining, even contradictory effects. A policy that is designed to encourage a specific type of resource allocation may be constrained or reduced to impotency by another policy that is designed to attain some other broad economic or social purpose.

It should be clear, therefore, that the process of resource allocation and investment is so widespread and all inclusive that all important government policies affect it. However, it is useful to identify other kinds of economic policies, not usually incorporated into monetary and fiscal policies, that have as their basic objective the resource allocation process of a country. First, there are the investment priorities, usually incorporated in the economic plan or annual budget, the extent to which government funds are allocated to some programs and projects and denied to others. The schedule of investment expenditures in a country's budget represents the most visible aspects of its policies for resource allocation and investment, but resource allocation in the private sector is also an essential and visible allocation process. The criteria for allocating investment resources have been discussed (see chapter 3, "Allocation of Resources") and may be summarized briefly. Primary attention must be given to economizing the use of the scarce resource, capital, to considerations maximizing the social marginal productivity of capital, to maximizing future investment funds, and to maximizing employment opportunities. The mutual constraints among these emphasize the need for coordination of the many policies that affect resource allocation.

Second, there are those policies that encourage or permit entrance into the market for some investors and prohibit or constrain the entrance of others. Granting industrial licenses to some entrepreneurs or agencies of government to build selected factories and withholding consent from others clearly involves implementation of investment policies. The creation and use of development banks, and the formulation of their rules for loans, are all decisions that represent investment policies of government. Import licenses for capital equipment of new projects, tax holidays, and construction permits are other operating manifestations of a government's investment policy through controlling the entrance to the market. In fact, the priorities that the government adopts in the use of foreign exchange, discussed in the next section, often are the clearest reflection of its investment policies. By granting foreign exchange to some and withholding it from others, by making foreign exchange low priced for some investments and high priced for others, a government reveals its investment policies far more concretely than in its political statements and published planning documents. Third, government establishes or modifies the institutions that encourage and allocate savings and investment. Banks, money markets, and insurance markets require positive action of government, both in their establishment and in their continuing operations. Special banks for industrial development and agricultural credit, rules for the use of commercial credit, interest rates, criteria for credit worthiness, government programs for the establishment of agricultural cooperatives, allocation of credit for fertilizer and similar government efforts—all reflect policies that the government adopts to shape the nature of resource allocation.

Finally, it is useful to emphasize that the climate of investment is not merely the product of broad national policies implemented through monetary and fiscal policies or by special institutions designed for that purpose. Resource allocation decisions are made at all levels of the economy and are affected by all levels of government. The application and enforcement of the property laws of the country obviously affect the creation of privately owned capital. Improved technology generally requires newly formed capital whose owners rely on the right of exclusion, the rights of owners to exclusive use of the capital and to protection in this use. The indirect effects of many governmental policies on resource allocation may be more important than the direct effects. Thus, failure to maintain law and order in rural areas, low interest rates only for large businesses, the acceptance of "legal black markets," nonenforcement of health and sanitation factory laws, low official rates of foreign exchange, and similar policies and conditions usually have more influence on the total allocation of resources than priority investment lists issued by the government. Similarly, some of the monetary and fiscal policies may be more influential in resource allocation than direct government policies. Thus, low official exchange rates may push resources toward intensive investment and low import duties on capital and/or tax holidays may also increase this tendency. Unsympathetic administration of policies to procure government supplies from small enterprises may have more important effects on the climate of investment than any announcements about the need to encourage small businesses. Resource allocation is an operational process that involves all production enterprises. Since resource allocation is a continuing process, affected by almost all important government policies, the role of government becomes critical. The imperfectly formed markets of the less developed countries are usually inadequate carriers of price signals to guide resource allocation in those production sectors that primarily involve private investment decisions. Even in the economically advanced countries, market determination of investment patterns must be adjusted to take into account social costs and benefits usually not adequately reflected in market prices. For investment decisions that have large external economies or that must reflect the potential demand of the sections of the population that are not yet part of the effective demand in the market, government policies to shape the composition of resource allocation must take on a special role.

Sectoral Policies

Sectoral economic policies are directly aimed at affecting the activities of a specific economic sector, such as agriculture, industry, mining, power, transportation, communication, and services. Since the entire economy is divided into such sectors, every economic policy affects some sector. Many of the important sectoral policies have already been mentioned. Yet it is useful to consider certain economic policies as sectoral when their purpose is to affect primarily one or two related sectors.* Economic sectors are no airtight compartments, but are

_____

*This shows the underlying analytical weakness of classifying economic policies by fields. Clearly, resource allocation policies are "sectoral" in that any specific resource allocation affects a specific sector. However, custom and some descriptive usefulness press in the direction of retaining a classification that mixes up method and purpose.

subparts of the economic subsystem, closely interrelated and mutually interdependent. It is important, therefore, to realize that sectoral policies cannot be examined satisfactorily in isolation, in a single sector. The economic policies that are designed primarily to affect agriculture usually have important impacts on other, closely related sectors. It is a major thesis of this book, for example, that agricultural policies and industrial policies cannot be separated operationally, that considering one sector without the other can lead to the wrong policies. Sectoral policies are analytical constructs, for purposes of presenting important policies that affect primarily a single group of related economic enterprises. Analysis, however, requires a broader view than a single sector.

The sectors most commonly used are: agricultural, industrial, mining, power, transportation, communication, trade and service, health, education, and welfare. Sometimes particular circumstances require subdivisions of the above sectors, as when the industrial sector is divided into large and small industry sectors, or the agricultural sector is subdivided into regional subsectors that reflect different geographic conditions. Product sectors may be subdivided into consumers' and capital goods. Sometimes analysis requires division into government and private sectors. The sector breakdown used in any analysis reflects the kinds of problems to be analyzed, and in reality is often determined by the kind of data available.

Clearly, each sector and subsector has problems peculiar to its own operations, and each has problems that are common to all. It is almost impossible to separate economic from political and social considerations. For example, land use and land tenure policies are more than economic policies; they represent primarily the political and social forces and institutions that are the major framework for the economic policies. The agricultural cooperatives, the agricultural credit bank, the systems for producing and distributing the new agricultural inputs of fertilizer, insecticides and improved seeds are necessarily related to the arrangements for providing credit and judging credit worthiness. Policies establishing rural works programs, including the procedures for selecting workers, are closely related to the systems of land tenure and income distribution. Government policies for providing essential services to agriculture must necessarily relate to transportation, power, and communication, the basic economic overhead facilities of every economic subsystem.

Sectoral policies arise, consciously or unconsciously, from the operations of the different ministries of a government. The decisions to designate certain types of enterprises as reserved for government operations, schemes for licensing or controlling imports and similar governmental activities require different reasoning in the different sectors that soon result in each sector having its own policy constraints. Very early in the development process the government must develop ways of handling pressing sectoral differences, and some part of the government becomes designated as the center of concern for each sector, even if sectoral ministries are not established.

Policies for each sector can be analyzed in terms of their differing impact on production and productivity. Thus, policies that influence entrance to production may include land tenure policies for the agricultural sector, licensing for the industrial sector and the general policy in transportation that all rail facilities will be publicly owned and operated. Price policies may affect products of the industrial, power, and transportation sectors, but not the agricultural sector. Import policies as they relate to the factor market may have wide sectoral differences that require separate analysis by sector. Public administrators in each sector necessarily become familiar with the general and specific policies that affect their sectors; and administrators form a part of the process that must continually be formulating, implementing, and evaluating economic policies.

Foreign Exchange Policies

Policies relating to the acquisition and use of foreign exchange are among the most important economic policies that a government must formulate and administer. Less developed countries characteristically are confronted with critical shortages of foreign exchange. The capital goods they need in order to achieve a higher level of technology are generally produced in the developed countries which means they must acquire sufficient foreign exchange to pay for these imports. The exports by which foreign exchange can be earned tend to increase at a slower rate than the demand for imports so that the governments are forced to allocate foreign exchange in accordance with some priorities. Foreign exchange policies could be considered a special part of monetary and fiscal policies, so intricately are they tied to all of the monetary and financial operations of a government. Taxation policies, for example, must be considered not only for their effect on earning foreign exchange. Government expenditures must be considered in terms of domestic currency and of foreign exchange. Indeed, many countries develop foreign exchange budgets to be considered annually, together with the regular budget. So widespread are the requirements and uses of foreign exchange that policies relating to its acquisition and use affect all important sectors of the economic subsystem.

The importance of foreign exchange policies can be demonstrated by considering some of their major purposes or the kinds of economic problems that involve control of foreign exchange.

1. As a scarce resource, foreign exchange must be allocated with reference to some priority determinations, either by government or by the enterprises that earn the foreign exchange. In nearly all of the less developed countries, all foreign exchange earned by private enterprises must be turned over to the government in exchange for domestic currency. All legal users of foreign exchange must therefore secure it from the

government; and, implicitly or explicitly, all foreign exchange is used on the basis of priorities established or accepted by the government. These priorities shape the composition of imports; they can eliminate imports considered nonessential luxuries and can emphasize imports essential for consumption or for capital formation. By the nature of these priorities, certain domestic industries can be created and others suppressed or eliminated. Import licenses can be issued in accordance with policies that encourage certain groups and discriminate against others, such as policies that limit certain licenses to nationals of the country, or to small business enterprises, or to enterprises located in a certain geographic area. Priorities for the use of foreign exchange are among the key economic operating policies of a government, and the formulation and implementation of these priorities reach down into many of the layers of administrative machinery.

2. Among the priority considerations for the use of foreign exchange must be the economic stabilization objectives of government. Foreign exchange may be allocated to reduce certain prices and to meet critical shortages that cause violent fluctuations in the economy. Imports to meet famines are conspicuous examples of these crises, but far more common are the considerations that must be given to the flow of adequate imports of raw materials, spare parts, machinery, and energy requirements. Violent fluctuations are costly, disruptive of planning and of efforts for increasing production and productivity.

3. The use of foreign exchange must be part of a government's efforts to stimulate capital formation, both from domestic and foreign resources. Foreign exchange may be made available to encourage investment in specific kinds of industrial plants, or for the importation of essential inputs. Foreign exchange may also be denied to imports that would compete with domestic production to protect existing investment and to avoid use of resources in the creation of unnecessary facilities. Foreign exchange policies must also relate to transfer of profits and depreciation funds held by foreign-owned concerns in order to avoid excessive foreign exchange losses through transfers or capital flight.

4. Government policies must help exports in order to increase foreign exchange availabilities. Thus, export subsidies, multiple exchange rates, and export bonus schemes become part of the numerous foreign exchange arrangements by which governments attempt to encourage exports.

5. Foreign exchange policies are often designed to raise revenue. Such regulations as multiple foreign exchange rates often establish a spread between the buying and selling prices of foreign exchange that are meant to absorb windfall profits, to subsidize certain kinds of exports, and to transfer some of the profits from the exporters to the government.

6. Foreign exchange policies often are directed at achieving some political as well as economic objective, to enlarge a trading market area, or to give preference to some countries.

So widespread are the requirements and uses of foreign exchange that the secondary effects of foreign exchange policies are often more important than the direct effects. For example, efforts to limit the use of foreign exchange to those enterprises that can use it most efficiently may result in concentrating production in the hands of large enterprises and may seriously distort economic and political power. Efforts to eliminate the use of foreign exchange in certain luxuries may create a powerful smuggling operation with a greater hidden loss of foreign exchange. Policies that prohibit specific imports may result in the creation of local production facilities that are both undesirable and difficult to control. Maintenance of class and group interests can become directly related to foreign exchange controls and the political impact of such vested interests may soon become major considerations. The administration of foreign exchange policies thus presents extraordinary difficulties to the government. It utilizes an inordinate amount of administrative capacity and seems to be a constant source of major and minor crisis. So profitable are the right pieces of paper for an enterprise that they continuously attempt to influence the allocation decisions of administrators. Hidden ways to compensate appropriate officials for favorable decisions include jobs for relatives, favors to family businesses, trips for profitable investment, and promises of jobs after retirement from government services. These, together with the more obvious gifts and favors, create a powerful force toward cynicism and corruption in administration that is difficult to counteract. Efforts to reduce or eliminate these undesirable tendencies require more detailed checks and balances, more scrutiny of detailed administrative decisions, and consequently a process that is still more demanding of the limited administrative capacity of a government.

When foreign exchange policies are badly designed and inadequately implemented, their effects can indeed be costly to a country's efforts to increase productivity and improve income distribution. Not only will such inadequate policies utilize an excessive amount of administrative capacity, but they tend to encourage the development of production capacity that can only exist under continued public protection or subsidy. Generally, protective efforts by government have both desired and undesired results, but the latter tends to loom larger as it becomes a more established segment of a country's economic subsystem. The hidden subsidies and protection implicit in the implementation of many foreign exchange policies adversely affect relative prices of the factors of production and create windfall profits that are difficult to recapture by taxes. They usually interfere with the development of efficient production, creating a production system that cannot compete in world markets and that resists improvements in technology, both fatally dangerous tendencies of an economic system.

Market Policies

Market institutions are among the most important economic institutions that a country must develop in order to achieve a satisfactory rate of economic growth and improve income distribution (see chapter 7, "Market Institutions"). This type of institution, often quite intangible and difficult to analyze, is by definition the path toward improved use of factor inputs, of increased product sale and of more efficient use of financial resources. All important economic policies affect some aspects of market institutions. Government to a large extent establishes or accepts the rules and procedures by which market institutions operate, acts as an enforcer of these rules, and as an arbitrator in disputes about their interpretation. No significant market institution can operate without government recognition and acquiescence, if not support. This applies to clearly illegal market operations as well as markets formally proposed and supported by the government. Government not only establishes rules or accepts their establishment and enforcement; it is a most important element in establishing the climate in which the market institution must operate. This climate of buyers and sellers strongly affects the expectations and the discount rates applied to future returns by investors. The importance of market climate must be recognized as an important element in improving productivity.

Market institutions perform many economic functions. They ration supplies of consumers' goods among consumers having both the willingness and the capacity to pay a price for them. Markets are the major means of allocating production between commodities and therefore allocate the different factors of production among their various potential uses as these factor inputs try to maximize their incomes. Thus, market institutions govern to a large extent the relative quantities of specific kinds of labor and capital inputs that are made available and, in a basic sense, are the major institutions for distributing income.

Government policies for the control and influence of market institutions may be classified into direct or indirect, although some policies have both direct and indirect effects. Direct policies are those that the government clearly recognizes as having as their major purpose the shaping of a market institution. These would include policies that establish criteria to determine which enterprises or individuals can participate in a specific market's activities and the rules for participation and operation. Examples of such policies vary from broad major policies established at the highest political and financial levels to specific actions by local authorities. The policy to limit insurance transactions in a country to nationals of that country, to exclude foreign-owned banks from engaging in commercial loans, to limit the stalls in the village market to local inhabitants and similar market actions are examples of direct policies. Rules for ensuring standards for weights and measurements, sanitation rules, and rules for auditing and accounting of financial market operations illustrate more general types of direct market policies of government.

While direct market policies are numerous and important, they are far outweighted by indirect market policies, policies that are directed at other economic institutions or at other aspects of economic control, but that indirectly have important elements of market policies. Indeed, their most important impact may be on how they affect market institutions. Clearly, the most important of these are price policies; so important that they are discussed separately below. Other illustrations of indirect market policies are industrial licensing and import licensing. Nearly all important monetary and fiscal policies, if they are effective, strongly affect many market institutions. Any policy that affects the capacity of enterprises to compete in their factor or product markets must necessarily affect the relevant market institutions. Thus, policies that restrict imports in order to ensure domestic markets for domestic producers are effective only when they shape the market institutions in which these practices must operate. Reducing or eliminating the quota of foreign exchange for cosmetics may strongly affect the retail market that encompasses hundreds of small shops. The extent to which monopoly in a market, either total or partial, is supported or accepted by government may be an important way of looking at the indirect market policies of government. Thus, some policies may have both direct and indirect impacts on market institutions. The important point to emphasize is that many economic policies of government can best be understood by identifying their direct and indirect effects on various market institutions.

Price policies, because of their widespread use, are not usually considered as market policies. Yet their effect on specific market institutions is often their prime objective. Several different kinds of price policies should be identified. Often governments to meet objectives that are more social and political than economic establish fixed prices for essential goods or services, such as fair prices charged by Fair Trade Stores. The object is usually to reduce prices, to provide some counter measures for the effect of scarcity or hoarding and to ensure a more desirable distribution of the product. Wholesale and retail price markups are frequently established with the same type of objective to affect or limit sales to the public in a socially favorable manner. Even the use of marketing boards for the major export products or participation in international commodity agreements can be classified as price policies that are best understood as market policies of government. Differential taxation, customs duties, and export bonuses are other illustrations of price policies that by their nature reflect general or specific market policies of government.

Black markets, the illegal market institutions that spring up around controlled markets, are not a phenomenon limited to the less developed countries. As any businessman or any government official of the more developed countries can testify, they are a universal phenomenon, in some ways evidence of man's ingenuity and drive to make a living. Yet their appearance is often an indication of some malfunctioning of accepted market institutions, and their existence and acceptance often form a part of the market policies of government. Grey markets, the euphemism for illegal markets that have been more or less formally accepted by government, are nearly always the shadow of all controlled markets, and the role of the public administrator in their existence is as much a moral and social problem as it is a problem of administration. "Black" and "grey" are generally inefficient. They usually involve the generation of enormous profits, distributed in a way that is scarcely desirable socially and by definition almost impossible to tax for the public benefit. Rationalization of these markets, that they are essential to successful operation of economic enterprises, merely emphasizes the inadequacy of the existing legal market. It may be impossible in some circumstances to eliminate or even reduce the importance of a black market, but government administrators can recognize that this reflects to a large extent the inefficiency of the market institutions they are supposed to administer or support. Only through the more efficient operations of legal market institutions can the black market be eliminated or reduced to negligible proportions.

Labor Policies

In this context "labor" refers to workers, as distinct from owners and managers, an imprecise distinction, but generally understandable. Workers' wages form the largest part of the payment to the labor factor input, which includes all human factor inputs. Since wages are a primary element in income distribution, economic policies that are defined as labor policies play an important role in economic development. They affect production and productivity, capital accumulation, and economic stability.

Government labor policies are defined as those economic policies that affect workers and their wages, both indirectly and directly. Thus fiscal policies that stimulate the creation of new jobs also affect workers; any economic policy that affects production also affects the workers involved. But policies that attempt to control directly the number of workers employed, the wages they receive, their freedom to shift jobs, or to form unions are somewhat different from other economic policies, although they may be closely combined in their operations and have many interrelated consequences. In considering the labor policies of a government, it is particularly important to remember that government policies can be the result of either action or inaction. A government that makes no attempt to control the level of wages is following a wage policy just as much as when a government prohibits an increase in wages. Announced labor policies may be quite different from the policies that are implicit in what is actually happening in the labor market. Labor policies may be divided into employment policies, wage policies, union policies, working conditions and training policies.

Employment Policies

Employment policies are usually implicit rather than explicit. Governments designate full employment as one of the major economic objectives, recognizing that most families live from the wages of their members, and that welfare is improved generally as the number of workers are increased. In the less developed countries, full employment is a long-term dream; the immediate objective must be an increase in employment, as high an increase as possible. Thus, most of the employment policies really arise from the other kinds of economic policies that affect production, for example, the monetary and fiscal policies and the resource allocation policies. The actual employment policies in effect are more the resultant of all other economic policies than of any specifically titled employment policy. It is, therefore, quite logical and important to analyze the economic program of a government in terms of its implicit employment policies. Here the question of whether the objective of increased employment conflicts with increased production can be examined in terms of what is happening in the country. Do the investment and tax policies increase present employment sufficiently, or are they pushing in the direction of capital-intensive investment that may increase employment more rapidly in the future? Are the foreign exchange rates charged to importers encouraging the substitution of imported capital for workers? These are questions not easily answered and technical analysis must be supplemented by reasonable judgment. Experience from the developed countries may often be misleading. In the developed countries problems of unemployment may focus on how the unemployed labor force can be improved to meet the changes in the economic system. In the less developed countries, there must be added the view that the unemployed labor force must be used to change the economic system into a higher productivity system with improved income distribution.

More specific employment policies are illustrated by government rules about the employment of foreigners, the discharge of workers, and the employment considerations in the issuance of licenses or loans. Often, historical experience and current pressures create policies that attempt to limit the employment of foreigners and reduce the need for foreign experts by upgrading the training of local workers. Quotas and other restrictions on the migration of workers between countries are a common occurance, created by the desire to reserve employment opportunities for citizens. Restrictions on discharging employees often arise from antiforeign feelings, when large foreign investment and world market fluctuations focus on possibilities of mass layoffs of workers for what seem to be irrelevant reasons. Government employment policies may be expressed by import licenses issued to maintain industries that would otherwise close and discharge its workers, and by agreements to issue industrial licenses and make essential loans providing a certain level of employment is reached. Project approval for foreign aid may also be influenced by employment considerations. Announced employment policies of government are likely to be highly general and more of a future goal than a guide to present action. The actual employment policies of a government are expressed in the operation of all of its economic policies, indirectly and implicitly, rather than directly and explicitly.

Wage Policies

Wage policies are often more implicit than explicit, and form what has been termed the vague "incomes policy" of a country. A government usually establishes an incomes policy through its tax, investment, resource allocation, and market policies far more frequently than it does through any announced wage policy. Publicly wage policies are likely to be strongly influenced by welfare and public support considerations. Minimum wage laws are often expressions of goals and polemic arguments, rather than specific operating guidelines. A government cannot announce that it wishes to lower wages paid in industries, when the apparent goal is to raise wages and thus improve living conditions. But by raising the prices of products consumed by workers, governments can affect the level of wages and thus implicitly establish a wage or incomes policy. Here governments are faced with economic and political difficulties so complex as almost to defy either analysis or reasonable solution. If a country wishes to achieve a high level of investment, it is clearly undesirable to have general wage levels determined by what the most prosperous industries can pay. The best way to treat industries that have excessive profits may not be to raise their wages to absorb these profits, but to levy taxes if they are producing for an export market or to lower prices if they have a monopoly in the domestic market. This is, of course, more easily said than done. In the absence of trade unions or government pressure or monopolies, the general level of wages in industry would be determined by the level of agricultural income, since by paying something more, the towns can get all the labor they want. But trade unions, government pressure, and some degree of monopoly are nearly always present. Government wage policies that are explicitly announced will generally tend to be politically determined rather than based solely on economic considerations. It is in the implicit wage policies revealed in the operation of other types of economic policies that a government's wage policies are really revealed.

Union Policies

Union policies are generally more easily identified than employment or wage policies. Unions are defined as organizations of workers established to improve the wages and working conditions of their members.

Governments generally accept the pressures for unionization that exist as a matter of fact and rarely pass laws prohibiting the formation of unions. However, laws prescribing the form unions may take, their control, and administration, are quite common in all countries that are attempting to industrialize.[1] As in the case of the employment and wage policies, union policies are most realistically analyzed not by examining the announced policies but studying the ways these and other economic policies are carried out. Unions have too many important social and political capabilities to be considered only as economic institutions. Governments that are interested in continuing in power cannot neglect these other aspects of unions, particularly the potential and actual political power that is associated with large groups of people. The evaluation of union policies as they affect production, productivity and income distribution is so definitely contextual, almost unique to each country, that almost all generalizations appear vague and nonoperational. A country that is trying to develop itself rapidly is necessarily a changing country. Labor unions can be a force for stability, a force for influencing the behavior of large numbers of people who need channels to express their aspirations and frustrations. Unions are often associated with the nationalism that also focuses on protest and eases hardships. Unions become part of the new institutions that make development possible, with their political role probably more important than their economic role.[2] It is not surprising then, that the government feels compelled to participate in the establishment of the rules and procedures under which unions are formed and operated. Governments license unions, establish the rules of collective bargaining, establish the accounting procedures and fund control of unions, and often provide for arbitration for disputes that cannot be settled by collective bargaining. Some countries have established compulsory arbitration arrangements in an attempt to forestall costly strikes. Unions' internal controls and financing are a favorite subject of government regulation, since the role of protector of the individual workers against tyrannical leadership fits well with the desire of government to mold union leadership for its own political purposes. In many of the less developed countries, unions have become para-public institutions, with open, direct supervision by government or by political leaders. In other countries, the same basic condition may exist but control is less open and obvious. Fierce strikes, sometimes in government-owned industries, also reveal that government control is less than complete.

Labor unions are increasing in importance and power in the less developed countries. Public administrators must implement government economic policies in the presence of these institutions and must therefore learn how to work with them.

Development planning under democratic auspices must accept as a major variable the growth of labor unions. These organizations are likely to be highly political and inbred with a radical ideology. They will inevitably impose some costs upon the community and reduce the practicable rate of investment. However, if properly handled, they perform the vital function of channeling worker protest into socially useful forms and help prevent the subversion of democracy.[3]

Working Conditions and Training

Working conditions and training are an important area of labor policies, one that lends itself admirably to misuse and futility. The aims of improving working conditions and providing for adequate training are so obviously close to improving the welfare of large numbers of people that they are easily stressed in political platform and government press releases. Their attainment in operations is much more difficult and costly and the gap between goals and achievements is often painfully obvious. Countries tend to pass laws about working conditions, safety and health standards, and social security involving unemployment, disability, and retirement benefits. These are generally more important as ultimate goals than as immediate operating programs and are usually limited to a relatively small number of workers, with scanty financing. The training and welfare policies of the government are often part of the general education, health and welfare policies, discussed below.

Health, Education, and Welfare Policies

Policies that are directly devoted to health, education, and welfare matters are generally considered noneconomic. Yet they have important economic costs and consequences. Their purpose is to benefit people directly so that examinations and evaluation policies go far beyond their economic aspects. Primarily, policies of these sorts are identified with the social and political values of a country, with the institutions that are only incidentally economic. Schools, hospitals, and clinics require revenue use and involve expenditures and often some market operations. Factor inputs are used, specialized capital and human inputs are required. And as in the case of all important aspects of a society, government participation of some sort is a significant element in operations. Government policies are frequently the most important framework for these operations. There is little need to demonstrate these assertions, since they are obvious to even the most casual observer. In the context of this chapter, it is useful only to point out that many of these government policies have important relationships to the operations of the economic subsystem and to the attainment of increased production and productivity and improved income distribution.

Health policies that importantly affect the economic system are quite obvious. As discussed in chapter 4 in the section on "Health and Education," the improvement of the health of human inputs in the

320

production process can add significantly to the efficiency of production. It was also pointed out that helping people to improved health required no economic justification; it is a completely acceptable end in itself. Yet there are many health policies that require economic analysis in order to maximize the returns from the use of scarce resources, not the least of which is the required public administration input. Large modern health institutions, such as medical centers, hospitals, and medical training and research facilities, are very expensive to establish and operate. Their use must be contrasted with the feasibility of expanding local health clinics, particularly in the rural areas. This is not an either-or choice, but a problem of balance and of impact on future improvements. Policies that provide improved health services depend largely on widely dispersed health delivery systems which involve an unusual amount of administrative capacity, as do all retail delivery systems that provide services to a large number of individual consumers.

Education policies are eagerly accepted as the very essence of modernization, as indeed they are. Yet it is clear that there is questionable ability to adjust the formal educational structure to the needs of economic growth. Large quantities of resources are often unwisely used in education. Of course, this is only one and not necessarily the most important of the objectives of education, and the system may be justified by attainment of other objectives. Moreover, policies that relate to manpower planning go beyond the formal educational system. They must include apprentice training and on-the-job training programs, which are other important methods a country utilizes to train workers for modern industries. The large amounts of resources, including public administration, that are being devoted to education in the less developed countries are being challenged in many countries, not so much to reduce them but to make their use more relevant to a changing society.

Welfare policies include guidance for a broad variety of activities, many of which involve important public administration relationships with the modernizing of the economic subsystem. For example, many of the less developed countries have adopted social security laws, modeled after those in force in the economically advanced countries. The operational scope of these policies is generally more limited in the less developed countries, because resources are so limited and the need for improved welfare is so widespread. In adopting these policies, the intention is often to indicate the direction the country wishes to go rather than to devote scarce resources for immediate use by welfare activities. There are some programs for the handicapped, some minor unemployment compensation schemes, some subsidized retirement schemes, but mostly the welfare policies of this type are notional, indicating what will be done after more plentiful resources are available.

There is, however, a broad group of welfare policies relating to labor that currently has an important impact on economic institutions. Laws that prescribe minimum acceptable working conditions and factory laws require large capacities for inspection, and if vigorously enforced, would usually require large alterations in factory facilities. Minimum wage laws, designed to improve the welfare of handicapped and marginal workers, may have the effect, if enforced, of increasing costs and of limiting jobs for marginal workers. All labor laws which affect workers' ability to organize and bargain for wages and working conditions are in effect welfare laws, although they are not usually classified as such. However, government policies that affect workers as factor inputs are justified primarily as guidance for efforts to improve the lot of the workers, and can therefore be classified as welfare policies.

The purpose of this section is only to illustrate the wide variety of health, education and welfare policies that affect the operation of economic institutions, even though their primary purpose may not be their economic costs or results. To evaluate their importance to economic growth, it is essential that long-run and indirect benefits be considered as well as their short-run, direct benefits. Their costs are usually visible; they generally increase direct operating costs. Often, however, they decrease costs in an indirect way, such as reducing absence and turnover due to illness or unhappiness. It is almost impossible to determine quantitative measures in monetary terms of the benefits of health, education, and welfare activities. Efforts to do so have had limited success and usually strain the limits of credibility of the data and procedures. They attempt to prove what should need no proof, that it is worthwhile to help people become healthier and better off.

NOTES

1. See Sidney C. Sufrin, Unions in Emerging Countries: Frustration and Politics (Syracuse: Syracuse University Press, 1964).

2. For a discussion of these features of unions, see Bruce H. Millen, The Political Role of Labor in Developing Countries (Washington, D.C.: The Brookings Institution, 1963).

3. Walter Galenson, ed., Labor and Economic Development (New York: John Wiley & Sons, 1959), p. 13.

11

THE PROCESS
OF PUBLIC
ADMINISTRATION

THE MEANING OF PUBLIC ADMINISTRATION

Administration, in the words of Bertram Gross, one of the most imaginative analysts, is "the complex process through which administrators try to guide the activities of people in an organization toward formulating or achieving some accepted pattern of purposes." This is a modern concept of administration, not the traditional one. There are several key words and phrases in this definition that require emphasis:

"Complex process" means much more than supervision or direction. It includes the totality of guidance within an organization, including planning and evaluation as well as direct operations. It includes taking into account the external as well as the internal aspects of the organization, its relationships with its sponsors and clients as well as its own employees.

"Formulating or achieving" includes more than implementation of policies. It includes the effect that operations have on policies as well as the reverse.

"Accepted pattern of purposes" needs further elaboration because organizations have many purposes, some that are means of achieving others, some that contradict or constrain others. Different people give these purposes different priorities and interpretations. There is a mix of purposes that form a pattern that, if the organization is to operate in a rational (nonchaotic) way, must be generally accepted by the people within the organization and by the people outside of the organization with whom it has some relationships.

To show how loose and widespread the term "administration" has become, it has been pointed out that administration is involved wherever more than one person tries to achieve something through common action. Administration is the work of managers of organizations; it is the job of public administrators to manage the work of government agencies. Public administration, as used here in this book, simply means the policies and practices of public agencies as expressed in the activities of its administrators. Admittedly, this is so vague and broad as to be indeterminate in a definitional sense. Governments do or have done practically everything that a human society can possibly do and therefore the scope of this definition of public administration can include all kinds of human activities from the most specific to the broadest, from the crudest depravity to the most sublime virtue. Teachers in the field of public administration will, of course, be properly unimpressed with this definitional ambiguity and vagueness. If, as it has been said, "public administration is a subject matter in search of a discipline," definitions as imprecise as this are of scant help.*

No one seriously questions the existence of public administration as a real activity. Obviously, governments exist and operate, and the real world is full of the problems of their operation. In attempting to understand these operations and to evaluate and predict their import, governmental operations can be defined many ways. The traditional division into legislative, judicial and executive functions of government may be useful in explaining, although at a preliminary level only, the general nature of governmental operations. Clearly, these broad functions are so interrelated in every important problem that they cannot be kept separate for long in any serious analysis of government functioning. The executive and legislative functions of government are so interwoven in the way a government operates that no hard and fast lines can be drawn between them. For some purposes, the analysis of governmental operations can be limited to the executive functions, with strenuous efforts to exclude the political and legislative aspects. Thus, the analysis of staffing problems can usefully be limited to the civil service, although it will be recognized that the staffing of the legislative and judicial functions are both critical and have similar as well as different problems. Since this book attempts to analyze governmental functioning as it affects economic growth, there is no need to exclude legislative functions, which in many countries are closely related to economic policies. Thus, the scope of public administration used here is as broad as the scope of the whole political system, as reflected by governmental policies and practices.[1]

---

*Is this definition any more specific? "In its broadest context, the practice of public administration embraces all executive acts subject to political control, performed by public agencies, officials or employees. It could exclude purely political acts such as running for office, collegial action in debate, and voting in legislative assemblies. With few exceptions, administration is the work of the executive branch. . . ." Herbert Emmerich, "The Scope of the Practice of Public Administration," Theory and Practice of Public Administration: Scope, Objectives and Methods (Philadelphia: American Academy of Political and Social Science, October 8, 1968), monograph.

There are many different ways of looking at this complex process of administration. Traditionally, books on administration attempted to divide the work of guiding an organization into similar clusters or categories of activities that have some common technique or objective. For each of these categories, the description of the activities generally lead to the formulation of some operating principles or doctrines that appeared to be the lessons of experience. Thus, Henri Fayol, one of the earliest of the modern traditional writers on management and administration, proposed the following elements: forecasting and planning, organizing, commenting, coordinating, and controlling. Appropriate definitions of these elements would cover all the useful activities of administrators and could serve as a framework for all the description and wisdom, real or fancied, about the administrative process. Later writers combined or subdivided these elements, seeking categories that would permit the formulation of principles of laws of administration. The most famous of these, developed by Luther Gulick,[2] expanded Fayol's elements into seven categories, labeled POSDCORB, after the first initials of planning, organization, staffing, directing, coordinating, reporting, and budgeting.

In the first comprehensive textbook on public administration, Leonard White gave four assumptions that were basic to this viewpoint:[3]

1. "Administration is a single process, substantially uniform in its essential characteristics wherever observed." Therefore, it is not necessary to study separately municipal administration, state administration, federal administration; while there may be many noteworthy differences in these, basically management by government administrators is of the same cloth all over.*

2. "The study of administration should start from the base of management rather than the foundation of law." Starting with law makes administration emphasize its legal and formal aspects, rather than its operational characteristics. While law, particularly administrative law, sets limits to public administration and is certainly a major influence, it is to the management function that public administration must turn if it wishes to derive improvement from systematic study.

3. Administration is still primarily an art but attaches importance to the significant tendency to transform it into a science. The modern administrator has a great deal of equipment and systematic knowledge

---

*White did not directly confront the difficult question: Is public administration sufficiently different from the management of other types of complex organizations to justify a separate study or discipline? In many ways, his answer was "No, there is no difference in the management." Yet he continually wrote about "public administration" and did not hesitate to emphasize the public part of the phrase.

to assist him in his work. Science is transforming the methods of administration and moving away from rule of thumb empiricism to ascertained principle. The science of management seemed quite imminent to White and he knew that this development would strongly shape public administration.

4. It is often assumed that "administration has become and will continue to be the heart of the problem of modern government." This assumption is based on a further assumption, that administration can itself be essentially nonpolitical and therefore substantially independent of the political stresses and forces that set limits and constraints as well as priorities for administrative actions. So complex is the rule of government that there may be need to modify the biological analogy; perhaps public administration must be conceived as only one of the hearts of the problem of modern government.

Obviously, management of government agencies may have many similarities to the management of all other types of organizations. The useful generalizations that have taken the place of principles or doctrines are equally applicable to government agencies and to business organizations, to religious organizations and to citizens groups. Yet each type of organization brings relationships and patterns of objectives that are also different from other types of organizations. Sometimes it is useful to stress similarities; sometimes the differences are emphasized in order to analyze special problems peculiar to one type of organization. The emphasis of this book is designedly narrow in a functional sense; it emphasizes a small but important part of governmental operations. The relationships of government operations to economic growth have some peculiar aspects that require particular emphasis on the "public" part of the concept of public administration. Some, but certainly not all of the generalizations that are currently derived from general administrative analyses, have been emphasized in order to concentrate on selected relations of government and economic growth.[4] Thus, public administration is considered one kind of administration, very important and in many ways very different from other kinds of administration.

The traditional view of the administration of an organization was that of a hierarchy of authority, with control from the top down. The purpose of the hierarchy was to utilize its authority to get the job done as efficiently as possible. Individual jobs could be analyzed to see that the nature of each job was clearly understood by the occupant of the job, his supervisor, and fellow-workers. Individual workers were supposed to try to operate in the job as efficiently as possible, with financial incentives, at least in the private sector, to encourage job efficiency. There was a basic assumption of economic rationality; that is, workers respond to reward for efficiency and penalties for inefficiency. Workers were supposed to be willing to adjust to the needs of the job and were "production motivated; they accepted the purpose of the job as the production of the goods or services involved, as specified by their supervisors."5 Within this general view of administration, the attempt was made to summarize operating wisdom into principles or doctrines of administration, general rules or relationships that were universally true to a sufficient degree to warrant being followed by all administrators of organizations. Exceptions and the need for adjustment in specific cases could always be found, but these principles were basic considerations that had a high, direct correlation with administrative efficiency. As they were better applied, efficiency would increase. These principles were not advanced as rules to be applied mechanically, or as laws that portrayed natural or immutable relationships. Rather, they were basic, influential relationships that improved efficiency; they were supposed to provide a useful framework or reference for consideration of specific operational problems.*

It is impossible to summarize these principles of management without appearing to oversimplify their meaning, and thereby doing them and their authors an injustice. Most of the principles appear obvious and sensible, almost common sense applications of administrative experience in any kind of sizeable organization:6

Unitary direction—There should be only one supervisor for the work of any one person. To have more than one supervisor is confusing and will lead to inefficiency.

Control—Control of an organization comes from the top down. All operating decisions must go down, from superior to subordinates, following the hierarchical lines of authority.

Policies and implementations—Policies for an organization are also divided on a hierarchical basis, with subordinates implementing the policies established by those in superior authority in the hierarchy.

Functional departmentalization—A large organization should be divided into separate departments on the basis of important functions to permit specialization and to simplify the flow of authority and responsibility.

Delegation—Good administrators delegate authority and responsibility to their subordinates.

Line and staff—The operation of an organization can be divided into line functions, which are directly operational in producing the main output of the organization, and staff functions, which are specialized advisory services to those responsible for supervising the line functions.

---

*In the meaning of "principles" that suggest only working rules of conduct which wide experience seems to have validated, a number can be stated. Their exact formulation, however, is difficult and controversial. See Leonard D. White, Introduction to the Study of Public Administration, 4th ed. (New York: The Macmillan Co., 1955), p.

Span of control—An administrator can have only a relatively small number of people directly reporting to him. Too many direct subordinate means loss of control. In a properly organized hierarchy, there will be a pyramid type of organization, with each descending layer of administrators responsible for a limited number of lower level administrators.

MODERN ANALYSIS OF ADMINISTRATION

The principles developed by the traditional writers on administration have been questioned by present day analysts and have been largely deprecated.[7] Current textbooks may discuss these principles, but usually in a watered-down form that minimizes the universality of the generalizations. The attempt to discover basic rules about administrative activities has largely ended, and today's students of administration are content with posing some "currently useful generalizations" that point out similarities and differences in administrative activities that may help the thoughtful administrator. Most current writers in administration agree that the traditional views of administration are too narrow and that the position in an organization cannot be separated from the person who occupies the job. To separate position and occupant is to make the human occupant resemble a commodity, which is both morally and analytically wrong. Modern administrative theory seems to emphasize three aspects:

Administration deals with people and their behavior, rather than with things or with analytical constructs. Thus, problems of values, interests, motivation and interpersonal relationships become part of administration. People are not commodities or mere physical inputs; they also represent part of the output.

Administration functions in an environment which affects the inputs, the operations, and the output of all organizations. Internal management cannot be separated operationally from external relationships.

Administration cannot be reduced to a set of rules that can be applied automatically to guide the operations of an organization. Administration is contextual; it is shaped by the immediate aspects of a particular situation. The kinds of generalizations that can be applied to most administrative situations tend to become versions of moral precepts. While they are important and cannot be disregarded, they furnish little guidance for specific operations.

Within these three aspects, modern analysts vary greatly in the degree to which they establish a systematic framework for describing the administrative process. Some, for example, reject the division of the administrative process into clusters or groups of similar elements,

and prefer to discuss administrative activities under such broad categories as the role of organizations, the structure of organizations and
the operations of organizations. In the first section, such subjects as
the importance of organizations in modern society, the complexity of
organizations, the theory or models of organizations, the role of hierarchy and the different kinds of hierarchies would be discussed. The
structure of organizations would discuss specialization of work, coordination, decentralization, and organizational planning. The third
of these would discuss the relationship to the environment, the questions of leadership, power and politics and the social issues relating
to organization management. Within these broad segments, there were
many opportunities to discuss such subprocesses as decision making,
communications, motivation, and achievement.*

CURRENTLY USEFUL GENERALIZATIONS ABOUT ADMINISTRATION

This brief summary of the scope of administrative analysis is given
to furnish a setting for a more detailed discussion of several major analytical concepts and useful generalizations that can apply to public administration and economic growth.

---

*One of the most imaginative attempts to synthesize an entire
schema within which all the elements of the management of the administrative process could be analyzed is that of Bertram M. Gross, The
Managing of Organizations (Glencoe, Ill.: The Free Press, 1964).
Gross sets up a three-tiered classification:

Tier 1—Broad functions, operating in all parts of administration
      (a) Decision making
      (b) Communications

Tier 2—General functions, based on broad objectives
      (a) Planning
      (b) Activating
      (c) Evaluating

Tier 3—Specific administrative techniques, used by administrators
      These are operational entities, such as production, bud-
   geting, accounting, personnel, marketing, research, and
   so forth.

The Role of Decision Making

Many modern analysts have made decision making the cornerstone of the analysis of the administrative process. As the approach to social science became more behavioral in view, and as the concepts and tools in the related fields of psychology, political science, sociology, and anthropology became more precise and experimental, attention was focused on how individuals and groups weigh their choices of alternative activities and decide to act one way rather than another. To administrative analysts, the key operation in the administration of an organization was the flow of decisions that administrators made, with negative decisions as important as positive decisions. By learning how decisions are made it may be possible to learn how to improve decision making, and thus improve administration. All of the other aspects and activities of administration, such as planning, activating, and evaluating, or the more subdivided processes of planning, organizing, staffing, directing, coordinating, reporting, and budgeting of the POSDCORB are based on decisions made by some administrators. The study of how these decisions are made is therefore basic to understanding and improving all of these groups of administrative activities.

The focus on decision making must not be viewed too narrowly. It cannot be a mechanistic view, which regards inputs and outputs of the decision as automatic and inevitable: insert the right inputs and secure the right decision. A study of decision making must be based on concepts of rational human choice, with full consideration given to behavioristic rather than mechanical assumptions about human behavior, human motivation, and human value systems. In this point of view an organization is "an extension of individuals making choices and behaving on the basis of their understanding of their environment and their views."[8] Not only is decision making the point at which all activities center, but its analysis permits examination of why things are done rather than just how. The operational bias is made clear, as in this point by Simon: "The emphasis on the action process in traditional studies of administration tends to emphasize getting things done and neglects the 'choice that precedes action,' the decision what to do, rather than how to do it."[9]

In studying decision making, the role of the decision maker may be too complicated a unit of analysis. So may be the actual decisions made, since they reflect many different assumptions, postulates and conflicting evaluations. While decision making is not mechanical, it is also not necessarily rational. There must be a full recognition that cultural and social influences are present at all points in the process, and that impulses, emotions, and intuitive judgments operate along side of computations, comparisons, and the most rational types of considerations. Pure or complete rationality is theoretically possible, but assumes complete freedom of action, perfect information, and perfect timing. These rarely if ever exist in reality, and therefore real decisions are a mixture of rationality and intuition, emotion and judgment; there is a degree of rationality and irrationality, and, on important decisions at least, complete rationality is unattainable.[10] But rationality remains a powerful tendency; administrators try to be rational, to base their decisions on the weight of the information available and the goals to be achieved.

Rational Decision-making Model

The assumption that administrative decisions generally have a large element of rationality makes it useful to examine a simple model of a rational decision, to see its form and important components.[11]

Identification of the problem: Why make the decision? What will be solved? Who will it benefit or satisfy?

Objectives and their priorities: What should the decision achieve? Of the many objectives, which are the most important? Which are the best? What are the alternative objectives?

Policies and means required for achieving each of the objectives: How can each of the objectives be attained? What means must be used?

Cost benefit assessment: What are the consequences of each objective? What will it cost to attain each objective? What will the benefits of each objective be? What are the alternative cost-benefit comparisons?

Decision: What is the option that gives the greatest relative benefit and the fewest relative disadvantages?

The difficulty in applying this model is obvious. It assumes a kind of situation that no administration really confronts, complete information about costs, benefits, and alternatives, complete control of necessary resources (no time problem) and no capacity for intuition and emotion. Administrators would know all options and all possible consequences for every decision. It is clear that while this model may be useful as an analytical construct to show tendencies, it cannot be used to describe the decision-making process that takes place in actual operations:

Goals are multiple, often contradictory and each goal often forms constraints on other goals. Their priorities are often determined or at least strongly affected by forces, even orders, from without.

Information on objectives, costs, and consequences are usually far less than perfect and even the limited information available often cannot be used effectively. Also, information is costly to acquire and compute, and often cannot be used effectively.

Timing problems generally enter into decisions as serious obstacles to securing and evaluating the necessary information.

Relationships with other agencies and interest groups including the "public" often set contradictory constraints and limitations on both assessments of options and objectives.

The personal emotions, ambitions, values, and loyalties of the administrators enter into assessments of priorities and evaluation of information.

The procedures of the organization and related organizations, with
precedents, formal channels of information and hierarchical authority,
affect the communications flow and the alternatives that are operating
options.

The Decision-making Process

The fact that the process of decision making does not often approach the pure rational model does not make the effort rationally unimportant. Administrators try to act rationally and defend their decisions
with statements outlining their rationality. It would be useful to have
a simple model that could be applied meaningfully, but thus far the mod
els and their variables have been so strained and indeterminate that the
serve more to provide hope for further analysis than for current understanding of the process. There is a clear difference between an "optimum" decision, which is the best, and a "satisfying" decision, which
seems to be some point between rational and irrational, one that is not
optimum but seems reasonably satisfactory considering the circumstances, resources, processes, and possible consequences.[12] The
differences in reality from any abstract model of rational decision
making are so varied, complicated, and important that starting with
the model and attempting to understand relationships among the de-
viating variables appears to be beyond existing analytical capacities.
Thus, no single model seems to be adequate. Too many variables affect
and determine the many possible models, as Sharkansky points out:

> Some of the features that preclude the rational model may also
> preclude any other single model of decision-making from attain-
> ing universal use among public agencies. The variety of inter-
> ests that are brought to bear on the decisions of most agencies
> and the variety of functions, resources, personnel and clientele
> that one finds among agencies are likely to create marked dif-
> ferences in the ways that agencies make their decisions.[13]

While the absence of a satisfactory model makes the examination of
the decision-making process less than systematic and complete, some
useful insights into the process have been advanced and explained:

(1) The importance of defining the problem is obvious. Every decision is made to meet a problem or a complex of problems, using the
term "problem" in its widest sense, including how to achieve objectives
Understanding the full nature of the problem is a long step toward evaluating possible solutions. Often the hardest part of a job is defining
the right problem, right in the sense of existing circumstances and satisfactory solutions. An agency that is operating inefficiently may have
many side issues that affect its operating efficiency, together with the

relatively few basic difficulties that must be examined and confronted. Most problems are really clusters of problems that apparently can be subdivided into an infinite number of subproblems. The existence of complex problems is inevitable; many stem from the numerous objectives that every large organization necessarily seeks to achieve. The formulation of the problem for which a decision is required is, implicitly or explicitly, the first phase of decision making. However, it is not a true phase, with clearly marked limits, because the problem may be modified as its answers are being developed and put into effect.

Problems may deliberately be kept vague and fuzzy to avoid sharp confrontations and demands for solutions that are undesirable or not suitable. In other words, problems are often defined with the resources available for their solution in mind. Thus, there is no laboratory solution where cause and effect can be neatly isolated and studied. The definition of the problem to meet the apparently available solution is a common administrative occurrence. This becomes more evident as the level of the organization involved in the decision rises. Limits and constraints are set on the definition of problems by expectations both within the organization and from outside of the organization. These influences mold the premises that an administrator makes and the way he computes the information he has available to arrive at the decision he makes.

(2) Routine procedures are designed to reduce the level of decision making. "Routines are decision rules that specify which of the numerous inputs that might be relevant are actually considered in making decisions."[14] These specify the importance that is to be assigned to each type of variable, and identify the level at which the decision will be made. Implementing the policy involves procedures that are established to organize the activities of the organization in the direction desired and to select the levels and channels of information flow and points of decision making. How these are routinized often determines the quality of the decision, the degree of correctness, however that is measured. Routine also determines, to a large extent, the amount of administrative capacity that will be utilized in making the decision. For example, a routine may require that every letter from a business requesting an exemption from an existing rule must be seen by the head of the agency, who must personally approve the response. This administrator may add to the routine or clarify it by specifying the kinds of information that must be attached to the file when it is sent to him, including a proposed reply, who should approve the proposed reply or at least comment on the proposed reply. A series of minor decisions precede and accompany the final decision, ranging from what materials accompany the correspondence to major concurrences or disagreements with the proposed decision. The routine cannot specify all that happens, but generally shapes the nature of the administrative action and is a major determinant of the quantity of administrative capacity that will be utilized.

(3) Justification is an integral part of the decision-making process. It may not take the form of a formal announcement and it may not even be written; but an administrator, even if only to himself clothes his decision with reasons. Important administrative decisions are usually so complicated that it is necessary to adjust opposing views, to consider the objections and disadvantages of a possible decision as well as its benefits. The compromises involved in every important decision require references, implied or expressed, to cost-benefit analysis or to effectiveness in some form which appeals to rationality. The fact that future decisions and actions are usually affected also enter into the need for rational justification as part of every important decision.

(4) Administrative decisions have a tremendous range and involve high level and lower level administrators. Important decisions are always cooperative efforts, even though only one person may issue the decision and claim sole responsibility. To mass whatever information is used, the alternatives possible, the assessment of consequences and policy formulation generally requires many subdecisions or preliminary decisions. The exact specification of the division of responsibility for a decision is often quite different from reality and from the amount of work involved. Final decisions are often predetermined by the lower level decisions specified in the procedures. Thus, important decisions are cooperative efforts, the product of some kind of group interaction. This brings in all the complications of coordination and tensions, most of which must be handled by routine procedures. If not, each major decision throws the organization into a crisis operation, neglecting almost all other business but the decision at hand.

(5) The routines established influence the final decision, but do not necessarily determine it. Formal routine procedures generally have a large rational element, but the informal aspects of routine procedures, the deviations that performance adds to written rules of procedure, are often as important as the formal routines. There are also tendencies built into the decision-making process that may not seem rational from the viewpoint of the top level of administrators, but are rational from lower level viewpoints and affect an influential part of the informal procedures. Among these are the tendency to spread the risk by involving others who might share the responsibility of mistakes and the tendency to push decisions upward, so that the top administrators really make the final decision and therefore take much of the formal responsibility. Routines, formal or informal, that encourage spreading the risk and pushing decisions upward clearly utilize more administrative capacity than do routines that provide check reins of these tendencies.

(6) There are also tendencies toward conformity that are characteristic elements of administrative decision making, tendencies that operate against innovations and large deviations from precedents. The absence of all the elements of a pure rational decision, such as complete information, full evaluation of all alternatives, and full assessment of all consequences, means that all administrative decisions have large areas of uncertainty that involve judgment. The routine procedures

established to channel decision making and its concomitant information provide an emphasis on precedents, on what has happened in similar situations. Clearance procedures that spread information and check possible consequences also spread the risk and try to reduce the dangers of wrong decisions that may hurt the organization in its efforts to achieve its objectives. The administrative decision-making process becomes incremental, focusing on small changes from previous decisions and previous policies. One of the ways of adjusting decisions to conflicting opinions within an organization is to avoid sharp changes with accepted policies and practices, to see that each decision is only a small change from a previously acceptable and approved position.[15]

In general, decisions are based on availability of information and the computational capacity available to deal with the information. This makes communication and the flow of information a critical element in decision making. The decision premise accepted by the administrator is a direct function of what he knows or learns, as processed by his ability to handle information. A good deal of administrative capacity is therefore devoted to establishing and maintaining the flow of information. The evaluation and interpretation of this information is the computational capacity involved in the administrative process. The individual administrator has a limited computational capacity. His knowledge is limited, and his ability to combine, select and interpret information is limited. Capabilities for information flow and interpretation must therefore be built into the administrative process, and these must focus on providing the right administrators with the right information, in the form that will enable him, with his limited computational capacity, to make the right decisions.

Quantification is one of the prime methods of assembling or summarizing information in a form that aids decision making. Data that are not quantified are often difficult to summarize and even more difficult to analyze. There are many problems in establishing units of magnitudes that are meaningful through time as well as in interspatial and in interform comparisons. In decision-making terms, quantification is an attempt to convert a variable or the characteristic of a variable into meaningful units that can be compared or manipulated in analysis. By itself, quantification requires examination of the variable with a view toward some kind of measurement, and is therefore a force in the direction of more careful examination, more precise observation. But quantification can also be undesirable, it can provide the wrong information or give a false sense of correctness and accuracy. Some characteristics are not yet quantifiable in meaningful terms, although astonishing progress has often been made in the fields of psychiatry, sociology, and social dynamics. With the increased emphasis on electronic devices for data processing, quantification as a means of assisting administrators has received a powerful stimulus. In spite of frequently misplaced and immature forays, the drive toward quantification is largely salutory and useful. Quantification, if it can be achieved in appropriate units and with adequate validity, is a major means of assisting decision making.

In using decision making as an approach to the study of the administrative process, the key is to identify the critical decision centers and the channels of communication. These can be studied in terms of their operational adequacies and inadequacies. Their operations and the improvement of these operations must necessarily depend upon an evaluation of their effectiveness or efficiency, whichever is possible or appropriate. Thus, in studying the decision-making process and the flow of information, it is necessary to have criteria on which to base evaluations of adequacy and effectiveness. These criteria need not be quantified, and overemphasis on quantification can easily be counterproductive, with less rather than more information the result. Yet appropriate quantification is clearly one of the best ways of improving the flow of information and increasing the capacity of both senders and receivers of information.

Communications in Decision-making

Communication has definite channels that can be identified and studied in even the most chaotic-appearing organization. These channels may be prescribed by regulations, the formal channels, or may be unorganized, unauthorized, and accidental, the informal channels of communication. Both types, formal and informal, inevitably exist in even the most strict kind of organization, and both types are important. Information moves along these channels between points of origin to points of decision and points of control with all kinds of counterflows and responses. Because modern communication theory is largely based on engineering, particularly electronics, many engineering concepts and terms have been utilized, as if information was a flow of energy or a liquid or gas. Thus, terms such as "feedback," "loop" and "circuit" arise from engineering application, with useful results in understanding the flow of information. But often too much is made of this similarity to physical flow and the communication system may be viewed too mechanically by communication specialists. The substance as well as the shape of the flow of information is important, and both are strongly influenced by and influence the zest and drive of the organization.

Formal information channels are of course more subject to control and shaping by management than informal channels, but the latter cannot be neglected and it is not impervious to management influence. Leadership is strongly associated with control to channels of communication. Contrary to popular opinion, official channels of communication are usually more efficient than informal channels. The rumor that spreads like lightning through the informal channels may impress one with its speed; but the effectiveness is more apparent than real, since only small bits of information, widely changed in distribution, get through the system rapidly. Management is wise to recognize and even use the informal channels, but by far most attention must be paid to the quality and quantity of the official information flow as it relates to computational capacity at decision points. To be most effective, flows must help reduce the choices of policies that are under consideration to reduce indeterminacy. The quality of the decisions made, and therefore the degree of efficiency and effectiveness of the organization, is determined to a large extent by the adequacy and validity of the information flow. But a good communications system does not just happen. It takes deliberate management planning and implementation to decide on form, frequency, and clearance of information. Mechanical means, personnel, and spatial arrangements must be made to fit the communications flow into the operations of the organization. Control of the duplicating machines may be just as strategically important to top management as control of the financial disbursing authority.

As one moves to the top of the hierarchy in an organization, information is needed in a more aggregative form. Top management cannot consider the day by day operating detail that a subunit supervisor may need to allocate work to individual workers and evaluate individual productivity. While electronic data-processing technologies have greatly greatly increased management's computational capacity to process and summarize detailed data, it is just as true as it ever was that too much detailed information may be just as harmful to proper administration as too little information. Decisions by subunits or by departments tend to foster subgoals and instrumental objectives, that is, objectives whose value lies largely in their attainment in order to achieve other objectives. Division of work and specialization of function, the necessary attributes of growing size and efficiency of organizations, must be associated with specialized channels of communication. Division of work and specialization require stability of organization, and the development of subgoals that are instrumental to the whole organization's goals. Where communication is poor, control of subunits is more difficult and less effective. It is clear that the influence of an organization's goals on the decisions of its administrators, particularly in the decentralized aspects of decision making, depends to a large extent on the communications system of the organization.

Decentralized Decision Making

Since decisions are based on the availability of relevant information and the computational capacity available to deal with the information, every complex organization or subsystem develops its own balance between centralized and decentralized decision making. These are of course relative terms; what looks like a process that is preeminently decentralized may appear quite centralized by comparison with another organization. Routine procedures designed to reduce the level of unimportant decision making may screen a highly concentrated authority for all important decisions. Centralized decision making may thus set the limits and rules for more detailed, less important decisions for which routine procedures are established. This distinction between centralized and decentralized decision making, while relative and difficult of precise definition, is of great importance to operations of complex organizations and requires particular emphasis as related to the economic subsystem. The production of goods and services in a country and the correlated distribution of income requires a tremendous number of interrelated economic decisions. Practically every person above the infant and child age participates as a seller or buyer in the billions of buying and selling transactions that make up the constant flow of decisions. These decisions vary from unique, important decisions, such as to build a large factory or incorporate a new development bank, to innumerable, small decisions, such as to buy a pair of shoes or a piece of candy. Production decisions range from accepting a particular style in a government plant and producing 5000 garments to producing a single dress for a specific customer. The tremendous number and range of economic decisions must be viewed as a flow of interrelated decisions, channeled by economic institutions that have been developed to facilitate the production and distribution of economic goods and services.

The more complex and numerous the decisions become, the greater the need for developing the proper mix between centralized and decentralized decision making. In a single organization, with few participants, with few and simple objectives, and clearly understood roles of participants, the decision-making process can be almost entirely decentralized. As these characteristics become more complex, there is an operating need for common understanding and direction that creates the need for central decision making, however universal its participation by individual members may be. When organizations become sufficiently complex to require specialization of management, questions of authority and control, of multiple objectives and flow of information require a mix of centralized and decentralized decisions. Clearly, all decisions cannot be made at the top. In the complex economic subsystem that even the least developed country has become, the innumerable economic decisions to produce, to price, to sell, to buy and to exchange must be characterized by a mix of centralized and decentralized decisions. In a decentralized decision-making process, more detailed information can be available at the more numerous decision points to be processed by more people. In the rules and procedures established for decentralized decisions, the implicit judgment is made that the centralized decision making for these decisions are either impossible, or more costly. Since computational capacity to handle the mass of information necessary for decision making is at a premium, the pressure to decentralize what are considered the less essential decisions become reflected in the procedures to routinize operations, to focus central decision-making capacity on important decisions that limit and control routine operations. It may well be that an efficient decentralized decision-making subsystem requires an efficient centralized sector to establish the degree and limits of the decentralization.

Multiple Objectives

Every organization has multiple objectives or goals. This is so obvious intuitively that it would not be worth pointing out, except that in specific instances there are pretensions that an organization has a single, clearly recognized and accepted goal. From the very nature of human organization, a single goal is impossible; and to insist on a single objective is to fail to recognize one of the basic considerations about the administration of an organization. Organizations are complex, interacting entities, where the desires and objectives of the individuals, the group, and the organization, are in a continuous state of formulation and adaptation. There are long-run and short-run objectives, objectives that arise from individuals' needs and objectives that form the formal purpose of the organization; there are social goals as well as organizational goals, immediate, instrumental, and proximate goals as well as ultimate objectives. This complexity is present in any organization; and the larger and more important the organization is, the more complex and diverse its objectives are likely to be.

The identification and classification of organization goals form parts of many descriptions and fields of thought, including moral theology, philosophy, and history, as well as all of the current social sciences. No matter how wide the study of organizational objectives is made, there are always more distant perspectives that move towards the ultimate purposes and questions of human existence. In the study of administration it is obviously impossible to ignore these ultimate perspectives, yet there is a need to examine organization objectives from an operational point of view, to encompass the pattern of objectives in a way that can be related to the decision of administrators, to the flow of information, and to the process of administration. Ultimate objectives are influential and may set perimeters or limits, but they can only be interpreted within more operational assessments of an institution's objectives.

Multiple objectives may be and are often contradictory in effect. Partial achievement of one objective may actually oppose the achievement of another. If not actually contradictory, there usually exists some mutual constraint between objectives because the existence of one objective serves as a constraint upon achieving another objective. Thus one objective of an institution may be to maximize its profits; but, as a constraint on this, there may also exist the objective of paying its workers a living wage and improving their well-being as much as possible. Social objectives often contradict or constrain individual or specific organizational objectives in the short run, at the same time encouraging or complementing them in the long run. It does not take much imagination to list numbers of contradictory and mutual constraining objectives that form the interrelated mesh of an organization's objectives.

To divide into categories the complex of organizational objectives has some analytical advantages, even though they cannot be readily divided in actual operations. Bertram Gross, who has pushed this type of analysis probably as far as current capabilities of the social sciences permit, has developed seven broad clusters of objectives:[16]

1. Satisfaction of interests—The interests of all parties concerned must be considered, workers, administrators, clients, society, and so forth.

2. Output of services and goods—The basic reason for the establishment of an organization; what it is supposed to produce.

3. Efficiency or profitability—The comparisons of outputs with inputs.

4. Investment in organizational viability—The improvement and survival of the organization.

5. Mobilization of resources—The capacity to acquire and utilize the inputs required to achieve the organization's objectives.

6. Observance of codes—The achievement of kinds of behavior that are acceptable to the organization.

7. Rationality—The objective of utilizing as effective a process as possible, the achievement of a desirable action pattern.

These clusters form a pattern of objectives, with all types of adaptations to short-run and long-run time periods. One purpose is always a constraint or an influence on other objectives. To be operational, that is, to affect an organization's operating decisions, an objective must involve some purposeful commitment to do something in order to achieve a desired future state. To list an organization's objective as "to improve the well-being of the citizens of this community" may sound well in public relations releases but is not operational unless specific actions are directed toward this end. An organization's pattern of objectives can be and usually is interpreted differently by each administrator and by each associated organization in its environment. One administrator may emphasize minimizing costs of production to the exclusion of almost any other organizational objective. Another may emphasize good relations with parliament in order to insure the continuation of adequate budgets; and he may therefore ignore almost completely the objective of reducing costs of production. Some long-run, ultimate objectives are usually merely assumed to be operative, while administrators tend to concentrate on more immediate, more visible objectives. An organization may stress the importance of expanding its services to reach all people who need them, but this may not be operational. No administrators may be given any authority or responsibility for expansion; and each one may concentrate on narrower, more immediate objectives, such as reducing clients' complaints or improving the operating conditions of the clinics. Many times, the process of selecting the objectives to be emphasized is the essence of the decision-making process, the major job of top management.

Commitment to attain objectives must also be considered in operational terms, since verbal commitments are usually of limited value. Operationally, commitment to achieve an objective is measurable by the means that are devoted to achieve a future situation. Moral commitments are of course important and basic to any kind of society; but moral commitments without implementation are difficult to justify, even philosophically. In a government agency, the complex pattern of objectives makes commitment difficult to measure, but this does not eliminate the need for recognizing the importance of the commitment of resources in relation to this pattern of objectives. The existence of a pattern of objectives and the emphasis needed on the different parts of this pattern are clearly involved in the decision-making process and communication flows of an organization.

Formal and Informal Aspects of Organizations

The formal aspects[*] of organizations are those prescribed by authority. These generally include the more visible and acceptable objectives of the organization, its legal status, and the division of labor among the different parts of the organization. The schema of hierarchy within the organization is also prescribed by authority, the distinctions between superiors and subordinates and the flow of authority and chain of command. This also usually involves the span of control; that is, who reports to whom and who gives and receives certain kinds of directives. The formal rules for an organization generally establish a "polyarchy" with multiple kinds of authority rather than a simple hierarchy, where each subordinate has only one superior. The phenomenon of multiple subordination is the rule rather than the exception.

The informal aspects of an organization are those relationships between individuals and between parts of the organization which are not prescribed by formal authority but develop to modify and supplement the formal aspects. They arise on the basis of experience, on opportunity, on friendship and extra-organizational contacts, on personality elements and on chance. Communication flows are inevitably a part of these informal aspects of an organization, and decisions are influenced outside the formally established lines of communication and direction.

---

[*]There is a reluctance to use the term "structure" because it has an architectural, hence static, concept of an organization. An operating organization is neither static nor impersonal, which may be the connotation of the term "structure."

Every organization develops these informal aspects. Every experienced administrator recognizes the extent and importance of these relationships and channels; to ignore them would be to guarantee administrative failure. While the informal aspects of an organization may appear chaotic and confused, they must be considered operationally together with the formal aspect which they supplement and modify. This can provide a more systematic perspective of the informal aspects and can permit their incorporation in an analysis of the administrative process of an organization.

Operating authority and capability are determined and allocated by both the formal and informal aspects of an organization. The emphasis on human relations, including motivation, participation and satisfaction, which is the distinctive mark of modern administrative analysis, emphasizes the importance of the informal aspects of an organization's operations. It is through these informal aspects that participation in decision making is broadened and made more effective. Every study of improving human relations in the administration of organization emphasizes the importance of increased participation at all levels of personnel. Consent and acquiescense is far more efficient and meaningful than reluctant acceptance or manipulation. The need for self-fulfillment, self-development, for loyalty, and for status are integral parts of work at any work level. This is particularly true at the middle and higher levels of administration, where informal relationships tend to be very important operationally. The depth and extent of participation varies tremendously and is difficult to measure, but a recognition of its importance as part of the informal aspects of the operations of an organization is clearly both necessary and important.

Critical power within an institution, the ability to influence activities, is always dispersed. Every institution is thus a cooperative effort, a type of democracy. Obviously, some institutions are more authoritative than others, but only in theory would it be possible to imagine an institution that operates on a fully authoritarian basis. Even military units recognize the importance of cooperation, individual initiative, and dispersion of authority, although the attempt may be made to limit these to minimal areas. Thus, the informal aspects affect decision making and communications and are necessarily involved in the ability of an organization to provide its output and attain its objectives.

Policy and Implementation of Policy

There is general agreement among modern students of administration that there can be no operating separation of policies and their implementation. The belief in such a separation is a myth based on superficial observation and improper logic. Developed largely by government officials who wished to continue their employment regardless of changes in political leadership, it served as a philosophical rationalization for the maintenance of a hierarchical chain of command which seems so basic to any organization. But even in that most formal hierarchy of organizations, the military, the separation of policy and implementation has been seriously questioned. Philosophically, the question resolves itself into the age-old question of the separation of means and ends. This discussion was settled a long time ago in favor of the view that separation in real life is impossible. Some means predetermine their ends, while ends always affect means. Too, most ends are instrumental to other, more ultimate ends. Thus, the objective of increasing per capita GNP is an instrumental end, an ultimate end being the well-being of the people. Furthermore, means tend to become ends, as in the case of power seized by a group in order to achieve specific ends, then often become an end in itself, the maintenance of power. While in any specific analysis it may be useful to discuss ends and means separately as conceptual constructs, in real life the separation of ends and means is operationally impossible.

Policies are of course not objectives; they are guidelines or directives to help achieve certain objectives. Thus, policies can neither be separated from the objectives they are designed to help achieve nor from the implementation they are designed to guide. Policy implementation necessarily involves a degree of attainment of the objectives. But since objectives are usually multiple, contradictory, and time-bound, with long-range, ultimate objectives differing substantially from more immediate objectives, the achievement of one goal (for example, high production) may result in the loss of another goal, increased quality. Lower unit costs may mean increased worker unrest. Increased savings may result in increased consumption in the future; but in the present, a reduction of intended consumption may be the result. The conflict between objectives at any level of generalization cannot always be settled in operationally meaningful terms by appealing to ultimate objectives, such as the well-being of the people or security.

The pattern of objectives that organizations necessarily have must be viewed as a mix, with different intensities and time spans and of varying operational significance for each level of administration. At the top level, consideration of expenditures for attaining the objective of viability of the organization may be meaningful and operative. To the supervisor of the messenger service, this objective may be as vague and ineffectual as such ultimate objectives as "well-being of the nation" or "improving international relations." Yet at each level what administrators do makes up part of the policies of the agency. The mix of objectives that is finally achieved in an organization may be as much due to lower level implementation of decisions as to highest level policy decisions.

While policy and implementation cannot be separated operationally, they can be discussed separately and work assignments are often made on the basis of this verbal separation. Clearly this type of separation is only part of policy formulation and not necessarily the most important part. The operating policies of an agency arise from what that agency thinks and does. Just as the decision to adopt a policy and then to do nothing about its implementation is a different policy than the one formally adopted, so doing something without a specified policy also involves policy, implicitly, or explicitly. In an important sense the implementation or nonimplementation of a decision encompasses within itself meanings that are implicit or explicit, variations in interpretation and intensity that can have important effects on operations.

Administrators, by the nature of their work, become involved in establishing and modifying policies. They necessarily participate in policy determination, regardless of any statement in the formal procedures that may prohibit this. Participation in policy does not detract in any way from the role of an administrator. Nor does it diminish in any way from the role of an administrator. Nor does it diminish in any way the usefulness of a continuing civil service that is protected against the spoils system of political job appointments. It does emphasize, however, the need for a mobile, sensitive civil service with more important criteria than seniority for the selection of key operating personnel. Since a neutral administration is not possible, even theoretically, operations occur in a climate that is really a continuum from strong support through diminishing support and increasing opposition to strong opposition. Since objectives are multiple and often contradictory, the continuum represents a multidimensional mix of opposition and support, often undefinable by the administrator himself. To be neutral generally means avoiding the extremes of the continuum, neither strong (or visible) opposition or support. This kind of neutrality is possible, of course; but it is not necessarily the best climate for engendering successful operations. It misses taking advantage of one of the major lessons in human relations, the usefulness of proper motivation and interest in getting work done.

The fact that administrators are involved in determining as well as implementing an organization's policies has one other facet that deserves noting. There is a relationship, important operationally, between the level of work and the harm that may be caused by accepting the myth of separation of policies and their implementation. At low clerical levels, the policy implications of action or nonaction are often quite small. A messenger does not need to know the contents of the message he delivers, although he may be a better messenger if he has been taught the general communication policies of an agency. A division head, on the other hand, can only separate policies from implementation by confining himself to the most mechanical formulation of his functions; and even such work often has important policy implications to others within and outside of the organization. The recognition that policy and its implementation are inseparable operationally does not mean that all policy decisions and discussions must include everybody in the organization. Formal discussions and decisions may involve any set of participants and may be quite selective, depending upon the nature of the problem. Cabinets may discuss public ownership with and without senior civil servants. Yet in a real sense of the term, the policies and implementations of an organization are set by its operations. How these policies are determined and implemented is simply the essence of administration.

Development Administration

The importance of adequate public administration for economic growth was quickly recognized and emphasized. Development is an additional responsibility of government, as pointed out in this report:

> Countries which have not attained a satisfactory standard of service in respect to historic government functions . . . [will] find themselves burdened with the necessity of development and effecting complex defense, agricultural, public works, industrial welfare and other undertakings. The inadequacy and incompleteness of their administration [will] generally be a far more serious barrier to economic progress than lack of resources or the absence of modern scientific and technical skills.[17]

The term "development administration" has recently become fashionable. It is used rather loosely to apply to the activities of governments to achieve development or modernization, terms that themselves require more adequate definition. Like many colorful expressions, the term development administration has a value in calling attention to the special importance of public administration in the modernization process, but it may add little to the tool kit of analytical concepts. Too often, it is merely a slick expression for good administration, or for administration that is adjusted to the needs of the country. Probably the most useful application of the term is to apply it to goal-oriented, change-minded administration. Thus, development administration can be the administration of change.*

---

*It may be useful to consider the definitions of the term given by several authors, as follows:

> Development administration is a carrier of innovating values. As the term is commonly used, it embraces the array of new functions assumed by developing countries embarking on the path of modernization and industrialization. Development administration ordinarily involves the establishment of machinery for planning economic growth and mobilizing all allocating resources to expand national income. New administrative units,

If the term "development administration" is to have usefulness in communicating some special ideas about the type or style of administration, it must have some distinguishing characteristics that differentiate it from other kinds of public administration. Every government, regardless of the level of its economic production, faces changes that affect its operations. Every government announces a wide variety of goals that it claims dominates its policies. To limit the meaning of development administration to goal-oriented, change-minded administration is to lose much of the descriptive value of the term. Even the

---

frequently called nation-building departments, are set up to foster industrial development, manage new state economic enterprises, raise agricultural output, develop natural resources, improve the transportation and communication network, reform the educational system, and achieve other developmental goals.

Merle Fainsod, "The Structure of Development Administration," in Irving Swerdlow, ed., Development Administration: Concepts and Problems (Syracuse: Syracuse University Press, 1963), p. 2.

"The process of guiding an organization toward the achievement of progressive political, economic and social objectives that are authoritatively determined in one manner or another." Edward W. Weidner, "Development Administration: A New Focus of Research," in Ferrel Heady and Sybil L. Stokes, eds., Papers in Comparative Public Administration (Ann Arbor: Institute of Public Administration, University of Michigan, 1962), p. 98.

". . . organized efforts to carry out programs or projects thought by those involved to serve developmental objectives." Fred W. Riggs, "The Context of Development Administration," in Fred W. Riggs, ed., Frontiers of Development Administration (Durham: Duke University Press 1971), p. 73.

". . . a set of administrative objectives for development administration includes: an innovative atmosphere, the combining of planning (thinking) with action (doing), a cosmopolitan atmosphere, the diffusion of influence, the increasing of toleration of interdependence, and the avoidance of bureaupathology." See Victor A. Thompson, "Administrative Objectives for Development Administration," Administrative Science Quarterly 9 (June 1964): 91-108. But why aren't these definitions of "good administration" for any country, whatever its level of development?

most economically developed country, the United States, is attempting to reduce poverty, to improve income distribution, to rebuild its cities and to improve the quality of its lifestyle. The resources spent on economic development in the United States probably exceed that spent in all of the less developed countries combined. Yet to describe improvement-minded administration in the United States as development administration would be to decrease the usefulness of the concept and necessitate the use of another adjective to apply to the administration of the less developed countries as they attempt to increase their economic production and improve their income distribution.

To be most useful, development administration can be applied not only to goal-oriented, change-minded administration, but only to those countries that have as a top priority the change from low productivity to much higher productivity levels, sustained over a reasonably long period of time. The level of economic productivity in which the public administrator operates is the essence of the need for distinguishing between other types of public administration and development administration. Low economic productivity introduces special kinds and intensities of problems, political and social as well as economic, that make of development administration a useful concept. Is public administration in the less developed countries sufficiently different from that in the more developed countries to make it worthwhile examining these differences and attempting to identify useful operating generalizations? An unambiguous answer is difficult to give. The public administration of any government is both complex and contextual. Each country is unique, and its public administration appears unique. The similarities that exist in their administration are often possible of analysis only at very high levels of generalization, partaking more of moral precepts than operating generalizations. If development administration is to be a useful concept setting off certain kinds of administration from others, it must be limited to the administration of those countries that are seeking development and are starting at low levels of economic productivity. Development administration is the conscious study of the conditions of public administration in the less developed countries. It is the study of what can be expected of public administration in the particularly difficult cases of the less developed countries.

Fred Riggs has advanced a view of administration that provides a systematic basis for a concept of development administration.[18] In his judgment, the key to understanding the operations of administration in a society attempting to modernize itself is to examine the degree of "defraction" or specialization of function. The hypothesis is based on what he calls "structural-functional" approach. Structures of organizations refer to patterns of behavior, and an organization with "structure" is one whose behavior pattern has become a standard feature of a social system. A structure reacts with other structures, and this

347

reaction is termed its "functions." When an organization performs many different functions, it is functionally diffused and unspecialized; when it performs a limited number of functions, it is functionally specific. Generally speaking, traditional societies have "diffused" organizations while modern societies have specialized organizations. The measurement of this degree of "defraction" is the best way to view the degree of modernization.

A transitional society is one that contains a strong mixture of both traditional and modern organizations. In attempts to modernize, many forces operate in the direction of creating new organizations with specific functions or in directing existing organizations to specialize their functions. These concepts permit descriptions of the many variables that are associated with increased diffraction, variables in political, social, and administrative development. The variables are of course interrelated, and often are merely different facets of the same basic phenomenon, development. By relating environmental variables to administrative behavior, it is possible to describe meaningfully the relationship between political development and economic development and the role that government must play in a transitional society.

Organizational Development

The current emphasis on the human relations aspects of administration has led to an interesting and useful variant titled "organizational development," which may be characterized as the 1970s development of applying behavioral science to the management of enterprises.[19] Every government agency faces change in both its internal operations and its external relationships. These changes constantly affect the jobs that people do within the organization. To remain viable, always a major objective of any enterprise, the management must constantly change to adjust to the continuing changes within and around the enterprise. Some changes can be anticipated and management must constantly prepare itself for oncoming changes that offer the enterprise an opportunity to do a better job, to produce more of the goods or services for which it is established. The mechanistic view of organization—that it is a system of simple cause and effect, is only partially true and is generally inadequate. Organization is also a complex system of uncertainties and probabilities, with human beings interrelating emotionally to their work and to their fellow workers. The object of organizational development is a conscious effort on the part of management to integrate the human interrelationships with the technical systems of the organization, to seek out innovative processes for the purpose of initiating actions that will adapt better to changes in the environment. "Organization development can be defined as a process of planned change. Used correctly by managers, it is an approach that enables an enterprise to adapt effectively to the demands of internal and external reality."[20]

Organizational development is a continuing process, not a one-time action. It focuses on the individuals in the organization, usually the top level and upper middle management. The concept of a system approach to an organization is basic to the process, the view that organization is an open system of many interacting parts and individual managers must see themselves in relationship to the system. An understanding of motivation and of the need for individuals to satisfy their hopes for improvement and achievement is a basic element in establishing organizational development. The management of an enterprise that is attempting to adopt organizational development as a continuing process will usually establish a team of consultants staffed by inside managers as well as by outside consultants. The team will identify some major operating problems that require changes and will examine the human and power relationships involved in the problem and its possible solutions. Examination of alternative lines of action and selection of the best alternative follow the usual problem solving procedure with assessment of the changes being made. What makes organizational development different is the emphasis on how individuals can change their relationships among themselves and to the organization by increasing their desire for growth and achievement and by improving their relationship to organization. The continuing nature of the process, the emphasis on individual motivation and power relationships among key management people in the organization, gives to organizational development a focus that concentrates management's efforts to seek those organizational changes that will improve operations.

EFFICIENCY IN ADMINISTRATION

Ancient writers on society and government had a great deal to say about how well or how ill government operated. Governmental operations affected, even controlled, almost all aspects of society, and the level of well-being often was a simple function of how well the king and his servants performed their jobs. Reference to these evaluations are as old as writing, and many of the early masterpieces of social analysis are extensive treatises on public administration. For many centuries criticisms and advice to public administrators have included concepts of efficiency and effectiveness, although these specific terms are of fairly modern origin.[21]

At first, modern writers on administration have emphasized efficiency in administration. When public administration became a special field of conscious observation and sustained writing, one of the maxims was "in the science of administration, whether public or private, the basic good is efficiency." Frederick Taylor (1856-1915) in his emphasis on "scientific management" related labor input to product output. He pushed the increase of efficiency through work study, standardization of tools, selection and training of workers, piece work payment and improvement of supervision and planning. Efficiency, product per man-hour, was the prime operating objective of management, the measure of good or bad management. Other writers, notably Henri Fayol (1841-1925), Luther Gulick, and Lyndall Urwick emphasized efficiency beyond the factory. They placed the attainment of efficiency high among the objectives of public administration. Implicit in much of their writing was the assumption that management efficiency could be separated from the output of goods and services. Administrators produced an "intermediate product," one that was distinguishable from the final output used by clients or customers. Thus, administrators could be efficient, even if their product was not desirable, or was manifestly ill received by society.

The emphasis on efficiency, regardless of the nature of the output, aroused a great deal of opposition. In its simplistic form, the emphasis was antisocial and not acceptable to most social analysts. Efficiency for what? Efficiency to do evil, or oppress people and pile up wealth or keep a tyrannical government in power was scarcely desirable by most standards. A single value organization oversimplifies the whole question of purpose and human motivation and therefore cannot exist. Thus, efficiency by itself can only be an instrumental objective, a limited means of achieving something else that must be evaluated as useful or desirable. Now, while studies of public administration clearly involve efficiency, its description and evaluation are made only a part of the analysis and often so overlapped with other aspects of purpose and operations as to become almost invisible.

One of the major reasons why the concept of efficiency has been demoted in the analysis of public administration is its difficult application to government operations. Efficiency is simply a shortcut concept of relating input to output. A process is judged efficient when its output has a satisfactory relationship to its cost, which is merely one way of measuring input. Intuitively one feels that this is a reasonable concept; why incur costs and use up scarce inputs if the output, the product, is not valued by the intended consumer, and if the output is not worth the cost? One process is more efficient than another when the ratio of its output to its input is higher. Thus, efficiency is always a relative concept. There can be no absolute efficiency, except as a theoretical or mathematical construct. When a process is called efficient there is implicitly involved some standard for reference, and either the word "more" or "less" is usually implied.

Efficiency must not be confused with effectiveness, although the two concepts are quite related. Effectiveness refers to the degree to which an operation achieves its objectives, and thus is not directly related to costs. A machine may be very effective in lifting large loads; but it may be quite inefficient by comparison with other available machines. The two concepts are often confused because costs are so important in evaluating performance that they are often implicitly included in the analysis; they are taken for granted. When a process is labeled very effective, it is often assumed that cost considerations are taken into account. Yet that assumption permits some imprecision in language that is not desirable. Efficiency and effectiveness are two related but different concepts, both useful if properly used. "Cost-effectiveness" is a useful evaluative concept in those administrative situations where it is possible to measure the effectiveness of the operation without specifying its output, or where the specific products produced are not really the relevant output.

The concept of efficiency is most clearly applied in mechanical processes, where the inputs and outputs are easily identified and measured. Thus, the efficiency of a motor can be measured in the pulling power per unit of fuel consumed or in the energy delivered per unit of fuel input. The concept is more difficult to apply to economic production but is still useful for analysis. Output per man-hour, per machine, and per dollar of capital invested are common measures of efficiency. In terms of economic development, higher productivity really means a higher efficiency, more output of goods and services from the available inputs of land, labor, and capital. An improved technology, which is the major source of economic growth, is merely a way of combining the factor inputs more efficiently to produce a larger output from the same quantity of inputs. A higher per capita GNP, in these terms, merely means more product per person, the result of greater efficiency in production.

It is clear that efficiency is directly related to rational economic activity. The effort to minimize or reduce the use of inputs and to maximize the outputs is an effort to increase efficiency. Unfortunately, efficiency is one of those useful concepts that lends itself to simplistic, unreal use. While its application to machines and other inanimate inputs is acceptable, human outputs and inputs are a different matter. Man cannot be treated as a commodity, even though in some of his activities he buys and sells his services as if he were a commodity. The concept of efficiency applied to human inputs must include consideration of the well-being of man as a major purpose of the production process. Simple and rational as the analytical concept of output compared with input may be, the difficulties of measurement and quantification are in actual practice very great, and detract significantly from its usefulness and acceptability. This is particularly true in the application of the concept of efficiency to public administration and is the main reason why efficiency is no longer given the emphasis it received by earlier analysts.

Several kinds of measurement difficulties arise. First, there usually are many different inputs and outputs of a complex process. In economic production, inputs can be any one of the three basic factors, inputs, or any identifiable part of them. Employment, man-hours, machines, machine-hours, acres of land—all are examples of the kinds of specific inputs that can be used. Similarly, output may be a mix of products and series of varying quality and timing. This means that measures of efficiency can be computed in many different ways, sometimes with conflicting or contradictory interpretations. The selection of the units used to measure efficiency is a matter of judgment and purpose and may therefore predetermine the conclusions to be reached. Output can be measured against man-hours worked or total cost, and these ratios may be quite different. For example, where expensive machines are used inefficiently, production per man-hour worked may be improving, but total cost per unit produced may also be going up, each a measure of efficiency but with contradictory tendencies. Clearly, each is measuring a different aspect of efficiency. Agricultural output per acre changes quite differently than agricultural output per farm worker, and different conclusions can be made about efficiency because the two ratios are necessarily different aspects of efficiency. Very often, the inputs or outputs selected are merely the ones that can be measured most easily, rather than the best suited for the particular analysis.

A second type of problem, far more difficult than the first, is the fact that many important inputs and outputs are difficult or impossible to measure. These may include costs and benefits that have psychological impacts but are not directly measurable in market transactions. It also includes the wide variety of important services that are only indirectly measurable by usual standards. For example, the health of a worker that is jeopardized by a dangerous industrial process may not be a measurable input, nor is the air pollution that may result from the operation of a copper smelter. Sometimes it is possible to estimate the quantities of inputs or outputs of this type, but usually the most that can be done is to recognize their existence and attach some adjective such as "large," or "small," or "insignificant," or "serious" to them. Some processes produce the type of external economies that simply cannot be measured, either directly or by surrogate variables. While some analysts have tried valiantly to measure the real output of educational systems, it must be admitted that useful as these attempts are they provide little help in evaluating the efficiency of these schools. A school system that can be measured by the number of students or number of graduates per monetary input still leaves many questions unanswered about the efficiency of the school in terms of training or education success. All measures of efficiency have limitations; and where inputs and outputs are so difficult to measure, the measures of efficiency have limited usefulness. This is particularly true to public administration, where both the inputs and the products of the process must remain difficult to measure.

Traditional accounting and budgeting methods are usually inadequate to provide guidance for the administrative decisions of government agencies. Even the adoption of new types of management accounting and costing methods, helpful as they are, do not fill this gap completely. Government administrators by the nature of their position, must include significant social costs and social benefits in any calculation of cost-benefit analysis. The conceptual and computational tools developed by economists and engineers are helpful in assessing large scale investments in commercial enterprises, and these can be used in many kinds of governmental operations, particularly water power development and transportation. Cost-benefit analysis is a type of efficiency measurement. It can be applied, sometimes in abbreviated form, to practically all kinds of governmental operations.[22] Even where costs or benefits are external economies, nonmeasurable by market operations, they can be evaluated in nonquantitative terms and considered in the decision. It is wrong to assume that only quantitative measurements can be included in the mass of useful information that must be processed by the decision-making capacity of an organization.

Joint costs are also a difficult problem in the measurement of efficiency and cost-benefit analysis. These are common costs that can be applied logically to several kinds of products, with no operating data to record the degree to which each product uses the common facility. For example, railroad tracks are used by both freight and passenger trains. What share of maintaining the tracks should be allocated to each type of service? If freight trains are twice as numerous, should they bear twice as much of the cost of roadbed maintenance? Should it be on a per passenger-mile and per ton-mile of freight basis? If so, how many ton-miles of freight equal one passenger-mile in terms of use of railroad-bed? Joint costs are quite common in all large production operations with diverse products. Joint costs are often distributed arbitrarily, with historical precedent given as the most usual basis. Since history so often provides instances of the wrong kind of economic judgment, a historical basis for allocation of joint costs in measuring efficiency or cost-benefit analysis is not likely to provide optimum guidance.

These measurement difficulties have combined with questions of purpose and objectives to reduce if not eliminate the role of efficiency as the basic evaluative criteria of public administration.

> It is difficult to criticize on logical grounds the concept of increased productivity—getting all you can for your money. However, the fact remains that the word efficiency has acquired a stigma which causes it to be avoided in many circles, principally because of its association with the single value system. This was a philosophy of human motivation which viewed labor as a commodity, each individual being his own agent operating within the laws of the market place. Under this single system of values, owners and managers did not view themselves as their brothers' keeper and regarded themselves and their enterprises as insulated from the broad problems of human welfare.[23]

Public administrators are forced to consider the limited role that efficiency measurements assign to social costs and social benefits. Since many public enterprises arise from market inadequacies and social need, it is obvious that market measurements are often of limited usefulness in evaluating the desirability of many types of governmental operations.

Yet there is a basic inconsistency here that must be faced. If public administration is a critical input in economic growth and has become the limiting factor in many situations, then the efficiency of its use must be of critical importance. Just as improving the quality of the labor input is a key complementarity to the use of new capital equipment and the adoption of an improved technology, improvement in the quality of administrative input and economy in its use is required to achieve higher production and productivity. Efficiency of some government operations may be more difficult to measure than efficiency in a private sector enterprise whose entire production is sold in the market, but efficiency in government is no less important than in business. Efficiency, however measured, must be fitted into the complicated pattern of objectives which governmental operations have, even though they may be significantly different from those of most private sector enterprises. This is being done, consciously or unconsciously, at all times. It is important that these evaluations and judgments of efficiency be carried on more openly and consciously with improved techniques and with full realization of their importance to economic growth.

The concepts of efficiency and effectiveness in administration are attractive in theory but so controversial and difficult to apply that their use is clouded. Rationally, their value as basic aspects of public administration is unquestionable. If the objectives of a government agenc are desirable, efficiency and effectiveness in operations have real, worthwhile significance. By adding the phrase "if the objectives of a government agency are desirable," the age-old debate between ends and means becomes much less sharp, and attention can be focused on the usefulness of the concepts in actual operations. The difficulties inherent in measuring the output of government operations has been alluded to many times. Not only do they usually consist of services difficult to measure, but their evaluation presents problems that, thus far at least, have escaped our analytical tools. The problems of valuing such public goods as security, justice, and free movement are only slightly more difficult than measuring pure water and pure air. These difficulties in concept and application have relegated the actual measurement of administrative efficiency to relatively low level, routine work, with little effort to apply the concepts directly to larger, more difficult administrative operations. Yet indirectly and sometimes unconsciously the application is made. Remarks about the general inefficiency of certain government operations are commonplace, but usually reflect momentary irritation rather than the conclusions of systematic analysis.

It may have been an exaggeration to state in the preceding paragraph that not much has been done to measure administrative efficiency and effectiveness. Most administrative systems do make efforts to evaluate efficiency and effectiveness, but this is done in nonquantitative terms and with vague criteria. Principal reliance is placed on some evaluation of the expenditure process, since that is something tangible that can be observed and measured. How well an agency of government expends its funds is vague because the term "well" can be given many meanings. Staying within the budget, avoiding illegal diversions, gaining public recognition, avoiding trouble—all these are coupled with the production of specific outputs. Although budgets and other expenditures controls are ancient means of judging efficiency, these types of financial controls are often blunt tools, too crude to really measure what should be measured. Although they clearly serve useful purposes, they are not at their best in measuring either efficiency or effectiveness.

Recently, greater emphasis has been placed on measuring cost-benefit relations in public administration. Specifically, there has been a strong effort to develop budgeting into a process that not only allocates financial resources but which also permits more careful evaluation of efficiency and effectiveness. While this emphasis is too recent to permit thorough evaluation of its results, there is no doubt that it has already had a salutory effect on the process of controlling and evaluating public administration. In its most advertised form called Planning–Programming–Budgeting (PPB), it is currently being attempted by many agencies of government; and its concepts and relationships are being discussed in many public affairs journals.[24] Briefly, the basic elements of PPB are: (1) Defining the major programs of each agency, (2) Identifying the principal outputs of each program, and (3) Establishing records that show the use or expenditure of the inputs as they relate to the production of the outputs.

The difficulties of PPB are immediately apparent, and they cannot be dismissed lightly. They tend to concentrate on the inability to specify very important outputs, and the inability of the usual type of records to show very real but nonfinancial inputs and costs, such as political costs, social impact, and undesirable redistributions of income and power.[25] PPB tends to emphasize those inputs and outputs that can be counted, and therefore may give a false sense of exactness and precision to what can at best be a semblance of what it tries to measure. This of course is the charge made against all attempts to measure man and his activities, the inability to encompass all aspects of human thinking, feeling and acting; and it is a serious charge. Yet PPB with its partial analysis has many advantages. It focuses evaluation of progress and efficiency on program objectives and not merely on expenditures. It creates the need for a discussion of objectives and the need to evaluate progress toward those objectives. It provides administrators with opportunities to discuss subunit contributions to agency programs. As with most administrative processes, its wise use adds to administrative capabilities, while untutored, brash use leads to waste and less capability. It is not a costless process.

Recently, rising administrative costs in most countries have stimulated interest in the productivity of public administration operations. Productivity is of course involved in almost every question of cost-benefit analysis, and is closely related to work-load analysis. A recent symposium on productivity in government[26] has imaginatively explored the dimensions of the problems, and demonstrated the progress that has been made in measuring administrative productivity. For a surprisingly large proportion of administrative operations in the United States at both federal and local levels, it has been possible to develop meaningful units of work and output that permit measurement of operations and provide some basis for judging changes in productivity. The most widely used measurement process was manpower planning, followed by workload measurement, unit costing and overall productivity measures. General productivity measures were devised, but their limitations were carefully noted. While significant progress has been made in developing some measurement of productivity for public administration, there is a great deal more that must be learned before this type of evaluation is of widespread usefulness. The fact is that measures of administrative productivity lend themselves to misuse so easily that they must be utilized with the greatest care. The quality of an output is often neglected or mismeasured, yet quality is of the essence of the services provided by governmental agencies. An increase in the letters distributed by the mail services may be a significant increase in output, but for most governmental agencies such an increase without reference to the substance and quality of the mail would be a relatively meaningless measure of output. Productivity can be measured many ways, and there is a danger that a partial measure of productivity will be mechanically interpreted to the serious harm of the governmental process.[27] Efficiency is always subject to the basic question, efficiency for what?

ADMINISTRATIVE CAPACITY AND FEASIBILITY

Concepts of Administrative Capacity and Feasibility

Administration is the process of "achieving desired results through organizations." Administrative capacity must therefore be the capacity to achieve the desired results. This makes administrative capacity not only a function of the process of result achievement but also what it is attempting to achieve. Limited objectives, or easily achieved objectives, mean that a given capability is high in adequacy when compared with the job to be done. This may sound oversimplified, and in many ways it is. Yet its importance is often overlooked. Simply reducing the targets or objectives of a production unit does not increase its capacity to produce. Yet it is true that capacity measured in an absolute sense is an impossible concept to apply to administration, as it is to any complex process. Capacity involves measurement and measurement involves criteria even though those criteria may be judgmental in character and impossible to quantify. A water tank can have its capacity measured; an organization or a country can elicit a judgment about its administrative capacity to achieve certain objectives, or can be compared with other organizations. However, the fact that administrative capacity is impossible to measure with unequivocal units and is therefore difficult to judge does not eliminate the need for that concept or reduce its widespread use.

In the operations of government there is a constant appraisal of administration capacity. This is most visibly reflected in efforts to assess the feasibility of new or additional programs, projects or policies. At budget time, requests for additional personnel or directions for cuts in personnel are presumably based on judgments of capacity to do the assigned work, although other criteria are certainly involved. Specifically, when new projects or programs are proposed, and when development plans are assembled and negotiated, the question of administrative feasibility is constantly raised and assessed. Judgment about feasibility thus is another way of looking at administrative capacity. Almost every country that has tried to speed up modernization is familiar with the need to examine proposals for new government operations in terms of administrative feasibility, as well as in terms of the more familiar financial resource feasibility. In a real sense, administrative feasibility can be considered a resource problem, the availability of adequate human and organizational resources. Judgment about feasibility is an exercise in evaluating administrative capacity against some implicit or explicit patterns of objectives.

It is quite simple to see how administrative capacity and feasibility are necessary elements of the acceptance or rejection of a specific program or project. It is somewhat more difficult, but just as essential, to recognize this necessary element in the consideration of a policy. Obviously, the operational aspects of policies differ. Some policies will require no particular related operations; they may merely announce the priorities to be assigned to activities already occurring, or they may only change relative costs in existing markets. Other policies may involve additional operations that require significant administrative capacity for their implementation, such as the policy to initiate the allocation of foreign exchange to individual importers. Sometimes the administrative capacity involved is in a separate unit of government and sometimes it is diffused throughout government and throughout the entire public and private subsystems of organizations. When administration capacity requirements are very diffused, they tend to be overlooked or are considered almost costless. Governments have a tendency, quite understandably, to disregard private sector administrative requirements for implementing government policies, although the complaints from the private sector are usually vocal and piercing. Here again the real difficulties in evaluating a diffused administrative requirement should not hide its existence and costs. Administration is a scarce input in the production process because it involves both financial and human resources, and its scarcity and cost are facts that must be faced.

The achievement of a rapid, satisfactory rate of economic growth requires many new government agencies and greatly expanded government operations. This, of course, raises questions of administrative capacity, as expressed in judgments about administrative feasibility. So familiar are governments with this problem, and so difficult do they find it to confront, that most of them have developed stereotyped language to give the appearance of attempting to do something constructive about it. Most development plans have chapters and sections that explain the seriousness of the scarcity of administrative capacity, the dangers of continuing to neglect this scarcity, and the general steps that must be taken to improve the situation. Intentions to improve selection and training of administrators and the determination to pay more attention to the implementation of these intentions are nearly always part of every comprehensive development plan. It would be wrong to imply that these are only paper promises; many governments are making determined efforts to improve administration. Yet it is the judgment of most observers that the requirements for increased administrative capacity are probably growing as fast or faster than the actual capacity of governments to perform the operations required for modernizing a society. Thus scarcity of administrative capacity is believed to remain one of the most serious obstacles to higher production and productivity.

There is an obvious difference between the total administrative capacity of a government, and capacity in a specific sector, program or project. If it concentrates its capabilities, almost any country can do a specific job that is given the highest priority and that everybody else must help expedite. Every country is familiar with situations where a specific program, mismanaged and relatively unsuccessful in achieving its objectives, is suddenly vitalized by important personages and decisions. Additional resources are assigned and new management and new priorities for resources and attention are provided. Administrative capacity for that program becomes more adequate so that progress, and even successful achievement may be assured. The cost to other operations of government may be great or may be negligible, but usually these costs are too diffused to be visible, and they are therefore considered relatively costless. It is operationally important to consider overall administrative capacity of the country somewhat differently from that of a single program or institution, or even different from a group of such institutions. The joint concept of administrative capacity and feasibility that is applied to a country or a significantly large segment of the government, is a "macro" view, a large aggregative concept that can be examined only at higher levels of generalization. The "micro" view, the administrative feasibility of specific programs and projects, has different variables and determinants. Both views are important, both are interrelated, but their differences should not be overlooked.

Overall (Macro) Administrative Capacity

The evaluation of administrative capacity of a country attempting to achieve modernization is so vague and formless a process that it is difficult to find useful for operational guidance. Most of what has been written on the subject consists of generalities that are intuitively obvious and operationally useless. They furnish little guidance to administrators and analysts who must constantly face aspects and side effects of the scarcity in administrative capacity. Administrative capacity to achieve more rapid economic growth is obviously limited and in short supply. Government plans for economic programs are often not implemented adequately and objectives are not achieved because government activities are not of the required quality and quantity. The evaluation of this scarcity can have no hard or fast rules, no mechanical procedure for attaining an answer. No check list or cook book can be devised to assess overall administrative capacity and form judgments of what specific policies and actions must be taken to improve macro-administrative capacity.

Yet improvements in administrative capacity can and are being made. Vague and complicated as the administrative process is, it is susceptible to conscious improvement, as well as the improvement that comes indirectly from associated and related changes. Improvement in capacity may come from experience, although this is not inevitable. It may also come from changes in recruitment, changes in training plans, changes in governmental structures. Unfortunately, in a real, operating sense, improvement in administration capacity to achieve modernization is greatly influenced and is even dependent upon changes in the whole social structure. The type of bureaucracy developed, the flow and distribution of power in the whole system, changes in the social structure, changes in the value systems and social practices—all these are some of the important determinants of administrative capacity for achieving modernization in a society. While it is sometimes possible for administrators to affect these determinants consciously and directly, usually these basic changes reflect the functioning of the whole society and lie far beyond the questions of administrative capacity to achieve rapid economic growth.

To add to bewilderment and frustration, it is always possible to demonstrate that situations of surplus administrative capacity exist alongside acute shortages. These are nearly always a part of the administrative system that is continuing to do low priority, even worthless work, administrators who invent things to do when their real tasks have been diminished, administrators who create false urgency situations to preserve their status and absorb resources. Administrative capacity is not a mobile resource capable of flowing automatically to the point where it can yield the greatest return. Macro-administrative systems are generally sluggish, responding slowly to change in their objectives. Consequently, there are always idle resources, difficult to identify and difficult to move to other operations where additional capacity is needed. Search for these surpluses often involves the questioning of administrators' prerogatives and of codes that make it difficult to perform an inside scrutiny. These surpluses are often cited as evidence that administrative capacity in total is not strained, but this is a mistaken view. An administrative system attempting to operate above its capacity, with inadequately trained staff and faltering communications flow, is characterized by pools of underutilized capacity that the system does not assess properly.

Macro-administrative capability for development must be reviewed as a whole system. This permits examining the total process as it is determined by a group of interrelated variables. Changes in one variable affect the others; and in judging total capability, the attempt must be made to assess and judge these relationships. The system's approach is only a framework; it does not by itself provide the coefficients and parameters, the measurement of actual relationships and constraints. At this macro level, little work has been done in quantifying any determinants. Practically nothing has been done that enables the systems approach to answer operating questions such as how much should be expended on training of administrators; what kind of training should be given? Should recruitment be only at the junior levels or should there be "lateral" recruitment? Nevertheless, a system approach is useful at the overall level, with its large aggregative approach to major problems, because it makes possible two things: (1) It permits a senior administrator to aggregate or sum up, however nonnumerically, the impressions, cautions, and conclusions that reach him from less senior administrators who can deal with less aggregative, more specific programs and projects; (2) it provides an opportunity to search for related changes important to the evaluation of aggregated problems by indicating that changes in other variables may have important effects on any specific administrative problem under consideration.

It is impossible to separate administrative development from political development, except for analytical purposes. At macro-administration levels, the separation is even analytically impossible. How can such questions as improvement of civil service appointments, terms of service, structure of government agencies and attitudes toward social reform be examined in operational terms without references to social values and norms, political power, and problems of political participation? Yet available theories of political development are numerous, imaginative, and vague, too elusive thus far to be yoked with operating concepts of improving public administration. In the words of William Siffin: "The conceptions [of political development] do not lead to strategies and plans spelling out major levels of action that can be implemented by political actors existing in the real world."[28]

Three clusters of variables have been identified as assisting in his macro approach to evaluating overall administrative capacity:

Performance—These relate to the inputs and outputs of the system, the costs and types of inputs, the quantity and quality of inputs, the benefits and disbenefits that arise from successes and failures in achievement, the operating bottlenecks associated with failures.

Structure—These relate to the organization of the human and non-human resources that form the subsystems of the whole system, including the organizing practices, principles, the codes of conduct and operation, the guidance and communication parts of the subsystems, the degrees of participation by the different elements in the subsystems and the motivation and coercion influences.

Environment—These include both the immediate environment and the general contextual environment, consisting of other organizations on both the input and output sides of macro-administrative process.

Identifying these very broad groups of variables is only a slight advance in the necessary analysis of macro-administrative capacity. Within each group, the number and complexity of the variables requires much more identification and examination. So numerous are these variables and so different in scope, intensity, and visibility, that some very crude principles of selection must be used to sort them out. To list and describe all possible variables would be to set up an encyclopedia that would have little operational usefulness. It is necessary to emphasize what should be obvious, that the administrative capacity of a country is uniquely related to its history, culture, social structure and value systems. Therefore, discussions of macro-capacity quickly become a long array of general statements, closely ralated to moral maxims, that stress the need for improvement, the need for better coordination, the need for greater social consciousness, the need for paying more attention to cost-benefit analysis, the need for avoiding corruption and selfishness, and the need to learn from experience. Since no one can deny the relevance of these improvements, the operating task is to identify how to achieve them at a reasonable cost in a reasonable time span.

That the administration of a country necessarily reflects its social structure and value systems need not be accepted as an iron law that makes useless any operating efforts at improving macro-administrative capacity. The substantial differences in capacity between countries and between sectors or programs within a single country indicates that operating changes can be effective and worthwhile. They may even help bring about the general social changes that are basic to overall improvement of public administration. A government that is exhorting its people to be democratic and to open its economic and social opportunities for all classes of citizens is not likely to be very effective if it limits its key public administrators to the upper level, land-owning classes instead of opening recruitment to the civil service to all classes. Changing the image of government by increased participation by all classes of citizens requires far more than an active, sympathetic civil service;

but this may be an essential requirement whose absence may be fatal to any broad social advance.

The operating options to achieve an increase in the macro-administrative capacity of a country seems to be limited to the following:

Improvements in the Recruitment of Administrators

This usually involves the determination to open higher level government employment to new classes in society by changing the examination and selection systems. Where the usual entry channel is university training, it may mean changing the requirements for matriculation or changing the universities. In either case, deliberate efforts can be made to ensure that young people from classes not now represented in the bureaucracy are introduced into the system. The improvement in recruitment for higher level positions may involve lateral entry whereby experienced, successful people outside of government are brought into the administrative structure not merely as advisers or for short periods of time but as part of the permanent staff. The existence of a vigorous, lateral entry flow of additional staff raises, of course, questions of remuneration, seniority, and status of government and nongovernment employment, and these are quite difficult to confront. Yet if overall administrative capacity is to be improved, broader recruitment to the civil service is a necessary, if not sufficient condition.

Improvement in Training Administrators

This broad category of options to improve the overall administrative capacity is the simplest to support and the most difficult to justify objectively. Training of administrators is an ancient intellectual dispute, as was briefly discussed at the beginning of this chapter. Perhaps the only worthwhile training of administrators is done on the job, doing the work and watching other administrators. Even if this narrow view of training for public administration is held, it is possible to develop training programs that foster the lessons of experience and expand efforts to have more experienced administrators help guide the less experienced people. Staff colleges, institutes of public administration, special academies for accountants, finance personnel, village and agricultural administrators, and many different kinds of institutions have been developed to improve training. As in the case of most educational institutions, it is difficult to measure output in any terms that signify improvement in administrative capacity. Experienced observers have concluded that while these efforts are generally useful and well worth the cost, they meet only a small part of the total need. Usually, they are not adjusted to the specific country, with teaching materials and even teachers generally imported from more advanced countries. Their results have been useful, but quite limited.

Improvement in the Operating Procedures of Administration

There are many operating procedures in the assignment and use of administrators that have a marked effect on macro-administrative capacity. They include the number and type of cadres or services, and the flexibility of transfer between services. In many countries there is a colonial heritage of a select cadre for whom most of the key positions are reserved. This creates a type of elitism that is of questionable value to the general image of government and usually results in difficult morale problems with the other administrators who are not part of the elite services. It is generally accepted now that this system requires serious modification, but the cost as well as the benefits of changes are so important that this question can be examined operationally only in a specific context. Similarly, assignment procedures and the weight given to seniority are clearly related to the question of rapidity of personnel turnover. The procedure whereby a large number of administrators are constantly shifted from one agency to another and where the major basis for promotion is seniority rather than job effectiveness, may help achieve and reward experience and may help avoid corruption, but it also results in loss of specific experience and motivates toward conformity rather than innovation. Merely eliminating select cadres or reducing the importance of seniority does not necessarily mean an increase in administrative capacity; that depends upon what procedures and criteria are added to the administrative system.

Improvements in Morale and Integrity

Improvement in morale and integrity are basic to a general increase in the macro-administrative capacity. This kind of improvement is more an indirect result of other changes in society than the direct result of changes in administrative policies and procedures. For improvements in morale and integrity, ". . . profound changes are required in political and social attitudes in governmental structure, institutions, behavior and skill."[29] The examples set by the leaders of a society and the general tone of integrity and sense that a government establishes in its practices are probably more important than any specific order issued to eliminate corruption or to work more efficiently. Rigid enforcement of work rules relating to daily time sheets, illness and holiday absences, and work-load are relatively meaningless in a climate of laxity and failure of leadership to set firm examples of devoted administration. A general sense of social justice and commitment is far more important than petty time keeping rules, although the importance of the latter cannot be ignored. Morale and integrity of administration are so closely related to the social structure and value system as almost to be indistinguishable from them.

Continuing Evaluation of Administrative Capacity

One of the most essential elements of the improvement of macro-administration is establishing the ability to cope with administrative failures and crises. This ability is significantly different from establishing a program for improvement or review of administration. It represents assigning the requisite responsibility to some agency of government, either in the budgeting or in the planning areas of staff responsibility, that is on the lookout for administrative failures and crises. One would suppose that this would be an integral part of any budgeting or planning operation, but unfortunately the regular work in these fields always seems to squeeze out a continuing examination of administrative failures and crises. A "crisis" appraisal of any problem is usually deprecated as a second-best approach, just as medical treatment programs are not nearly as desirable as illness prevention programs. Yet operationally they are not substitutes for each other; they are complementary. It is necessary to make judgments on the return to investment of resources in each and to allocate the available resources accordingly. Operating entirely on response-to-crisis correctives will make it impossible to avoid many costly failures, although some are to be expected under any system. The continuous operation of a capacity to evaluate administrative failures and crises is an integral part of any comprehensive program to improve the overall administrative capacity of a country.

Specific (Micro) Administrative Capacity

It is far easier to examine and evaluate the administrative capacity of a project, a program, or even a single sector of the economy than it is to evaluate the overall administrative capacity of government. In fact, macro-capacity is so general a concept that the only way to evaluate macro-capacity may be by building up from individual sectors and programs to the total, by examining single sectors and programs and then aggregating them into a total picture. Some practices, such as government recruitment policies, or social class representation of administrators, may be susceptible only to overall change; but at operating levels, questions of feasibility and possible results of proposed changes must clearly be based on an examination of individual sectors, programs and projects. Macro-administrative capacity must be operationally related to micro-administrative capacities.

The basic reason for the reliance on a "micro" appraisal is intuitively obvious. Administrative capacity and feasibility is measured in relation to objectives. And the objectives of the total public administration system are difficult to state in concrete terms. They can only be stated in highly generalized terms, difficult to quantify, and difficult to relate to specific administrative personnel and practices. As the scale of generality is lowered, the statement of objectives becomes easier to specify and easier to associate with specific administrative functions. For example, it is easier to state the objective of a government seed improvement program than it is to make positive and clear the overall objectives of the Ministry of Agriculture. To secure the latter, the objective of all of the important programs and departments have to be summarized; and some additional objectives relating to co-ordination and general policies are also necessary. Obviously, both specific and general levels of objectives are necessary, and neither should be neglected. But it is no criticism of public administration to point out that many of its multiple objectives must be stated at high levels of generalization, difficult to quantify, and difficult to use in evaluating the administrative capacity required for their achievement.

The three clusters of variables that have been indicated as useful in assessing the macro-administrative capacity—performance, structure, and environment—could also be used in the "micro" approach. Somewhat more useful, because they break out some of the more important subclusters, are the internal and linkage variables proposed by the institution-building model (see chapter 7), leadership, doctrine, program, resources, internal structure, and the linkages relating each of these to the environment. Based on the description of these variables in chapter 7, an examination of each of these would permit an evaluation of administrative capacity. But these variables are almost impossible to quantify, and evaluation would necessarily involve judgment and experience with each specific instance.

There is a difference, of course, between actual and potential administrative capacity, between the capacity demonstrated in the past or the present, and that which will be either required or will be available in the future. The historical and the actual situation is always easier to evaluate than the future, in the sense that the potential is more subject to the swings of hopes and fears. Current and past performance, difficult as they often are to measure against objectives, are still the best indicators of future capabilities. By relating performance characteristics of even a few of the major variables to estimates of future requirements, it is often possible to form a composite judgment of future administrative capability. It should be clear, however, that the process is difficult and uncertain; and only its necessity justifies it. There is no way of avoiding the necessity of making a judgment about administrative capacity, whether this judgment is explicitly made or implicitly assumed.

An ambitious statement on the validity of appraising administrative capacity was prepared by an international group of scholars for the United Nations' Department of Economic and Social Affairs. While there is confusion in the analysis between macro- and micro-administrative capability, the analysis largely focused on the latter. By minimizing the traditional concepts of hierarchy and compartmentalized administrative analysis, attention was focused on administration as a scarce resource, an essential scarce input that had to be consciously allocated to yield the most return. General improvement of the administrative system was considered necessary, but it always involved costs that had to be examined and compared with benefits. "It must be stressed that although improvement of an organization may require changes in its structure or its relations with its environment, the basic purpose of such change is to improve performance."[30]

The three general areas of examination advanced by the Interplan group—(1) performance, (2) structure, and (3) environment—can be approached at varying levels of generalization, ranging from arms-length surveys, which are quite distant and general, to full-length appraisals, requiring detailed statements and analysis about each subunit. While all levels of analysis have their place, one level must permit a concentration on performance. This can only be done at a fairly detailed level, one that involves self-appraisal by participants as well as outside judgments.

Performance Analysis

The Interplan report stresses the multiple dimensions of performance, based of course on the multiple objectives that all significant organizations have. Major emphasis is placed on the relationship between outputs and inputs and on the need for stressing the measurement of performance in achieving objectives. Costs are a complex of market costs, social costs, and opportunity costs, while output is often difficult to define and measure. Quality must clearly form a part of the measurement of output, and measures of the public interest must also be involved in assessing the benefits of any government organization. The development of performance or program budgeting is an effort to establish conditions for performance analysis. Traditional government budgeting by categories of purchases (manpower, equipment, services, and so forth) helps little in analyzing either efficiency or effectiveness. Establishing some way of specifying outputs, whether tangible or intangible, and relating these to both costs and objectives is the essence of any performance analysis. To the extent that this is impossible to achieve in objective units and with valid data, intuition and judgment must be relied on. Few situations, if any, would exist where complete reliance could be placed on quantitative comparisons only. All evaluations of performance will involve substantial elements of judgment based on intuition and experience. Yet the assumption of an important degree of rationality makes possible the assertion that the availability of data on cost, production, and objectives in a more or less comparable form makes possible better assessments of performance, better than the assessments possible with less adequate information.

Structural Analysis

The structural analysis must be based on an analysis of people as well as things, since people are the prime resource. The internal structure is essentially based on these building blocks, people and things. The way these are prepared and arranged has a great deal to do with the effectiveness of performance. Organized in subunits that attempt to group similar functions, they often represent specialized functions, such as financial, accounting, and engineering, and there is as much danger of over-specialization as under-specialization. Only experience and judgment, viewed against performance, can test the internal structure of an organization. Only an examination of the flow of decisions and communication can identify bottlenecks and inadequacies, can assure the development of appropriate codes of behavior and values and can evaluate the adequacy of guidance subsystems in an organization.

Environment

The way an organization fits into its environment is stressed by the Interplan group as a basic dimension of administrative capability. Environment must be considered both as a "task" environment, immediate and operational, and a "contextual" environment, more remote and general. The task environment includes all the other governmental and nongovernmental organizations which are related either as they affect the inputs, the administrative process, or the outputs of any government organization. All significant internal variables have external linkages, and the task and contextual environments also usually include international linkages. The turbulence of societies in transition toward modernization are environmental facts that must be involved in any evaluation of administrative capabilities. Environment influences the quality and quantity of both inputs and outputs. For example, the existence of schools helps determine the availability of persons who can be trained as supervisors and foremen. The price elasticity of the demand for a product may help determine the product mix of a plant. External expectations and fears are important elements in administrative decisions. While the effect of environment on administrative capacity is obvious, it is also often neglected.

NOTES

1. For a wide ranging and thoughtful dialogue on this question, see Theory and Practice of Public Administration: Scope, Objectives and Methods (Philadelphia: American Academy of Political and Social Science, October 8, 1968), monograph; particularly the papers and the following discussions of Dwight Waldo and Stephen K. Bailey.

2. Luther Gulick and Lyndall Urwick, eds., "Papers on the Science of Administration" (New York: Institution of Public Administration, 1937).

3. Leonard D. White, Introduction to the Study of Public Administration (New York: The Macmillan Co., 1962), pp.

4. See for example, Bertram M. Gross, The Managing of Organizations (New York: The Free Press of Glencoe, 1968); Herbert Simon, Donald Smithburg and Victor A. Thompson, Public Administration (New York: Alfred A. Knopf, 1950); and John M. Pfiffner and Frank P. Sherwood, Administrative Organization (Englewood Cliffs, N.J.: Prentice-Hall, 1960).

5. For a brief but more complete discussion of hierarchy, see Pfiffner and Sherwood, op. cit., pp. 74-95.

6. For a far more adequate exposition of these "principles," see Harold Koontz and Cyril O'Donnel, Principles of Management (New York: McGraw-Hill, 1955).

7. See Herbert A. Simon, "The Proverbs of Administration," Public Administration Review 6, no. 1 (Winter 1946): 53-67.

8. Pfiffner and Sherwood, op. cit., p. 386.

9. Herbert A. Simon, Administrative Behavior, 2nd ed. (New York: The Macmillan Co., 1957), p. 1.

10. Ibid., p. 70.

11. This is based on the model suggested by Charles E. Lindblom, The Policy-Making Process (New York: Prentice-Hall, 1968).

12. James March and Herbert Simon, Organizations (New York: John Wiley & Sons, 1959), p. 140.

13. Ira Sharkansky, Public Administration—Policy Making in Government Agencies (Chicago: Markham Publishing Co., 1970), p. 47.

14. Ibid., p. 55.

15. See Charles E. Lindblom, "The Science of 'Muddling Through,'" Public Administration Review 19 (Spring 1959): 79-88.

16. Gross, op. cit., p. 477.

17. D. Stone and Associates, "National Organization for the Conduct of Economic Development Programs," National Institute of Administrative Sciences (Brussels: 1954), p. 8.

18. Fred W. Riggs, Administration in Developing Countries: The Theory of Prismatic Society (Boston: Houghton Mifflin, 1964).

19. For a basic presentation and explanation of the concept, see W. G. Bennis, Organizational Development: Its Nature, Origins and Prospects (Reading, Mass.: Addison-Wesley, 1969).

20. Samuel A. Culbert and Jerome Reisel, "Organization Development: An Applied Philosophy for Managers of Public Enterprises," Public Administration Review 2 (March/April 1971): 160.

21. For an interesting survey of some of the major writing on public administration prior to the present century (such as Old Testament, the Mahabharata, Confucius, Plato, Aristotle, Kautilya, Nizam-Al-Mulik, Machiavelli) see Gross, op. cit., chapter 5.

22. See Martin S. Feldstein, "Cost Benefit Analysis and Investment in Public Sector," Public Administration 42 (1964): 351-72.

23. Pfiffner and Sherwood, op. cit., p. 98-99.

24. For an explanation of the concepts of PPBs, see the following: Charles L. Schultze, "PPB in Brief," in Politics and Economics of Public Spending (Washington, D.C.: The Brookings Institution, 1968),

pp. 19-34; Samuel M. Greenhouse, "The Planning-Programming-Budgeting System: Rationale, Language and Idea Relationships," Public Administration Review 26 (December 1966): 271-77; David Novick, Program Budgeting, Rand Corporation, 1966. Yet, for a view that reduces the significance of this development, see Gross, op. cit., pp. 617-19.

25. See Aaron Wildavsky, "The Political Economy of Efficiency: Cost-Benefit Analysis, Systems Analysis and Program Budgeting," Public Administration Review 26 (December 1966): 292-310.

26. See Public Administration Review (November/December 1972), particularly the following articles: Jerome A. Mark, "Meanings and Measures of Productivity," p. 747; and Thomas D. Morris, William H. Corbett and Brian L. Usilaner, "Productivity Measures in the Federal Government," p. 753.

27. See the article by Frederick C. Thayer in the symposium cited, "Productivity: Taylorism Revisited (Round Three)," Public Administration Review (November/December 1972): 833.

28. John D. Montgomery and William Siffin, eds., Approaches to Development: Politics, Administration and Change (New York: McGraw-Hill; Durham, N.C.: distributed by Duke University Press, 1966), p. 7.

29. United Nations, Department of Economic and Social Affairs, A Handbook of Public Administration: Current Concepts and Practice with Special Reference to Developing Countries, 1961, p. 6.

30. United Nations, Department of Economic and Social Affairs, Public Administration Division, Interplan—Appraising Administrative Capabilities in Development (ST/TAO/M/46), 1969.

12

GOVERNMENT CONTROLS

Government inputs* into the economic activities of a country are as varied as all other inputs. They vary in motivation, purpose, extent, method of communication, base of authority, point of impact, point of origin, point of influence, and in the part of the economic process affected. So complex are government inputs that no general classification that has been suggested is satisfactory. Classification for one purpose will often be impossible for another purpose and difficult even for a single well-defined purpose. The usual classification of government controls seems to be based on the degree of force or coercion used or implied. Leonard White's classification is both comprehensive and operational.[1] It is based on what government does, actual operating activities of government rather than on analytical constructs.

Noncoercive Forms of Administrative Action

Declaration of public policy—By stating and explaining public policy, government hopes to influence the actions of both public and private sectors.

------

*The terms "direction" and "control" are used interchangably here. It is important to emphasize that government influence is not necessarily restrictive, which is the usual connotation of the word "control." Direction can be invigorating and freeing, rather than only restraining. Yet the word "control" is more useful and avoids some language oddities, such as "direct direction" which grate on the eyes. Hopefully, by

Voluntary standards—By persuading interested parties to establish voluntary standards, public pressure is designed to press for compliance.

Demonstration—The identification of a preferred method or device is a basic method of influencing others.

Mediation and conciliation—These are noncoercive forms of official action to adjudicate disputes.

Compliance through publicity—The deliberate use of public approval or disapproval to channel government influence on economic activities is a useful, frequently used method.

"Yardstick" regulation—This consists of establishing a government operation that provides data for testing and measuring the performance of others, that is a yardstick.

Coercive Forms of Administrative Action

Inspection—Examination to decide whether something conforms to standards set by appropriate authority is an old process of government. Inspection places the initiative on the government to set standards for operations and to require that operators open their premises for inspection and comply with the result of the inspection.

Licensing—This process involves formal authority by the government to perform a function that is otherwise forbidden. The essentials of a licensing system involve (1) setting of a standard for the license, (2) prohibiting action of this type until a license is obtained, (3) establishing procedure for applying for license, and (4) granting a license to show adherence to the standard and conveying the legal right to proceed. The granting of the license may be perfunctory or may require detailed study.

Dispensing power—This is the administrative practice that dispenses or allows a deviation from an established pattern, such as remitting penalties, permitting variations from a zoning regulation, and reducing taxes. This dispensing power may be recognized by law or may be unofficial, as when an official decides on his own volition to overlook a minor misdemeanor. The essence of this type of activity is the discretion of the administrator, even though official and unofficial constraints may be present.

Directing power for individual application—This is a specific order for a specific purpose.

Rule making power—This is a directive to a group rather than an individual application. It may prescribe required conduct for all

occasionally throwing in the word direction, the emphasis is such that control is interpreted as both positive and negative, both encouraging as well as restraining.

engaged in a specified activity, not just any particular individual. It may issue broad rules or detailed regulations under these rules.

Administrative adjudication—This resembles the courts and consists of the activities of administrative tribunals designed to have coercive power and to make determinations on specified matters of interest to government. It is not a judicial court; it operates under different rules and with different constraints.

Sanctions—This is the penalty-giving authority, when rules and regulations are violated. It includes withholding and withdrawing as well as avoiding benefits. Sanctions are of course part of every method of control. Coercive sanctions represent the ultimate governmental activity in controlling activities for its citizens.

This scheme of classifying governmental controls by type or degree or coercion may be useful as a descriptive device, but analytically it has obvious defects. Each type has "border" problems; that is, defining the borders and avoiding overlapping is both difficult and hardly worth the trouble. Administrators perform several of these types almost with the same action and the degree of coercion usually provides little operational guidance. For example, tax commissioners who are applying administrative adjudication often have both demonstration and sanction powers. Sanctions are usually part of the rule-making power if inspection is part of the rule. Licensing authority sometimes involves dispensing power, as in instances where building permits are judged unnecessary. Unless one adopts the untenable position that the scale of coercive controls provides a scale of correctness (the less coercion the better the control and the more coercion the worse the control), there is little operating significance in such a classification scheme. Surely, effectiveness and efficiency related to the importance and priorities of the problem furnish far better criteria for judging the need or applicability of controls than these loosely defined degrees of coercion.

Basic Controls of Economic Activities

A far more rational classification was made by Robert Dahl and Charles Lindblom.[2] After discussing the problem of ends and means in social action, they presented seven ends which they accept as basic to their analysis—freedom, rationality, democracy, subjective equality, security, progress, and appropriate inclusion. To achieve these ends by social action requires rational calculation and social control, and the analysis of these processes leads into the classification of social control that affects economic activities. To these analysts practically all control is direct, since it affects the area of awareness of the individual in some form. What is usually called "indirect" control is really direct control through a chain of agents. There are four basic control techniques by government that affect a person's awareness:

1. Spontaneous field control—This is the basic control technique of a society and it is a paradox because it is not a deliberate, intended control. It is simply an unintended effect on people's field of awareness, the unconscious signals given about rewards and penalties, about what is best to do or not to do. Spontaneous here does not mean uncaused; rather, it means not intended for a purpose. At first, this technique of control seems contradictory and out of place, more like a technique of noncontrol. A little reflection will show that it is basic to all social systems. For example, the price system in a mixed economy works largely by spontaneous control. Thus, spontaneous control is the universal kind of influence on others' actions, and government actions play an important part in the spontaneous control to which all individuals and groups are subject.*

2. Manipulated field control—This is the deliberate action to influence the awareness field of another person by means other than command. It is done by manipulating signals about rewards and penalties.

3. Command—This is to affect "the response of a subordinate exclusively by virtue of a penalty prescribed by the controller for nonperformance of an implied or stipulated directive." It is of marginal importance because the way command is defined here, command does not involve reward for compliance but only penalty for noncompliance. In most civil laws, command in this sense plays a limited role in law enforcement.

4. Reciprocity—This is the mutual control that is common even in hierarchial organizations, where people control or influence each other.

These four fundamental techniques of control are advanced as the building blocks from which all social systems are constructed. There are other, distant, more roundabout methods of control that are labeled indirect. One or more of the four basic techniques described above can be used, not to influence actions of people directly, but indirectly, by affecting basic conditions. These include control to affect the personality, the role, and the agenda of a society. In a sense, these refer to long-range or fundamental changes that a major war or revolution may make, rather than those made as part of a process of deliberate planning.

Dahl and Lindblom proceed to show how the basic techniques of control are used by government to affect all of the basic processes for economizing within a society, classified into distribution of claims on resources, stabilization, choice, allocation, resource development and high resource output. The whole classification scheme is then focused

---

*This apparent paradox of spontaneous control will seem a little easier to understand if the word "influence" is substituted occasionally. Individuals are influenced by all kinds of governmental actions that are unintended.

on how the price system, control of leaders, and bargaining among leaders affect the six basic processes of economizing. While the basis of the analysis is a set of fairly abstract concepts, with a somewhat difficult language because of the use of familiar words in an unfamiliar way, the description of the way government affects economic activities is revealing. But the approach in this classification, as in White's classification given above, is not focused on the problem of evaluating the scarcity of public administration.

IMPLEMENTING ECONOMIC POLICIES

Economic policies are defined and made real by their implementation. The feedback of information from the implementation process must be used to evaluate and modify continuing policy; to fail to do so almost assures policy failure. The instruments used in implementing economic policies are so varied in scope, intensity and purpose that any system of classification contains overlapping categories and questionable assignments. For purposes of description, the instruments available to governments have been grouped into nine reasonably homogeneous categories, roughly arranged by the extent of direct involvement of government in enterprise operations. But, as will be readily seen in the brief discussion of each category, this classification is too uncertain to bear any interpretation of desirability.

The nine categories devised for presenting the multivariate instruments used to implement economic policies are:

1. Direct operations
2. Expenditures
3. Subsidies and grants
4. Licenses, permits and charters
5. Loans
6. Insurance
7. Taxes
8. Regulation of business practices
   (Codes of performance)
9. General climate for economic enterprise.

Government economic policies are generally implemented by the joint use of these instruments, whether or not the government deliberately chooses to do so. A policy that at first appears to be implemented by a simple licensing procedure may soon become involved in taxes, loans, subsidies, regulations of business practices and, by its publicity, may become an important element in establishing the general climate for economic enterprise. This is why, in the illustrations of these instruments given below, there is frequent reference to other instruments and some actual overlap in classification. What appears on the surface to be one instrument may in reality be another so that they cannot be separated operationally.

Direct Operations of Government

Some economic policies can be implemented by government ownership and management of economic enterprises. The government provides the financial resources, makes the entrepreneurial decisions, provides the general policies and management, and presumably takes the profits or losses. Policies that are related to the use of this instrument vary from basic ideological convictions to attempts to meet short-term shortages of certain goods or services. The belief that the basic services of a utilities nature, such as power, transportation, and communication, should be owned and operated by the public, is accepted by most of the less developed countries, even those that are determined to have a large private sector. Products that require large investments that must be paid off over long periods of time often result in government enterprises. A need for marketing capacities may cause a government to establish marketing and storage facilities for basic crops. The feeling that credit is not properly furnished by the existing credit institutions may lead to a decision to establish a government credit enterprise. Where the private sector is not performing an important function to the satisfaction of the leaders or of the public, an easily understandable instrument is direct operation by government.

Where the basic ideology of a country determines that all or most of the economic enterprises will be directly operated, as in Communist countries, this instrument of economic policy implementation is fairly well prescribed for the public administrator. This is not true for most of the less developed countries, which often have to choose between the public and the private sectors. Most of the less developed, non-Communist countries that ventured into large efforts at government ownership and operation have found this means of implementing economic policies less than easy and often less than desirable. Too many of the enterprises have been unprofitable and obviously inefficient in achieving their main objectives, increased production and productivity. The question of evaluation, however, must be made in terms of "opportunity costs"; what is the best alternative given up by choosing a direct government operation? There has been no acceptable study that permits empirical evaluation of direct government operations of economic enterprises. In the Communist countries, there is a built-in assumption of the desirability of government ownership and operation. Economic myth has been added to economic and political ideology in so complicated a manner that there apparently is no simple way of sorting out the question, even in fairly broad terms. Considerations other than efficiency, largely related to social purpose and welfare considerations, are often more important than financial returns to investment. Therefore, the evaluation of the costs and benefits of direct ownership of production entrepreneurs tends to be general impressions, based on assumed values.

Several general considerations warrant examination. The organizational form of the direct government operation usually receives a great deal of attention, as if it were a determining factor in successful institutionalization. The most common form of organization is the public or quasi-public corporation, with most of the functions and objectives enjoyed by private corporations. Not infrequently, the board of directors and top management are appointed by government, and most of these corporations report, in varied ways, to cabinet members and to ministries of government. The purpose of the corporate form is to free the enterprise from the rules and procedures of government that are supposed to reduce operating efficiency and to prevent government operations from being "business like." The corporate form of organization for a production enterprise appears to be more suitable than the usual type of government bureau or department. The internal flow of authority and decision making in the corporate structure is more understandable and more concrete in terms of production and productivity than the usual government agency. The title "corporation" has of course no magic operating significance, and the business organization need not necessarily be a formally organized and chartered corporation. What is significant is that an enterprise that focuses on production and productivity of an economic product tends to require a type of organization that is less defused, more specialized, than the usual government agency. Thus, the tendency that most countries have shown to establish corporations to operate government-owned production units is probably on the whole beneficial. Yet the success of public corporations has been quite limited, and casts doubt on the desirability of continuing to multiply public corporations. This doubt does not arise from an ideological view about government ownership, but rather from the conviction that the opportunity costs are too high, that there are better ways of getting the job done, that there are built-in tendencies for inefficiency that cannot be overcome except at a high opportunity cost. The major difficulty is that while the public corporation is visualized as a separate, largely autonomous organization, free from most government rules on staffing, financial controls, procedures, and decision making, in actual practice, most of the governmental features are carried over into public corporations.

Staffing

The area of personnel is one in which the public corporation is supposed to have the most advantage over the usual type of government agency. Selection and promotion of government employees are characterized by nonefficiency considerations that the newly organized corporation is supposed to have the ability to avoid. Theoretically, this is true and there are many cases of this type of potentiality. Yet there are too many cases of nonrealization of the potential to make this avoidance a matter of chance. There seems to be a forceful tendency to incorporate most of the effects of government personnel policies into public corporations, even if the written law does not require this. The staff is substantially made up of government career people, attracted by higher salaries but still subject to the disciplines and prejudices of their former careers.

Financial Controls

The financial controls developed by government are largely focused on objectives of accountability and avoidance of illegal decisions. They seem to be based on the assumption that given any opportunity, the prime purpose of a government worker is to utilize the government's financial resources for his own benefits. While this may be an important objective, it is far from the total objective in a modern production unit, which needs financial controls designed to expedite efficient use of resources and to implement managerial decisions. The complexity of government policy financial controls are often added to problems of budget and general financial planning that are the province of ministries of finance, leaving the public corporation with the worst of two possible worlds.

Government Procedures

The development of procedures for doing all the routine operations of any organization takes time and effort. Public corporations tend to adopt government procedures in an apparently effortless way. But the results are not effortless, because government procedures in the most routine activities are not noted for their efficiency or speed. Procedures for getting supplies, setting up communication channels, and allocating housekeeping responsibilities seem to come from government in unchanged form with all their customary delays and inefficiencies.

Decision Making

The design of the decision-making process in public corporations is frequently the exact copy of that in government agencies. This means that the government agency's tendency to pass decisions upward, to avoid responsibility by involving as many people as possible and to check on the political aspect of decisions, is repeated in an organization which was established to avoid these characteristics in its decision making. Enough experience has been achieved to warrant the assertion that adopting the corporate form does not necessarily eliminate and may not even reduce the problems of the decision-making process that is slow and too centralized. Government ownership of large industrial complexes in developing countries will necessarily involve government deeply in the process of resource management, and then political considerations will tend to supersede economic criteria in the decision-making process.

The tendency to adopt without much improvement the rules and practices of government agencies is associated with several other tendencies that must be considered in evaluating public corporations. Because they usually involve large, important operations and are often staffed with senior government officials who know their way through the jungles of bureaucratic controls, public corporations tend to be favored by government control and allocation. Whether it is access to foreign exchange, licenses to import, speed in allocation of freight cars, space on airplanes, or any of the multitudinous licenses, permits, quotas, and services that government agencies ration or allocate, public corporations are more alert, more knowledgeable and more influential than most of the other corporations in securing the right piece of paper from government. When inflation requires a reduction in investment expenditures, when foreign exchange crises require sharp, arbitrary reductions in commitments, the public corporation is in a good position to resist these curtailments and protect its plans for expenditures. This may not be a bad outcome, if these public corporations are better than the average enterprise in their use of scarce resources and in the relative value of their output. If this superiority does not exist in fact, then this tendency to be in a protected position represents a diminution of the efforts to optimize use of scarce resources.

Public corporations tend to be monopolistic; that is, they generally are selected for operation in areas where no other production enterprise is likely or is permitted. Monopolies, with competition almost non-existent or at best quite limited, have less pressures exerted on them to minimize costs and maximize returns. Because they are monopolistic and are so closely related to the centers of political authority and power, they can probably mold their environment somewhat more readily than most private enterprises. They are less liable to bankruptcy as a penalty for inefficiency, less liable to change of management because of a reduction in production. Because of their more protected position, they may get away with many inefficiencies that can be hidden from public scrutiny under the cloak of government secrecy rules. Some tensions in the opposite direction are also present, the public corporation may have parliamentary scrutiny, the finance ministry and other government agencies may provide some useful checks, and the public enterprise may be more in the public eye than a private entrepreneur would necessarily be. Yet the point is worth making that the drive toward efficiency through rewards and penalties is probably less present in public corporations than in private enterprises.

The desirability of public corporations as the appropriate structure for direct ownership and operation of production enterprises has been widely accepted by the less developed countries. Political considerations often press in the direction of establishing public corporations, since it is easier to point out that any excessive exploitation by the public corporation is eased by having profits accrue to the owner, the nation. Yet more sophisticated political leaders and civil servants have learned from observation and experience that public control of private enterprise may provide a better form of organization and operations for many products and services whose output must be accelerated. Without learning the formal concept from economics, they have come to realize that opportunity costs, difficult as the concept is, have a real place in determining the emphasis on public corporations.

State trading corporations are a growing form of government imple-mentation of economic policies. Where pricing and distribution prac-tices of private traders seem too costly and too complicated to control, governments organize trading enterprises, often with monopolies in their fields. Selected imports and exports, with their tendency toward mo-nopolistic and windfall profits, are usually the products chosen for the state trading corporation. Marketing boards for basic export commodi-ties, such as rice, rubber, cotton, cocoa, tea, timber and tin, are fairly common instruments for implementing government economic poli-cies. Dissatisfaction with prices paid to producers, or with the dis-position of profits received from fluctuating world prices, make this type of instrument a major element in implementing government policies. The establishment of "Fair Price" stores, to distribute essential foods in a time of scarcity, is another illustration of trading enterprises es-tablished by government to implement its economic policies.

Joint operations with private owners, usually foreigners, are a growing device for many governments. Often, it is the result of at-tempting to reconcile two conflicting policies, the policy of minimizing foreign involvement in essential enterprises, and the recognition that the government or its nationals are not yet capable of operating the enterprise in question. Joint enterprises provide some opportunity for gaining experience while utilizing foreign skills in operations, for being influential in policy decisions without taking full responsibility for management decisions.

Government Expenditures

Implementing economic policies by means of government expendi-tures is an instrument easily recognizable and commonly used. Govern-ment procurement of goods and services is usually between 10 percent and 20 percent of total GNP, and these purchases, like any other ex-penditures, can have a strong effect on the implementation of economic policies. Where government economic policies involve such measures as price support and acquisition of specific kinds of capacities for services (storage, transportation, power, and so forth), expenditure of government funds is a natural component of the policy. Attempts at stabilization of the economy and the stimulation of economic growth through government expenditures are common objectives of the fiscal

379

policies of government. Most of the social policies of a government involve a considerable expenditure of government funds.

However, government expenditures are more than direct instruments for carrying out government policies; they are a measure of the implementation of other, less direct economic and social policies. Not only will the scope and extent of government expenditures influence the general economic climate of the country, but they reflect the degree to which a government can coordinate its efforts to attain its multiple objectives. Obviously, government expenditures on such programs as health, education, and welfare are an indication, although not the sole measure, of its determination to push improvements along those lines. Government expenditures on foreign skilled technicians reflect its evaluation of programs to train local technicians. Government expenditures on imports reflect on its policy to minimize the use of imports. Government procurement policies reflect strongly on its efforts to encourage small businesses or discourage monopolies. The price paid for government supplies is a measure of the implementation of government price policies. For example, where a government is attempting to fix the wholesale and retail markup of manufactured products, government procurement must assure dealers that products sold to the government will meet these directives. By paying higher prices, government may be providing direct or hidden support for domestic industries. Government procurement can by loose favoritism and outright corruption set a tone and standard that is more influential by example than the direct transactions themselves.

Subsidies

Subsidies are government grants of resources to enterprises to encourage or support their activities. Direct subsidies are open grants of government funds; but most subsidies are disguised or hidden and are often disclaimed, even denounced, by government. Direct subsidies are usually easy to identify and measure. They represent conscious, although not always willing, actions on the part of the government. Thus, when the budget allocates funds for establishing a public corporation, the initial allocation of funds may be considered a subsidy to the corporation. But when a public corporation, through business losses needs replenishment of its working capital, the funds allocated by the government can be considered in effect a subsidy, even though some governments carry them on their books as loans. Direct subsidies are usually associated with products or services that have a high component of public interest, since the subsidy must often be defended publicly. That is one reason why hidden subsidies, discussed below, are often substituted for direct, open subsidies.

Hidden subsidies are as varied as the ingenious mind of man can devise, largely because of a desire to prevent recognition as a subsidy.

Government can in effect provide a subsidy to an enterprise by paying a higher price than the market warrants for its procurement. In this way, it is transferring government funds as a grant to the recipient enterprise for products or services that it considers desirable, even though the grant is disguised as a market transaction. The borderline between grants of government funds and lower costs is so difficult to draw that it often disappears under actual operating conditions. Thus a government, to encourage the establishment of a specific type of enterprise, may provide a location in an industrial estate at a very low price. This, in effect, is a disguised subsidy, a grant equal to the difference between the price the government charges and what that location would be worth on the open market. Similarly, when the government makes development loans at concessional rates, it is in a sense providing a disguised subsidy in order to encourage development. It is clear that hidden subsidies of government funds are a widely used, well accepted instrument of implementing economic policies, even though the hidden nature of this instrument may lead to its abuse. Hidden subsidies of government funds are powerful instruments of policy implementation, difficult to identify and even more difficult to evaluate.

Even more difficult to identify and evaluate is an extension of the hidden subsidies into the area of nongovernment resources. Through implementing an economic policy, the government may often provide for a transfer of private resources to a recipient, without the knowledge of the owner of the resources. Thus, when the government guarantees to a domestic producer that his market will be protected against competition from imports, even though his product is higher priced, a hidden subsidy may be involved. The government has arranged, in effect, a grant from the buyers of the product equal to the difference between the domestic market price and the previous imported price. Price support subsidies may be direct or hidden. When the government provides import permits and the related foreign exchange at the low, official exchange rate, a disguised government practice that enables an enterprise to buy its imports at less than the market price or sell its products at more than the market price involves a hidden subsidy.

This should make it clear that the concept of a subsidy, direct or hidden, cannot be automatically considered as undesirable or as a weakness of the system. All economic subsystems involve numerous varieties of direct and disguised subsidies. Their desirability or undesirability must be measured by their economic impact, the comparison of their costs and benefits. Many useful, even essential objectives necessarily involve governmental subsidies, direct or hidden. For example, where education is carried out by both publicly financed and privately financed schools, the publicly financed schools could be considered as receiving a subsidy from the government. When educational institutions are exempt from property and income taxes, they are in a sense receiving disguised government subsidies. Where economic enterprises are concerned, economists tend to favor direct, open subsidies so that the play of market forces can be more easily interpreted by the suppliers and sellers. Hidden subsidies tend to disguise relative scarcities and make efficient responses to market signals more difficult.

Many public administrators are involved, consciously or unconsciously, in the provision of these direct and hidden subsidies. The enforcement of the government's rules that make the subsidy a real gain to the enterprise is often a major function of officers at all levels of government, from the national to the most distant local office. Subsidies, direct or hidden, are so sought after that they tend to involve the worst aspects of favoritism and corruption in administration. The hidden, implicit value of the subsidy appears only as the opportunity for enlarged profits at apparently no cost to government, which is clearly a deceptive way of evaluating subsidies. Wherever subsidies increase the cost of providing goods or services, they must be evaluated to determine their desirability. Spreading the increased cost over a large number of buyers does not reduce the cost; it merely makes it more difficult to measure and less likely to arouse protests. While the evaluation of the desirability of certain subsidies may go far beyond economic matters, the economic aspects cannot be neglected. As a country becomes more sophisticated in its market structure, its financing and its administration, the role of direct and hidden subsidies in implementing economic policies probably increases, and the involvement of government administrators becomes more strategic.

Licenses, Permits and Charters

Licenses, permits, and charters are probably the most ancient instrument of implementing public policy. These consist of conferring permission on a specific person or enterprise to undertake a certain operation, conduct a business or perform a specified task. The exact differences between the three forms of conferring permission is too vague to be of operating significance. Charters are usually more unique and formal documents, specifying purpose and rights in more grandiose terms as in the charter to establish a development bank approved by a parliament. The terms, licenses and permits, are used almost interchangeably with licenses somewhat more formal.* In all three terms, the basic reality is that under various kinds of authority, public administrators issue or sign documents that permit some person or enterprise to undertake some action that is sanctioned by the government. Implicitly or explicitly, there are penalties for those who undertake this action without proper approval.

---

*Here, the term "license" will be used to mean all three types of documents.

Licenses generally have three functions: (1) to limit the number of recipients, (2) to ensure that the recipients meet minimum standards, (3) to collect funds. Licensing decisions are made at all levels of government, from national cabinets which decide on major industrial licenses to local officials who issue permits for petty traders. The number and variety of licenses necessary to carry out economic activities in the underdeveloped countries is large and somewhat alarming— alarming because the issuance of licenses is time-consuming and involves a significant use of administrative capacity. Licenses are likely to tend toward the direct control, the specific control, and the discretionary control. Thus, licenses tend toward absorbing more administrative capacity than would more indirect, general and nondiscretionary controls. Few indeed are the licenses that are issued automatically, merely upon application. Each petitioner for a license must have his document examined, his credibility evaluated, his competence judged, and his timing approved. The need for judgment and the opportunity for delays not only demands a reasonable, flexible system, but provides numerous opportunities for special favors and administrative discretion. The operation of an efficient licensing system for anything other than the most trivial or routine matters (dog licenses, car licenses) is both difficult and infrequent in any country. In the less developed countries, where administrative capacity is so scarce an input, it is almost unique to have licenses issued without a corollary system of tips and outright bribes.

Loans

Loans are far more acceptable than subsidies, although loans at concessional interest rates and overly mild repayment provisions can be considered hidden subsidies. Loans are a preferred instrument of implementing economic policies because they appear businesslike and efficient. All good businesses expect to make and repay loans. Economic development is in the minds of many persons synonomous with building new capital capacities. Loans to acquire new capital are not only generally acceptable, but frequently considered by the public as a sign of progress. Government loans are usually made at less than local market interest rates and terms, with the government often absorbing some of the risk of the enterprise. So common and so useful are loans as an instrument of implementing government economic policies that practically no one objects to this instrument. It is the specific use of the instrument that warrants careful scrutiny; for government loans are often highly profitable, largely monopolistic and vigorously pursued. Even more than licensing, the review of loans is an individual process, no matter how careful the rules and arrangements are stipulated. Loans to business enterprises, whether in the public or private sector, require long examinations and detailed justifications. System loans, such as loans to cooperatives or to housing applicants, may require less detailed examination at national levels, but far more detailed examination at local levels. As in the case of licenses, each loan application requires careful review at some time or other, and, more than licenses, requires continuing observation for repayment and conformity to the loan provisions.

Government guarantee of loans is a mild variant of the loan instrument. It is usually reserved for large loans, primarily for loans made to private enterprises by international agencies. Here, government administrative requirements may be significantly less than direct government loans, but only because the loans are larger and fewer. If government guarantees were given to small loans, there is reason to believe that the involvement of public administrators would assume much larger proportions. Government may wholesale the operation by making large loans or guarantees of loans to specialized banks, which in turn may retail the resources to its ultimate users. This is commonly accepted as good procedure. However, it merely shifts the consideration of individual loans to another bureaucracy, from government staff to bank staff.

Loans are not only a way of transferring government resources, they can be used to implement many other economic policies. Loans to private enterprises may be used to implement a policy that the private sector should be a vigorous part of the economy. Restraints on certain kinds of loans will often limit the extension of private enterprise into kinds of enterprises the government wishes to reserve for public enterprise expansion. Loans to small enterprises may seek to avoid the entrance of large enterprises into a specific sector. Loans may also contain provisions for standards of operation that express economic policies. Thus, loans may not be made to enterprises that do not have adequate provisions for training local nationals for the higher management positions. Loan agreements may specify what rates of profit and depreciation may be repatriated to foreign countries. Because of their widespread use and general acceptance, the management of loans is an area in which public administrators frequently devote much of their time.

Insurance

Insurance is a new type of instrument for implementing economic policies and is therefore infrequently used. Insurance is a method of absorbing the cost of risk, which is an element in almost all economic activities. In small, unspecialized operations, the risk is so deeply embodied in the usual activities of the participants that it generally cannot be identified and evaluated. As production becomes more specialized, risk becomes more clearly identifiable. Entrepreneurial risk is universally recognized, but the identification of special kinds of entrepreneurial risks is one of the corollaries of modern production practices. Risks of production include risks of usual competition for factor inputs and for finding adequate buyers, but they also include risks of fire, theft, and loss through changes in exchange rates, through expropriation, war, and closing of markets. The more an enterprise can identify and pass off to someone else these different kinds of risks, the more likely he is to reduce his costs of operation.

Insurance is a method of spreading risk, so that if the risk eventuates in a loss, the specific burden is reduced or eliminated. By absorbing or spreading the risks, governments reduce costs for enterprises in both the private and public sector. In the public sector, insurance is often implied rather than specifically identified. A public enterprise engaging in foreign trade may not need separate insurance against expropriation of its shipments or reduction in the value of the foreign exchange it earns. Its position as a government agency based on government resources may make it a self-insurer without much need for greater risk spreading.

Government insurance at concessional rates may be a way of disguising a subsidy. Thus, to encourage exports and reduce the costs of doing export business, governments may provide insurance on shipments to foreign customers at less than commercial rates. If losses to the government result, they are made up discretely by additional transfers from the government budget. Insurance against fluctuation in foreign exchange rates can be provided by a system that permits exporters to claim local currency at the rate approved at the time of sale or of shipment, regardless of the market rate at time of settlement.

Thus, insurance by government is not always in the form of an insurance document; it may be the spreading of risk or assumption of usual commercial risk by the government through its process of controlling resources and market transactions. Insurance as a means of implementing economic policies will increase in usefulness as the economic system becomes more complex. Risk is an inherent part of production for the market. Just as control of entrance to the market affects the scope of competition, so insurance is a way of consciously spreading risk and making its cost more easily appraised and absorbed.

Taxes

Taxes are a favorite instrument for the implementation of economic policies. Not only do taxes raise revenue to permit expenditures for economic objectives, but differential taxes discourage or encourage all types of expenditures in the private sector and can affect income distribution. Taxes are difficult instruments to use because they have numerous effects on different elements in the economy. A tax to raise funds may tax poor people too heavily. A tax to discourage certain investments may result in unemployment for some people. A tax holiday to encourage investment may reduce essential revenues. A tax on luxuries may induce illegal production. The incidence of taxes are rarely simple and the nee for government revenue may often outweigh considerations of equity.

Taxes, no matter how their basic laws are written, become apparen to the public in the actions of the public administrator. No country has ever succeeded in developing even a simple tax that is automatic, divorced from the involvement of the officials who administer the tax. Practically all taxes are painful from the outset, since they involve a transfer of resources from someone to the government. At best, they are considered neutral, if they can be passed on to someone else without loss or without too much effort. Hence, the role of the public administrator is particularly important in the use of this instrument to implemen economic policies. In the administration of taxes lies the clearest example that public administration is contextual; its administration depends to a large extent on local conditions, institutions, relationships and value systems. To transfer tax policies from developed to underdeveloped countries without serious adjustments is bound to be harmful How a tax is administered is as important as why it is levied and often determines its direct economic impact on costs, prices and market trans actions.

Direct Regulation of Business Practices

Government regulation of business practices is a widely used instr ment for implementing economic policies. Practically no sector of the economy is free of laws and regulations that prescribe what must or mus not be done while undertaking production and distribution of goods and services. Indeed, it is difficult to distinguish between direct regulatio and those regulations which involve licenses or taxes. However, there are many broad regulations that have a surprisingly important impact on the efficiency of economic transactions. An example is the provision fo standard weights and measures, so that transactions can be readily understandable and consistent. This seems like a simple matter, yet the establishment and enforcement of standard weights and measures is a troublesome administrative matter in many areas of the world, particularly in rural areas where local officials are involved. General regulations about price fixing, price margins for wholesale and retail markups regulations about showing prices and ingredients of products, pure food and sanitation laws—all are examples of government regulation of business practices that have significant impact on a wide range of economic activities. Laws and the administration of the laws defining rules for land ownership, land use and the rights of tenants are important. Policies for the operation of agricultural cooperatives and the credit they receive and give will often determine how the proceeds of improved tech nology will be distributed among the large farm owners, the small farmers, and the landless laborers. Policies that initiate rural works programs and their method of selecting projects and the workers employed on these projects will be an important element in determining income distribution, particularly the ability to reach the lowest levels of income recipients.

It is an obvious truism that regulations require administration and sanctions for those that violate the regulations. Too many countries are prone to adopt highly advanced regulations, modeled after the most advanced thinking, without regard to the problems of enforcement and administrative requirements. Thus, minimum wage laws, factory laws, pure food laws, standard interest rates and laws for regulating the collection of debts are often more expressions of social purposes than of regulation of business practices. Regulations that require permits or licenses, such as certificates of sanitation for restaurants or licenses for electricians, are often so impossible to administer that they lose credibility very rapidly and, as issued, are merely the basis for widely accepted gifts to the issuing officials. In no other instrument of implementing economic policies is it so important to assess the feasibility of ascertaining the necessary administrative capacity before it is used. In no other instrument does the work of enforcement and sanction reach so many of the lower levels of administration. Public administration is the essence of successful operation of this instrument, and public administration is a scarce input and must be allocated as carefully as any other scarce input in the production process.

Codes of performance are one of the general ways of attempting the regulation of business practice. The government may promulgate such a code, or may encourage voluntary adoption of a code by the participants of the industry. Examples of government-adopted instruments are zoning codes, which establish some of the rules under which construction can be carried out. Usually these include requirements for permits and inspection of plans. The code may cover a single industry or a separate function of many industries. Sanitation codes for restaurants may be voluntary or, more likely, government issued. Fair trade practices may be adopted by an industry with the support of government. Many times the codes may be unwritten, understood generally and enforced by voluntary acceptance. Thus, there may be an unwritten code governing the allocation of market sites and the enforcement of zones of trade. Competition may be severely limited by customary codes voluntarily accepted by participants in the trade and only incidentally enforced by government officials. Where codes have been developed to preserve the status quo in maintaining the existing structure of economic functions, the code may be quite harmful to the general effort to improve productivity and income distribution. Government officials often unconsciously are part of the enforcement of customary codes that tend to preserve inefficiencies and prevent improved income distribution.

General Climate for Economic Enterprises

The selection and use of instruments to implement economic policies inevitably brings with it a general climate within which all economic enterprises, public and private, must operate. It would be difficult to exaggerate the need for considering this general climate, so important is it and so directly is it related to the adequacy of public administration. The right climate will stimulate enterprise, encourage capital formation and new technology; and the wrong climate will do just the opposite. A general feeling that the government will arbitrarily seize and punish any enterprise it feels is endangering public interests, loosely defined, will do more to destroy the adoption of new technology than any instrument the government can adopt to encourage necessary changes. The general climate for economic enterprise is not set by a pronouncement of grand objectives and good intentions. It is set, by and large, by the totality of a government's actions toward economic enterprises in both the public and private sector. All of the previously discussed instruments enter into the general calculation of the climate for economic enterprises and a loose balancing and net accounting is made by the operators of the enterprises. This evaluation will vary from group to group, from class to class and from industry to industry. Large industries may net the evaluation one way while small enterprises may reach the opposite conclusion. It is not unusual to have a different evaluation for a single enterprise and for its total sector. So intangible is the general climate for enterprise that governments may find it impossible to shape it directly, but must depend on the evaluation of its numerous ways of implementation of economic and general policies. For the general climate of economic enterprises is determined, not just by economic policies and their implementation, but by many noneconomic policies, particularly the changing value systems and political developments that are so important a part of a developing country.

Four generalizations may be given to accept how governments affect the general climate for economic enterprises:

1. Basic economic policies have an important, underlying effect on the climate in which economic enterprises operate, in addition to any direct economic impacts. Thus, monetary policies, such as interest rates and availability of credit, may have important indirect impact on the confidence of entrepreneurs in making investment decisions. Projections of future income returns is the basis of capital formation and discounting the uncertainties of future production and sales is the essence of entrepreneurial decisions. Government's monetary policy is always an important element in evaluating the future of the economy.

2. Investigation and publicity are commonly used tools of enforcement of government policies. By providing favorable or unfavorable publicity, government can often implement economic policies directly and indirectly. Appeals to patriotism and nationalism are quite common, but their use is often to preserve inefficiencies rather than to improve the general business climate. Moral suasion is important, but is so often used on trivial matters that it is suspect as an effective continuing element in policy implementation.

3. The demonstration effect of effective leadership and efficient administration cannot be overlooked as a basic element in establishing a general climate favorable for economic enterprises. Unfortunately, while few would deny its obvious importance and relevance, even fewer would confirm its actual use. A climate of efficiency in public administration, demonstrated to the public by prompt and adequate implementation of economic policies, is a condition sought after but not attained by most countries.

4. The instruments used to implement economic policies affect and are affected by the economic forces operating in economic enterprises. The impact on production and productivity is determined to a large extent by how the selected instruments affect entrance into production, factor markets, product markets, technology, and financial markets. The efforts of economic enterprises to minimize costs and maximize returns, to achieve the multiple, often contradictory, objectives that all organizations necessarily have, are affected by the instruments selected to implement economic policies and how well these instruments are used. The acceptable mix of the objectives of an enterprise is often determined by government policies operating in conjunction with its own objectives. Public administrators must select the instruments that fit best into achieving an acceptable mix of public and private enterprise objectives. It should be clear, moreover, that the effectiveness of the public administration input is likely to be an important part of the effectiveness of the economic policy.

Some economic policies necessarily include the instruments that must be used to implement them, while others permit some choice of instruments. Thus, the fiscal policies focused on raising large sums of money for public investment necessarily mean using taxes primarily as an instrument, although the kind of taxes and the method of administering taxes may offer some options. Other economic policies, however, such as the policy to help small enterprises, or to increase employment, require several instruments in their implementation. The interrelationship of the instruments for implementing economic policies and, indeed, the complex nature of most economic policies, often means that these instruments will be used in a contradictory fashion. Government loans may stimulate enterprises that are being constrained by certain government rules. Permits may be denied to enterprises that have been approved for government loans. Sometimes these contradictions represent lack of coordination, but often they are the result of having to choose between different objectives. The efforts to expand production may lead to issuing permits for construction where the shortage in foreign exchange may lead to rejecting the application for import licenses of some necessary equipment for the expansion. Coordination of government control activities is clearly an essential part of the selection of the instruments for implementing economic policies.

CHARACTERISTICS OF GOVERNMENT CONTROL

Basis of Classification

The fact that public administration is a scarce input must be related to the way this scarce input is allocated and used. The usual assumption that the scarcity of this input is recognized and its use minimized is of dubious validity. No doubt most governments recognize the importance of this problem because they are constantly confronted with its painful effects. The steady appearance of short-falls in performance, the constant reiteration by international agencies and bilateral foreign aid programs of the need for improved administrative performance, the continual confrontation of different effects of poverty and low efficiency in production—all of these situations combine to ensure that governments are aware of the basic inadequacy of public administration and that not enough is being done to overcome it. It may be impossible to measure in unambiguous terms whether this inadequacy is growing or decreasing, but it is clear that much more must be done to improve performance.

It is sometimes considered useful to distinguish between "long-range" and "operational" direction by government. This distinction is difficult to identify. Long-range direction usually refers to basic government influences that slowly determine the characteristics, form or objectives of the economic institutions. These may be exemplified by the influence provided by inheritance laws, copyright and patent laws, and property laws for the religious institutions or for the extended family. These long-range directions are important and influential because they provide a framework within which economic activities are undertaken and they may affect operating decisions slowly and undramatically, but still in important ways. Operational direction and controls, as usually contrasted with long-range direction, are considered more immediate in their influence; they are visibly effective in the short run or some intermediate time period rather than slowly over the long run. But the distinction is of doubtful validity. Some specific government direction may be effective in both the short and the long run, and the distinction loses its analytical usefulness. For example, a change in the land tenure system, vigorously administered, may have both long- and short-run consequences to economic institutions such as corporations, land banks, large farmers, small farmers, and fertilizer factories. The production effect may be different in the short run and in the long run, and it may be important to keep this in mind. But government controls cannot be classified into long-range and short-range categories. The concept of government exercising operational control must therefore necessarily include both short-run and long-range changes and effects.

It has proven impossible to provide measures of public administration input, that can be compared directly with output, so as to minimize costs and maximize returns. Both costs and outputs are measured ambiguously, or are nonmeasurable in the sense of quantification used in the usual productivity measures. It may be possible, however, to examine the operational role of government and to characterize certain ways of direction and control as more efficient or less efficient in their use of the scarce public administration input.

For this purpose, it may be useful to take a single, easily recognized and important operating characteristic of government controls, and to consider it a "continuum,"* a graduation or progression of degree of intensity. By judging how this continuum is related to more or less use of administrative capacity it may be possible to propose some useful working rules for the more efficient use of public administration inputs.

The technique of a continuum showing some important characteristics of government controls is suggested for the following characteristics:

1. Direct or Indirect Controls
2. Discretionary and Nondiscretionary Controls
3. Specific and General Controls
4. Positive and Negative Controls

These characteristics of government controls are abstracted from the classification suggested by White and by Dahl and Lindblom. They are simplified, hopefully not oversimplified, to focus on features that can be recognized fairly easily, rather than on basic psychological relationships that are probably more accurate but far more subtle and therefore difficult to define and examine. They are not related to either degree of coercion or degree of effectiveness since these almost entirely depend on the specific situation for which the control is designed.

Direct and Indirect Controls

Probably the most useful way to characterize government direction of economic institutions is to assess the degree to which government is directly involved in operating these institutions. Direct involvement refers to participation at the management level in specific operation decisions.† Indirect controls refer to involvement that changes the environment in which the institution operates, with these changes affecting

---

*The continuum is an analytical device that is useful in illustrating the various intensities of a variable or characteristic, especially those that cannot be meaningfully quantified with common units, and as value, weight, and size. See Dahl and Lindblom, op. cit., p. 14.

†Sometimes the term "physical control" is used to mean substantially the same as direct control, as used here. The former term is

the operating decisions of the institution. An economic enterprise utilizes scarce factor inputs to produce the goods that are its production objectives. The operating decisions that the management of the institution makes can be divided into two types, at least in theory. These direct operational decisions encompass the decisions to hire certain people, to produce a certain mix of products, to set prices for the product, to make an investment in a new plant or to buy some new machinery. The environment within which the institution operates refers to such aspects as the prices and availability of transportation and communication interest rates, availability of money to be borrowed, intensity of competition, and the existence and type of marketing institutions.

While direct and indirect control may be separated conceptually, in reality most situations are mixtures that have elements of both. Thus a government tax may be so important and specific that it has the nature of a direct operating control. A government decision to have all fertilizer distributed by cooperatives, as in some of the states of India, is both direct and indirect control of many different economic institutions, such as cooperatives, fertilizer factories, banks, and the government agency importing fertilizer. Sometimes it is even impossible to assess relative importance of the direct and indirect involvement, with only the two extremes of the continuum distinguishable.

At the one extreme, complete direct government participation at an operating level, would be government-owned and -operated institutions, including government banks, government railroads or factories, and power plants. Obviously, in these cases government officials make all management decisions. But even here it is useful to recognize that government-owned and -operated institutions also operate within a framework, as do privately owned and operated institutions. This framework is affected by government controls for both government and private institutions. It is often asserted that certain kinds of government institutions should be permitted to operate "autonomously," by which is meant that these institutions should have no important, direct controls from government other than the usual influences and pressures generated by government for privately owned enterprises.

Examples of more or less direct and indirect controls are readily available. Direct controls include granting tax holidays to new factories, granting a loan at concessional rates to a specific institution, fixing the price of a specific product, the allocation to specific firms of scarce materials, import licensing of specific products for specific companies, and denying a certificate of essentiality to an entrepreneur

---

derived from the actual allocation of physical material to specific plants which is clearly direct control. Not that this definition is substantially different than that used by Dahl and Lindblom, discussed in the previous section. This confusion is regrettable but coining new language here would be even more confusing.

who wants to start a business. Examples of indirect controls include
establishing minimum wage rates for general categories of workers, setting interest rates for loans, instituting import and export taxes for
broad categories of commodities, and determining prices for such government supplied services as transportation and communication. Clearly,
the intent is to separate decisions within the institution and the environment within which the institution makes its operating decisions. Yet,
setting interest rates is internal "price fixing" and a direct operating
decision for a bank, while it is external and part of the environment for
businesses attempting to borrow from the bank. Similarly, setting railroad rates is direct control for the railroads, even though it may be
"indirect" for the users of railroad services.

The assumption is usually made that direct controls require more
specific information and more decisions than do indirect controls. The
obvious difficulties of conceptualization and measurement make this
impossible to be empirically verified, but experience seems to support
the generalization. Some illustrations may make this assertion more
real. An official of a production unit must know a great deal more about
the technology of that enterprise, the kinds of factor inputs it uses, the
actual and potential market for its product, and the options of its product mix, than does an outsider who does not have to make direct production decisions. The outsider may need information to assess the
possible results of changing interest rates or of raising taxes, but he
must rely to a large extent on the management inside the organization
to make the production decisions within the structure of costs and
benefits relating the enterprise to its environment. Indirect controls
can and usually do affect many enterprises at the same time. In this
sense, they may require fewer decisions per product produced.

Discretionary and Nondiscretionary Controls

One of the most important characteristics of government control is
the degree to which government officers are given discretion in application clearance. Does it have to be applied to everybody and at all
times? Can some people or institutions be omitted in the application
and can its usage vary in intensity? Again, this characteristic can be
considered as stretching along a continuum, an infinite gradation from
one extreme to the other. At one end of the continuum would be government control that applied to everybody, without exception, and is applied automatically and with equal intensity. At this extreme, application is automatic without any possibility of discrimination or selection. At the other extreme of the continuum would be those government
controls that are entirely at the discretion of the administrator, with
each application a separate decision based entirely on the judgment of
the government officers, and with no review of the decision. It would

393

be hard in real life to find illustrations of the perfect extremes, completely discretionary or completely automatic and nondiscretionary. Even the most rigid and explicit rule or control of government leaves some room for interpretation and exception. Even the most generally defined control has some limitation and review, however broad, in its application. Thus, every government control has both discretionary and nondiscretionary characteristics; it is the degree of discretionary application that is important and this is usually observable.

Illustrations of an extremely nondiscretionary type of control would be an excise tax, where, for example, a specific tax is placed on every package of 10 cigarettes produced regardless of who produces them or the market for which they are produced. There can be no question of a decision by an administrator to permit some production without taxes. Each such decision to omit the tax would be clearly illegal and therefore would be beyond this area of discourse.* As soon as the rule is relaxed to permit, for example, production for export or for military use without the tax, an element of discretion arises, since some production may not be clearly in those categories. At the other end of the continuum, an example of almost completely discretionary control is the issuance of a certificate of personal worthiness by a government official of an application for some government service. Even here, the discretion of the official must be fitted into whatever criteria of worthiness are established by custom if not by government regulation. It is difficult to imagine any kind of control that is completely discretionary, although from the viewpoint of the petitioner this often seems to be the case.

The importance of some degree of discretion in governmental control of economic institutions must be evident. First, it is useful to the administrator because it permits flexibility: no one establishing the criteria for the application of the control, whether it is a legislature, a cabinet member, a board, a commission, or a department, can visualize all of the operating situations faced by an administrator. Decisions have to be made, frequently based on situations or assumptions that were not considered when the directives were formulated. Consequently, the managers must be given some flexibility in the application of rules of behavior and decision making. This flexibility is often implied, rather than expressed in a detailed manner, and it is given the form of administrative discretion. Its necessity cannot be questioned, and its existence can be easily verified by even casual observation.

Yet the necessity for flexibility in application of controls brings with it two inevitable corollaries. First, there is the need for more operating information with which to make judgments about specific appli-

_____

*Administrators, like anyone else in the society, have the option of breaking the rule and becoming illegal. The discussion here must be limited to legal action.

cations, the excuse or reason for the discretion. Second, there is the increased possibility, indeed, the almost certainty, of some form of improperly influenced decision, thus corruption. The first corollary clearly involves more use of administrative capacity at the government level. The second corollary means a less efficient use of administrative inputs. The extent of discretion that administrators have in applying controls is therefore one of the characteristics of control that can be usefully examined.

The increased opportunity for corruption when discretionary controls are applied needs little empirical verification. This, of course, is not a phenomenon limited to the less developed countries. Governments have found that even in times of crisis, when the overwhelming importance of unselfish, honest administration is clearly evident, there are some officers who yield to cupidity, lesser loyalties, or to ill-advised pressures. The result is costly to the country in terms of the wasted production and administrative capacity. For the assumption can be made that corruption involves misuse of scarce resources in financial and product terms as well as in terms of administrative capacity.

Specific and General Controls

Specific and general government controls are related quite strongly to the degree of direct or indirect control, yet they are sufficiently different and important to warrant additional explanation. Some government controls are very specific, such as detailed orders about individual import licenses for specific goods from a given country. By comparison, an import license for a broad category of a commodity is more general. A general tax on the production of a class of products would be completely general. A specific import license can be issued for the importation of penicillin; a more general license can be issued, in the same product field, for antibiotics; and more generally, an import license can be issued for medicine and drugs as a broad product sector. In these illustrations, the operating aspect that is being emphasized is the extent to which specificity in government controls involves the use of scarce administrative capacity. The government decision to allocate resources to the broader category of medicine and drugs requires the individual importer to decide which specific drug to import. For him to achieve the same degree of success in ordering the import of the right kind and quantity of drugs, the information required and the end decisions would probably be the same. But as the government directive becomes more specific, more detailed information is clearly needed by government officials rather than at the importers' level.

Here, too, the existence of government-owned and -operated institutions must not be permitted to cloud this useful generalization. For purposes of this analysis, the government production unit is in the same position as the privately owned plant or factory. Government controls

395

may be specifically aimed at the government plant or may cover the government plant as well as all similar private plants. Thus, if there are both public and private fertilizer plants in operation, the provision for credit to the purchasers of fertilizer may be a general type of control for all fertilizer plants. The setting of a definite price for a specific type of fertilizer may be a specific control for both types of plants while the provision of a government loan at a convenient rate of interest to a government plant may be a specific government control that affects a single government plant only. The generalization that specific government controls utilize more government administrative capacity than do more general controls refers to agencies of government external to the production unit concerned. It is a useful generalization, regardless of whether the operating institution is in the public or private sectors.

Positive and Negative Controls

Some analysts, notably Gunnar Myrdal,[3] distinguish between positive and negative government controls. Positive controls are those that stimulate, persuade, encourage, or induce people or institutions to behave so as to achieve a desirable economic objective; the government control works by providing something. Negative controls limit or prevent something from happening; control is exercised by denying authority or prohibiting someone or some institution from using the necessary resources. Thus, a negative control occurs when the government prohibits the use of foreign exchange from importing certain luxury goods or when an entrepreneur is denied a license to expand his factory. A positive government control occurs when government grants a tax holiday for a new factory or issues an import license for copper wire to a firm that is making electric motors. Educational campaigns to encourage increased savings, the granting of subsidies to exporters, and providing credit on concessional terms are examples of positive government controls.

The tendency to categorize government control as positive and negative is in a sense a carryover from individual psychology, where positive or negative reactions can usually be classified with some meaning. However, when applied to governmental direction of the institutions responsible for the production and distribution of goods and services, the classification is strained and not very helpful analytically. A government control is usually both positive and negative at the same time. A decision to prohibit the importation of electric motors is a negative control for the enterprises that wish to import motors, but it is a positive control in that it stimulates domestic production of electric motors. It may give monopoly control through protected market and thus encourage the production of many more motors at a high cost.

Evaluation of Methods of Government Controls

Cost of Control

There are many ways to measure the cost of a control or of a particular control system. The most obvious one is the monetary cost, the cost of paying the salaries and necessary facilities of the government officials and agencies involved. While this kind of analysis has usefulness, particularly as far as budgetary operations and control of the government is concerned, it has very limited usefulness as part of this analysis of governmental control. Obviously the monetary cost of a control is important because the monetary cost may be excessive relative to available resources or other uses to which the money could be placed. Monetary costs of a control are usually very difficult to determine, since the process involves many joint costs spread over many controls and related operations. The direct monetary costs of control may be less important than the monetary opportunity costs, the monetary costs of the best alternative use of the administrative funds. Thus, though monetary costs are important, they fail to emphasize the most important aspects of the cost of government control.

The concept of cost is of course related to optimum use of scarce resources. Monetary costs are only one way of assessing relative scarcity of the factor inputs. Another and probably better way is to assess the alternative use that might be made of administrative capacity. While administrative capacity may be even more difficult to assess than monetary costs of administration, it has the advantage that it is possible to judge without a detailed monetary cost analysis, whether one option will use more or less administrative capacity than another option. Another useful concept is to think of administrative capacity in two levels, a higher level involving extensive training and significant decision making and a lower level involving largely routine and clerical work. These can be defined differently in each country, and even in each ministry. However, some meaningful communication occurs when a distinction is made between "high level" administrative capacity and "low level" administrative capacity, even if the dividing line is quite vague. In most developing countries, while there may be a relative shortage of both high and low level administrative capacity, the most critical shortage is at the higher level, where capacity expands most slowly and never seems to keep up with requirements. Lower level administrative capacity can be expanded more quickly, although even here, if this is done too rapidly, efficiency also seems to fall rapidly. In any case, the cost of a government control can be usefully evaluated in terms of its requirement for higher or lower level administrative capacity.

Effectiveness

The effectiveness of a government control is even more difficult to measure than its cost. Effectiveness must be measured in terms of attainment of objectives. A control used by government to attain a certain economic objective is effective to the degree that this objective is attained. But this can be a simplistic approach, ignoring all kinds of important complexities. Rarely are economic organizations geared to only one objective, and rarely do significant controls affect only one objective. It is often necessary to identify a whole pattern of important objectives, with the attendant difficulties of ranking them by importance. Objectives that seem quite important are often only instrumental objectives, a means of securing still more important and more ultimate objectives. An economic institution, such as a banking system, a cooperative system, an insurance market system, or a fertilizer production system, can have many objectives at the same time, all legitimate, worthwhile and even essential. An agricultural cooperative may be needed to stimulate the use of better seeds, to distribute fertilizer, to supply credit, to encourage savings and capital formation, to provide local participation and a local political framework, to reduce or eliminate a monopoly in fertilizer distribution, to lower prices of fertilizer, to strengthen the cooperative movement, and to provide administrative jobs for deserving people. Clearly some of these are more important than others, but at any one time, and under a particular set of circumstances, the priority assigned to these will vary considerably even if the same person assesses the priority. The priority will often be a function of the role of the person establishing the priority, his personal position, time horizon, and his vested interests.

In addition to affecting many different objectives, with different time horizons and to different degrees, controls also have side effects, both expected and unexpected. Thus, a wage policy that keeps workers' monetary wages constant, may have the objective of holding down consumption and increasing savings. The government control may be a system that orders all increases in wages be approved by a government official with general instructions to permit increases only as the cost of living goes up. The control system may be effective in its objective of holding down consumption. It may also encourage exports and increase capital formation because it increases profits from which so much of private savings is taken. The policy and its application may also increase unionization and stimulate agitation for government changes, which clearly may not be part of the objective of the wage policy. It may also so limit the size of the domestic market that production will be less than it would have been if more income had been distributed to the general consumers. There may be other side effects, such as capital flight and consumption. Measured narrowly against limited, mechanical objectives, evaluation of the effectiveness of government control may be illusory and misleading. The often caricatured statement of medical practitioners, "The treatment was successful, but the patient died," aptly expresses the difficulty of measuring effectiveness against too narrow a criterion of success.

Difficult as it is to do, the only rational criterion for evaluating the effectiveness of a control is to assess the degree of achievement against all its important implied and expressed objectives, together with an evaluation of the side effects of its application. Time will often be an important consideration, as when controls are supposed to have immediate rather than long-term effects. Comparing the effectiveness of the alternative systems of control often involves assumptions as to honesty, hard work, and degree of interest that are even more difficult to appraise than they are to conceptualize. Yet they often become the most essential element of the appraisal of effectiveness. For example, many efforts at control involve the objective of being fair to all contenders, as in the renewing of applications for a limited quantity of foreign exchange. Here fair refers not only to nondiscrimination, but also treating each person with justice, so that each receives his legitimate portion, with legitimate measured in terms of moral and ethical rights. The concept of being fair to all often involves direct rationing, where the assumption is made that information will be sufficient to permit the rationing decisions to be more equitable than any alternative distribution method. The usual distribution method is some form of market mechanism involving some degree of competition between claimants, so that the transactions become a means of deciding who will receive the scarce item. In a sense, using the market mechanism in this way is "rationing by price," when price is the only criteria used for distribution. But constraints often temper the market mechanism, and effectiveness of any type of administrative method of control must be measured against a pattern of objectives, and not just against one.

The degree or effectiveness of government control will vary greatly from time to time and from situation to situation. At one time, a specific government policy may have a strong impact on production, influencing it to move in a particular direction. At another time, the same policy may have no effect at all, or may even influence the industry to operate in a totally different direction. This variation in effect is largely the result of the numerous forces that influence economic decisions. For example, at one time a government policy to support wheat prices at a given price may be quite effective in encouraging production. Under different supply and demand situations the following year, the identical government policy may be completely ineffective and may even have contrary effects on production decisions. These variations in timing and effectiveness make analysis difficult. In no way do they detract from the obvious reality that government policies and practices are strongly influential, even critical, in the decisions important for production and distribution of economic goods.

Using these two concepts, cost and effectiveness, it is possible to assess some of the characteristics of government controls.

Evaluation of Direct and Indirect Controls

Direct controls tend to be costly controls at both high and lower level administrative capacity. Direct controls usually involve detailed operating information and detailed operating decisions. The officials who issue import licenses must examine the data submitted by each firm. They must form judgments on past history of the imports of the firm, the potential use of the license and the effect of granting or not granting the license and the effect of granting it. Lower level administrative capacity is utilized to handle and classify the large flow of papers, to code, accumulate, and keep records of the results and to compare them with previous results. By contrast, a more indirect method to attempt to achieve the same result would be to determine the total amount of foreign exchange that would be available for a particular class or group of imports and then to auction and import licenses off to the highest bidder. Leaving aside the question of effectiveness of the two methods, the indirect method would usually require less administrative capacity, both at the higher and lower levels, than would direct control.

While it is reasonable to assert that direct controls tend to be more costly than indirect controls, the judgment about effectiveness is much less apparent. Indirect controls often have many side effects. They raise so many new questions, often unanswerable, that direct controls seem to be necessary by the very nature of the unanswerable questions. For example, auctioning off foreign exchange in accordance with different priorities seems simple enough and clearly less demanding of administrative capacity than direct approval of each import license. But how can the following questions be answered? Will auctioning of foreign exchange choke off new entrants, thus creating or supporting a monopoly by the existing firms? Will the larger, richer firms be able to drive out the smaller firms, thus tending to create a monopoly and also creating losses of business and employment in the smaller firms? Will the imports tend to concentrate in certain geographic areas, or among certain ethnic or social groups, to the detriment of presently disadvantaged areas and groups?

These and similar questions of the effect of indirect controls seem more difficult to appraise than similar questions about direct controls. They often lead to the conclusion that only by direct controls can government not only restrict the use of foreign exchange to the priorities it assigns, but also avoid creating or enlarging socially difficult problems of concern to government. To disregard these questions would be impossible. Direct controls seem less prone to unfortunate side effects than are indirect controls.

There is one additional feature of direct controls that should be mentioned. Direct controls seem to be a favorite among colonial powers. In their calm assumption that they obviously knew best what was needed by a colony, colonial administrators would almost automatically use direct control methods. Law and order and tax collection, which were

400

their major areas of concern, clearly lent themselves more easily to direct methods of control than do modern economic systems. To the extent that significant economic institutions needed control, it was done by owning and operating such institutions as railroads or banks, and by specifically excluding competition from foreign nationals. Entrepreneurs from the metropolitan country were to be encouraged and left to their own ingenuity to exploit the advantages of having a colony. This was of course the basic economic purpose of having a colony. Many of the public administrators of the developing countries were trained in this administrative philosophy. Many of the concepts and procedures left as a heritage by the colonial forces were in the direction of using direct controls, as compared with the less reliable, more illusive indirect controls.

The apparent ease with which important side effects are taken into consideration in direct controls seems to lead inevitably to the conclusion that though they may be more costly, direct controls are more effective. The problems of concentration and fairness, and of geographic and ethnic location, are too important politically and socially to be ignored or resisted. Coupled with the heritage from the more simple colonial days, this feature tends to push public administrators in the direction of direct rather than indirect controls in economic institutions. This belief, that direct controls are more effective than indirect controls, more fair and less likely to breed politically unpalatable results, seems to be part of the psychology of public administrators in the developing countries.

Coupled with this preference for direct controls is a suspicion, sometimes even a fear, of market mechanisms as a means of allocating decisions. Whether organized as separate special institutions or as parts of economic institutions having marketing functions, market mechanisms assume that significant decisions are made at the locus and time of the transaction. Buyers and sellers make decisions about the transaction that attempt to manage costs and returns so that they adjust to market conditions. If public administrators distrust this mechanism and can substitute their own decisions for the decisions achieved through a market mechanism, they will tend to rely more on direct controls which they will feel are more effective in achieving worthwhile objectives. The colonial heritage of associating the market mechanism with capitalistic exploitation and colonial imperialism adds to the tendency toward using direct controls.

Yet it would be a mistake to assume that this assumption of higher efficiency of direct controls is usually valid. The evaluation of effectiveness cannot be separated from the fact that direct controls involve more administrative capacity. The observable facts seem to be that direct controls are often so costly and so ineffective that they represent one of the major bottlenecks in achieving higher production and productivity. They can fail to achieve their expressed objectives and they may prohibit better adjustments to supplementary objectives and side effects.

Their capacity to meet the problems of concentration, fairness, and location is more apparent than real. By apparently concentrating on meeting the broader, supplementary problems, direct controls often sacrifice achievement of the prime objectives of the economic institution, the efficient production of goods and services.

In summary, direct controls, as they are used in most of the developing countries, seem to be more costly and less effective than indirect controls. In some cases, obviously, this is not true. There may be no good substitute for a direct control, and the administrative capacity assigned to it may be adequate to do an effective job. More typically, direct controls are only marginally effective in meeting the complex side effects inherent in such controls. Furthermore, they absorb an astonishing amount of administrative capacity, both at the higher and lower levels of administration.

Evaluation of Discretionary and Nondiscretionary Controls

Discretionary controls are usually more costly in terms of administrative capacity than nondiscretionary controls. Not only is more operating information required to make competent discretionary decisions, but the number of such decisions that must be made by government is tremendously increased. Similarly, the level of decision making moves higher with increasing amounts of discretionary control. That is, the utilized administrative capacity tends to be at higher levels if discretionary controls are used in place of nondiscretionary controls. An illustration of this tendency would be the situation of granting tax holidays for new industries. The completely discretionary method of control would be to allow all would-be entrepreneurs to apply and have each application examined. Those that meet criteria of essentiality, location, financial backing, and experience would be approved for receiving tax holidays. The opposite philosophy of control, a total nondiscretionary system, would publish the kinds of products for which specified tax holidays would be given priority locations and minimum requirements in financial backing and experience for each location. Approval would be given automatically to all meeting these requirements.

The difference in cost is obvious, but the difference in effectiveness is not so obvious. The discretionary system would be costly in terms of higher level administration. It would also have the unfortunate facility of making corruption more likely. The nondiscretionary system would require less high level administrative capacity and more lower level capacity, assuming a greater volume of applications. In terms of effectiveness, it is obvious that the choice of controls depends upon some assumptions of efficiency. If there are enough administrators who are reasonably efficient in the application of the rules at their discretion and if the favoritism and corruption do not expand unduly, then a discretionary system may be more effective than a nondiscretionary one that applies rules automatically. This is particularly true if the data necessary for analysis of the effects of the controls are inadequate or even nonexistent and if the estimates of the monetary costs of the impact of the rules are seriously in error.

It is an unfortunate reality that few economic policies can be implemented automatically because of their complexity. There usually are many significant variables to be considered, with timing so important that it becomes a dominant influence. Where this occurs, responsible administrators constantly plead for flexibility, the ability to adjust decisions to changes in relationship and timing between the many variables. Because of these complexities, it is not easy to compare controls that emphasize automatic or nondiscretionary administration with other controls where the discretion of the administrator is emphasized. The cases are so different in objectives and complexity that the comparison is of limited usefulness.

Yet there is a considerable area where nondiscretionary controls can achieve substantially the same effectiveness or even greater effectiveness than discretionary controls. The crux of the problem lies in so selecting the criteria for application that the flexibility is focused entirely on those matters where only discretionary judgment can sort out the important and determining variable. Thus, the focus becomes the selection of the mix of discretionary and nondiscretionary aspects of the administration, a mix which permits giving as much emphasis as possible to nondiscretionary controls. Examples of this mix can be selected from many levels of administration. In issuing licenses for construction, small buildings of specified dimensions can have licenses automatically approved in a nondiscretionary procedure, while larger buildings require individual consideration and some discretion. Procurement of small magnitude may be authorized at lower management and field levels, making the process of approval nondiscretionary at higher levels of administration. The auctioning of the foreign exchange to be used by a specific part of the economy makes the approval of the individual sales nondiscretionary, while the determination of the foreign exchange allocated to each part of the economy is a more discretionary act of administration. Because of their large requirements for high level administration, as well as their propensity toward encouraging corruption and discrimination, the use of discretionary controls must be carefully applied to those cases where they cannot be reasonably replaced with more automatic criteria.

Evaluation of Specific and General Controls

Since direct controls, as discussed above, tend to be specific, while indirect controls tend to be general, a good deal of the evaluation of the degree of specificity of controls has been covered. Specific controls are more narrow than more general controls, and are usually more related to concrete problems. Their appeal is this concreteness and apparent simplicity. When a manufacturer of small tools cannot meet

the price competition of imported tools, it seems easier to help him by
cutting his taxes, giving him a subsidy, or raising the import tax on
hand tools than to look to changes in the foreign exchange rate for a
remedy. If his were the only case to consider, this might be true. But
if producers of many different kinds of goods are similarly affected, to
handle each of these through specific subsidies, grants or specific import duty increases may be both costly and ineffective. Under these
circumstances, the answer might lie in a general rise in duties on broad
classes of imports or in the reduction of domestic costs relative to imports that comes from a devaluation of the currency. It seems safe to
generalize that while specific controls are often required to meet special
purposes, administrators should constantly strive to replace many of
them with broader types of control, which are less costly in terms of
administrative capacity and which often can be just as effective.

Evaluation of Positive and Negative Controls

There is no reason to believe that either positive or negative controls have any inherent advantage in cost or effectiveness. To the extent that one seems to be better than the other in cost or effectiveness,
it will be because of differences in directness, discretion, or specificity.
A positive control that provides a tax holiday for a new plant is not necessarily more costly or effective than a negative control that prohibits
the use of foreign exchange for importing luxury goods. The comparison
of costs and effectiveness cannot be clarified by any reference to the
positive aspects of one control and the negative aspects of the other.
Because negative controls seem to set limits within which other means
of decision making can operate, they appear, in general, to be more
effective and less costly. But it will be seen upon examination that the
critical characteristics are not the negative aspect of the controls, but
rather the degree of directness and discretion.

Summary of Evaluation of Characteristics of Control

Thus far, the comparison of the characteristics of government controls have led to the following conclusions:

Characteristics of Control	Cost		Effectiveness	
	More	Less	More	Less
I. Direct	X		I	I
Indirect		X	I	I
II. Discretionary	X			X
Nondiscretionary		X	X	
III. Specific	X			X
General		X	X	
IV. Positive	I	I	I	I
Negative	I	I	I	I

X indicates where judgment would indicate the characteristic of control would be.
I indicates indeterminate, where no judgment can be made.

(1) From this presentation, admittedly partial and subjective, improvement of controls seems to be in the direction of more indirect controls, more general controls and more nondiscretionary controls. Obviously, the needs and capabilities of each country vary, and in any specific situation the opposite characteristics of controls might be required. Empirical observation shows it is useful to group specific, discretionary controls, which require a great deal of high level administrative capacity, and to cover them with a general rule that is more automatically applied. Where it is possible, the shift from discretionary to nondiscretionary controls clearly reduces the amount of administrative capacity required and reduces the total number of decisions that are made by government. There is an implicit assumption in this generalization that if the number of decisions to be made by a government can be reduced, the fewer decisions it does make will be of better quality, more efficient and better result-producing. This appears to be a reasonable assumption in most situations.

(2) It should be clear that the choice of the control characteristics does not have a fixed relationship to the basic economic philosophy of the country. Capitalism does not mean the absence of control and communism or socialism does not mean full control. Capitalistic countries must provide guidance and direction to their economic institutions, just as do socialist countries. All countries use market mechanisms to encourage economic transactions and all use economic institutions to organize and direct these transactions. The degree of directness and discretion in controls is no less the concern of the "market" economy of the United States and United Kingdom than it is of the "centrally directed" economies of the USSR and Yugoslavia. The notion that indirect controls are capitalistic because they seem to assume a market economy with a profit motive is misleading. Even in a socialist country, or in any country that tries to eliminate private profits, attention must be given to efforts to economize on scarce factor inputs to maximize returns and to stimulate and reward efficiency.

Conceptually, it is not correct to assume that a centrally directed economy necessarily involves more direct controls than a market economy. Experience has shown that indirect economic controls can be used effectively by socialist economies, and as the productivity has gone up they have moved increasingly in that direction.* The recent moves to

_____

*The recent experience with the Lieberman plan gives management broad objectives, rather than specific physical targets. Its purpose is to give plant management more determination in the mix of production and more motivation to emphasize quality rather than quantity of production.

405

utilize profits in certain production units as a measure of managerial efficiency shows the growing realization in the USSR of the usefulness of indirect controls.

(3) Government controls have a tendency to increase over time. This tendency seems almost biological, as if controls breed controls in some strange nonorganic fashion. If this tendency were not so costly to a society, its overall impact would be one of amusement, as if humans play at being serious about their objectives. The existence of legal and illegal loopholes or avoidances are constantly brought to the attention of public administrators, and constant efforts to improve efficiency and achievement are frequently associated with apparent requirements for additional controls and directives. For example, it is obvious that no industrial licensing board or commission can have all the technical competence it needs to judge the technical competence of the proposals it receives. Some system must be established to have the proposals either accompanied by technical instructions made by competent technicians or else the board must refer the proposals to other government agencies that do have access to the appropriate technicians. Initially, the question is raised of judging the competence of the technical advice. Who decides who is a competent sanitary engineer, capable of certifying that a particular proposal meets certain general standards? Do all engineers require licenses in order to assure that incompetent engineers will not certify the wrong kind of standards? To assure technical adequacy, do all construction plans need to be approved by certified architects?

(4) Governments are tempted by the apparent simplicity of direct, specific controls, as compared with the use of indirect controls to achieve the same purpose. Indirect controls seem to lend themselves to all kinds of subterfuges, to undesirable and more or less illegal diversions that enterprising businessmen dream up to their advantage. Thus, if it is clear that the country cannot afford to construct as much as everybody wishes, it seems much easier to set up a control that requires all construction (or construction that contains some critical materials, such as cement, steel, pipe, wire) to have a permit from a board. The board then can establish criteria for its operation, prohibiting certain kinds of construction (motion picture houses, luxury housing) and specify constraints and limitations on other types of construction, which may include location, certificates of essentiality, and costs. This direct control, specific and discretionary in its operation, seems far simpler and more effective than attempts to use indirect tax rates, import licenses, and control of banks and loans to indirectly guide available resources toward desirable fields of construction. Clearly, the effectiveness depends upon the efficiency of the control board. Its operations could be more effective than general, nondiscretionary controls, if it is well staffed, with sufficient professional advice, free from undue political pressure, reasonably free from corruption, and its priorities and criteria articulated with the economic plan for the country. But this

406

happy state of operation is frequently absent, and therefore a judgment must be made of the options and of the alternative degrees of effectiveness and efficiency. No nonambiguous way has been developed to study and measure these degrees of effectiveness and efficiency. Empirical observation seems to justify the general conclusion that many developing countries would benefit from a shift away from direct controls toward indirect controls.

(5) The effectiveness of indirect general controls is related to the availability of market mechanisms. Setting a very high interest rate on certain kinds of loans, so as to discourage investment expenditures of that kind, is a futile operation if there is no way in which the loans are made. Setting a minimum monetary wage on a particular kind of labor is futile if that labor always receives its pay in terms of a share of the product. While there are many indirect and general controls that do not rely on specific market institutions or mechanisms to make them effective, these are not nearly as numerous or effective as the others that do rely on routine market operations. As a country develops, its market mechanisms must necessarily develop. The increase in production and productivity can only come from changes in technology and in institutions that necessarily involve more and better ways of exchanging goods and services; these better ways are the developing market mechanisms. It is as impossible to visualize a country achieving a growing capacity for production without improved transportation and communication as it is to have a country achieve its modernization goals without increasing its capacities for exchanging goods and services. Thus, in those developing countries that are so lacking in market mechanisms that direct controls must be utilized, the development of production facilities will unquestionably be associated with the ability to shift over to more indirect, general controls.

NOTES

1. Leonard D. White, Introduction to the Study of Public Administration, pp. 467-94.
2. Dahl and Lindblom, Politics, Economics and Welfare (New York: Harper, 1953).
3. See Gunnar Myrdal, Asian Drama, chapter 19.

ABOUT THE AUTHOR

IRVING SWERDLOW is currently Professor of Economics and Public Administration at the Maxwell School of Syracuse University. He teaches graduate courses in economic development, economic planning and development administration. He has degrees in economics from the University of North Dakota (B.A. 1930) and the University of Wisconsin (Ph.D. 1939). While at the Maxwell School he has served as a consultant in South Asia and Africa, helped inaugurate and operate the Pakistan Administrative Staff College and directed several research projects on institution building and development administration.

Before joining the faculty at the Maxwell School, Professor Swerdlow served in several government and international agencies involved with development and rehabilitation. For nearly four years he was economic consultant to the Government of Burma, emphasizing progress reporting, capital programming and plan implementation. In the Marshall Plan Agency he was Director of Office of Statistics and Operating Reports and worked in both Washington and Paris. After the war, Professor Swerdlow was Budget Director, Director of Reports and Records and Deputy Controller of the United Nations Relief and Rehabilitation Administration. Prior to the war, Professor Swerdlow was an economist, statistician and administrator in the War Production Board and in several of the welfare agencies, such as the Federal Emergency Relief Administration, the Federal Surplus Relief Corporation, the Works Projects Administration and the National Youth Administration.

PLANNING FOR DEVELOPMENT IN SUB-SAHARAN
AFRICA
Ann Seidman

AGRICULTURAL DEVELOPMENT PLANNING: Economic Concepts, Administrative Procedures, and
the Political Process
Willard W. Cochrane

ECONOMIC GROWTH IN DEVELOPING COUNTRIES—
MATERIAL AND HUMAN RESOURCES: Proceedings
of the Seventh Rehovot Conference
edited by Yohanan Ramati

INDUSTRIAL DEVELOPMENT: Handbook of Planning
and Implementation Techniques
Richard S. Kaynor and
Konrad F. Schultz

AID PERFORMANCE AND DEVELOPMENT POLICIES
OF WESTERN COUNTRIES: Studies in US, UK,
E. E. C. and Dutch Programs
Overseas Development Institute
(edited by Bruce Dinwiddy)